THE

ETERNAL PRESENT

OF SPORT

DANIEL A. GRANO

THE
ETERNAL PRESENT
OF SPORT

Rethinking Sport and Religion

TEMPLE UNIVERSITY PRESS
Philadelphia • Rome • Tokyo

TEMPLE UNIVERSITY PRESS
Philadelphia, Pennsylvania 19122
www.temple.edu/tempress

*Page iii: Photograph by Eadweard Muybridge. (Public domain image accessed from
Dover Publications.)*

Library of Congress Cataloging-in-Publication Data

Names: Grano, Daniel A.
Title: The eternal present of sport : rethinking sport and religion /
  Daniel A. Grano.
Description: Philadelphia : Temple University Press, [2017] | Includes
  bibliographical references and index.
Identifiers: LCCN 2016042737 (print) | LCCN 2017010940 (ebook)
  | ISBN 9781439912799 (cloth : alk. paper) | ISBN 9781439912805
  (pbk. : alk. paper) | ISBN 9781439912812 (E-Book)
Subjects: LCSH: Sports—Religious aspects.
Classification: LCC GV706.42 .G73 2017 (print) | LCC GV706.42 (ebook)
  | DDC 796—dc23
LC record available at https://lccn.loc.gov/2016042737

Printed in the United States of America

020918P

For Dee and Anthony

CONTENTS

ACKNOWLEDGMENTS

THIS BOOK HAS BEEN more than six years in the making. It began with an idea that I first presented at the International Association for Communication and Sport (IACS) Fourth Summit in 2010. Along the way, I received support from many generous people, only a fraction of whom I have the space to name here.

I begin with my colleagues in the Department of Communication Studies at the University of North Carolina (UNC) at Charlotte, where I have been a faculty member since 2004. I am especially grateful to Debbie Baker, Jason Black, Cris Davis, Loril Gossett, Sandy Hanson, Min Jiang, Dean Kruckeberg, Rich Leeman, Shawn Long, Cliff Scott, and Ashli Stokes for their support. I especially thank Rachel Plotnick and Maggie Quinlan for reading parts of this book, and Jon Crane for being a trusted friend and mentor on all things critical and political. Finally, I owe many thanks to my graduate research assistants, Corey Kelly and Meghan Snider, for their hard work.

Also at UNC Charlotte, I benefited greatly from the support of two colleagues and friends from the Department of Religious Studies—Sean McCloud and Joe Winters (Joe is now at Duke University). Both contributed centrally to my thinking on religion and theology.

I received my Ph.D. in rhetoric and public address from Louisiana State University (LSU) in 2003, and my LSU family played a central role in this book, as in much of my professional and personal life in the academy. First and foremost, I thank my LSU mentors, Andy King and Ken Zagacki. It is my sincere hope that this book reflects the scholarly values they instilled in me. For their support throughout my career, I am grateful to Ruth Bowman, Wesley Buerkle, Jon Croghan, Jason Munsell, Danielle Sears, Laura Sells, Tracy Stephenson Shaffer, David Terry, Shaun Treat, and Justin Trudeau. I owe special thanks to Mindy Fenske for our ongoing conversations about sport and the body, Lisa Flanagan for her support on both academic and family fronts, Christi Moss for helping me to understand purpose in academic life, and Gretchen Stein for helping me to map out this entire book on a yellow legal pad at a conference in Memphis.

The communication studies discipline has provided a home for my scholarship and support from more people than I can acknowledge here. For their help on important parts of this book, I thank Megan Foley, Pat Gehrke, and Samuel McCormick. For their support as mentors and friends, I am grateful to Bill Balthrop, Barb Biesecker, Carole Blair, Tom Frentz, Josh Gunn, Ray McKerrow, and Mary Stuckey.

The influence of thinkers from interdisciplinary sport culture studies is evident throughout this book, and the openings they have established for sport-related scholarship have made my own work possible. I am especially indebted to scholars in the growing area of communication and sport, including Meredith Bagley, Karen Hartman, Abe Khan, Kate Lavell, Korryn Mozisek, and Ray Schuck. I cannot overstate my gratitude to Andy Billings, Mike Butterworth, Tom Oates, and Larry Wenner for their support at every stage of this project.

I am grateful to the editors and staff at Temple University Press, who have been generous and able guides through the review, revision, and finalization process. The two anonymous reviewers who read early versions of the manuscript helped me to improve it substantially. To the many people in academia who have supported me but whose names do not appear here, I offer my sincere gratitude.

Finally, I am very fortunate to be surrounded by loving family members. They all helped me immeasurably as I wrote this book during a period of significant personal challenges. Much of what I know about the value of hard work and kindness I learned from my parents. My brother, Ken, and I share interests in religion, ethics, and philosophy. Our conversations about work-related things always make me a better thinker. More importantly, nobody makes me laugh harder. Finally, and above all, I dedicate this book to my wife, Dee, and my son, Anthony, my greatest sources of inspiration.

THE

ETERNAL PRESENT

OF SPORT

1

INTRODUCTION

Sport and
Negative Theology

IN ONGOING SCHOLARLY and popular debates over the relationship between sport and religion, one consistent theme is that sport is "religious" insofar as it provides an escape from politics. This can take a couple of basic forms, each at opposite ends of a broader spectrum. Academics or popular critics interested in radical social change often characterize sport as an opiate that obstructs emancipation. Conversely, scholars, theologians, or media commentators sympathetic to sport might celebrate its capacity to transcend the terror and boredom of quotidian existence (work, sleep, bills, interpersonal conflict, partisan strife, and so on). This book is an effort to move away from both of these positions in order to rethink sport-religion relationships in dialectical terms. For an initial sense of what I mean by this, consider some basic problems with each of the above versions of sport as religious escape.

The image of sport as an opiate borrows from Marx's most famous metaphor for religion while ignoring the tensions that the metaphor summarizes.[1] The result is a condemnation of sport as an institution that pacifies citizens and inhibits their development of political consciousness. Marx, per common readings of his argument in "Toward a Critique of Hegel's Philosophy of Right," stated that religion was "the opium of the people" and that "the abolition of religion as the illusory happiness of the people is the demand for their real happiness."[2] Critiques of sport have taken a parallel form. For example, Terry Eagleton wrote in an opinion piece for *The Guardian*:

> If every rightwing thinktank came up with a scheme to distract the populace from political injustice and compensate them for lives of hard labour, the solution in each case would be the same: football. No finer way of resolving the problems of capitalism has been dreamed up, bar socialism. . . . Like some austere religious faith, the game determines what you wear, whom you associate with, what anthems you sing and what shrine of transcendent truth you worship at. Along with television, it is the supreme solution to that age-old dilemma of our political masters: what should we do with them when they're not working? . . . [F]ootball these days is the opium of the people, not to speak of their crack cocaine. . . . Nobody serious about political change can shirk the fact that the game has to be abolished.[3]

Eagleton's proposal is not at all unusual. There is even an apocryphal story that Marx concluded, after watching a game of cricket, that there would be no socialist revolution in England if the masses could be anaesthetized by such a bourgeois activity. The story is often repeated as fact, illustrating, as Ben Carrington notes, "the widely held perception concerning the inherent incompatibility of sport with politics."[4] The main problem with such arguments is that they isolate sport from the broader structure of social relations within and through which it exerts unique but also interdependent ideological force, and then treat it, in a deterministic way, as the linchpin that by necessity must be removed if the larger structure is to come apart. This represents a common failure, as Carrington argues, to view sport "in complex relation to the wider historical conjuncture and the contingent set of social relations that produce it."[5] As Stuart Hall defines it, a *conjuncture* is "a period in which the contradictions and problems and antagonisms, which are always present in different domains in a society, begin to . . . accumulate" around a point of rupture. Conjuncture includes the aftermath of that rupture, relevant processes of social change, and "challenges to the existing historical project or social order."[6] Without some conception of conjuncture, there can be only a limited critical or cultural studies of sport. If sport is complicit with "ideological manipulation" and ultimately "devoid of any counter-cultural elements, let alone transformative potential," then the only point in critiquing it is to expose it as a site for false consciousness.[7]

To study sport's relationship to broader conjunctures is to go much further. Such a study requires what Lawrence Grossberg calls (in his exhortation to cultural studies critics) a "radical contextualism" wherein we assume that "the identity, significance, and effects of any practice or event . . . are defined only by the complex set of relations that surround, interpenetrate, and shape it." In this sense an institution or practice like sport cannot be "isolated from its relations"; it must be understood instead "as a condensation of multiple determinations and effects."[8] From there, scholars interested in sport culture can take an important additional step: to demonstrate that sport condenses these effects in ways that exert *unique force* across a broader structure of social relations. To cite some examples from my book: sport is a site that conditions hyperawareness about the transitory nature of bodily capacity, time, and labor production; reliance on specialized modes of audiovisual capture (e.g., instant replay) makes sport a proving ground for problems of human perception, institutional authority, and historical judgment; elite competition stages the most consistent, dramatic tests of progress in human potential, while also throwing light on the technological, medical, and governmental interventions behind such progress; and controversies over competitive eligibility bring into public view debates over the indeterminacy of gender, sexuality, and ability that were formerly raised almost exclusively by activists and academics.

These and other debates uncover long-standing contradictions and problems, which are often condensed in sport in the form of religious ideals like "witnessing" or "transcendence." Thus my book proceeds from two basic premises: (1) at present, elite televised sport is in a moment of conjuncture in which conflicts inherent to several of its most foundational religious (or, as I define the term shortly, "theological") images and tropes are becoming visible and crystallizing around points of rupture and (2) processes of historical change related to these ruptures illustrate how sport is a context that produces uniquely powerful religious antagonisms and transmits them across an interrelated set of cultural practices and institutions.

Of course sport does not only create conflict. It can and often does serve as an opiate in the most negative sense, but this does not preclude its oppositional potential. As Andrew McKinnon argues, the phrase "opium of the people" has been made "undialectical" due to a tendency to translate it, through contemporary sensibilities, as a reference to drug-induced passivity or escape. At the beginning of the nineteenth century, opium was "largely an unquestioned good": a beneficial medicine affordable for the poor as well as a source of inspiration for artists and poets. Marx used it himself to treat various illnesses. By the end of the century, however, it had become "demonized" due to social concerns over "baby doping" (the use of opium to soothe children, a practice driven largely by women's working conditions and pharmacists' marketing efforts), illness, and addiction. Marx formulated his opium metaphor between these periods, thus capturing dialectical tensions between its implications as "blessed medicine" and "recreational curse": "Religious suffering is at the same time an expression of real suffering and a protest against real suffering. Religion is the sigh of the oppressed creature, the feeling of a heartless world, and the soul of soulless circumstances. It is the opium of the people."[9] This summarizes, according to McKinnon, Marx's dialectical thinking: religious suffering *simultaneously* expresses and resists "real" suffering—that is, suffering grounded in the material, social conditions that produce religion, and to which religion is a response as well as a shaping force. Expression and resistance constitute an "unstable equilibrium," an "indivisible whole" in which each part influences the other.

This, McKinnon argues, is what ordinary translations of the opium metaphor miss: a "dialectical movement, in which opium, as a condensed signifier, brings together both expression and protest in one moment."[10] Religion cannot be abstracted from the conditions of its social, political, and economic production. Neither, then, can it be seen to merely give voice to an illusory world outside those conditions. As "a sigh that bears witness to oppression," religion reflects and deepens the inequitable structures that it constitutes (and that it is constituted by), while at the same time providing an image of an alternative future.[11] Max Horkheimer summarizes this perfectly in his essay "Thoughts on Religion": "The concept of God was for a long time the place where the idea was kept alive that there are other norms besides those to which nature and society give expression in their operation. . . . Religion is the record of the wishes, desires, and accusations of countless generations."[12] The capacity for religion to express a radical or "wholly other" alternative to the present state of affairs was "perverted," Horkheimer argues, after Christianity "became the bedfellow of the state." Even so, traces "of the drives and desires which religious belief preserved" could be "detached from [their] inhibiting religious form and become productive forces in social practice."[13]

This process of detachment and reinvention summarizes my basic approach to religion throughout this book. In each of the chapters that follow, I attempt to map out the social, economic, and historical conditions under which certain religious drives central to sport have become sources of profound disruption for the very institutions—leagues, governing bodies, media companies—that have historically cultivated a profitable religious idealism. This disruption is not only the work of critical scholarship; it is also apparent in the efforts of journalists, fans, players, and other members of sport institutions who recognize that crises surrounding several of sport's highest religious ideals provide unique opportunities for activism and change. I maintain that reconsidering sport-religion relationships in this way is commensurate with appreciating sport as a site for political unrest.

Operating from a different ideological standpoint, sport culture scholars and theologians have often celebrated sport's capacity to ritualistically transport adherents out of the profane patterns of everyday life and into the sacred time of live events. In these cases the sacred is posed as superior to the quotidian, existing as a unique and separated source of hope and order. For example, Charles Prebish argues that sport turns "chaos into cosmos" and provides "a place of safety from the ghosts and demons that populate ordinary space"; Michael Novak maintains that both religion and sport lift us toward an experience "full of exhilaration, excitement, and peace . . . more real and more joyous than the activities of everyday life—as though it were *really living* to be in sacred time" as opposed to the "jading of work, progress, history"; Joseph Price views the U.S. sport calendar as a series of ritual transitions "from the chaos of secularity to the cosmos of sport, from cultural malaise to corporate hope"; and Eric Bain-Selbo writes that the sacred time of sport is "simply more meaningful and valuable than other time."[14] The mechanical tedium of quotidian life *desacralizes* the world, and sport offers a chance—perhaps one of the last remaining chances—to "*resacralize* our lives."[15] Harry Edwards goes so far as to claim that sport is the only "universal popular religion in America," and the idea that sport might supplant denominational religions, or has already done so, is common among sport culture scholars and popular commentators alike.[16]

Scholars in sport culture are increasingly calling into question these moral and temporal distinctions between profane and sacred. In their recent book *Religion and Sports in American Culture*, Jeffrey Scholes and Raphael Sassower argue that there is "mounting evidence that the sacred and secular do not operate in two separate domains in twenty-first century culture" and that anyone looking to "cleanly separate the religious from the non-religious" in sport is likely exaggerating the distinction in order to pick a fight.[17] Such a fight can certainly be principled. Robert Higgs and Michael Braswell worry, for example, that conflating religion and sport distorts the moral potential of faith, transforming it to the avarice of competition:

> The danger of attempting to make sport a religion, even one qualified by the word "popular," is the distinct possibility of an opposite effect, legitimizing religion as sports, trivializing the grand purposes of religions in spite of failures that all human institutions experience. Having the world's largest congregation or Sunday school, becoming top dog in the manner of national championships, and providing services for membership can easily become more important than providing services "for the least of these" in a community.[18]

Higgs and Braswell propose rethinking the sport-religion relationship as akin to that of "oil and water, which seems analogous to Jesus's metaphor of the things of Caesar and the things of God."[19] The problem with this proposal is that, much like Eagleton's proposal, it is mostly a thought experiment. Religious, state, and corporate institutions have been working together for too long to make separation realistic. In fact, the presumed boundary between sacred and profane has been breached by the very people who would seem most opposed to profaning faith via commerce, such as religious leaders and proselytizing athletes.

As William Baker explains, sport and religion have developed together through a history of mutually beneficial accommodations: Puritan requirements for quiet reflection on Sundays were lifted, and Sunday is now one of the most important sporting days in the U.S. week; believers shifted their attitudes toward celebrations of the flesh in sport, especially as pleasurable spectacles afforded religious leaders an opportunity to proselytize; sport reformed from a background of wanton violence to adopt moralistic rules and structures, sanitizing both games and bodies (e.g., testing for performance-enhancing drugs); and, understanding its influence over visibility and alumni support, denominational colleges and universities enthusiastically integrated sport with religion.[20] These accommodations are apparent today in the popular branding of Evangelical Christianity in, for example, major- and minor-league baseball "Faith Nights," where athletes testify to their faith and church leaders give away bobble-head dolls of Biblical characters like Noah, Moses, and Samson.[21] Since the mid- to late nineteenth century, the idea of "muscular Christianity"—a characteristically Christian commitment to health and masculinity—has been aligned with athletics on the premise that sport was an arena for Christian outreach.[22] In 1858 prize fighter Orville "Awful" Gardner (thus nicknamed because he had bitten off an opponent's ear in a barroom fight) testified to his Christian conversion in a New York City church and used his celebrity to convert others, becoming one of the United States' first muscular-Christian athletic evangelicals.[23] Today his heirs hold group prayers on the field after games, and offer up their talent as a public testament to God's grace.

Not all people of faith are on board with these partnerships. Thoughtful debates among theologians about the ethics of public prayer in sport, for example, point to a more general unease about such interdependencies.[24] These are important and meaningful philosophical problems, but the focus of my book is on the practical economic and historical conditions under which sport reconciles religion and the market.

The boundary between sacred and profane is porous in sport, even if we attempt to draw it at a formally theological or denominational level. We run into similar problems when characterizing sport as a form of "civil religion," a construct that captures some of the importance of sport's religious imagery but often simplifies its politics.[25] As Sean McCloud argues, studies on sport as popular religion are often characterized by functionalist understandings of religion.[26] To borrow from James Carey, sport culture studies are "functionalist" when they treat ideology "as a device for releasing tension" and satisfying needs, rather than as something connected with larger "structural forces."[27] The frequent focus in sport culture studies on profane-to-sacred transport summarizes this functionalist tendency most clearly. By no means do I view such studies as ingenuous or illegitimate. They capture a very real experience central to sport participation, one that I have had myself at ballparks and stadiums, with family and friends. My concern is with the ontological assumption upon which profane-to-sacred transport is founded—that the sacred is separated from and morally or experientially superior to the profane—and the related idea that the *essential* function of religion in sport is ideological escape.

Given the realities of contemporary sport media production, the more sustainable position is that sacredness is both a product of "profane" cultural forces (e.g., economics, politics, media representation) *and* an expression of hopefulness and desire for separation from those forces. This is part of a more generally dialectical view of sport and religion. The idea is not to resolve a metaphysical fight in the direction of either religion or materialism but to recognize that in terms of practical, cultural production, these forms of experience and commitment are interrelated; they create irresolvable tensions that mobilize a variety of social practices, ranging from proselytizing to forming labor unions.

In response to both of these predominant visions of religious escape I propose approaching sport-religion relationships through the lens of negative theology. Not to be confused with Apophatic theology (a project of characterizing God through negations), the negative theology I refer to comes out of the so-called theological turn in critical and cultural theory, philosophy, and literary theory and traces back to thinkers in the Frankfurt School.[28] Negative theology is a critique of history and a practice of interpretation ideally suited to understanding the problems and possibilities of conjuncture in elite televised sport. It advances two premises that I find especially important. First, it opposes interpretations of social experience as *either* metaphysical *or* materialist. It allows, instead, a back-and-forth migration between religious images, terms, and ideals and their secular, economic, and politicized analogues.[29] Second, it recognizes a process whereby theological images become detached from their institutional appropriations and mobilized against the very notions of historical progress they have traditionally upheld.[30] Negative theology interrogates several assumptions underlying the antagonisms and ruptures within, and projecting out from, present-day elite sport. An overview of those assumptions provides an initial sense of how and why negative theology might be both practically and theoretically important as a critique of history and as an approach to interpretation, especially in light of current states of unrest in elite televised sport. This discussion serves as a preview of my approach in the coming chapters.

Sport and Negative Theology

The term "theology" is ordinarily associated with the systematic study of the nature of God or with justifications of religious belief and doctrine. Theology in this sense is fideistic, apologetic, confessional, and denominational. It is a discipline predominantly identified with churches and seminaries, and less (as debates among scholars in religious studies suggest) with secular academic institutions.[31] In contrast, critical and cultural theorists invoke the term as a framework for locating a radical or "wholly other" alternative to our current moment, in which market logics have penetrated every aspect of public and personal experience.[32] Theology in this sense is largely materialist, secular, and atheistic.[33] These two conceptions of theology represent divergent projects (save for their intersections in leftist movements in twentieth-century Judaism and Christianity, or in contemporary liberation theology).[34] Yet they share a common lexicon for imagining history in fundamental contrast to the present day. What critical and cultural theorists are attempting to capture in theology, then, is the insistence that the present state of affairs is not inevitable, that other possibilities for social and political order exist and can be realized in our own time.[35] The most immediate context for this second sense of the concept is the theological turn in contemporary philosophy, critical and cultural studies, and literary theory, a moment that incorporates the projects of diverse thinkers like Giorgio Agamben, Slavoj Žižek, Jacques Derrida, Alain Badiou, Terry Eagleton, and others. As Roland Boer notes, this moment has been curiously disconnected from the theological thought of earlier Western Marxists such as Ernst Bloch, Walter Benjamin, Theodor Adorno, and Max Horkheimer.[36] Among the rare exceptions have been reengagements with Benjamin, particularly in the writings of Agamben, Žižek, and Derrida.[37] I do not examine the reasons behind this disconnect, nor do I investigate any one of these thinkers' larger theological projects beyond their relevance to my own book.[38] My interest, more broadly and more practically, is in how critical theorists have looked to theology to recover capacities for historical critique that seemed foreclosed in their particular philosophical and political moments.

I am not looking to advance negative theology as a grand theory of sport and religion. My approach throughout the book is more characteristically strategic: I rely upon theorists and concepts from the Frankfurt School and from the more recent theological turn based on their relevance to the particular contexts and problems that interest me.[39] My thinking is especially influenced by Benjamin because he connected theology, history, and media technologies in a way that is relevant to problems of religion in elite televised sport. But I do not view an association between sport and negative theology as necessarily Benjaminian (especially since Benjamin never wrote about sport, and guessing at his thoughts on the topic seems beside the point). Negative theology is, for me, a theoretical "wager about what will work" to address some very specific problems.[40] What justifications can we locate, from within current sport culture contexts, for moving away from the position that religion serves essentially as an outlet for ideological escape? What related insights can we gain about the processes of change, and the foreclosures of those possibilities, currently underway in elite sport? And on what terms can we project alternative futures?

Sport, Conjuncture, and Theology

For thinkers of the contemporary theological turn, theology offers a potentially radical alternative to the current social order at a moment when theorists debate whether any approach to criticism or activism can be invented that does not simply reinvest in the political and discursive structures it opposes.[41] This capacity to imagine a "wholly other" alternative to the present state of affairs traces back to the thinkers of the Frankfurt School, even if that connection is not always acknowledged.[42] Max Horkheimer wrote that a theological perspective allowed critics to conceive of "something other than the world, something over which the fixed rules of nature, the perennial source of doom, have no dominion."[43] As Eduardo Mendieta summarizes, critical theologies have been characterized by a "refusal to grant immanence the last word."[44]

Sport might seem the last place one should look for hope for an alternative future. Many fans, players, and commentators perceive sport as ideally "apolitical" (and thus attempt to prohibit political discussion), while many academics perceive it as "actively *anti*-political" (and thus dismiss it as a context for social change).[45] In practical terms, neither position is sustainable. Political struggles break through all the time, and the impossibility of their containment means that sport projects an idealized image of society (a level playing field, a separated time and space that transcend difference and inequity) and at the same time stages constant profanations of that image. Thus, as critical and cultural scholars have long insisted, sport is not merely a site for repression. It can also, as Ben Carrington argues, "under specific circumstances, offer a space through which oppositional politics could be fought and won."[46]

Another way of putting this is that sport can and should be studied in relationship to broader historical conjunctures, especially as an institution that exerts unique influence across a complex structure of social relations. As Stuart Hall defines it:

> A conjuncture is a period in which the contradictions and problems and antagonisms, which are always present in different domains in a society, begin to come together. They begin to accumulate, they begin to fuse, to overlap with one another. The ideological becomes part of the economic problem and vice versa. . . . The aftermath of the fusion, how that fusion develops, its challenges to the existing historical project or social order . . . *all* of that arc constitutes conjuncture.[47]

Of interest are the processes by which these tensions and contradictions begin to "accumulate" or "fuse" at a specific historical moment, becoming conspicuous or legible in such a way that they precipitate protective responses from powerful officials, or activist mobilizations, or legal challenges, or predictions of alternative futures. Conjunctures do not guarantee radical change. They do, however, open spaces for potentially new conceptions of historical reality.[48]

Hall emphasizes that "in a conjuncture, different kinds of contradictions can play the leading part, but they never define it entirely."[49] While I am making the case that religious antagonisms are central to broader crises in elite sport, then, I also recognize that it is a series of *interrelationships* between religious idealism and various practices of production (political, economic, technological, medical) that are beginning to fuse together in this arena.

Although he does not use the same vocabulary of conjuncture, Benjamin implies something similar in his conception of the "now of recognizability." What Benjamin adds (and I cover shortly) is a way of thinking about how theology relates to the accumulation and fusion of contradictions at particular historical moments. In *The Arcades Project*, he argues that the claims and burdens of the past can "attain legibility" or "accede to legibility" as images, but "only at a particular time"; "each 'now' is the now of a particular recognizability."[50] On this "now" Benjamin writes:

> It's not that what is past casts its light on what is present, or what is present its light on what is past; rather, image is that wherein what has been comes together in a flash with the now to form a constellation. In other words, image is dialectics at a standstill. For while the relation of the present to the past is a purely temporal, continuous one, the relation of what-has-been to the now is dialectical: is not progression but image, suddenly emergent.—Only dialectical images

are genuine images (that is, not archaic); and the place where one encounters them is language.[51]

Images in this "now" are dialectical because they force a confrontation between an idealized version of the past and the present reality.[52] In such moments, ideal and actual history do not split apart or diverge but rather *come into constellation*, and their imagistic juxtapositions constitute a disruptive legibility. The result, Benjamin hoped, would be a political awakening wherein the "secret affinity" between "what was" and "the now" would finally "disclose itself."[53] These constellations represent "dialectics at a standstill" because even as the images that constitute them emerge from a historical continuum, the resulting tensions are not resolved teleologically (that is, they are not synthesized or rendered as a new image of progress). Rather, the now of recognizability represents a "contracted" moment during which, as Samuel McCormick explains, we are able to step outside the flow of sequential history and experience the contradictions of a time when "the actuality of the present and the potentiality of the future begin to intermingle."[54]

This sounds abstract, but it actually describes a condition of practical possibilities. Benjamin insisted that a historical object had to be "blasted out of the continuum of historical succession" to force a "confrontation" between that object's past idealization and present reality.[55] Under such conditions our "now" could be "charged to the bursting point" with dialectical tensions, and past images could gain "retroactive force" and work against the continuity of progress through the present.[56] This is, as I argue throughout this book, what is starting to happen around religious images central to elite televised sport.

My consistent point of reference for this process is the athletic body. As historical (and, as I cover below, theological) objects, athletic bodies represent a presumably natural continuum of ever-advancing human potential. Sustaining that image requires, as I maintain in Chapter 2, a continuous flow of historical successions: of record-breaking performances, of newly emergent stars, of increasingly superendowed bodies. A temporal disruption or cut in that continuity represents at least two important possibilities: (1) that some practice of sport cultural production (e.g., audiovisual capture, biotechnological enhancement, labor struggle) has constituted a unique moment of legibility around long-standing but typically concealed antagonisms and (2) that this is a moment of risk, when progressive social change and reinstatements of idealized history are both possibilities.

Hall emphasizes that a conjuncture is a "narrow period of crisis" that occurs between the "relative stability" of a dominant social formation and the appearance of "cracks" in that formation. Central questions for any conjuncture, then, are how long it will last and in what directions its constitutive struggles and attempts at resolution point.[57]

Similar considerations of time and opportunity were important for Benjamin. As he warned in "Theses on the Philosophy of History":

> The true picture of the past flits by. The past can be seized only as an image which flashes up at the instant when it can be recognized and is never seen again. . . . For every image of the past that is not recognized by the present as one of its own concerns threatens to disappear irretrievably.[58]

The now of recognizability is, as McCormick puts it, *a time in which time is running out.* In order to "make a difference in the present," the image must compel immediate action; we must understand that "recognition is not enough."[59] The changes that may emerge from our own moment of recognition are part of an uncertain future. But this does not mean that the critic's or the activist's obligation to respond can be deferred. There is urgency to act in the present, since the moment opened by the image is already passing by.[60] In addition, dialectical images and objects are visible not only to activists or critical scholars. They are also available for appropriation by the very institutions they threaten to undermine.[61] This means that critical and cultural work on sport, just as with any dominant popular institution, operates under a "logic of 'no guarantees.'"[62] The relations that shape history and social experience are not essential or inevitable, and this means that political struggles can and will change them. But the results are always uncertain. This is not to romanticize contingency or indeterminateness: any new structure of relations will be *real* in the sense that it will exert material force over peoples' lives.[63] The idea is to recognize that our "now" is not inevitable and then, in Grossberg's words, to gain a "better understanding of where we are so that we can get somewhere else (some place, we hope, that is better—based on more just principles of equality and the distribution of wealth and power)."[64]

As Hall argues, ideological struggle does not involve the wholesale displacement of one unified system of thought by another. Rather, movement toward a new historical stage occurs within a terrain defined "by the existing balance of social forces," the unique shape of a "concrete conjuncture" within which political action is limited. The balance of forces can be changed, but there are no "final guarantees" regarding the direction or results of that change due to the "'openness' of historical development to practice and struggle." Hall is not elevating change as intrinsically good. Rather, he is acknowledging the limits of what we can claim or predict about new configurations that may or may not emerge from the crises of a particular conjuncture. Ideological struggle matters not because it guarantees results in advance but because it exerts *real, material force* within, through, and perhaps against existing relations of power.[65]

Borrowing from Grossberg, my hope is that theology might serve as a resource for constructing "possibilities, both immediate and imaginary" out of the concrete historical circumstances we confront in contemporary sport cultures. Theology should not be viewed as a totalizing theoretical framework for understanding sport. More modestly (and also more practically and materially), it summarizes antagonisms basic to sport cultures that are currently *in the process of* crystallizing around points of rupture. I view it as a framework especially suited to the moment this book captures.

As an example for thinking through sport in terms of conjuncture, consider Jean-Marie Brohm's seminal collection of essays *Sport—a Prison of Measured Time*. Brohm's essays were written in response to conditions between 1968 and 1972, a period of heightened debate over "bourgeois institutions and values" brought about by events like the 1968 workers' strikes in France, the Vietnam War, and controversies over the 1968 and 1972 Olympic Games.[66] Brohm saw these debates penetrating sport and thus creating a condition where consensus over its political purity had broken down: "Sport can no longer be naïvely treated as a value unaffected by the political and ideological class struggle. Sport is now a *central political issue* in the social conflicts of our time. Things can no longer go along in the same way."[67] Scholars of the contemporary theological turn have identified similarly a moment of crisis wherein discussions over what constitutes progress in a capitalist society can no longer proceed in the same way. The book *Paul's New Moment*, for example, opens with such a scene: in the aftermath of the 2008 global financial crisis, "the capitalist world is coming apart at the seams" and "the perils of greed built into the very heart of the structures of capitalistic commodification" are exposed; yet serious critiques from the Left have been marginalized. For critics invested in the theological turn, theology seems one of the few disciplines through which one can seize on this moment and "mount an uncompromising stance against capitalism and its supplement, neoliberalism."[68] If, as critics of the contemporary theological turn insist, theology is an appropriate response to conflicts in contemporary capitalism, I think that that response should include sport, especially because sport so effectively sublimates the competitive avarice of the market—physical labor, individualism, violence, productivity—into religious imagery.

Brohm recognized that the crises surrounding sport in his own moment would develop beyond the scope of his writings, but he indicated that it was "already possible to discern some general tendencies which can only be aggravated in the future."[69] I write from a similar position, not knowing how the crises that interest me will turn out but confident that there are underlying, emergent patterns that point toward opportunities for productive conflict and change.

Negative Theology and Sport Culture Criticism

The conception of theology that critical theorists advance is "negative" in at least two senses that I view as important to sport-religion relationships: a negative theology (1) counters interpretations of social experience or economic production that take place through binary understandings of profane vs. sacred or immanent vs. transcendent and instead recognizes how these categories of experience are dialectical and (2) outlines a process for detaching religious images, tropes, and objects from their institutional appropriations and mobilizing them against the very notions of historical progress they have upheld. Both are built on a principle of negation basic to critical theory. The critic identifies a historical object (say, an athletic body) that is made up simultaneously of proclaimed unities (e.g., "natural" advances in human-athletic potential) and internal contradictions (e.g., biotechnological enhancements). My use of "human-athletic" here (and throughout the book) summarizes a common articulation between dreams of human progress and measurements of athletic achievement, an articulation that constitutes idealized tropes like transcendence while at the same time mobilizing a host of profane political and economic interventions. Creating awareness around the conflict between idealization and actuality represented by (and operating within) the object reveals how that object "fails by its own standards." The hoped-for result of negation is a *positive* alternative to the present state of affairs, an alternative currently foreclosed by the seeming unity of the object and the broader structure of social relations that it holds together.[70] To be clear, these are not the only elements that might fall under negative theology, whether the reference is to the Frankfurt School or the more recent theological turn. They are elements that I find especially relevant for sport culture criticism, and it is in this specific sense that I review negative theology here.

Interpretation: Hovering between Materialism and Religion

Critics interested in a negative theological approach often look for convergences between religious and materialist ideas when they read texts.[71] Adorno describes both his and Benjamin's view as an "inverse" theology that is "directed against natural and supernatural interpretation alike."[72] And Benjamin writes that when theologically examining works of art, those works must be interpreted with attention to "their political aspects as much as their fashionable ones, their economic determinations as much as their metaphysical ones."[73] The general idea of critical theologies is, as Rudolph J. Siebert summarizes, to allow "religious and theological contents to migrate . . . into the secular discourse" of various academic disciplines and "into communicative and even political praxis."[74] These migrations enable the critic to hover, as David Kaufmann puts it, "between the twin perils of uncritical piety and materialist reduction."[75]

This hovering is especially important for sport because arguments about religion and ideological escape—whether articulated as opium or as profane-to-sacred transport—are premised on a separation between the immanent world of politics and the mythic time of games. As Richard Gruneau warns, setting apart sporting experiences as superior or more hopeful in contrast to the depressing, commercialized, or instrumental nature of profane existence causes critics to treat religious imagery as "*outside . . .* the process of active history," so that "the meanings encoded in play, games, and sports become depoliticized and recreated in mythic forms that have powerful ideological overtones."[76] This problem is especially represented through the influence of Mircea Eliade in scholarship on sport and religion.[77] Eliade assumes an experiential and moral separation between sacred and profane that is characteristic of the functionalist assumptions I critiqued above: "Religious man [*sic*] lives in two kinds of time, of which the more important, sacred time, appears under the paradoxical aspect of a circular time, reversible and recoverable, a sort of eternal mythic present that is periodically reintegrated by means of rites."[78] Here "circular" and "sacred" time run parallel but separately through the human condition, and "reintegration" involves ritualistically tapping into the sacred as an ontological structure universal to all cultures. This ontological separation suggests that experiences are "religious" in the sense that they transcend the influence of ordinary cultural forces.[79]

As religious studies scholars insist, in contemporary commercial media production the borders between profane and sacred or immanent and transcendent have become so "clearly porous" that distinguishing between these categories is now an "unhelpful" and "unsustainable" basis for criticism.[80] Accordingly, conceptions of sacredness or transcendence must attend to the specific conditions of power, culture, and mediated production within which they are constituted.[81]

Specific to sport, Scholes and Sassower argue that "the sacred and secular do not operate in two separate domains" in twenty-first-century sport culture. "If," they suggest, "one is unable to cleanly locate and separate the religious from the non-religious, as was once thought possible," then one is justified in turning one's attention toward how religious values and experiences of time "are expressed in culture," where the secular and religious continuously co-opt one another.[82] This is not to say that denominational institutions and sport leagues are the same thing, or that attending games and observing sacraments carry the same implications for belief and spiritual commitment. Relationships between sport and religion can be figurative, but they are not arbitrary. They must be understood within specific contexts: for example, where the proselytizing and commercial interests of Evangelicals and sport leagues converge, or where an advertising campaign appropriates religious images to promote a mega-event. Each sport culture context presents a unique challenge for delineating religious and secular imagery and identifying the particular ideological interests served by their figurative and denominational constructions, their intersections, and their attempted separations.

Within these contexts, particular theological images, tropes, or objects can come to represent or condense the complex social relations that constitute a conjuncture. They become theological, in this sense, when they represent the act of making experiences *sensible* by interpreting back and forth between immanence and transcendence, the material and the metaphysical. As Kenneth Burke argues in *The Rhetoric of Religion*, "Theological principles can be shown to have usable secular analogies that throw light upon the nature of language."[83] Drawing on a foundational analogy between "words" and "The Word," Burke writes: "What we say about *words*, in the empirical realm, will bear a notable likeness to what is said about *God*, in theology."[84] When we talk about the "supernatural" or the "ineffable," then, our words are "necessarily borrowed from . . . the sorts of things we can talk about literally . . . (the world of everyday experience)."[85] Extending Burke's focus on the supernatural, Joshua Gunn argues that this analogical movement between immanence and transcendence is essential to the way language works, even when describing the most mundane experiences.[86]

Sport discourses are often structured around the same analogical movement. It is not hard to find journalists or fans celebrating the supernatural (a record-breaking performance that defies physics or stretches the horizons of human possibility) in terms of the material world (muscular physique, technologized training, measured time). Or, moving in the opposite direction, economics and politics constantly encroach on what fans and journalists view as protected territory: the sacred, the transcendent. Also, as sport culture scholars have long emphasized, content-level parallels between sport and religious institutions are readily apparent. In his seminal book *Sociology of Sport*, for example, Edwards details correspondences between "traditional religions" and sport: both have saints (iconic departed figures), ruling patriarchs (owners, coaches), gods (star athletes), high councils (governing bodies), scribes (journalists, broadcasters), "seekers of the kingdom" (fans), and shrines and houses of worship (arenas, stadiums, halls of fame).[87] To read these parallels descriptively—simply classifying religious and secular overlaps—would be to miss how they signify deeper structures of thought and experience and, moreover, how they represent the constant potential for contradiction and rupture.[88]

Benjamin saw in theology a form of experience that enabled the transformation of "elements of archaic myth" into "keys for deciphering" material, political potential.[89] As Susan Buck-Morss emphasizes, this approach aimed at drawing on the constitutive relationships between worldly and religious phenomena while avoiding the oversights of a worldview that compartmentalized materialism and theology. In Benjamin's view, theology keeps Marxism from falling "into positivism," while Marxism keeps theology from falling "into magic."[90] Benjamin maintains tensions between the theological and materialist poles of his thought to avoid either of these excesses.[91] His refusal to resolve their inconsistencies has made for uneasy reception of his work. As James Martell puts it, Benjamin has been "too mystical for the Marxists and too Marxist for the mystics."[92] This sounds like a perfect middle ground for critics of sport and religion.

History: Theological Critiques of Progress

A negative theology rejects idealizations of history as teleologically or divinely guided progress. Rather, history is a catastrophe that violates the very religious ideals it is so often structured around. In response, the critic is to use theological images *against* the progress-oriented histories they support in a recovery or reappropriation of those images' suppressed political potential.[93] In sport this reappropriation would mean rejecting the continuity of human-athletic advance, insofar as it is supported through theological tropes like eternity, transcendence, and revelation. In recovering the suppressed political potential of these tropes and reading them against the grain of progress, a negative theology actually aims at a *positive* alternative to the present: a refiguring of social relations invented out of possibilities not totally defined by the prevailing economic, political, or symbolic structures of our own time.[94]

In "Theses on the Philosophy of History," Benjamin famously depicts the problem of progress through Paul Klee's painting *Angelus Novus*. The angel is turned toward the past; while most people perceive history as a cumulative succession of events, he sees it as a "catastrophe," a continuous piling up of unaddressed wreckage. The angel "would like to stay, awaken the dead, and make whole what has been smashed," but the storm of "progress" propels him violently toward the future.[95] As Michael Bowman argues, the "crucial question" for Benjamin was "how to shake off the burden" of this catastrophe, how to rescue the truth content of the past from the "ash heaps of history." This boiled down "to a question of how to 'read' [history's] ruins," both as a form of criticism and as a "model of social praxis."[96]

For Benjamin, the work of addressing the true disaster of history falls to historical materialists, whom he distinguishes from "historicists." Historicists empathize with the victors and in doing so affirm a view of history as linear and cumulative progress, which hides the lasting imprint of past injustices in the present.[97] Historical materialists, by contrast, "seize hold of a memory as it flashes up at a moment of danger" and use it "to explode the continuum of history."[98] In order to "win" against the march of progress, the historical materialist must, Benjamin insists, enlist "the services of theology."[99] This is, again, characteristic of a more generally negative theological approach: a call to recover and reappropriate the suppressed political potential of theological images. As Gunn writes, Benjamin's aim is to deploy these images instrumentally, as "rhetorical effect[s]" designed to "keep the past alive in the present" and motivate change.[100] For Benjamin, theology aids the historical materialist in recognizing that the past is always unfinished, that every generation inherits responsibility for its unsettled debts.[101] In failing that responsibility we allow the dead (the literally deceased, as well as the anonymous and voiceless) to die again.[102] Here negative theology's *interpretive* refusal to resolve tensions between religion and materialism becomes a framework for attitudes toward historical change.

These problems of progress pervade sport, especially (as I argue from Chapter 2 forward) surrounding images of human-athletic advance and their attending theological tropes. The seemingly immutable (ahistorical, transcendent) nature of that advance serves as a constant justification for forward historical motion in sport. Very few cultural institutions make the past so seemingly naturally obsolete because very few institutions build their histories so thoroughly around moving, competing, measured, and evolving bodies. Under certain conditions, however, the "stigmata of past experience" inscribed on athletic bodies can become legible *through* those theological ideals that ordinarily obscure the catastrophes of historical progress.[103]

Athletic Bodies as Theological Objects

Elite athletes represent especially powerful embodiments of theological conflict. Buck-Morss notes that for Benjamin, a historical object has no inherent theological meaning. Rather, theological meaning emerges only out of an object's construction in a specific context. When an object's representation of some utopian hope (e.g., human freedom) "is brought together with its historically present form, the double focus illuminates both . . . [the] utopian potential and, simultaneously, the betrayal of that potential."[104] The simultaneous representation of promise *and* betrayal is important, as it relates to the object's capacity to force a dialectical confrontation: to act, in Benjamin's words, as a "force field in which the confrontation" between an idealized past and present-day truth "is played out."[105] Thus, our "now" can be "charged to the bursting point" with dialectical tensions between ideal and actual history.[106] For Benjamin this confrontation "makes up the interior (and, as it were, the bowels) of the historical object."[107] Under certain conditions the conflict between ideal and actual history churning *within* a historical object foments energies sufficient to create a "breaking point," a wakening disruption that "bursts forth" from the historical continuum.[108] In conceptualizing athletic bodies as theological images, then, I am suggesting that they encapsulate these conflicts and energies, which are variously suppressed or made visible across multiple representations and historical contexts.

The theological construction of athletic bodies is especially apparent where sport condenses the broader tensions of capitalist production. Even the most damning assessments of sport have allowed that athletic bodies might constitute (more than merely reflect) crises that move political and economic struggle forward.[109] Brohm, for example, critiques sport as repressive at every level, its ideals "naively peddled" as cover for its actual dramatizations of capitalist violence.[110] Yet he also recognizes that sport is central in bringing that violence to light, as athletics index the body's greater relationship to capitalism:

> Apart from the act of labour, the dominant and fundamental way man [*sic*] relates to his body in state capitalist society is through sport—inasmuch as it is through the model of sport that the body is understood in practice, collectively hallucinated, fantasised, imagined and individually experienced as an object, an instrument, a technical means to an end, a reified factor of output and productivity, in short, as a machine with the job of producing the maximum work and energy. And it is precisely this competitive sport and the conception of the body which it exemplifies which have now entered a *period of continuous crisis.*[111]

This is a good summary of the basic interrelationship between athletic bodies and conjuncture. As Brohm argues, athletic bodies both "refract" and "aggravate" the political, economic, and social conflicts of which they are a part.[112] Elite athletes, then, do not simply mirror crises in capitalist production. By representing a "double focus" on idealization and instantiation, they embody tensions sufficient to disrupt historical continuity.

Athletic Bodies, Audiovisual Capture, and Unconscious Optics

Benjamin's image-based views on theology and history coincided with his interest in photography and film.[113] According to Peter Gilgen, the imagistic potential to explode the historical continuum and the technology of film are "structurally homologous" in Benjamin's thought.[114] More generally, Benjamin understood the enhanced visibility of images in both theological and technological terms. The "lightning flash" of recognition created by dialectical images was, as Buck-Morss explains, "like illumination from a camera flashbulb," and the "images themselves" developed over time.[115] Photography, film, and electricity provided metaphorical understandings for the "shock" experience of recognition.[116]

These connections between historical memory and media technologies are particularly apparent through Benjamin's conception of "unconscious optics." Identifying the various interventions of film capture—expansions of space through the close-up, extensions of movement through slow motion, isolations of the subject—Benjamin writes, "The camera introduces us to unconscious optics as does psychoanalysis to unconscious impulses."[117] Miriam Hansen notes that unconscious optics mobilize a form of memory that sneaks in "through the back door," bringing "involuntary recollection" to bear against the archiving and forgetting of history. This is in line with Benjamin's larger project of "redeeming the possibility of experience in an irrevocably transformed world" by tracking that possibility through its very "agencies of transformation," including media technologies.[118]

Particularly important for my purposes, unconscious optics make the moving body a subject of close examination. As slow motion extended movement, it revealed previously imperceptible details of the body. Benjamin writes: "Even if one has a general knowledge of the way people walk, one knows nothing of a person's posture during the fractional second of a stride. The act of reaching for a lighter or a spoon is familiar routine, yet we hardly know what really goes on between hand and metal."[119] In sport the same technological advances in capture have affirmed progress-oriented histories by encouraging habitual associations between the capacity to gaze at beautiful athletic forms and the ability to recognize the transcendent advance of the human species.[120] As I argue, however (particularly in Chapter 3), specialized techniques of audiovisual capture such as instant replay pair aesthetic evidence of human-athletic advance with a persistent historical anxiety, a *forensic* urgency to apprehend history in the moment of its production. Thus in sport we find a convergence between Benjamin's unconscious optics (enhanced examinations of bodily motion through a stoppage of time) and the potential for historical critique (the dialectical image becoming visible in that stoppage) within the most basic habits of capture and visibility that sport sustains.

Audiovisual capture imbues athletic bodies with theological meanings that often support, but also might undermine, the continuity of historical progress in sport. A freeze-frame image of two swimmers reaching for the wall in an Olympic final, or a slow-motion replay of a football player dragging his toes inbounds for a catch in the Super Bowl, provide granular looks at how moving bodies shape history in sport and how their status is arbitrated through a combination of capture (in still photography, instant replay and slow motion, and online video) and collective witnessing by fans, journalists, coaches, players, and commentators, who clothe optical revelations in the language of transcendence. Following Jennifer Hargreaves and Patricia Vertinsky, I assume that the body's relationship to sport history can be fully appreciated only through a focus on "the body-in-movement," including considerations of how "physical culture"—the body's "anatomy, its physicality, and importantly its forms of movement"—constitute sport's basic purposes.[121] Only by attending to these movements can we appreciate athletic bodies' roles in shaping and undermining sport histories.[122] As Jaime Schultz demonstrates in her history of women's sport, attention to even the most "ostensibly banal" elements of physical culture (e.g., hairstyles, fashion, equipment) can instigate ideological clashes around "points of change": moments when specific elements of the athletic body coincide with "larger cultural currents" to constitute "progress . . . strife, backlash, and regression."[123]

Religion/Theology and Elite Televised Sport

I do not provide in this book any single, guiding definition of religion in relation to sport, since this would involve debates and encumbrances that are unnecessary for my argument.[124] Instead, I rely on a connection between religion and theology offered by Eduardo Mendieta, which directs attention to the institutional and symbolic interrelationships between the concepts. "Religion," Mendieta writes, "is an institution, not just because it coalesces into churches, sects, and proselytizing movements, but also because it provides societies with . . . common languages through which to addresses their hopes and discontents"; religion constitutes "a world view that inflects and refracts every lived movement within the lifeworld." Theology gives *expression* to that worldview; it is the "medium in which religion is able to speak and disclose its truth content."[125] Given this proximity between worldview and expression, I use "religion" and "theology" somewhat interchangeably. When I do, I mean to imply a focus on both institutional contexts and their productions of discourse. An institutional and symbolic understanding of religion and theology acknowledges the role that sport institutions like commercial media, governing bodies, or leagues play in producing and appropriating theological images. The difference between such official appropriations and my own project is that I am invested in how to put theological expressions "at the service of a critical social theory."[126]

I acknowledge that I am operating with a loose definition of religion. As Dominic Erdozain argues, works on sport, religion, and the body too often "stretch" religion across multiple contexts to form the misleading image of a "unified sea of faith." It is more accurate, he argues, to chart how religious formations and changes come through "dominant traditions" like Evangelical Christianity.[127] This is an important point, especially because religious ideals do not come out of thin air; they are produced, as I argued above, within and through institutional contexts. At the same time, much of the religious meaning in popular, mediated sport is analogical. A given religious image might borrow from denominational beliefs, but its power often plays out through figurative appropriations of those beliefs, which are mobilized for particular ideological purposes in particular contexts. This is the case, for example, with "witnessing" and "transcendence," as I suggest in Chapters 3 and 4. At the same time, denominational institutions may borrow from the religious power of sport to advance formal faith commitments, as with partnerships between Evangelical Christian organizations and sport leagues. Among the most productive facets of a negative theology, in my estimation, is that by resisting categorizations like civil and denominational, or profane and sacred, it retains the capacity to capture context-specific and nuanced mobilizations of religious imagery and belief at the level of cultural, material production.

My focus throughout this book is on elite televised sport (for the reader who suspects that references to television harken back to old media, I cover the contemporary shape of televisual production in Chapter 3). This is not because I believe that elite competition constitutes all of what matters as sport (it leaves out, for example, participatory sport, amateur sport, and fitness cultures), but because elite sport is a primary cultural source for images of transcendent human potential. That potential is assigned most powerfully to athletic bodies, which incarnate many of the most utopian dreams for the human condition: evolutionary leaps in physiological and spiritual capacity, liberation from the laws of physics and time, perfectibility. Elite *televised* sport is important because these dreams are constituted through audiovisual capture. In fact, as I suggest in Chapter 3, elite sport has served throughout history as a primary site for the development and application of specialized technologies, which, ever since Eadweard Muybridge's famous experiments with instantaneous photography in 1872, have aimed at capturing the secrets of bodily motion. Elite sport makes no sense apart from audiovisual capture and televisual representation; these are the means of production through which *proof* of ever-advancing human potential is represented, and through which competitive tests of that potential are staged. At the same time, elite athletic movements provide the raw evidence that audiovisual technologies record, freeze, and reveal. When I write about "elite televised sport," then, I am referencing a structural interdependency between bodily movement and audiovisual capture that lies at the heart of sport-religion relationships.

I am also referencing the potential problems that commercial media production poses for sport's religious idealism. Elite competition stages ultimate tests of human potential while at the same time (and relatedly) attracting massive corporate and governmental investments in broadcasting and content rights, advertising, medical and technological research, and training programs. The same bodies that presumably transcend species limits or political division also serve as sites for these investments: as billboards for corporate sponsors or nationalist rivalries; as machines conditioned, tested, and modified for specialized labor; as icons of domination and economic superiority. This simultaneous representation of religious idealism and market-based avarice is inherent, as I maintain throughout this book, in the very means of production in elite televised sport, but it becomes disruptively legible only under certain conditions. In the coming chapters I attempt to understand these conditions.

My focus on elite televised sport requires some caveats. First, elite sport predominantly implies sport as developed within wealthy nations, which have the economic, technological, and medical infrastructures necessary for competitive success on national and international levels. I analyze international sport in Chapters 3 and 4 (and to a lesser extent in Chapter 2) but my primary focus throughout the book is on U.S. sport. This is primarily because I am a U.S.-based scholar and these are the contexts I am most familiar with. My intention is not to endorse the hegemony of wealthy (and especially Western) nations but to analyze contexts where intense concentrations of capital, medical and technological intervention, and state sponsorship are contributing to particularly acute and highly publicized crises.

Second, elite sport predominantly implies sport as represented by and through a small handful of "wealthy organizing bodies and leagues" (e.g., the International Olympic Committee [IOC] or the National Football League [NFL]) that, as Brett Hutchins and David Rowe write, have the capacity "to attract and afford the highest quality athletes who can deliver mesmerizing athleticism on a consistent basis."[128] In packaging and promoting athletic spectacle, the NFL, for example, attracts more viewers than any other programming type—sport or nonsport—on U.S. television, thus folding together representations of elite performance and intense concentrations of political controversy.[129] The crises that interest me emerge from these organizations' increasing struggles to promote and regulate idealized conceptions of sport. Any possibilities for change have to be considered, however, against the fact that these organizations have been built through interdependent relationships with the state, the legal system, media conglomerates, technology companies, medical organizations, and other institutions. As a result, leagues and governing bodies have immense resources for responding to and appropriating public controversies.

Finally, elite *televised* sport captures problematic relationships between corporate media production, consumption, and dominant masculine notions of natural athleticism. In a recent update to a twenty-five-year longitudinal study, Cheryl Cooky, Michael Messner, and Michela Musto note that "coverage of women's sports in televised sports news and highlights shows remains dismally low."[130] There are signs that audiences for elite women's sporting events are expanding. The 2015 Women's World Cup Final between the United States and Japan, for example, averaged 25.4 million viewers in the United States, making it the most viewed soccer game (men's or women's) in U.S. history.[131] Moreover, attention to women's sport is not simply an every-four-years phenomenon exclusive to the World Cup or Olympics; there is evidence that elite women's sports are attracting sustainable and growing audiences in annual leagues as well (including, for example, professional basketball, professional soccer, and college softball).[132]

Overall, however, the ratings dominance of men's sports persists. Sportswriters, corporate media producers, and fans often take this as a sign that men's bodies can simply do more spectacular things, and so men's sports create greater demand in the marketplace. This presumption is reinforced by inattention in coverage, by the persistent ways in which "female athletics are constructed as an inferior product" to the more "naturally" exciting performances of men, and through the normalization of masculine assumptions in sport media workplaces.[133] Elite physicality is presumptively male, so much so that when women athletes' performances are *too* elite (record-breaking, or parallel to those of their male counterparts), their gender becomes subject to suspicion. The result is that the religious assumptions about human-athletic advance I critique in this book are disproportionately related to men's bodies and men's sports. This is not intended as an endorsement of the status quo. In fact, as I argue in Chapter 4, one of the most important crises in elite sport surrounds the continuum of challenges to supposedly natural or pure athleticism issued through the participation of female, transgender, and intersex athletes, as well as athletes with disabilities. Even so, given the current state of televised production, the most publicized crises of contemporary sport condense predominantly around men's competition.

Overview of the Book

The chapters that follow offer a response to the problems of sport and religion I have outlined above. In each chapter I demonstrate how negative theology provides a practically and theoretically useful critique of religion and conjuncture in elite televised sport.

Chapter 2 focuses on the uniquely obsessive preoccupation with legacy that characterizes elite sport, especially as condensed in the tropes "greatest ever" and "all-time." I argue that legacy debates represent the more general importance of constructing *eternity* as a form of temporal experience. More specifically, I maintain that eternity relates to fans' or journalists' desires to bear witness to a continuum of advancing human-athletic potential running through present time, a desire to appreciate how an accomplishment in *this moment* might relate to the expanse of *all-time*. Initially, eternity may seem to be about remembrance, about the stability or permanence of the historical record, especially because it so often attaches to anxieties over legacy. In fact, it is about the *constancy* of human-athletic evolution and the related guarantee that any person, living at any time, will get to experience its latest manifestation. What elite sport makes eternal is not the record but the cycle of evolutionary advances. The result is that the historical record becomes an archive of outmoded figures (former record holders, defunct physiques). According to the truism that all athletes "have their time," even the most legendary players will become mere rungs on the evolutionary ladder.

Chapter 2 is built, then, around a counterintuitive premise: eternity is produced in sport through forgetting and planned obsolescence. As Paul Connerton argues, planned obsolescence is a form of forgetting inherent to capitalist production, wherein "the ever increasing acceleration of innovation for the purpose of consumption produces ever larger quantities of soon to be obsolete objects," and the discarding of those objects is essential to how the market operates.[134] In sport, planned obsolescence is central to the continuous, commercial production of religious expectation, including interminable and profitable debates over legacy as well as scheduled and marketed anticipation of the next revelation in athletic advancement. Accordingly, Chapter 2 establishes a problem of forgetting that is basic to elite sport, a continuity mapped to the seemingly immutable advance of human-athletic potential. The argument I make in this chapter is that this image of immutability powerfully influences conceptions of elite athletic bodies as theological objects and potentially conceals the processes of historical production and institutional intervention that go into their creation. The chapters that follow, then, map particular cultural conditions under which the apparently ahistorical essence of human-athletic progress comes apart and processes of institutional intervention become popularly legible.

Chapter 3 is about the nature of witnessing in sport in light of debates surrounding instant replay. As John Durham Peters argues, "witnessing" is a term that captures the "questions of truth and experience . . . and the trust-worthiness of perception" that come with viewing the world through audio-visual capture.[135] As a religious ideal, witnessing relates commonly to images of profane-to-sacred transport (especially in the form of live participation and anticipation), but also to anxieties surrounding the status of "being there" at a moment of live revelation, an experience of time that, according to many critics, replay desacralizes. In contrast to the problems of historical continuity I examine in Chapter 2, the most distinctive and important quality of replay is that it *stops* continuity, introducing a cut in time that, depending on one's viewpoint, either ruins the "natural flow" of games or helps to fulfill sporting bodies' responsibility to "get history right" before it is too late and the outcome becomes a permanent part of the historical record. Benjamin argues that disrupting the continuity of historical progress requires changing the speed at which historical images flit through the present. If the flow of those images is slowed or brought to a halt, they might crystallize in "a constellation saturated with tensions."[136] This is, I argue, the basis of instant replay's importance: it stops the flow of live time, alters the ways in which we see elite sport, and in doing so creates the basic conditions for struggling over issues of historical authority, visual evidence, and present-oriented action.

In Chapter 4 I analyze controversies surrounding "technological doping," a relatively recent construct in ongoing debates over performance enhancement and antidoping regulation. The term refers, in its most straightforward sense, to the use of a technological aid (for example, a wearable or prosthetic technology) to gain a competitive advantage. In a more complex sense, technological doping represents, I argue, a specific stage in a series of ongoing social agreements on performance enhancement, a moment when the qualities of secrecy and visibility associated with doping are undergoing changes that point toward the challenges and possibilities of transhumanist sport. I maintain that the implications of this moment can be profitably understood through Martha C. Nussbaum's distinction between "internal" and "external" transcendence. For Nussbaum, internal transcendence provides a backdrop against which human excellences can be meaningfully pursued, as it marks out "finitude" in relation to the limits of the human body (e.g., pain, aging, death). By contrast, Nussbaum rejects as "incoherent . . . the aspiration to leave behind altogether the constitutive conditions of our humanity, and to seek for a life that is really the life of another sort of being," a desire that she associates with external transcendence.[137] Her case relates especially to athletics, where achievement has value only relative "to the context of the human body, which imposes certain species-specific limits and creates certain possibilities of movement rather than others." What is the meaning of achievement, then, for a body that "transcends" these limits (say, through extrahuman or "unnatural" technological modifications)?[138] This is the basic problem confronting contemporary elite sport, a problem that technological doping especially sheds light on.

My argument in Chapter 4 tracks a succession of stages in the institutional and popular agreements surrounding doping, leading up to and through technological doping. Each stage represents changing problems of human-technological integration in sport: from human bodies and technological aids as separated systems, to wearable technologies as integrated but removable devices, to prosthetics as more fully integrated with "organic" body parts, and finally to the integration of transhuman and cyborg athletes into mainstream (e.g., able-bodied, categorically gendered) competition. Throughout the chapter I analyze problems and difficulties that come with referencing the body as a context for deriving species-specific limitations to transcendence. Despite the common moralism surrounding performance enhancement, doping represents, in John Hoberman's words, a "tacit agreement" between officials, medical professionals, and athletes who wish to reap the social and economic benefits of elite performance while also attending to popular idealisms surrounding the "purity" of sport.[139] In this sense those forms of technological intervention, which mark a "transhumanist" moment in elite sport—a moment of transition toward a posthuman state, when athletes' bodies are becoming more fully integrated with biotechnologies—are a significant source of anxieties but also a logical extension of institutionalized desires for limitless performance.[140] I conclude Chapter 4 with a consideration of the future implications of external transcendence in light of challenges posed to supposedly natural athleticism by biotechnologies, transgender and intersex athletes, and athletes with disabilities.

The National Football League (NFL) is currently in the midst of a crisis over traumatic brain injury (often summarized as a "concussion crisis") that has many commentators contemplating the "death" of the league as the most powerful sport media empire in the United States. In Chapter 5 I argue that ruminations over the NFL's fall can be understood in light of the league's tendency to revisit its beginnings. In more general terms, I view the NFL as an example of how sacred origins might serve as both reservoirs for idealized memory and scenes of foundational injustice. Origins represent the desire for an essentially pure beginning that can be revisited and refreshed to cleanse the sins of subsequent history. But origins might also contain an institution's founding crimes, a taint of barbarism that transmits forward and becomes legible at specific historical moments.[141] The traumatic brain injury crisis is, I argue, one such moment.

The NFL has historically constructed and maintained idealized versions of its past through NFL Films (the league's in-house production company) and through partnerships with entertainment industry directors, producers, and production companies. A significant part of the league's commercial success relates to its masterful production of mythic historical accounts, which it refreshes as a resource for regular brand maintenance and a vehicle for responding to publicity crises. Yet the brain injury crisis is exceeding the league's typically firm ideological control. In this way, the NFL represents how perpetual return to idealized beginnings might expose the discontinuities and corruptions of an institution's rise, resulting in a gradual and condemning retelling of its official history. To get at these problems of origin I analyze how the league's earliest moments of commercial ascendance in the late 1950s were simultaneous with its undermining of players' collective bargaining rights, and how resulting struggles over long-term health-care and disability benefits are becoming uniquely legible through the brain injury crisis.

Chapter 6 concludes the book by proposing a set of theses about negative theology and sport, using as its touchstone a brief account of current legal and activist challenges to the amateur ideal in elite college athletics (especially in football and men's basketball). For more than a century, the National Collegiate Athletic Association (NCAA, the most powerful organization governing college athletics in the United States) has run some hybrid version of a free-market and nonprofit (educational) institution. Within this system the organization has negotiated increasingly lucrative media agreements and licensing deals, while also barring college athletes from market-rate compensation, due-process protections, and collective bargaining rights. That system is, as one journalist put it, "on life support," due largely to a series of activist and legal challenges led by current and former college athletes.[142] These challenges come at a time when the so-called arms race in big-money college athletics (an effort between universities and conferences to compete for television dollars, elite players, and top coaches) has created conspicuous spending on athletics buildings, practice facilities, stadium and arena expansions, and multimillion-dollar coaches' contracts. As Joe Nocera of the *New York Times* writes, all of this spending constitutes a "glaring, and increasingly untenable, discrepancy" between the compensation given to football and basketball players and the profits reaped by "everyone else in their food chain."[143]

From these challenges to the amateur ideal I extrapolate, with an eye to the preceding chapters, a set of theses regarding sport and negative theology. These theses are particular to the historical and cultural moment captured in my book, but I also offer them as more general guides for understanding, critiquing, and perhaps acting on significant changes surrounding religion and elite sport cultures.

2

GREATEST EVER

*Eternity, Forgetting, and
Obsolescence*

It is August 2008 at the Summer Olympic Games in Beijing, China, and Jamaican sprinter Usain Bolt has, in the words of *Philadelphia Inquirer* journalist Phil Sheridan, transcended the "time-space continuum."[1] Bolt has run so fast, has so thoroughly dominated his opponents in breaking world records and winning gold medals in the 100- and 200-meter races, that multiple witnesses are testifying to a reordering of time and the potential of the human body. *Salon* writer Gary Kamiya compares watching Bolt run to "looking over Shakespeare's shoulder" while he wrote *King Lear*, "sitting next to Isaac Newton when the apple fell from the tree," and being with Gustav Mahler as he composed his Fifth Symphony. Bolt has "turned in the greatest individual athletic performance of our time, and one of the greatest ever" a feat that so fundamentally shifts "the horizon of human possibility" that the brain is not calibrated to appreciate it fully.[2]

Journalists promise that even if Bolt's records are broken, their imprint will "last forever," but there is a representative urgency to situate his accomplishments.[3] Are they the greatest achievements in track and field history? Is he among the greatest Olympians of all time? Even if only intuitively understood, there is always a sense after moments of elite athletic performance that memory and historical status are at *immediate* risk. As John Fiske suggests in his book *Television Culture*, this risk is characteristic of televisual events: by focusing on achievement they "compress time" and shift attention to the "performance-climax that produces the result." Characters and narratives only "'live' in their

moments of performance," creating the smallest of windows to stake a historical claim before attention shifts to the next event.[4]

Heading into the 2012 Summer Olympic Games in London, the question
of Bolt's legacy is reopened, the eternal status of his accomplishments only
four years earlier already in doubt. Bolt has lost twice in the Jamaican trials to
his younger teammate Yohan Blake, and journalists are questioning whether
he is already being passed by the next advance in the athletic evolutionary
chain.[5] If Bolt does not win again in the 2012 games, he can be dismissed as
a flashing "phenomenon," a "freak," a temporary star.[6] But Bolt does repeat,
becoming the first track athlete to complete the so-called "double-double"
with gold-medal performances in the 100- and 200-meter races. Now he cannot be dismissed. He is officially an Olympic legend. Journalists exult once
again: Bolt has "made a mockery of everything we previously believed about
. . . the limits of the human body"; he has transcended race, nationality, and
religion by representing humanity at large, "defining what is possible within
the limitations of the species."[7] Bolt, who is delightfully irreverent, claims
the same status for himself: "I am a legend. Bask in my glory."[8] But he also
seems aware that he is caught up in an inevitable historical progression. Asked
whether he will compete in the 2016 games in Rio de Janeiro, Bolt is unsure:
"I think I've had my time." In 2016 he will be thirty years old, while his Jamaican teammates, who are his closest competition, will be only twenty-six.[9]
Track and field legend Edwin Moses warns that Bolt must stay out of the 2016
games or risk his legacy by giving younger competitors the chance to overtake
him.[10] Moses speaks from a position further along the historical continuum.
He understands that the difference between 2012 and whatever future Bolt
faces is the inevitable *replaceability* of his body.

Bolt went on to compete in and dominate the 2016 Olympic Games.
Having achieved, in his own assessment, "immortal" status, he announced
his retirement. Andy Bull of *The Guardian* suggested that the timing for
Bolt's departure was appropriate, as the "cracks" in his physical ability were
starting to show: his speed was no longer special, and he had dominated
his competitors due primarily to a psychological advantage.[11] Such focus on
Bolt's elite ability and inescapable decline summarizes sport history's most
basic article of faith: a continuum of evolving human-athletic potential runs
through our own moment, and the present generation bears witness to its
latest stage of development through a succession of rising and declining stars.
It also illustrates how forgetting is a seemingly inevitable part of sport historical production. As Bolt conceded in 2012, all athletes have their time,
and when that time is up it is important to bow out gracefully. A player who
resists retirement after a clear decline in physical skills is said to be hanging
on too long. What sets apart all-time greats is that they remain *citable* as time

passes. In interview after interview, athletes express their wish for legacy in this limited sense: they hope that whenever the history of their sport is discussed, they will be brought up "in the same sentence" with the greatest to ever play. Thus, while questions like those surrounding Bolt's status among the "greatest ever" Olympians are to some extent about remembrance, they also help fans and journalists to anticipate the *next* revelatory advance in athletic progress. Sport programming providers capitalize on this anticipation by selling the consumption of live games, highlights shows, online debates, and commemorative specials as opportunities to witness history in the making. Fans negotiate the passing relevance of their favorite stars and teams with the excitement of new revelations, and constant historical turnover comes with a fundamental reassurance: no matter which present we live in (this moment, or the present to come) we will be granted the opportunity to witness signs of human advancement in their very moments of production.

As Walter Benjamin recognized, such an evolutionary view of history requires proclaiming the past as completed, a finished step in the ever-unfolding march of human progress.[12] This is especially apparent in sport because that unfolding is punctuated at such abbreviated intervals. As we learn from Bolt's example, in the four-year gaps between 2008, 2012, and 2016 athletes can be assigned eternal status, risk losing it, regain it, and risk losing it again, as the very continuum of human advancement they reveal also overtakes them. As long as the naturalness and inevitability of that process is maintained through the image of an ever-evolving body, we are stuck with a limited capacity to recognize in the present the traces and residues of past political and economic inequities that remain unaddressed in our own time.[13]

This chapter is about these problems of forgetting as they surround the supposedly immutable progress of elite athletic bodies. My main concern in this chapter is to outline some of the most basic processes of sport media production that suppress the dialectical potential residing in athletic bodies through their capacity (as I covered in Chapter 1) to force confrontations between the highest promises of religious idealism and the betrayal of those promises in actual history. Beyond simply presenting a problem, my hope is to map out—in some detail—those patterns of sport media production and fan expectation that mobilize a constant turnover of events and star athletes, in order to understand the particular conditions under which these patterns might be disrupted. My argument is that an image of eternity—as frequently condensed in the tropes "greatest ever" and "all-time"—sustains historical continuities central to the economic and social interests of elite sport institutions. This image is especially tied to elite athletic bodies, which provide primary sources of visual, performative proof that humanity is advancing through successive stages of evolutionary development.

Although this may seem counterintuitive, debates over "all-time" are not principally about remembrance or preservation of the historical archive. They are about a form of purposeful forgetting, what Paul Connerton identifies as a "*planned obsolescence* built into the capitalist system of consumption," where "the ever increasing acceleration of innovation for the purpose of consumption produces ever larger quantities of soon to be obsolete objects" and where the discarding of those objects is essential for how the market operates.[14] Fredric Jameson similarly associates planned obsolescence with late capitalism and with larger problems of memory—"namely, the disappearance of a sense of history, the ways in which our entire contemporary social system has . . . begun to live in a perpetual present" where the media relegate "recent historical experiences as rapidly as possible into the past."[15] Forgetting is not just a failure to remember or commemorate. It is often a problem of selective representation, a particular and ideologically directed use of partially recalled history.[16] In elite sport, eternity is a form of forgetting that expresses desires to live during and bear witness to a continuity of advances in human capacity.

This chapter is divided into two parts. The first offers a broad look at productions of eternity with reference to the 2008 sport season, examining how conceptions of succession, circulation, and eternity in the works of Kenneth Burke and Bruno Latour provide fitting ways to read those productions.[17] This first part frames a general understanding of eternity that I apply, in the second part, to a close reading of two NFL Network (NFLN) commemorative specials: *The Top 100: NFL's Greatest Players* and *The Top 100 Players of 2013.*[18] While any number of sport seasons or commemorative specials might contain similar evidence about how eternity is produced, the cases I focus on in this chapter are particularly illustrative. The 2008 season was at the time (and still sometimes is) referred to as the greatest season in the history of sport, so it featured uniquely concentrated debates around questions of legacy and history. The NFL's *Top 100* lists represent how the United States' most powerful sport media empire structures its practices of historical production around a succession of constantly replaceable bodies and legacies. In addition, the 2008 sport season and NFL lists emphasize how legacy is staked in a finite window within which individual athletes self-reflexively grasp for eternity.

Part One: Succession and the Immutable Progress of Athletic Bodies

Surveying the 2008 sport season during a weekly appearance on National Public Radio (NPR), *Sports Illustrated* journalist and HBO correspondent Frank Deford perfectly summarized the tension between eternity and succession that characterizes sport: "It's really quite amazing the attention that sports fans pay to legacy, to how their favorite has-beens rank for posterity. History is history, except for sports." As he explains, "The present is always playing the past" through a persistent need to ask, "Who is the greatest of all time?"[19] Australian sportswriter Michael Cowley wrote similarly that "past versus present is . . . sport's greatest contest."[20] Deford was responding to widespread claims that 2008 was the greatest sport season ever. While remarking that he would typically associate such talk with standard sport "sophistry," Deford conceded that 2008 had legitimately presented fans and journalists with "an absolute glut of brilliance."[21] The NFL's New England Patriots were looking like the greatest team in the history of football, and perhaps of any sport. They were undefeated in the regular season and had won more games than any team in league history. Tennis star Roger Federer, perhaps the greatest player in history, had lost to Rafael Nadal in an epic Wimbledon match that was rated by observers as the greatest Wimbledon final ever and perhaps the greatest tennis match of all time. Tiger Woods, evaluated by journalists as the most dominant golfer ever, dramatically overcame a knee injury to win the U.S. Open. U.S. swimmer Michael Phelps was proclaimed the greatest Olympian ever after winning a record number of gold medals at the Summer Games in Beijing. And Jamaican sprinter Usain Bolt ran so fast that he tore a metaphorical hole in the fabric of space and time.

Most of this has to be reconsidered in hindsight. Eleven days after Deford's appearance on NPR, the Patriots lost to the New York Giants in the Super Bowl (though sportswriters made an easy enough pivot and labeled this one of the greatest upsets of all time).[22] In 2010 Tiger Woods confessed to multiple extramarital affairs and has struggled ever since to return to his former level of dominance.[23] After a second-round defeat at the 2013 Wimbledon to the player ranked 116th in the world, Roger Federer's legacy is being questioned, and there are concerns that if he does not retire soon, he could "incrementally slip [toward] also ran status."[24]

Despite all their attention to legacy questions, journalists and fans intuit that debates over "greatest ever" and "all-time" are as much about forgetting as they are about remembrance. Why bother, then? Because, as one journalist insightfully put it, sport supports a "lust to share one's lifespan with nothing other than the Greatest, the Brightest, the Best and the Most Momentous, as if somehow the glory will rub off on the observer, like excess aftershave."[25] To live in this kind of present, some image of constancy has to run through successive changes in the historical status of athletes and teams, especially when participants know those changes are coming. Most devoted sport fans have experienced, in repetitive cycles, the sentimentality attached to a fading career alongside the excitement of witnessing the next great performer, the precariousness of all-time in the fading attention of the present. That image of constancy, I argue throughout this chapter, is the ever-evolving athletic body.

While attention to memory may characterize other cultural institutions, sport has no equal when it comes to obsessions with legacy. Turn on any network dedicated to sport in the immediate afterglow of an elite performance and you will see flash polls, a cobbled-together top-ten list, and a panel of retired athletes, all adjudicating its historical status. This is just a microcosm of constant efforts to mark, measure, debate, and recall history through commemorative specials, "all-time greatest" lists, interview shows, and so on, whether the accomplishment or event under examination occurs during a sport mega-event (an Olympic final, a Super Bowl) or a mundane afternoon baseball game. In terms of persistence and consistency there are no parallels in politics (imagine every legislative controversy or major speech being ranked on an all-time list on a weekly basis); in film, music, or art (where greatest-ever lists are published at longer intervals); or any other popular cultural institution. The closest approximation may be the entertainment histories produced by VH1 like "I Love the 80s" or "Best Week Ever"; while sport has a similar self-consciousness, however, its constant remaking of history is not purposely ironic.[26]

In *The Rhetoric of Religion*, Kenneth Burke explains constant attention to the present by offering an analogy between time and eternity. Drawing similarities to the structure of a sentence, Burke compares "time" to the sentence's individual and transient signs, and "eternity" to the sentence's larger meaning. To provide an immediately relevant example: if I say, "Lionel Messi is one of the greatest soccer players of all time," "Messi" serves as a transient sign. His name is interchangeable with a certain number of alternative possibilities, but the sentence has meaning beyond this one example; it invites a formulaic sport cultural debate over all-time greats. It is within the *formal* properties of that debate that sport media producers can shape an image of perpetual and successive progress through our present moment. As Burke writes, eternity is experienced when we take transient signs as evidence of a broader, more essential continuity:

> The succession of words in a sentence would be analogous to the "temporal." But the *meaning* of the sentence is an *essence*, a kind of fixed significance or definition that is not confined to any of the sentence's parts, but rather pervades or inspirits the sentence as a whole. Such meaning, I would say, is analogous to "eternity." In contrast with the flux of the sentence, where each syllabus arises, exists for a moment, and then "dies" to make room for the next stage of the continuing

process, the meaning is "non-temporal," though embodied (made incarnate) in a temporal series.[27]

In sport, the continuity of a "temporal series"—as one era's greatness is surpassed by the next stage of development—proves that the work of transcendence is always unfinished, that human potential is being, and will continue
to be, pushed to its outmost boundaries. All focus goes to the present-day
incarnation of the sequence in the person of the athlete, whose exploits make
the advancement through the next stage knowable. To follow from Burke, the
present becomes "immutable" only when an ongoing succession of tangible
details—words, bodies, statistics, events—make the newest emergence legible,
then dissolve away to create room for the *next* emergence.[28] What becomes
meaningful is the process of succession itself, a process that is "non-temporal"
not because it occurs outside history (as suggested in ontological notions of
sacredness or transcendence), but because it appears to be irreducible to any
one moment.

The eternity that programmers produce—the endlessly renewable excitement of witnessing the *now* of historical production—requires making room
for the next emergence in an uninterrupted continuity. That continuity is by
no means inevitable, however. There is always a possibility, Burke writes, for a
"*temporal* contradiction" between time and eternity, an "interval" in "the suc-
cessiveness of time" that opens up possibilities for social change.[29] The challenge for sport media producers and institutional officials is to foster profitable
obsessions over history without cultivating critical attention to the processes
underlying historical production or introducing stoppages or intervals that
would allow the past to become more fully legible. To appreciate how producers and officials, as well as athletes and fans, negotiate this challenge, we need
to understand the athletic body's immutability as an effect of circulatory patterns in historical and mediated production.

As Cara Finnegan writes, "circulation" is a term that helps critics to focus
on how images or discourses acquire meaning both in the immediacy of a
specific rhetorical context and through transfer and reproduction across multiple contexts and events. Importantly, circulation does not merely *transmit*
meaning as a passive conduit; in asking where, how, and why images and
discourses circulate, we can understand better how they "become inventional
resources in the public sphere."[30] It is through correspondences between technological production and circulatory patterns that programmers, commentators, and fans inscribe beliefs about immutable progress onto athletic bodies.

Describing the formation of scientific and religious images, Bruno Latour
argues that the small details and decisions that go into an image's production
are encoded into visual forms that are transferable across multiple contexts.

Latour calls that process of inscribing smaller traits into a larger, mobile form "trans-formation." In detailing the work of preparing a scientific image, for example, Latour writes that a "hundred or so intermediary steps" will be taken in the image's construction, and then there "will be the gradual *disappearance*" of those steps as the image takes on a seemingly essential or ahistorical shape. Immutability is the effect of all those intermediary steps becoming invisible as the form circulates across texts and contexts. Parallel with Burke's explanation of how the sequential particulars of time are transformed into the immutable present of eternity, Latour argues that the apparently essential nature of a religious image is actually a product of "successive transformations": "What is kept constant from one representation to the next is morphed . . . into the *thing itself*. . . . This, then, is the ultimate paradox of a historical mediation that provides access to what is then seen as an inaccessible, ahistorical, and unmediated essence."[31]

Rather than signifying permanence and constancy, immutability is about concealing actual works of historical and institutional intervention in a continuity that *appears* essential. By retaining some constants and allowing other details to dissolve from memory, producers are, in Cara Finnegan and Jiyeon Kang's words, able to hide the work of "human hands" in the creation of a religious image, sustaining the image as "an immutable object of adoration."[32] In sport the work of human hands includes an entire system of institutional interventions that have gone into constituting the body's supposedly natural, evolutionary, or transcendent advancement. To borrow from Finnegan and Kang, athletic bodies contain histories of these interventions, but dominant institutions "rely on the concealment" of those histories in order to sustain the "truth" of advancing human potential. To critique a religious image's apparent immutability, then, the details of its production have to become legible.[33]

Legibility is not universally disruptive, however. As I emphasize in the coming chapters, conjuncture in elite sport depends on the accumulation of problems and contradictions surrounding particularly foundational assumptions about athletic bodies' status and meaningfulness within broader structures of media, state, technological, medical, and labor production. By "foundational" I am referring, in part, to the various essentialisms (naturalness, humanness) that uphold athletic transcendence, but also to the deeper points of retreat that fans or journalists or governing body executives can move to as questions emerge about the proclaimed values of competition. And in elite sport the most apparently irreducible truth that establishes a floor beneath problems of contradiction or antagonism is the evolutionary progress of human-athletic potential. This truth contains a certain amount of deterministic power: it establishes an essence untouchable by the fluctuations of politics, scandal, or new technologies, and it offers a guarantee that sport will never be completely lost as a source of uplift *out of* those fluctuations.

The importance of institutional interventions is not lost on fans, journalists, or players. In fact, much of the work of human hands is made visible through frequent attention in sport media coverage to improvements in diet, training, and performance enhancement. These details are not irrelevant, but under most conditions they seem to be of *secondary* and *temporary* importance to the transcending arc of human potential. Even the most insightful popular critics of sport tend to preserve the assumption that an unmediated constancy enables the progress of athletic bodies. Journalist Dave Zirin's book *Welcome to the Terrordome*, for example, offers a typically sharp critique of the various institutional interests surrounding steroid use in Major League Baseball (MLB). Zirin notes that team owners' greed drove a desire for more home runs, leading to changes in the depth of outfields, a more tightly wound ball, and a smaller strike zone. Innovations surrounding performance-enhancing drugs, especially after the U.S. federal government deregulated the supplements industry through the Dietary Supplement Health and Education Act (DSHEA), made steroids a widely available means for furthering the production of home runs and improving injury recovery, while owners and other MLB officials turned the other way. Zirin allows that each factor helps to explain the increase in home runs. But then there are the facts of "basic evolution." As Zirin writes:

> Players are also just better than they were eighty, fifty, twenty, even ten years ago. . . . [I]t is a well-recognized fact that—in every sport from running to swimming—athletes get better over time. The male winner of the 1932 Summer Olympics swimming gold medal in the 100-meter freestyle wouldn't even make the Junior Olympics team today. If Babe Ruth were alive, he would be a fat guy watching baseball on TV. If Ty Cobb were alive, he would be laughed off the field for holding his bat with his hands about six inches apart. It is just a different game.[34]

All of this evidence—swimming speed, body composition, technique—implies the work of historical forces greater than the sum of institutional controls; one way or another, the 1932 Olympic swimmer, Ruth, and Cobb would have become obsolete, as today's athletes are "just better" and are improving in shorter and shorter historical intervals. This image of an ahistorical evolution is coming to a point of rupture, as I argue in Chapter 4, due to recent shifts in the conspicuousness of performance enhancement, but the durable image of an irreducibly natural athleticism makes the implications of that conspicuousness uncertain.

Reflecting on the 2008 season, Deford argues, much like Zirin, that the tendency to "bow to the numbers and worship the immediate" is unfair to past athletes but is also a sign of inevitable advances in athletic capacity: "With his times from 1936," Deford notes, "[track and field legend] Jesse Owens wouldn't get near the Olympic starting blocks" in 2008.[35] *New York Times* journalist Dave Anderson argues similarly that debates over whether the 2008 New England Patriots were the greatest team of all time are senseless because changes in players' bodies make comparisons across historical eras impossible.[36] For Deford, this regular habit of measuring individuals and eras against one another is a "parlor game" inherent to sport, where fans assume that athletes are always improving and "records are made to be broken."[37] In no other institution, Deford insists, is this assumption so powerful: "The issue of pre-eminence in sport is heightened because, of almost all the institutions in the world, it's about the only one where it is accepted that the principals are getting better all the time. In sports, it's an article of faith that somebody paints a better Sistine Chapel ceiling about every other weekend."[38] To reinforce his point, Deford asked listeners during a radio commentary: "Remember when, oh, about five minutes ago, Roger Federer was surely the best tennis player of all time? Now, all of a sudden, he may not even be considered the best player of his generation."[39] In fact, the 2008 Wimbledon final between Federer and Rafael Nadal was considered at the time the greatest tennis match in history, but Nadal won; for observers, this signaled "the dawn of a new era," a sign of the end of Federer's reign.[40] In 2008 *Sunday Age* journalist Will Swanton described Federer's decline: once considered the best athlete in the world, Federer was perhaps not even the world's best tennis player; younger stars were "circling like sharks," Federer's health was failing, and it could have been that he was never "as good as we thought, capitalising on a soft era."[41] In a 2013 retrospective titled "Federer-Nadal Rivalry on Its Last Legs," *Sports Illustrated* writer Bruce Jenkins noted that Federer's 2008 Wimbledon loss affirmed questions in the tennis world regarding his toughness that had become "eternally valid" when Nadal soundly beat him in the 2008 French Open final a month earlier.[42]

Nostalgic attachments to past sport heroes persist, but they are easily trumped by technologically focused celebrations of the body's progress. As Kimberly K. Smith suggests, people who resist historic advancement enabled by "ever-improving technology" might open themselves to charges of nostalgic opposition to progress, emotional attachment to an outmoded past.[43] That charge does not always come through explicitly in sport (certainly stories about sport heroes "back in the day" can induce some eye rolling), but it is implied in concessions to the inevitability of athletic evolution. Like Zirin, Deford, or Anderson, many journalists, fans, coaches, and players might like to retain a memory of the past but feel they are up against the undeniable forces of progress. Consider, for example, Dick Vermeil, former head coach of the NFL's Philadelphia Eagles, St. Louis Rams, and Kansas City Chiefs, commenting on the idea that the 2008 Patriots are the greatest team of all time: "I believe [the Patriots are] the best team. . . . [T]hey've won all their games, more than anyone has ever won . . . and they've done it in a more sophisticated league. . . . I like to say that the 1976 Cadillac was a beautiful, wonderful car. But compared to the 2006 Cadillac, it can't compete."[44] On technical grounds Vermeil is right. Presuming direct competition as a primary measure of sport's "greatness," contemporary players and teams would overwhelm most of their predecessors. And contemporary athletes have to assume they will be overtaken, in kind, by some future turn in the evolutionary cycle. This is how British swimmer Simon Burnett explained Michael Phelps's dominance in the 2008 Olympics: "[Phelps is] from the future. His father made him and made a time machine. Sixty years from now he's just an average swimmer. But he has come to this time to mop up."[45] Burnett's time machine depicts a realistic scenario for sport fans: sometime in the future, we will look back on today's great athletes and perceive them as low-tech.

In establishing human advancement as an irreducible truth, these evolutionary images sustain continuities central to economic production in elite televised sport: endlessly renewable cycles of rising and declining stars, interminable debates over legacy, seasonal turnover, regularly scheduled anticipation of live games, and constant production of commemorative specials. There is common awareness in sport of a finite duration—often referred to as an athlete's "time" or a team's "window"—within which players can make a historical mark. When their physical skills deteriorate, they are typically either forced to renegotiate their contracts or are cut by their teams; players routinely respond by accepting that elite sport is a business and that their value to the organization was always contingent on continuing productivity. Fans' praise of players will turn to criticism at the first hint of a downward turn in physical ability, at which point they claim that the players have had their time and need to step aside for someone younger. Forgetting and obsolescence are the expected costs of evolutionary forces presumed to overtake all players and teams. The athlete's time mirrors the life cycle of emerging and degenerating technologies.

No athlete is immune to such encroaching obsolescence. A player who sustains a period of dominance is always subject, in the very moment of her or his declining skills, to legacy doubts. When Tiger Woods played through a knee injury to win the 2008 U.S. Open, commentators glowed over the television image of his toughness and determination. The *Washington Post*'s Thomas Boswell wrote that Woods "simply decided to ignore [the pain] out of some Special Forces code of honor" inherited from his father, Earl Woods, a Vietnam War Green Beret who taught Tiger how to play golf. "This day," Boswell continued, "was about a son honoring the memory of his hard-bark dad. . . . This was boot camp and jungle and show-me-what-you-are-made-of-kid for Tiger."[46] The image of Woods willing his body to victory circulated as evidence that he may have been the greatest athlete of all time. Journalists compared him to Muhammad Ali, Pete Sampras, Pele, Babe Ruth, Wayne Gretzsky, Michael Jordan, Lance Armstrong, Martina Navratilova, and Jim Thorpe, among others, and Woods topped several lists as the most dominant athlete in any sport, ever.[47] After the revelation of his extramarital affairs late in 2009, Woods did not win a golf tournament again until 2011 (when he dropped out of the top fifty in the world rankings for the first time in his career); at the time of this writing, he has yet to win another major.[48] Legendary golfer Nick Faldo and iconic British Broadcasting Corporation (BBC) commentator Peter Alliss both argued that Woods has lost his "aura," and a common theme in current commentaries is to question whether he will ever return to dominance.[49]

To borrow from Latour, sport culture debates over all-time or greatest-ever athletes constitute a "series of transformations for which each image is only a provisional frame."[50] Urgent questions over whether a particular accomplishment counts for eternity, and debates over what standards to use in determining that, signal some awareness that as an image flits through our own moment, some elements of it will be lost to the past. This is part of the urgency and desperation to make status judgments in the immediate aftermath of elite athletic performances: if a given accomplishment or figure deserves consideration for all-time status, the time to record history is *now*, before the affective intensities of the moment and the bodily evidence for recognizing transcendence simultaneously fade away.

For athletic bodies to become more than provisional frames in a series of successions, the continuity of historical production has to slow down or come to a stop. As Benjamin emphasizes, the "flow must come to a halt" so that the conflicts and struggles of the past can "crystallize into a shape" that is "immediately present."[51] Under such conditions athletic bodies might signify the burden of still-unresolved historical struggles rather than the immutability of progress. Much depends, as Ronald Greene writes, on the "differential speeds of circulation and duration of attention" that define larger communication patterns.[52] This is the problem I move to next, with the hope that a close reading of the NFL's *The Top 100: NFL's Greatest Players* and *The Top 100 Players of 2013* specials provides a more detailed illustration of the processes of transformation, succession, and immutability outlined above. Specifically, I expand on how sport media production makes athletic bodies provisional frames in a broader continuity, before I briefly preview the focus of the remaining chapters: the cultural and historical conditions under which that continuity comes to a halt.

Part Two: Succession and Eternity
in the NFL Top 100

Sport programming features all-time and greatest-ever lists for everything: upsets, blunders, college football and basketball players, soccer players, baseball pitchers and hitters, quarterbacks, most-hated athletes, dirtiest athletes, black athletes, women athletes, Mexican American athletes, left-handed athletes, and so on.[53] At least two factors make the NFL and its *Top 100* lists stand out within these broader production patterns: (1) the NFL has been the most popular sport league in the United States for the past several decades, and (2) the growth of that popularity is attributable to branding strategies that have focused, in part, on "mythopoetic" productions of league history.[54] Particularly relevant for the *Top 100* lists, the NFL has for decades relied on its in-house media production company, NFL Films, to tell "stories about professional football in a self-consciously epic mode."[55] The lists I analyze below were produced by NFL Films for broadcast on NFL Network (NFLN), the league's official television network.

NFL Films has served as the league's production arm since Commissioner Pete Rozelle incorporated it in 1964 as "a promotional vehicle to glamorize the game and present it in its best light."[56] Most of the iconic images and sounds associated with professional football—including John Facenda's melodramatic narrations about mythic scenes and great warriors, field-level shots of players running in slow motion, tracking shots of spiraling footballs dropping into receivers' hands, soaring orchestral music punctuated with grunts and collisions—have been produced by NFL Films. In addition, many of the practices associated with contemporary sport media production originated with the innovations of NFL Films founder Ed Sabol and his son Steve Sabol. Starting with the 1964 season, NFL Films shot regular-season and playoff football games with an increasing number of cameras (with one always dedicated to slow motion) and from multiple overhead and field-level perspectives.[57] For a contemporary nationally televised NFL game, more than twenty cameras and forty replay machines capture action from various angles.[58] The images captured by all of these cameras have long been included in NFL Films–produced histories like the *Top 100* lists. Television series produced for NFLN, such as *America's Game* (which commemorates recent

Super Bowl seasons and teams) and *A Football Life* (which profiles key figures and moments from the league's past), represent contemporary realizations of Rozelle's original vision: ghostly figures wander through billowing mist; great moments are replayed against epic soundtracks; hardened coaches remember and weep.[59] Through both of the *Top 100* commemorations examined here, NFL Films continues its longer project of mythologizing professional football through audiovisual capture and examinations of players' bodies.[60]

The *Top 100* lists I analyze here detail how the NFL incorporates reflexivity over its own practices of historical production, but within a continuity that dissolves political tensions surrounding the league's past. Commentators gesture toward labor disputes or racial inequities as temporary bumps in professional football's otherwise continuous rise as the United States' most popular game (some of those tensions are analyzed here, and Chapter 5 is devoted entirely to NFL history and the league's current crisis over brain injury). My analysis starts with an all-time list—*The Top 100: NFL's Greatest Players*—in order to detail the league's creation of a broader eternity. Then, I analyze a shorter timeframe—*The Top 100 Players of 2013*—to demonstrate how the *now* of NFL history succeeds from that eternity.

The Top 100: NFL's Greatest Players

Each episode of *The Top 100: NFL's Greatest Players* opens with choppy violin music and an overhead shot of a white slide reel cycling through a sequence of numbers printed in black at its outer edges. The filaments of a light bulb flash on before a panning shot shows piles of unorganized slides sitting on top of an empty canister. The pace of the music and the shot sequencing picks up as the work of arrangement begins. There are close-ups of old audiovisual technologies replaying game highlights. Beams of light project from the lenses of 16-mm film projectors, highlighting dust particles in the air. There is an audible buzzing and whirring matched to unevenly turning reels. Slide canisters turn notch by notch with a clear *click*. An archivist (we see only his hands) carefully sorts the documents, flipping through pages of still photos, arranging and inserting slides, and marking, cataloguing and organizing images; interspersed with this activity are close-up images of the smaller gears and lenses of the cameras and slide projectors. Moving and still images of players from the *Top 100* list, captured in film, television, and photography, flash across the screen. This focus on audiovisual replay prefaces the basic format of each player feature in *The Top 100: NFL's Greatest Players*—a presenter is assigned to each figure and, as he or she testifies to that player's importance within league history, television and film highlights, still photos, and audio broadcast clips support the presenter's claims. This relationship between testimony and audiovisual evidence is important for assuring viewers that the one hundred players chosen were worthy of the list and that the smallest details of their on-field exploits will prove it.

The introductory focus on old technologies and the labor of recovering and sorting archived items also characterizes the producers' approach to remembrance. In a press release announcing the series debut, the NFL suggested that the question "'Who is the greatest player in NFL history?' . . . links generations and resonates with all NFL fans." To properly select one hundred players from thousands of candidates who played in the league's "modern" and "pre-modern" era (the dividing line is usually drawn between the culmination of the 1966–1967 season in Super Bowl I and the full merger of the American Football League [AFL] and NFL in 1970), NFL Films employed a "blue ribbon panel" of current and former coaches, players, league executives, football media experts, Hall of Fame voters, and league historians. The result, argued NFL Films president Steve Sabol, was "the holy trinity of a good sports documentary series—action, analysis and reminiscence."[61] The idea was to mobilize every resource at the league's disposal, including recovery of key moments from dusty archives and old media, to create an *official* record of the NFL's ascent as the United States' most popular sport.

The Legacy of Prototypes

Football players are evaluated in terms of both attributes specific to their positions and how their productivity raises the level of play for the larger offensive or defensive units to which they belong. As with sport labor practices in general, football emphasizes a "high degree of specialization and standardization" to mark the value of individuals' labor within a larger system.[62] Football players in particular are evaluated according to position-specific prototypes composed of an ideal height, weight, speed, arm length, body mass, hand size, agility, and intellect, as well as a repertoire of techniques that facilitate the repetitive performance of specific functions. Such close attention to replicating movements constitutes within scouting communities and fan bases alike a "kinesthetic imagination" regarding function- and role-specific body types and kinesthetic repertoires.[63] In sport, highly organized schemes for evaluation, training, and coaching develop muscle memory and reliable repetitions of technique, while technological interventions (techniques for measurement, diet, supplementation) aim at isolating and reproducing traits associated with reliable and task-specific productivity. These processes of controlling for and producing certain kinds of bodies and functional movements change with advances in a given sport, such that elite athletes are commonly regarded as prototypes who embody both the lineage of previous models and the necessity of constant updating.

As Nick Trujillo suggests, treating football bodies as machines for "industrialized production" raises the same problems I have associated with planned obsolescence. A player's value is defined in relation to present and future production (according to the sport cliché that "you're only as good as your last game"); the violence of football accelerates the inevitable breakdown of the body, which situates both commodity value and memory within the time of a typically short career.[64] In football, then, prototypes represent one of the few images through which to recover memory *after* the time of expired labor production. Prototypes become symbolic reserves for memory by punctuating an unfolding series of derivative kinetic repertoires that can be traced forward into our own time. Athletes have a chance at being remembered beyond the time of their physical productivity when their expansions of movement and performance become traceable through the movements and performances of present-day players. In this sense, a player attains "legacy" by becoming citable as a progenitor of an athletic type in a specific line of succession. What an athlete who qualifies for eternal status often leaves behind, then, is less a figure—a *person*, whose cultural status invites attention to the details of a specific historical moment and, perhaps, to the imprints of that moment's struggles, longings, fears, compromises, and hopes on its most elevated characters—than a bundle of mechanical traits transferable across multiple visual forms, bodies, and historical contexts.

All-time greats are praiseworthy, then, because they performed a repertoire of position-specific movements that revealed new possibilities for production to future generations. Contemporary players add their own virtuosity to the repertoire to make yet further advances possible. In *The Top 100: NFL's Greatest Players*, for example, we are told by the narrator in a segment on Baltimore Colts player Lenny Moore (#94) that Moore's "versatility allowed him to line up at half back or flanker, blazing a trail for the likes of Bobby Mitchell, Roger Craig, and Marshall Faulk." Film replays show Moore lined up at both positions from field-level and overhead vantage points, running deep pass patterns and breaking through the line of scrimmage with equal skill. Each clip appears as a grainy template for contemporary offensive stars. Similarly, in a segment on Minnesota Vikings and Chicago Bears defensive lineman Alan Page (#43), we are told by journalist Steve Rushin that Page "revolutionized the defensive tackle position." At the time, defensive tackles were limited to smaller lane assignments (responsible for controlling a few feet of space at the line of scrimmage), but Page was more mobile, working across different gaps and swimming through blockers. A video replay shows Page lined up across from an offensive guard; the video freezes as a white arrow is superimposed, identifying Page; the replay restarts and Page cuts to the right of the guard, goes around another blocker, and sacks the quarterback.

Similar expansions are attributed to players who forced scheme innovations by revealing new possibilities for movement and contact. For example, New York Giants linebacker Lawrence Taylor (#3) was, according to a narrator, "a new kind of linebacker, one the league had never seen," whose "freakish athleticism" opened new possibilities for defensive pressure and made NFL offensive units change their blocking schemes. "Revolutionary" changes in defensive schemes are attributed similarly to the play of Tampa Bay Buccaneers linebacker Derrick Brooks (#97) and New York Giants linebacker Sam Huff (#93).

In several profiles innovations in movement are connected with rule changes to encourage more downfield passing, an aspect of football ordinarily associated with the game's increased popularity for television audiences. In a segment on Pittsburgh Steelers cornerback Mel Blount (#44), for example, former Cincinnati Bengals tight end Bob Trumpy explains that Blount was so good at "eliminating the receiver, on a play by play basis" that new rules for contact were instituted to favor greater offensive production. Journalist Michael MacCambridge describes Elroy "Crazylegs" Hirsch (#87) as the progenitor for contemporary offensive skill-position players and downfield passing schemes. And Dallas Cowboys owner Jerry Jones credits San Diego Chargers and Cowboys wide receiver Lance Allworth (#38) with influencing football "maybe as much as any person ever" because he was the face of the "wide open" American Football League (AFL).

Even as the prototype signifies a body valued through specialized labor production and technological advancement, claims about the body's intrinsic spiritual worth are common throughout sport histories.[65] Indeed, the most enthusiastic testaments to sport's greater meaning are reserved for movement repertoires through which the athlete achieves an apparent jailbreak from the material limits of the body, its ordinary anchoring to time and thought. In light of the foregoing discussion on immutability, this is the athletic body in its most essentialized, *religious* form: movement transcending history. Consider, for example, the testimony of jazz musician Wynton Marsalis, who draws parallels between the running style of Detroit Lions running back Barry Sanders (#17) and the flows of spontaneous art:

> In the arts, greatness means that you're able to develop your skills to raise our—human beings'—level of consciousness, and our horizon of aspiration, to a higher level. We say, "Wow, we didn't know that could be done." Now you start talking about somebody like Barry. . . . [H]e has almost a Zen approach to it. Things you had never seen, that umpty umph, that thing you can't describe, it's an eloquence [that can't be put into words].

Marsalis speaks as video replays feature Sanders weaving through defenders, breaking tackles, spinning, juking, stopping and starting, displaying brilliant and spontaneous creativity. An interview clip features Sanders talking about turning off his conscious mind, improvising in the moment. Marsalis returns:

> It's metaphysical. And that's where you *are* the thing. And when you become that thing you don't have to think. Because it is transcendent, the figuring out things is transcendent . . . to just what we call the "is-ness"; you are here in this moment and you are the living embodiment of that thing *in action.* . . . When you don't think, you're on a higher level than if you think, because the thought takes you away from the thing. And in music it's the same way, because if you're thinking and you're playing something, the second you stop playing what you're playing to think . . . you're automatically one step removed from the thing itself.

Here spontaneity in jazz and sport are parallel forms of true becoming, balancing between the practicalities of art and its metaphysics. Consistent with Latour's explanation of how religious images appear to be products of "ahistorical" and "unmediated essence," Sanders becomes "the thing itself"—rises to the essence or "isness" of the performative moment—by transcending the body's usual attachments to time and consciousness.[66] Marsalis describes Sanders as "the ultimate improviser" because he is "able to master his relationship" to small calculations "in the context of time." As in jazz improvisation, "There's no *time*, man. How much time you got between when the ball is snapped and somebody is tearing your head off?" Sanders cannot take back a move any more than a musician overwhelmed by chord changes can take back a note, so his virtuosity comes through in the tiny intervals between spontaneous decision making and its physical consequences. In testifying to Sanders's mastery over consciousness, Marsalis provides a model for appreciating the greater meaning of sport, its expansion of "our horizon of aspiration": sport's transcendence is revealed in movement, but only when you take out all of the intervals that bind ordinary consciousness to history. By taking leave of those intervals and their disruptions of flow, by getting fully caught up in the *nowness* of our own moment, we come to appreciate how figures like Sanders represent "the thing itself": a manifestation of the body transcending time.[67] These are legitimately moving experiences of elite performance.

Succession and the Politics of Selective Inheritance

Remembering through prototypes involves reducing athletic careers to selected images of movement and making those images transferrable *as constants* across multiple historical contexts. Focus on past inheritance is limited to only those qualities of movement that contributed to present-day innovations in labor production and to increasingly profitable forms of visual spectacle. Recalling Latour's argument that immutability is the effect of retaining certain features of an image "from one representation to the next" so that those features become "the *thing itself*," official sport histories allow traces of struggle over labor and social inequities *as well as* traces of an ever-evolving human potential to be indexed on athletic bodies.[68] But only the latter can achieve mobility and be carried forward if the true meaning of sport is to be appreciated. Accordingly, producers and commentators select from the careers of all-time greats primarily those features that compose an ideal image of inheritance in our own time. This is especially apparent in the ways that *The Top 100: NFL's Greatest Players* list quarantines problems of labor and racial struggle in the league's past, whether by excluding details of these struggles entirely or by partially highlighting them as markers of present-day progress.

As I cover in Chapter 5, NFL history has been shaped around significant labor struggles and the disproportionate power of league owners and the commissioner's office over a historically weak players' union. The implications of that history are now becoming disturbingly apparent in the brain injury crisis. *The Top 100: NFL's Greatest Players* brackets each player's timeline so that the details of labor struggles are not mobilized as inheritance and viewers are not troubled with the fact that those struggles touched even the league's most transcendent figures.

An immediate example: thanks to whatever extent Barry Sanders embodied the "isness" of sport (his performances were truly beautiful), Lions fans and Detroit sportswriters reacted to his unexpected retirement in 1999 by suggesting that his body and his labor belonged to them and that it was his obligation *as an all-time great* to sacrifice both until he reached obsolescence. Sanders retired at thirty-one years old, still in the prime of his career and only 1,457 yards short of Walter Payton's all-time rushing record of 16,726 yards.[69] Because Sanders had been a rare bright spot for the Detroit Lions, historically one of the worst franchises in the NFL, many fans and sportswriters viewed his early retirement (for which Sanders provided little public explanation at the time) as a betrayal. In an episode of *A Football Life* dedicated to his career, Sanders says in an interview that after ten years, and with the Lions struggling, he felt he had "run out of steam" and that his "drive and determination" were gone, so it made sense to stop while he was still healthy. Immediately after, we see a close-up shot of a newspaper headline—"Sanders Stains Image"—followed by a video clip of a Detroit sport talk radio host reading a fan's e-mail on the air: "Until yesterday O. J. [Simpson] was my least favorite NFL runner, but he only stabbed two people in the back."[70]

Sanders is presently looked upon as an icon, but his retirement remains the subject of speculation, as does the sense of loss over his unspent labor.

Perhaps the most prominent example of an icon remembered entirely apart from the politics of labor and long-term health is Baltimore Colts quarterback Johnny Unitas, ranked at #6 on *The Top 100: NFL's Greatest Players* list. During the special, a photo of Unitas playing in the 1958 championship game against the New York Giants depicts an otherworldly scene: Unitas's shoulders are tilted back to throw a pass, his right arm cocked at a 90-degree angle and his right hand cradling the ball, his left arm stretched out and his fingers pointing to the heavens, bodies of linemen falling all about his feet and stirring up plumes of dust, the focus pulled so that the crowd forms a blurred, apparitional backdrop. Journalist Frank Deford says:

> That *vision* of him, I think, was embedded in the American mind thereafter, and every quarterback since, whoever it is, one of the Mannings, Brady, whoever can be placed in that template. It all descends from Johnny Unitas on that December day in 1958. . . . It's not important, whether Unitas was the greatest. He is *the* quarterback for all time, in the same sort of category as Babe Ruth. Babe Ruth is *the* baseball player for all time, no matter what kinds of records are set, no matter what happens to the game. Unitas is the one and only now, and as such, he'll only be more legendary as time passes.

As I cover in Chapter 5, the legacy of the 1958 championship is more complex and troubling than offered here. Deford's praise of Unitas as "*the* quarterback for all time" fits, however, with the *Top 100*'s focus on eternity and succession. Unitas, Deford says, was a "working class" player in a working-class city: "We liked him because he was tougher than any other quarterback. The hits that Unitas took somehow added to the whole aura." Those hits also disabled Unitas, leading eventually to nerve damage and a loss of basic function in his right hand. Unitas applied for disability compensation from the NFL, but the league rejected him, sending an apparent signal to other retired players that they should not bother to file claims. As former Miami Dolphins running back Mercury Morris understood it, the league was saying, "If we can do that to Johnny Unitas, we can do it to anybody."[71]

The Top 100: NFL's Greatest Players deals with problems of race more subtly. In some cases it relies on the outright exclusion of historical details, but other times it highlights moments of racial struggle as part of a mostly *completed* series of victories over racism, suggesting that courageous individuals won respect for their on-field exploits within a meritocratic system.

The most obvious exclusion in *The Top 100: NFL's Greatest Players* is the NFL's institution of a color barrier between 1934 and 1946. The color barrier was erected through what Charles Ross describes as an informal "gentlemen's agreement among owners not to sign black players to contracts."[72] In the league's earliest years a limited number of African American players (no more than five in a single season) were employed "as drawing cards" but their participation became less important as the league's popularity increased in the 1930s. Ross notes that while there is no evidence of a formal agreement, there was clearly "unity between all NFL owners to keep black players out of the league."[73] Six players in the *Top 100* played through all or part of the league's color-barrier period: Mel Hein (1931–1945), Steve Van Buren (1944–1951), Sid Luckman (1939–1950), Bronco Nagurski (1930–1937, 1943), Sammy Baugh (1937–1952), and Don Hutson (1935–1945). Three others—Ernie Nevers, Red Grange, and Jim Thorpe—played in the early 1920s, when professional football had very few players of color.

More subtle exclusions come through the ways in which the *Top 100* negotiates the issue of racial stacking, which has a discernible impact on players selected for the list. Stacking is the over- and underrepresentation of players at certain positions according to racialized forms of evaluation. So, for example, white football players have disproportionately populated so-called "thinking" positions like quarterback and middle linebacker, while players of color have been disproportionately assigned to skill positions (e.g., running back, wide receiver) because of racist stereotypes about the intellectual superiority of whites as contrasted with the presumed physiological superiority of blacks.[74]

Commemorating the league's eternity in 2010 meant that stacking heavily influenced the list's choice of quarterbacks. The 2013 season (the commemoration of which I cover in the next section) featured the largest group of African American starting quarterbacks in league history: nine players out of thirty-two teams. In previous decades NFL teams had regularly forced successful black college quarterbacks to change positions as they entered the league, and many of the assumptions about intellect and "raw" athleticism behind these decisions remain prominent in the present.[75] Nineteen quarterbacks are on *The Top 100: NFL's Greatest Players* list, and all are white. Some played in the league's premodern era (#14 Sammy Baugh, #16 Otto Graham, #33 Sid Luckman, and #83 Norm Van Brocklin), and some straddled the premodern and modern eras (#6 Johnny Unitas, #51 Bart Starr, and #91 Fran Tarkenton). The rest were a combination of modern-era players (#4 Joe Montana, #20 Brett Favre, #23 John Elway, #25 Dan Marino, #46 Roger Staubach, #50 Terry Bradshaw, #80 Troy Aikman, #81 Steve Young, #90 Kurt Warner, #100 Joe Namath) and players active at the time the list was produced (#8

Peyton Manning and #21 Tom Brady). Former Houston Oiler Warren Moon is the only African American quarterback in the Pro Football Hall of Fame, and he was not included on the list. Incidentally, Moon has been derided by contemporary fans and journalists for pointing out racialized evaluations of quarterback prospects.[76]

By elevating nineteen white quarterbacks, *The Top 100: NFL's Greatest Players* secures as foundational and essentially associated with whiteness those attributes of movement, intellect, will, stability, and character that still define the highest realizations of the quarterbacking prototype.[77] For example, Indianapolis Colts and Denver Broncos quarterback Peyton Manning (#8) is credited with bringing a new "mental approach" to the position through tireless film study and in-game diagnosis of defensive formations. The presenter, Ravens linebacker Ray Lewis, says that Manning "has turned the art of quarterbacking into a science." Similarly, popular-culture critic Chuck Klosterman (who would normally mock this kind of sentimentality) gushes over Dallas Cowboys quarterback Roger Staubach's (#46) career as a Heisman Trophy winner, naval officer, Vietnam vet, and faithful husband: "There's probably never been a better role model that Roger Staubach, certainly in sports. He seems like the best possible American you can create. If you dreamed of having a son it'd be like Staubach." Quarterbacks are *the* archetypal figures of white athletic esteem in the United States. As Daniel Buffington summarizes: "More than any other position on the football field (and indeed most positions in other sports) quarterback has become virtually synonymous with leadership, knowledge of the game, and decision making under pressure—skills that run counter to dominant ideas about Black mentality."[78] The *Top 100* list provides reassurance that the die remains cast for the position's prototypical whiteness.

As assumptions about natural acumen have been undermined by the more recent success of African American quarterbacks, new labels—"running quarterback," "dual-threat quarterback," "mobile quarterback"—have been invented to recode older terms for stereotypically black movement repertoires. To be fair, several quarterbacks in *The Top 100: NFL's Greatest Players* list are identified as having traits common to running or mobile quarterbacks: Sammy Baugh of the Washington Redskins, Fran Tarkenton of the Minnesota Vikings, and Steve Young of the San Francisco 49ers. Only Tarkenton's profile, however, emphasizes his scrambling ability as a primary skill. More typical of evaluative schemes for contemporary quarterbacks, Baugh is praised for being able to throw accurately on the run (with accuracy assumed to be a result of technique rather than raw athleticism), while Young is identified as a talented runner who became *great* through his development as a passer. The order of these attributes matters a great deal: a real quarterback, according to increasingly intensifying responses to African American success at the position, must prove himself a passer *first*, and turn to running only as a secondary and complementary skill. Otherwise, as a depressing number of evaluations still suggest, reliance on genetic drives (signified through the *flight* response of running from the pocket) will supposedly stunt necessary processes of mental development.[79]

Outside the quarterbacking prototype, *The Top 100: NFL's Greatest Players* does a better job of resisting white brains/black brawn categorizations. For example, several African American players like Mike Singletary (#57), Willie Lanier (#53), Alan Page (#43), and Jerry Rice (#1) are praised for intelligence, will, and work ethic, and several white players like Fran Tarkenton (#91), Elroy "Crazylegs" Hirsch (#87), Red Grange (#48), and Lance Allworth (#38) are praised for elite physical traits. In addition, several profiles in the *Top 100* praise individual men of color for undermining racial stereotypes through their on-field exploits or postcareer activism. For example, Los Angeles Rams defensive lineman Deacon Jones (#15) is described as a player driven by experiences with racism in the segregated southern United States, and his resulting desire to violently "sack" the (white) quarterbacks of his day is addressed sympathetically. The segment on Minnesota Vikings and Chicago Bears defensive tackle Alan Page emphasizes Page's attendance at law school during his playing days and his retirement work as a Minnesota Supreme Court judge fighting continuing problems of racial inequity. Film of Page's office features Jim Crow–era news clippings hanging on the walls.

Wherever race is treated explicitly in *The Top 100: NFL's Greatest Players*, however, the NFL is presented as a colorblind meritocracy that has historically afforded opportunities for racial progress. Colorblindness has long set limits on racial contestation in sport by depicting sport as "a paragon of racial virtue" and at the same time an inappropriate forum for progressive racial resistance.[80] Exemplary historical figures symbolize both of these problems: presumably, they prove that talent trumps race (even if only because of coaches' and general managers' self-interest in winning), and they demonstrate that people who continue to bring attention to racism fail to appreciate and might even disrupt the progress of athletes earning their status within a meritocracy that rewards hard work and talent, not social activism. The importance of meritocratic opportunity is evident, for example, in the profile of Kansas City Chiefs middle linebacker Willie Lanier. Middle linebackers are frequently referred to as the quarterbacks of the defense due to their role in calling plays, reading offensive formations, and changing alignments; as such, the position has been historically subject to racial stacking. Lanier's presenter, Hall of Fame running back Floyd Little, says: "In the day . . . you didn't have a lot of African Americans playing middle linebacker. It was considered one of the areas that you had to have some intelligence." A video clip features Kansas City head coach Hank Stram saying that the team did not care about Lanier's race; they cared only that he could compete for a starting position. The narrator emphasizes that Lanier was easily accepted as a black middle linebacker because of his on-field production.

Marking racial progress through profiles like the one on Lanier, or those of Alan Page and Deacon Jones, suggests that changes came through isolated moments of struggle, where both structural barriers and the men who broke through them were provisional frames in the greater continuity of league history. The fact that the ordering of *The Top 100: NFL's Greatest Players* is based on the blue-ribbon panel's ranking system rather than on the time periods within which individual athletes played makes it especially easy to depict their efforts ahistorically, as moments that punctuated a struggle for equality imagined as mostly settled in our own time. Lanier matters *today* as a man who broke barriers as middle linebacker and opened the way for men of color to occupy the position in the modern league. Alan Page reflects the NFL's unique capacity for helping African American men to develop ideal body/mind complexes fit for both on-field production and postcareer pursuits in racial justice, each of these priorities presumably reflecting contemporary league values. Commemorating the struggles of players of color out of historical sequence makes each player's story an atemporal vignette, an image that once belonged to a specific historical milieu but that ultimately transcends the entanglements of that milieu to become relevant for eternity.

The Top 100: NFL's Greatest Players accounts for "all time" by throwing together players from different eras, shaped by different practices related to race, diet, conditioning, and scheme design, and writing them into a progress history that treats each as a transitional figure. The result is a diverse menu of remembrances that collectively trace the upward trajectory of the league's past into our present through bodies abstracted from their historical contexts. The superhuman, African American freak of nature and the white, blue-collar overachiever have historically been categorized by racialized and biologically deterministic forms of evaluation and, on that basis, assigned to inequitable structures for employment, salary, and organizational leadership. But these bodies are celebrated as *continuous* with a series of progressive historical leaps that presumably leave us, today, with a complex and diverse inheritance. Today's African American defensive end inherits a repertoire of pass-rushing moves and an acceptable disdain for quarterbacks from a player like Deacon Jones, himself recalled as a man who practiced a sanctioned form of black anger on the field. Today's undersized white quarterback prospect is given a chance by evaluators who can readily cite an all-time great like Joe Montana (#4 overall), praised in *The Top 100: NFL's Greatest Players* as a productive winner despite having "skinny little legs" and a weaker arm than his contemporaries. The trick for producing official sport histories is not to pretend that inequities never existed (or that they do not exist now) but to partially revisit them as a celebration of diverse lines of succession that enable parallel and equally diverse possibilities for athletic advance in our own time.

Legacy through Body and Media Technologies

Legacy is also traceable in *The Top 100: NFL's Greatest Players* through images of the low-tech bodies that preceded today's players: men covered in leather rather than high-impact plastic, fueled by moxie rather than supplements. Indeed, some of the most elongated, nostalgic moments of looking in the *NFL's Greatest Players* are reserved for figures from the earliest moments in the sport. The feature on Chicago Bears fullback Bronco Nagurski (#19), for example, opens with a black-and-white photo of Nagurski's face. The camera zooms in for a close-up of his large, square head, highlighting his prototypically masculine jaw, deep-set eyes, pronounced brow, thick nose, and skin. Author Jim Dent remarks that Nagurski's "forearms looked like a lot of peoples' thighs." The segment transitions to a photo of Nagurski in profile, shirtless, in a "thinker" pose. Highlights show Nagurski running violently through tacklers, wearing minimal padding and a helmet with no facemask; several of the offensive linemen blocking for him are not wearing helmets at all.

As I argued earlier in this chapter, such nostalgic longing is circumscribed in sport by the presumed inevitability of planned obsolescence. The *NFL's Greatest Players* preserves, however, a place for nostalgia by connecting it to the preciousness and uncertainty of memory in eras when audiovisual media were less developed and less widely available than they are today. Low-tech athletic bodies coincided with these eras, so remembering both technologies together—athletic bodies and audiovisual media—reminds viewers of the fundamental relationship between capturing movement and appreciating transcendence. Just as importantly, it reminds viewers that leagues and production companies exercise unique authority over memory because of their capacity to record, archive, select from, and represent images that would otherwise be lost to history.

This conjoined focus on body and media technologies and memory is evident, for example, in the profile on running back Jim Thorpe (#37). Thorpe's feature starts with a full-body photo that the camera scans from feet to head, featuring laced-up leather boots, thick pants with sewn-in padding, leather laces crossing at the crotch, a buckled belt, a long-sleeved shirt with padding at the elbows, and a football tucked under his left arm. Thorpe stares into the camera, his mouth straight, his jaw square, his nose flattened out, his hair unkempt. The outfit represents the minimalism of Thorpe's time, the physical sacrifices of a progenitor. Journalist Sally Jenkins explains:

> The fields were slower and boggier, they had terrible shoes, the jerseys were stuffed with flannel, and when they got wet they weighed fifteen pounds. [Thorpe] could run like that, with all that crap on, *my God*, how great he must have been. [Running back] LaDanian Tomlinson [#61 on the list, and at the time an active player] has it *much* easier than Jim Thorpe ever had it.

In distinguishing between Thorpe dressed in soggy flannel and Tomlinson encased in molded plastic, Jenkins describes a succession from sacrifice to inheritance. There is a protective impulse here: players from previous eras like Thorpe can never get their due unless we appreciate the influence of technology on their performance.

The segment on Thorpe reveals a desire not simply to *go back* to the past but to derive from the past a lesson about the relationship between technologies and forgetting. As the segment continues, Jenkins's focus on advancing body technologies dovetails with a focus on advancements in media technologies, making both considerations in the preciousness of sport memories. A short film clip of Thorpe punting a football plays on a loop as a narrator tells us it is the only footage of him known to exist. With only "faded photographs" to remember him by, there is not enough recorded movement by which to fully appreciate his legacy. Jenkins associates this lack of capture with the limits of acknowledgment: "We hear the faintest echo of what he was, but it's loud enough. Had anybody been there to see the real thing, I think we'd call him hands down the greatest player who ever lived." Jenkins's desire to derive memory and obligation from echoes and traces can become, as I argue in later chapters, a vital critical impulse. Within the framework of *The Top 100: NFL's Greatest Players*, however, her desire feels anachronistic, a nostalgic thought experiment grounded in contemporary ideals about audiovisual capture and performance.

The greater lesson on history and eternity to be derived from *The Top 100: NFL's Greatest Players* is that both obligations to remember and (in a related sense) directed practices of forgetting are accomplished by citing points of origin and succession traceable as legacy through the bodies of past and present athletes. Kept constant through these successive representations of greatness are those particular traits that signal an ever-expanding athletic potential. Looking back is about confirming the immutability of that expanding potential in our own time.

The Top 100 Players of 2013

The Top 100: NFL's Greatest Players initiated a new programming cycle for NFLN designed to provoke debate and build anticipation during a relatively slow period in the offseason. Every year since that program aired in 2010, NFL Films has produced successive, seasonal *Top 100* lists, and at the time of this writing the series is still going. Each list provides rankings based on the previous season and serves as a transition into the season that is coming up. The 2013 series, which I focus on here, ran from April 27 to June 27, shortly before the start of training camps in mid-July.[81] *Grantland* writer Bill Barnwell identified the 2013 version of the NFL's *Top 100* as an "arbitrary" and "now-annual feature during football's silly season."[82] As much as the *Top 100* lists stand out as "silly season" filler, they also illustrate how the most powerful sport media institutions match consumption with a constant recreation of history. Criticism of all-time and seasonal lists among fans and journalists might focus on problematic evaluative standards or superficial commercialism, but this does little to challenge official historical accounts. This is primarily because the underlying logic of the production process—the evolutionary premise behind constantly replaceable bodies and legacies—remains largely unexamined, accepted as an ahistorical reality.

Key to the NFL's success in making football the most popular sport in the United States has been a steady diet of consumer opportunities that stretch beyond the league's roughly six-month schedule of the regular season and playoffs (regular season games begin in September, and the Super Bowl is in early February). The NFL's schedule now extends across a twelve-month calendar of events that is built around the constant cycling in of new bodies.[83] Indeed, the NFL's version of spring renewal after its early February Super Bowl is the NFL Draft, a three-day, nationally televised event in which teams select collegiate prospects. Sport television networks and print outlets spend considerable time and resources covering the draft in the preceding months: detailing prospects' physical and mental attributes, running predictions through mock drafts, tracking rumors, and discussing teams' positional needs. The draft typically happens around late April, but anticipation is generated immediately following the Super Bowl as most major sport outlets air prospect-rating shows and behind-the-scenes profiles of the evaluation process.[84] The Scouting Combine, an event where collegiate prospects' physical and psychological attributes are measured through a battery of tests, drills and interviews, is broadcast live on NFLN in late February and covered by all major sport outlets.[85] The draft process also restarts fantasy football, as the most enthusiastic participants begin taking notes on prospects for drafts that will occur over the summer. Team "mini-camps" (short training camps) are scheduled through April, May, and June before full training camps begin in July. Preseason (exhibition) games run through August and up to the opening of the regular season in early September. The evaluation rituals surrounding collegiate prospects and team futures associated with the Combine and Draft extend through the April mini-camps to the end of the preseason, as sport journalists update prospects' development, assess emerging and declining veteran players, and preview teams for the upcoming season. The idea is to remove every interval, to make the entire twelve-month calendar a continuous experience of anticipation and consumption.

The seasonal *Top 100* lists that succeed *The Top 100: NFL's Greatest Players* special in 2011, 2012, 2013, and beyond each highlight the importance of time in relation to eternity. The image of today's athlete expanding a former player's repertoire of movements, or breaking long-standing records, is akin (going back to Burke's time-eternity analogy) to time *extending* or *stretching* eternity, pressing on the outward boundaries of human possibility.[86] Such temporal extension is discernible because of the citability of all-time greats. In that sense a list like *The Top 100: NFL's Greatest Players* offers a standard reference, a scriptural baseline for judging the athletes of our own time. The care that went into the *NFL's Greatest Players* list—the work of the blue-ribbon panel, the efforts at archival recovery and tedious sorting—is consistent with the importance of setting a foundation from which all future lines of succession can be traced. It is the *continuity* of those successions, however, that founds a capacity to live during, and bear witness to, the newest stages in human-athletic advance. This is my purpose in analyzing the 2013 list: to provide a detailed sense of the relation between time and eternity in elite televised sport.

For *The Top 100 Players of 2013*, as with the other seasonal lists, the 2010 program's blue-ribbon panel of writers, historians, and officials is replaced by a player-only voting system. This voting system allows NFL Films to highlight the experience of contributing to league history from the players' perspectives and, moreover, to feature players' reflexivity in regard to the small chance they have to establish themselves in the league's eternal timeline. While a panel of experts may seem more appropriate for judging the longer historical arc of eternity (from the presumed critical distance afforded by the passage of time), active players speak to the experience of history in the making.

Similar to the format of *The Top 100: NFL's Greatest Players*, there is a single introduction with which each episode in the 2013 list begins. In *The Top 100 Players of 2013*, however, memory is stored not on old media technologies but in a bank vault. We begin with a close-up of the vault being unlocked, large gears turning and locking pins retracting. The vault handle turns and the door opens slowly at first, white mist pouring out through a crack. Then the door flies open suddenly and the mist billows out. Fast, choppy violin music underscores the opening narration: "There are more than sixteen hundred players in the National Football League. Now the votes of NFL players will reveal the best of them. The top one hundred. The players submitted *their* rankings of the best players in the game today. The *players* voted. The *players* decided."

The viewer is taken inside the vault. Fluorescent lights flicker on, revealing rows of numbered safe-deposit boxes. Video highlights of active NFL players are superimposed on flat, square surfaces like deposit-box drawers and wall sections. In case it is not yet clear that the players voted on the list, the narrator repeats himself: "Their choices make up this countdown. The top one hundred players of 2013." The predominant image is not, as with the archivist's busy hands, of recovering lost footage and sorting through a mess of slides, film clips, and photos. Players' images are more immediately available, put into numbered rows of safe-deposit boxes so they can be easily retrieved should they end up qualifying for eternity. The work being done here is less archeology than proper filing.

In contrast to the format of the *NFL's Greatest Players* list, *The Top 100 Players of 2013* is composed entirely of player interviews, and each player testifies to his peers' worthiness *at that particular moment*. This means a persistent focus on the fleeting nature of status as each season turns over. Older players are declining in physical skill, raising questions about whether the sum of their career accomplishments adds up to all-time status; they are running out of time. Younger players represent the excitement of potential and future production, but they still have too much to prove. Players in between move up and down the list from year to year, highlighting the transitory nature of their peers' esteem.

This attention to the temporariness of status is the most important function of player-only voting. Active players bring both the ethos of expertise, via direct participation in the very moment being judged, and the changeability of being too far inside the moment to be held responsible for providing a longer historical assessment. They are, then, ideal spokespersons for the excitement of witnessing emergent stardom in our own time, and, simultaneously, for the fleeting nature of status and memory. Rather than marking a historical *loss*, however, that fleeting chance at status invites viewers to contemplate how exciting our own moment is. Much like the uncertainty associated with time and history before a live game—an event "about to take place" where the outcomes and the means of arriving at them are uncertain—an undetermined question of status requires immediate and intense attention.[87] During one segment, for example, a narrator refers to *The Top 100 Players of 2013* list as "a living, breathing document":

> Some names are constant [we see a video clip of New England Patriots quarterback Tom Brady]. Others appear once, never to be seen again [we see a video clip of Tim Tebow in a Denver Broncos uniform]. [A] fortunate few . . . manage to redeem themselves [a video clip features Atlanta Falcons quarterback Matt Ryan throwing a pass] with a return trip to the countdown.

Describing *The Top 100* as a "living, breathing document," and implying reference to past and future seasonal countdowns, invokes the interplay between permanence and change associated with ongoing productions of eternity. Someone like Tom Brady has already secured his legacy. He will be in the Hall of Fame when he retires, and he establishes the concrete possibilities of arrival. Tim Tebow is a cautionary tale. A great college quarterback at the University of Florida and a (quite literally) messianic figure for many sport fans, Tebow was drafted in the first round by the Denver Broncos in 2010 but is currently out of the league.[88] He appeared only once on the annual *Top 100*, demonstrating how abbreviated the time between devotion and irrelevance can be. Matt Ryan represents the possibilities between Brady and Tebow: not considered an elite quarterback just yet, Ryan was back on the countdown after a tough year, granted another chance to make his case for all-time.

Each player feature is formatted the same way, with imagery that extends the vault theme from the introduction: below a still image of the player is a metal locking mechanism, two bars connecting in the middle of the screen; the bars roll open to reveal the player's ranking on the 2013 countdown first, and then alongside it, his ranking on the 2012 list. By listing each player's current ranking next to that of the previous year, *The Top 100 Players of 2013* emphasizes the transitional nature of status in sport history. Based on season-to-season production, players move onto the list, fall off, or shift to higher or lower positions.

There is constant attention to how instantaneous these changes in status can be. Several players—including Seattle Seahawks defensive back Richard Sherman (#50), Kansas City Chiefs linebacker Justin Houston (#49), Houston Texans offensive lineman Duane Brown (#48), Washington Redskins quarterback Robert Griffin III (#15), San Francisco 49ers linebacker Aldon Smith (#7), and Houston Texans defensive lineman J. J. Watt (#5)—were not ranked in 2012. Their sudden ascent to the list in 2013 reminds viewers about the excitement of witnessing the earliest hints of a potential all-time great's emergence. Cincinnati Bengals defensive lineman Geno Atkins, for example, breaks onto the 2013 list at #36 after being unranked in 2012. Philadelphia Eagles guard Evan Mathis testifies to seeing the first signs of Atkins's potential in 2010 and argues that if Atkins "keeps playing the way he is . . . he's going to be one of the best of all time." Dallas Cowboys guard Derrick Dockery says that Atkins reminds him of all-time great defensive linemen like Warren Sapp and Leroy Glover, "all those guys who made a mark in the National Football League. He's heading in that same direction."

As with *The Top 100: NFL's Greatest Players*, tracing lineage involves attention to the smallest details of player- and position-specific movement repertoires as captured and represented through audiovisual media. In a feature on Arizona Cardinals cornerback Patrick Peterson (#33 on the list), for example, one of Peterson's teammates, defensive lineman Nick Eason, marvels at Peterson's level of play after only two years in the league. There is a transition to a split screen, with synchronized video replays to the left and right. On the left side we see Peterson readying for a punt return, catching the ball and sinking his hips, moving to the right to evade the first wave of tacklers. On the right is a parallel and simultaneous replay of Hall of Fame defensive back Deion Sanders (#34 on *The Top 100: NFL's Greatest Players* list) catching a punt and readying for a return; Sanders's level change, the angles of his shoulders and knees, and even his jersey number mirror Peterson precisely. Eason continues: "Knowing Patrick and knowing how competitive he is, if he continues to play I think he'll be up there with Deion." As Eason speaks the replays continue. The videos are synchronized so that Peterson and Sanders both cross mid-field at almost precisely the same time before running into their respective end zones for touchdowns. On the left side of the screen Peterson performs Sanders's trademark end zone dance—the "Deion Shuffle"—as a tribute; after a couple seconds of delay Sanders performs the original shuffle in the split screen to the right. About Peterson, Eason remarks: "Kid's amazing, man. He's gonna go down as one of the greatest players of all time in this league."

Just as younger players are coming into the league's present and developing résumés for all-time consideration, older players are aging off of the list. In the window between the 2012 and 2013 seasons, NFL Films captures a continuity of stars flashing up and fading through our own time. Every player on the countdown has to make a mark in the time between now and the end of his career, and the window is always closing. Between features on the #12 and #13 players on the list, a narrator describes the small chance at remembrance as seasons change: "The rankings on the top one hundred clearly indicate that greatness is difficult to sustain at the NFL level. Only seven players have been voted to the top twenty by their peers each of the last three years." Forgetting is especially inevitable because of the toll that football takes on the body. Prefacing a feature on San Francisco 49ers running back Frank Gore (#32), a narrator cites *The Top 100 Players of 2013* as evidence that for certain positions, like running back, age- and play-related decline are both predestined and quantifiable:

> If you take a look at the tenures of the *Top 100* players of 2013, you'll learn one thing: running the ball is a young man's game. The average NFL experience level of running backs appearing in the *Top 100* is four years. Compare that to six years for both wide receivers and quarterbacks. And seven seasons for *Top 100* tight ends.

The Top 100 Players of 2013 provides a small sample size, but football fans would readily recognize these numbers as representative of larger trends. Because running backs sustain so much damage from hits, their careers are short, as this narration suggests, compared to those of players at other positions. Consistent with the relationship between position-specific productivity and "greatness" summarized above, contemporary evaluators, general managers, coaches, and fantasy-football enthusiasts talk about running backs having a short "shelf life" and being "declining commodities" in the contemporary game.[89] Gore is credited with "bucking" this trend, but the narrator for his segment summarizes a good news/bad news scenario: Gore was productive in 2012, but he is not getting any younger; history will eventually catch up to him.

Similar prototype- and position-specific trends for declining physicality have caught up with older players throughout the list. Denver Broncos cornerback Champ Bailey (#53) dropped seven spots from the 2012 list because of signs that he had lost some speed. Chicago Bears defensive end Julius Peppers's ranking "tumbled" over the past two years, according to a narrator, from #10 in 2011 to #26 in 2012 and now (in 2013) to #54. New Orleans Saints defensive lineman Cameron Jordan says that Peppers could still be productive but that "his best days are behind him."

Other aging players are still clinging to relevance. A narrator tells us that Chicago Bears linebacker Lance Briggs's drop of eleven spots (from #72 to #83) may lead some to believe he is "past his prime," but his productive 2012 season showed he is still hanging on. Defensive back Charles Woodson, who played for the Green Bay Packers in 2012, had been cut by the team before the 2013 list was produced due to an injury that "sent him tumbling down the rankings" (from #36 to #85); although he was guaranteed to be a Hall of Fame player when he retired, Woodson was currently looking for work. An injury also moved Pittsburgh Steelers safety Troy Polamalu, another likely Hall of Fame player, from #19 in 2012 to #91 in 2013.

Figures like Woodson and Polamalu symbolize a persistent tension between Hall of Fame status and present-day relevance common in sport commemorations, reminding viewers, yet again, that the undeniable force of technological and evolutionary progress will overtake even sport's most elevated characters. For example, in the profile on Johnny Unitas in *The Top 100: NFL's Greatest Players*, presenter Frank Deford expresses confidence that Unitas's record of forty-seven consecutive games with a touchdown pass would never be broken: "It's more likely you'll get [New York Yankees great Joe] DiMaggio's fifty-six-game hitting streak record . . . broken than Unitas's forty-seven touchdown passes in a row. . . . [I]t's that extraordinary." Only two years later, New Orleans Saints quarterback Drew Brees (#11 in *The Top 100 Players of 2013*) broke Unitas's record, and the new benchmark was featured in Brees's profile. Similarly, Detroit Lions wide receiver Calvin Johnson (#3 in *The Top 100 Players of 2013*) broke Jerry Rice's seemingly secure single-season record of 1,848 receiving yards in 2012 with 1,964 yards. Writing for NBC Sports outlet ProFootballTalk.com, Michael David Smith cites *The Top 100: NFL's Greatest Players* to make sense of Johnson's achievement: "When NFL Network polled a panel of football experts two years ago to name the Top 100 players in NFL history, Jerry Rice came in first. So when a player breaks a record owned by Jerry Rice, that player has done something special."[90] And Eric Dickerson's (#52 on *The Top 100: NFL's Greatest Players* list) single-season rushing record of 2,105 yards was almost surpassed by the #1 player on *The Top 100 Players of 2013* list, Minnesota Vikings running back Adrian Peterson, who came up nine yards short after rushing for 2,097 yards during the 2012 season.

Calvin Johnson's and Adrian Peterson's 2012 performances were taken as clear signs of evolutionary advances in physicality, training, and medicine. At 6'5" and 236 pounds, Johnson represents a new prototype for a wide receiver's height, weight, and speed. In *The Top 100 Players of 2013* profile on Johnson, San Francisco 49ers defensive back Carlos Rogers argues that those physical attributes could eventually make Johnson the best wide receiver ever to play the game. Peterson's 2012 performance was especially impressive because he was recovering from a devastating late-season knee injury in 2011. Tampa Bay Buccaneers defensive lineman Gerald McCoy says of Peterson, "I don't think he's human. I think he's a robot." Philadelphia Eagles tight end Brent Celek insists: "If there is a human superhero, it's Adrian Peterson." And Buffalo Bills running back C. J. Spiller compares Peterson's healing powers to those of X-Men hero Wolverine.

Adrian Peterson, Calvin Johnson, and Drew Brees do not appear on *The Top 100: NFL's Greatest Players*. When the list was produced in 2010, each had a significant record of production, but their record-breaking 2012 performances were yet to come. If the list of *NFL's Greatest Players* were revised in 2013, all three players might need to be included. On one hand, such changeability illustrates the arbitrariness of condensing the "greatness" of our moment to one hundred slots, especially for a still-existing league. On the other hand, one hundred slots is a discernible temporal and spatial analogue for the finite nature of time and forgetting in sport. Players like Woodson and Polamalu are sliding off the bottom of the list, while younger players—many of whom were unranked in 2012—are finding their way on. All-time greats like Unitas and Rice may be remembered forever, but their citability is contingent on constant status threats from contemporary players. The bottom part of the seasonal *Top 100* draws a line. Dropping off does not mean being forgotten forever, as long as a player has submitted a memorable résumé, but it does represent movement to a different standard for remembrance: from the safe-deposit box (an ordered system for storage and immediate retrieval) to the archive (a challenge for archeological forms of recovery).

The small window in time captured by a seasonal list like *The Top 100 Players of 2013* provides individual athletes with a chance at staking a claim for eternity. That this chance is fleeting reflects the presumably natural order of histories made through emerging and expiring bodies. If only one hundred slots (or fifty, or ten, depending on the list) are available, then by the logic internal to capturing all-time on a finite index, some individuals will move up or down, and some will be replaced entirely. The NFL's *Top 100* lists mark the inevitability of forgetting in sport by synchronizing programming cycles with the immutable progress of athletic potential.

Conclusion

As long as athletic bodies index the inevitability of technological and evolutionary progress, histories in elite sport lack the "corrective" potential that Benjamin associates with theological images: the "mindfulness" that the past is not closed or completed and the capacity to make recognizable those historical conflicts and contradictions between idealization and actuality represented by, and occurring within, elite sport's most elevated figures.[91] To call the immutability of athletic advance into question, we might follow Latour and pay attention to the elements that are retained through transformations across visual media. The specific work of production that sustains an image's immutability—its textual qualities, contrasts, enhanced features, interpretations, efficiencies—can be critiqued as a series of choices in which some elements are kept "constant through transformations," while others are discarded.[92] Productions of sport history always involve selective remembrance, wherein producers or officials make choices (some conscious, some unconscious) of which historical details to include and which to discard or ignore, choices that make discontinuous elements of the past—details like labor disputes or social inequities that might disrupt the continuity of our present-oriented sense of progress—disappear into the athletic body's circulating form.

Through a continuity of transformations and successions, human-athletic advance remains the singular constant captured in sport historical production. That constancy grants producers a naturalistic warrant for selecting from athletic bodies and careers elements of movement or momentary political strife continuous with an immutable image of progress, and for erasing the discontinuous burdens of political struggle still relevant in our own time. If the conflicts between ideal and present history represented within and through athletic bodies are to crystallize and burst forth in the present, this continuity must come to a halt. In the next chapter I turn to the means of production through which stoppages in continuity and conditions for recognizability coincide most persistently in elite televised sport: instant replay. While replay does not itself undermine ahistorical idealizations of human-athletic progress (those challenges are the subject of Chapters 4, 5, and 6), it does form persistent disruptions that force attention to problems of historical authority and the burdens of visual evidence. This is, I argue, a basic condition for witnessing that becomes important throughout contemporary cultural crises in elite televised sport.

3

REPLAY AND THE NATURE

OF WITNESSING

GEORGE RETZLAFF CREATED the first in-game replay in sport television in 1955 for the Canadian Broadcasting Company's (CBC) *Hockey Night in Canada* program. Videotape recorders were not yet available (Ampex Corporation would introduce them the following year), so at the time a kinescope film—created by placing a motion picture camera in front of a TV monitor and recording the live broadcast—was the standard method for producing a segment for reproduction or replay. Retzlaff created a kinescope recording of a single goal that aired several minutes after the live play.[1]

Tony Verna invented the first *instant* replay while working as a director at CBS, and his innovation debuted on December 7, 1963, during the live broadcast of the Army-Navy college football game. The Ampex recorder had by then been available for seven years, but it still presented significant barriers to producing an instant replay. The director would need to see and mark the precise time when the action to be replayed started and stopped, record that exact segment to tape, and reinsert it (as replay) into the live broadcast. But the Ampex machine could not be cued so precisely. Verna's solution was to mark the tape with sound cues, transmitting one tone to the tape at the beginning of an action sequence and two tones at the end; these tones would mark a segment for replay while the game was flowing.[2]

Verna saw his opportunity after a scoring play by the Army team late in the game. The camera captured quarterback Rollie Stichweh running into the end zone. Verna heard his sound markers on the playback and saw clean video. When the instant replay came onscreen, announcer Lindsey Nelson famously shouted, "This is not live! Ladies and Gentlemen, Army did not score again." The explanation was required because of the instantaneous interval between the live play and the replay and because, as Verna explained, "those black-and-white video recordings playing in normal speed were indistinguishable from live video."[3] Even though visual enhancements like slow motion more clearly distinguish contemporary replay images from the live event, the experience of temporal and visual dislocation that Nelson addressed remains relevant today.

Only minutes separated Retzlaff's and Verna's versions of replay, but those minutes marked a profound difference in time. *Instant* replay made it possible to intervene within the flow of a game, altering experiences of live sport and creating a foundation for the video review systems that most people associate with replay today. When Verna died on January 18, 2015, journalists commemorating his career credited him with "remaking" sport television. The president of the Directors Guild of America said: "With the creation of instant replay . . . [Verna] changed the future of televised sports, and sports direction, forever."[4] In this chapter I focus on replay's influence over issues of vision and historical authority as these relate to the theme of witnessing.

John Durham Peters argues that of all the ways scholars have understood mediated experience (e.g., consuming, reading, viewing, decoding), "witnessing" most powerfully captures those "questions of truth and experience . . . and the trustworthiness of perception" wrapped up in viewing the world through audiovisual capture.[5] Television is an especially important medium for witnessing because it brings geographically and temporally separated publics together around a live event.[6] This remains true, I argue, even with the rise of networked and digital media, and particularly when it comes to live sport. Insofar as replay changes televised sport, it also changes the nature of witnessing and raises several problems related to memory and perception. What are the relationships between video evidence and the truth of historical events? What is the status of interpretive authority as judgment shifts from the human eye to the camera, from officials to fans? Replay persistently disrupts the continuity of live sport, and it is in relation to its stoppages that such problems of history and truth become recognizable. Journalists, league executives, and fans debate the nature of time, the fallibility of human perception, and the emptiness of history governed by machines. To revisit Walter Benjamin, disrupting the continuity of historical progress requires changing the speed at which historical images flit through the present: "the flow," as Rolf Tiedemann writes, "must come to a halt."[7] This is, I argue throughout this chapter, the basis of replay's importance: it stops the flow of live time, alters the ways in which we see elite sport, and in doing so creates basic conditions for struggling over issues of historical authority, visual evidence, and present-oriented action.

This chapter is divided into four parts. First, I examine the combination of religious and empirical values associated with live witnessing and replay capture. Second, I trace the rise of video review as both cause of and solution for emerging crises in the relationship between sight and historical authority. Third, I analyze how anxieties over perfection (of both sight and judgment) summarize a characteristically religious problem surrounding human-machine relationships in sport. Finally, I assess whether the forensic habits of viewing that replay fosters constitute conditions for meaningful social change. My focus throughout the chapter is not on any single replay text or event but on the larger patterns of production wherein witnessing takes shape as an audiovisual practice that encapsulates the limitations and possibilities of struggling over historical authority. To identify those patterns I focus on a sample of leagues and governing bodies with noteworthy histories of implementing and resisting video review: the National Football League (NFL), The National Rugby League (NRL) and Rugby Union, the International Cricket Council (ICC), professional tennis (including the U.S. Tennis Association [USTA], International Tennis Federation [ITF], Women's Tennis Association [WTA], the Association of Tennis Professionals [ATP], and the Grand Slam Committee), the National Hockey League (NHL), Major League Baseball (MLB), the Fédération Internationale de Football Association (FIFA), and the National Basketball Association (NBA).

Sport, Television, and the Metaphysical Value of Witnessing

In sport, witnessing is associated with the privileged status of *being there* at a live event: in the arena, at the stadium, or in the live co-presence of other viewers.[8] Positioned at the edge of an opening in time—at the moment the clock starts on a big game, for example—the witness anticipates a revelation of athletic greatness and is ready to testify to the experience both in the live moment and later, spreading the word to others who were not present. Peters writes that the "hard-core sports fan sweating the seconds . . . offers a profound lesson about the nature of time": the present is a framework for possibility and danger through which "possible futures come into being and vanish with every act," bringing the unmatched excitement of "an event about to take place." Seeing a sporting event with even the slightest delay can place the viewer in a "derivative role, a hearer of a report rather than a witness"; even though the game's details will be replayed endlessly in highlight shows, "the few seconds between occurrence and replay open up a metaphysical gulf in the meaning and quality of what is seen."[9] One must be there, live, at the precise moment when an elite athletic accomplishment disrupts quotidian time. Consider again Gary Kamiya's account (which I reference at the beginning of the previous chapter) of sprinter Usain Bolt's record-breaking performances at the 2008 Beijing Olympics:

> It's a strange feeling, watching history happen before your eyes. You know that you just saw something you will never forget, that will enter the pantheon of peak human achievements. You know it even as it happens, but it's too big to take in, because your brain isn't calibrated to register the truly extraordinary. You're going about your business, living your normal life, and suddenly something you've never seen before appears, and the horizon of human possibility moves back.[10]

Kamiya's testament highlights how the eventfulness of the live moment shocks the consciousness, providing a revelatory break from existing understandings of human limitation. This is clearly a televisual experience. Access to a rupture in time is possible through television's ordinary patterns of recording and display, which offer the possibility of something unplanned appearing on the screen.[11] The fact that sport regularly schedules this possibility in the form of games and events is central to the commercial value of live sport content.

Kamiya's testament is also clearly religious in the sense that it invokes the common ideal of sport transporting us from profane duration to sacred time. As I argued in Chapter 1, that ideal is problematic because it depoliticizes the religious meanings encoded in sport, abstracting them from the realities of economic and political production.

In fact, replay interweaves those seemingly transcendent qualities of witnessing with technology, flesh, mechanics, and the commodity value of televisual spectacle. As Margaret Morse notes, replay features bodies moving in a dreamlike world no longer governed by the laws of gravity or linear time. In slow motion, athletes glide and float "as if animated by some supernatural agency," overcoming the typical separation from nature and God, achieving the "spiritual grace" of machines perfected with "an aura of the divine." At the same time, replay elevates scientific (empirical, material) understandings of the body, movement, and elite performance that affirm technological access to events as they "really happened" and that mask productions of erotic desire and capital.[12] The dreamlike qualities of slow motion or freeze-frame movement are not separate from profane considerations like erotic gazing or technological measurement; neither is the replay image reducible simply to flesh or statistics. Witnesses ascribe evidentiary value to replay because it reveals the mechanics of bodies transcending the ordinary bounds of gravity and time *and* because it uncovers the most granular details of those mechanics for positivistic, historical scrutiny.

There is a long history of seeing sport through this combination of wonderment and empiricism. Indeed, the first successful capture of images previously imperceptible to the naked eye were Eadweard Muybridge's famous instantaneous photographs of galloping horses in 1872.[13] Although many stories behind why Muybridge produced the photographs are apocryphal, there is some consensus that Leland Stanford (the founder of Stanford University, who at the time was a wealthy industrialist) and millionaire Fred McCrellish hired Muybridge to settle a dispute over whether at any point during a horse's gallop all four of its hooves leave the ground.[14] Due to his innovations in high-speed photography and motion pictures, Muybridge is often credited as the inventor of the moving image, and athletic motion (that of horses, acrobats, runners) was a common subject of his experiments and public lectures.[15] As Rebecca Solnit writes, Muybridge's motion studies displayed bodies outside the bounds of gravity and fatigue, as "weightless images . . . dissected and reconstructed by light and machine and fantasy." In addition, Muybridge lifted the "veil of speed" that made the smallest details of movement imperceptible, creating new possibilities for knowledge about the body.[16] Phillip Prodger argues: "It was Muybridge, more than any other figure, who introduced what Walter Benjamin, decades later, termed the 'optical unconscious,' revealing that much of everyday life takes place beneath the threshold of our conscious awareness," including the drama of the "physical body navigating" calculated, measured space.[17] Marianne Hirsch argues similarly that Benjamin must have had in mind "Muybridge's series of still images of horses running, women walking, or men wrestling" when he became "concerned with the invisible that is present inside the visible, those bodily movements that are too minute to be discerned by the human eye and too automatic to impinge on human consciousness."[18] Here we find the most enduring and basic justification for replay intervention in sport: the camera displays the limits of human sight, and in doing so proves its worth as an "objective" arbiter of perceptual disputes.[19]

The replay systems featured in elite televised sport combine the empirical questions behind Stanford and McCrellish's dispute with Muybridge's revelation of a secret, otherworldly mechanics. Both the empirical and supernatural qualities of the optical unconscious are appropriated into the spectacle of contemporary sport media production, profitably anchoring games "in history and the real" while also increasing their spectacular qualities. Producers feature images of athletic bodies in slow motion or freeze frame to highlight their transcendent qualities, which, as Morse argues, seemingly set those bodies "apart from the world of production and the division of labor" and encourage a utopian view of human achievement that "disavows" commercial motives and maintains "the sanctity of sport." Yet the use of visual enhancement to construct idealized bodies also "'bares the device,' allowing the enormous capital investment in sport itself and in broadcasting technology to gleam through the 'live' event."[20] An especially important result is the conspicuous presence of specialized audiovisual technologies that disrupt the liveness of games in almost all contemporary elite sport. This includes both the obviousness of the technologies themselves—giant video screens in stadiums, multiple cameras, computer-simulated lines and boundary markers, slow-motion playback—and the rituals that surround those technologies, such as the coach's challenge or referees huddled around a video monitor during a stoppage in play.

The enhanced views provided to officials and fans for the sake of judgment constitute significant compressions of space and extensions of time: action close-ups isolate players from the broader context of the game, and slow motion lifts the moving body out of the speed and continuity of linear time, allowing officials and fans to go back and see more than they could in the live moment. These enhanced views bring viewers into a "hermeneutic process of scientific discovery" alongside referees, who are often looking at the same images (typically supplied by network cameras) in order to make a judgment.[21] In what Stephanie Marriott describes as a "live/not live" experience, viewers are enabled (or forced) to double back in time to peruse multiple angles, close-ups, and slow-motion clips along with on-air commentators, coaches, and exasperated players.[22] *Time* magazine writer Jack Dickey complained of this altered sense of time, citing a NHL rule that allowed officials to review a goal and then reset the game clock to the time the goal was scored: "That's right—game history can rewrite itself, as though the NHL were some sort of high-concept family-friendly comedy film. *Upon further review, those five minutes never elapsed.*"[23]

As Marriott explains, replay sequences make it so a game broadcast is "partially composed of an earlier segment of itself" that recurs as many times as a given play is reviewed. As commentators analyze various views of the play, its qualities of eventfulness and liveness change: the play is dislocated from its original, "'real' location in time" and reconstructed in the "now" of the viewer's experience, perhaps with very different meanings (e.g., as an overturned call or as a play deprived of its live excitement by repetitive delays).[24] Television replays create this "now" as a "shared perceptual space" by displaying common images for viewers, commentators, and officials.[25] It is within this discontinuous, shared space that producers foster a compulsion among these and other witnesses to seek out the truth of what *really happened*. And it is this constant, compulsive need to review and judge that so often frustrates fans, journalists, and league officials who argue that replay ruins the flow of games.

Journalist John McGrath summarizes this complaint perfectly, writing that the "replay machine first used in 1963 weighed 1,300 pounds, qualifying it as the heaviest can of worms in the history of the world"; it is an invention that has destroyed the pace of games, created an endless appetite for replay among fans, and caused as many disputes as it has solved.[26] The NFL—the organization most associated with embracing video review today—first experimented with replay in 1986 and decided to end it for the 1992 season after years of complaints that reviews killed the momentum and "natural flow" of games and led to "interminable delays."[27] In sports with less of a stop-start flow than football has (in the average NFL game the ball is in play for a total of only eleven minutes), the pace of play has been a more long-standing barrier to replay.[28] Soccer, for example, with its continuous game clock, is prized as a sport that "proceeds without interruption."[29] MLB has, until very recently, not had a game clock, and replay disruption has historically been viewed as a violation of the game's "natural flow," of its resistance to the growing "tyranny" of pace and speed in commercial sport.[30]

Even in sports like soccer and baseball, however, officials are forced to consider pacing concerns against the optics of replay. Responding to controversies over missed calls in 1999, MLB executive vice president Sandy Alderson noted: "You have to balance the texture of the game with the need to get every single play right. . . . We don't want to erase the human quality and we can't ignore the technology."[31] Similarly, NBA commissioner Adam Silver said in 2014: "Part of what makes for great NBA basketball is the flow of the game, and that flow is interrupted by instant replay. At the same time, we want to get it right." Silver proposed making replay reviews more efficient as the best way to negotiate this tension, articulating a common assumption in sport that the longer the delay, the more the drama of the live moment is reduced.[32]

The only way out of this bind is to propose restoring some imagined, pre-replay purity to sport. Bloggers and fans recognize (accurately) that replay opens intervals for advertising in otherwise continuous games (e.g., soccer, hockey, rugby).[33] Owing perhaps to associations between video review and the NFL, international sportswriters and fans commonly argue that replay stoppages represent an "Americanization" of their games—an invitation to rampant commercialism, technological "gimmickry," and a ruinous need for "absolute certainty" that has infected the North American continent.[34] That need for certainty is also commonly criticized in the United States. NBC sport columnist Joe Posnanski argues that the "real price" of replay stoppage is a growing litigiousness. "We used to just know," according to Posnanski, things like what constitutes a catch in football, but now these are subject to endless visual scrutiny. The more we rely on replay, the more we lose "the certainty of the game": the "natural understanding we all had" is replaced "with an endless appeal process and Talmudic wrangling over the most insignificant things."[35] This sense of loss is focused on the break in continuity, which changes the quality of witnessing. Instead of the eventfulness of celebration, the cheering of the crowd, the astonishment of the announcers, there is stoppage, rewind, calculation. Witnesses are positioned as surrogate officials evaluating forensic evidence rather than members of the elect gathered around an opening in ordinary time.

These qualities of televisual liveness remain relevant to sport programming even with ongoing shifts toward new, networked, and digital media. In their book *Sport beyond Television*, Brett Hutchins and David Rowe write that continuing preferences for viewing sport live guarantee "a level of popularity and commercial protection for rights-holders," since holding exclusive broadcast and distribution rights to live sport content means controlling "a rare source of 'must-see' content" (or "appointment television") in a condition of fragmented, dispersed, and specialized publics.[36] In his influential conception of "flow," Raymond Williams explains how television providers responded to competitive conditions by eliminating discrete intervals between programming units so that viewers can be "captured" in a total flow sequence.[37] Examples in sport might include everything from multiplatform, "wall-to-wall" coverage of mega-events like the Olympics or World Cup to a Sunday afternoon spent flipping through various regular-season games. Williams was writing at a time when three major networks still dominated U.S. television, before the influence of new recording technologies, cable and satellite television, and the Internet. Writing about television today requires an acknowledgment of how television texts "overflow" across interactive websites, mobile devices, and the various platforms of media conglomerates.[38] Yet capturing fans in a sequence of total flow—especially one that continuously directs fans to exclusive content—remains a relevant characterization of producers' aims. Thus, as digital television and live streaming services threaten broadcast companies' control over content, these companies respond by appropriating fans' and athletes' online participation (folding that participation into news and highlight shows, for example), by creating their own authorized streaming services, by suing over unauthorized distribution, and by threatening to negotiate lower-value contracts with sport leagues that stream broadcast content online.[39]

Even with these actions, there has been, as Hutchins and Rowe argue, a change in the "media sport content economy" from a condition of "broadcast scarcity"—wherein most programming was controlled by a handful of large corporations—to a condition of "digital plentitude"—wherein lower barriers related to cost and access bring more organizations, clubs, athletes, and fans into an active struggle over "the material and cultural possession of sport."[40] Yet this shift does not mean the demise of television. In countries like the United States (which has a small public-service broadcast sector and deregulated markets), media conglomerates continue to control most of the major networks providing sport content, and their ability to invest billions of dollars in exclusive rights contracts means that social media production still predominantly references and appropriates broadcast television texts.[41] To borrow from an Australian regulatory official, broadcast companies have recognized that they "can't control the arteries" (distribution channels, streaming services), so they have retained "control of the blood."[42]

Sport media scholars are rethinking "television" as a screen-based viewing practice that occurs across multiple devices (high-definition [HD] televisions, smartphones, tablets), platforms (streaming services, online television), and scenes (living rooms, bars, stadiums).[43] Replay has become particularly important within this new televisual reality. As Hutchins and Rowe note, the Internet changes every aspect of daily life, "yet somehow there are more types of television than ever before" (online and digital TV, 3-D TV, cable and satellite TV, "smart" Internet-ready TV), all affirming the continued "conceptual, material, and commercial significance of television." The result of television's various integrations with and adaptations to online and digital media is "a multi-layered reality" wherein the multiplication of screens and channels attracts more activity around and attention to live sport.[44] Williams's conception of flow has retained heuristic value thanks to his insistence that analyzing a programming text as a discrete whole misses the point that it is movement across and between texts, networks, and platforms that makes "watching television" a way of experiencing the broader values of a culture in relation to its technological means of production.[45] As Williams puts it, television has to be considered "simultaneously as a technology and as a cultural form."[46] It is across multiple screens and channels that replay images circulate and constitute problems of historical authority. Mobile devices and public screens increase the locations from which one can "be there" for a live game, and video hosting and social network services redistribute and extend the life of controversial clips.

The Rise of the Mechanical Witness
and the Mechanical Referee

Much is at stake in live sport. Once a play is over, it is a potential factor in the outcome of a game. Once a game is over, it is fixed as a win or a loss in the historical record. There is no retroactive justice in sport, no possibility of changing an official outcome after the live moment. Even if some unforeseen technology proves at a future date that a call was wrong, the judgment after the fact is purely academic. Consider Geoff Hurst's famous second shot against Germany in the 1966 World Cup final, which hit the underside of the cross bar, bounced down onto the goal line, and, after some initial uncertainty, was ruled a goal by the linesman. Hurst argued in a 2013 interview that if replay was available in 1966, it would have clearly shown his goal was good, preventing almost fifty years of German objections.[47] In fact, many of the technological interventions applied to Hurst's goal have suggested the opposite. For example, in 1996 engineers from Oxford University constructed an elaborate computer model to plot the ball's position along a virtual line derived from two separate, simultaneous video sequences of Hurst's goal. The result?—they were certain, by a range of at least 6 centimeters, that the ball did not cross the goal line.[48] In 2006, ITN Source, a video archive company, transferred the footage of Hurst's goal to high-definition video for the first time and claimed that the enhanced footage "settled" forty years' worth of dispute, clearly showing that the ball did not cross the line.[49] Hurst has maintained his stance and reminded critics that there is ultimately no way he can lose the argument: "They can't take [the goal] away now anyway. It is in the book."[50] Retroactive justice may be possible in rare cases of documented cheating (the International Cycling Union stripping Lance Armstrong's Tour de France titles is a good example) but even then there is a permanent hole in the historical record.[51] The impossibility of going back and redoing the competition means that we cannot say who won, only that the winner triumphed unfairly.

Within this context of irreversible history, replay provides access to the hidden optics of movement, space, and time. By putting otherwise imperceptible details on display, replay offers hope that those problems of past and future history contained in the live moment (the frustrations of previously unsettled errors, the unchangeable judgment of the referee) might be addressed decisively in real time. But this requires a shift in perceptual and interpretive authority from the human eye to the camera, and that shift is seen as both troubling and necessary in sport. In his recent history of replay, Dylan Mulvin helpfully summarizes sport-related ideas about video and historical truth in the form of two related figures: the "mechanical witness" and the "mechanical referee." The mechanical witness encapsulates "the ideological claims made about the video camera's disembodied position, multiple angles of sight, constant vigilance, and instant recall," all of which underwrite the presumed capacity of video to capture what really happened beyond the limits of the human eye and human subjectivity. With the rise of video review systems, these claims have been applied through the figure of the "mechanical referee" to problems unique to sport, particularly "the fallibility of the human perceptual apparatus in deciding matters of contact, boundary, and possession."[52] Both of these figures represent a formalization of the camera's historical role in settling disputes over athletic movement and perception, gesturing all the way back to Muybridge. And both represent ideas about perception and accuracy that have situated replay as a necessary and inevitable way of seeing elite sport.

Replay as Crisis and Solution

Mulvin writes that Verna's invention of instant replay in 1963 mobilized football (and eventually sport in general) as "a site for the public demonstration of the utility of video in forming new techniques of aesthetic and evaluative observation." As football publicized the value of video evidence for managerial and analytical purposes, sport-related approaches to recording and evaluating movement translated into military training, efficiency management for the workplace, and courtroom proceedings. Courts, in particular, adopted the rhetoric and logic of "indisputable visual evidence" as decisive in appeals cases, borrowing both "the system of judgment and the hermeneutic certainty" associated with video review in sport. The same logic translated back to sport, shaping contemporary video review systems as "miniature appellate systems" within which coaches and officials are responsible for determining the "truth" in a given sequence of actions.[53]

Mulvin borrows the term "mechanical witness" from Louis-Georges Schwartz, who (in his book of the same title) analyzes the history of evidentiary films and videos in U.S. courts. Among the various trends that Schwartz tracks is the development of video's evidentiary value *as video*—that is, as a medium that seems to reveal truth by virtue of its form. The truth value of video grew out of its contrasts with film, which preceded video in U.S. courtrooms, particularly during the 1940s and 1950s. Video was more readily incorporated into trials because of its portability; moreover, while lawyers could cast doubt over film images by suggesting they might have been edited before trial, video came "out of the camera ready to screen" and was thus "easier to authenticate."[54] Jurists still worried about manipulative editing techniques, but officials increasingly presumed the veracity of video evidence after decades of experience with preceding visual technologies (photographs, films) in courtrooms. By the 1970s "the moving image was no longer questioned as a means for bringing truth into court," and by the early 1980s "appearance, truth, and mechanical recordings of appearance and truth" were so "closely linked" that "videotape was convincing . . . precisely because it was videotape."[55]

In sport the truth value of video is presumed similarly and perhaps more powerfully: producers edit video sequences immediately, thus closing the gap between the event's occurrence and its representation. Moreover, edits and alterations of the original image are seen not as manipulative but as investigatory. Each additional angle, magnification, or slow-motion crawl reveals the unconscious optics of an event that the human eye could not capture in live time. The limits of human perception become especially problematic given the presumably natural, evolutionary advance of athletic bodies that I analyzed in Chapter 2. Indeed, as commentators ponder expansions of replay in a given sport, images of ever-improving athletic potential conflate with improvements in enhanced sight; bodily and audiovisual technologies advance along the same historical curve. John Walters summarized this conflation in *Newsweek*, writing that "as athletes become faster and as video technology evolves at an even faster pace, mistakes . . . are both more likely to occur and more prone to being exposed."[56] Former NFL running back Barry Sanders argued similarly that "the game has gotten so fast—I'm patting the modern athlete on the back here—that I think it's hard for officials to keep up [without replay assistance]."[57] As body and replay technologies are imagined together, these problems of speed become empirical, measured in fine-grained units of time and space. Consider a 2012 FIFA report on installing goal-line cameras to assist referees on goal calls:

> One of the challenges for referees is that the human eye can handle only approximately 16 images per second, which means the ball needs to be behind the line for at least 60 milliseconds. However, in some cases the ball is only behind the line for a few milliseconds before a player kicks it back or it rebounds back into the field of play, with the result that the human eye cannot see whether the ball has crossed the line. The ball can only be detected by the human eye at a speed of 12km/h or less, whereas nowadays players are able to shoot at a speed of over 120km/h.[58]

Recognizing these disparities between human perception and game speed, FIFA eventually implemented review technologies at the goal line for the 2014 World Cup. Will Oremus of *Slate* magazine wrote approvingly, "Humans are better than computers at a lot of things, but judging whether a fast-flying projectile has crossed a line is not one of them."[59]

Debates over implementing replay technologies rarely hinge on whether the technologies work. Concerns over angles, millimeters, or pixilation persist (most often articulated by hesitant officials), as do concerns that referees might misread or misinterpret the video image. But video's claim on reality is largely presumed. In fact, the prevailing problem is that replay images are *too revealing*. To understand why this is a problem, we need to revisit instant replay's 1963 origin story. Verna was motivated to invent instant replay because he wanted television viewers at home to see what he could see from the capture of multiple cameras. Without the additional perspectives supplied by replay, he could show viewers only *that* something happened (an incomplete pass) but not *why* it happened (the receiver tripped at the line of scrimmage). The reason behind the play was available on a separate piece of video, captured by a different camera, but there was no means of introducing that additional evidence into the continuity of the broadcast until Verna's successful manipulation of the video technologies that were available to him.[60] The solution to this issue—introducing additional video evidence into the flow of a live game—was initially intended to enhance the experiences of home television viewers. Verna said in 2013: "I didn't invent instant replay to improve officiating. . . . I invented it for a better telecast."[61] Yet his innovation provided the grounds for the appellate systems we are familiar with today.

Instant replay gave video an interventionist role, a capacity to insert enhanced judgment capacities into the live continuity of a game. That interventionist role did not then, and does not now, necessarily rely on a given sport having an official appellate system. In elite televised sport nearly every significant play is replayed and subject to analysis and commentary within the flow of a live game, as broadcasters keep adding new visual enhancements to increase the game's entertainment value. As a result, game texts take on forensic qualities for television and in-stadium viewers even if the referees do not use the enhanced images for official judgment. This is very much by design. Paul Hawkins, the inventor of the "Hawk-Eye" ball-tracking technology that has been successfully implemented into tennis, cricket, soccer, and several other sports, summarized how technology companies develop in-game video review in response to the demands of television:

> In general, we've found that broadcasters, who are in a competitive market, are eager to enhance production and give the viewers better value. Meanwhile, the sports' governing bodies are in a less competitive environment and are more reactive. The broadcasters are a great

marketing service for us, though: The governing bodies can see that everyone watching at home knows the correct call and the umpire doesn't.[62]

Governing bodies are reactive in the sense that they perceive replay as a threat to their authority over the outcomes of games, playoff seeding, historical record keeping, and other aspects of officiating control that sustain the value of sport content for broadcasters. Broadcasters are selling live sport on the basis that anything can happen and that outcomes will be determined by the agency of compelling athletes, not referees or league executives. Wading into the broader struggles over content control between large media companies and sport leagues, technology companies appeal first to the competitive interests of broadcasters, then rely on the evidentiary power of their replay images to create officiating crises. As an executive for CBS's NFL broadcasts put it: "We have the telephoto lens. We can slow it down[.] We can freeze. The human eye is like a 90-millimeter lens. I'm using 1,200-millimeter lenses. I'm really outgunning [the officials]."[63] Routing replay technologies through broadcast spectacle has proven remarkably effective. Over time the pressure of repetitively revealed errors builds up, and even those sports that have historically resisted video review systems eventually give in. In fact, the judicial value of replay often intensifies in sports where review systems are not in place, as the absence of options for official recourse elongates the life of a game text as an unaddressed (and unaddressable) piece of public evidence.

Consider the example of Major League Baseball. Historically averse to replay, MLB today employs an extensive and elaborate system for video review. Most journalists, players, and fans point to a 2010 game between the Detroit Tigers and Cleveland Indians as decisive in that change. Detroit pitcher Armando Galarraga was one out away from throwing only the twenty-first perfect game in MLB history when umpire Jim Joyce incorrectly called Cleveland shortstop Jason Donald safe at first base. The historical weight of the error was instantaneous. Minutes after Joyce's call, a succession of replays showed Donald clearly out from multiple angles, with each look prompting one of the Detroit TV announcers to ask, "Why is [Donald] safe?" and then, as the gravity of the error set in, to gasp, "Jim Joyce—no."[64] MLB's replay system was limited at the time to boundary questions (whether a ball was fair or foul, whether a ball had left the playing field, and whether a home run call was subject to fan interference), so the images replaying on the in-stadium screen could not be referenced to overturn the call.[65] Joyce saw his error just after the game ended, and said, "I feel like hell. This is a historical call and I kicked the shit out of it. . . . I feel like I took something away from that kid and I don't know how to give it back."[66] The permanence of the error weighed on him immediately.

Galarraga was gracious. He accepted an apology from Joyce after the game and told him that "nobody's perfect," which became the title of a 2011 book that the two men co-authored.[67] That moment of apology and forgiveness made national news as a sign of the instructive value of baseball: in the absence of perfection, the nation received a lesson on grace and accountability that parents could pass on to their children and that "self-righteous" world leaders could learn from as they negotiated conflicts in the Korean Peninsula and the Middle East.[68]

Even so, calls to expand instant replay beyond boundary judgments intensified after Joyce's error. The call was deemed one of the worst in MLB history, and journalists consistently connected it with an infamous call blown by Don Dekinger in the 1985 World Series (also at first base), which has often been viewed as decisive in the Series outcome. Dekinger himself joined a chorus of prominent media personalities who argued that MLB could no longer sustain its long-standing resistance to replay after the Joyce incident, not when contemporary replay technologies would have made a correction on Galarraga's behalf so easy.[69] As in other sports without extensive appellate systems, televised replays were out in front, serving to both display and condemn an error so egregious that it would inevitably mandate video review.

Commentators also called on MLB to overrule Joyce's call and grant Galarraga a perfect game retroactively. A *Wall Street Journal* editorial suggested that God created baseball's perfect game "as a hallowed rebuke to the sensible every-day notion that life isn't perfect" and that by refusing to amend the record, Commissioner Bud Selig would cause "this taint, this blot, this imperfection" to "hang over baseball forever."[70] Father Raymond J. de Souza, a columnist for Canada's *National Post* and a Catholic priest, made a more formally theological case: this was "a beautiful opportunity—so rare that it should not be squandered—to correct the past, to right a wrong, to make perfect what was imperfect," a chance to get as close "in the natural world" as one can "to the supernatural grace of absolution: the erasure of a mistaken past."[71] A fan writing to the sports editor at the *New York Times* argued that the "real . . . injustice" would be "considering the 'official' result carved in granite rather than fixable with an eraser."[72] And White House press secretary Robert Gibbs joked that Galarraga might be granted his perfect game by executive order.[73]

Yet the outcome could have been amended only in live time. *Detroit Free Press* reporter Drew Sharp suggested that Galarraga probably would not want the call reversed "two days later" because the moment was already gone and could not be recreated after the fact.[74] Mike Lopresti of *USA Today* wrote that overturning bad calls is as messy as "looking at spilled milk and trying to choose which drops go back into the glass."[75] And the *New York Times*'s George Vecsey depicted a slippery slope whereby Selig overturning Joyce's "ghastly call" could lead to a commissioner "sitting in the stands overturning a call in a World Series" during the game or even the following day when everyone was flying home.[76]

The Galarraga case neatly summarizes the value of video intervention in a moment of substantial metaphysical weight. The clarity of the call, the stakes of the perfect game, and the availability of indisputable video evidence all highlighted what critics saw as an arbitrary, self-imposed limitation for historical correction. The argument that replay technologies already exist and reveal everything to viewers is commonly directed against leagues and governing bodies that resist video review or employ it in a limited way. *Everyone can see what really happened.*

MLB's refusal to reverse Joyce's call became more problematic than the call itself, a sign of technophobic stubbornness that would eternally stain the game. According to many critics, that dogged attachment to tradition puts organizations like MLB on the wrong side of a new technological age. *Scotland on Sunday* writer Jeff Connor argued, for example, that British sport was troubled by "an endemic suspicion of new technology"; in an age of video review, "soccer and rugby [were] still happy to let a part-time, middle-aged, baggy-panted amateur, looking for a few bob to augment his schoolmaster's salary, make decisions that could win or lose a World Cup."[77] U.S. law professor Jonathan Turley wrote on his blog that resistance to replay demonstrated how sport was a last refuge for "the world's troglodytes resisting the simplest of technological advances."[78]

If audiovisual technologies expose the fallibility of officiating, then these same technologies can (indeed must) be used to ensure fair and accurate outcomes. This is the basic logic of replay expansion in sport. Consider *Washington Post* journalist Adam Kilgore's understanding of the causes and solutions behind officiating difficulties in MLB:

> Baseball's problem with umpiring has more to do with television cameras than the umpires. The numerous angles, in tandem with the technology available to production crews, turn every missed call into an obvious screw-up and every obvious screw-up into an outrage. It is hard to say if umpires are worse now than before, but they have never looked worse. The problem, of course, presents its own solution. The technology that exposes umpires could also eradicate the scrutiny they fall under. The same replays fans use to decry incompetence could simply be put to use and correct mistakes as they happen.[79]

The solution to problems of replay becomes more replay. This is the characteristically homeopathic logic through which video review permeates elite televised sport: to borrow from Peters, "the disease and the cure are in cahoots."[80] Replay reproduces itself by promising the possibility of perfection (fairness, accuracy, objectivity) *and* by supplying the forms of redress for its inevitable failures to deliver. Once replay is implemented as an appellate system, its status is secured as both problem and response in a compensatory loop: television companies feature new technologies that allow viewers to see more, officials implement the same or similar technologies to address new visual problems raised in broadcasts, and the ongoing push to expand replay corresponds to advances in specialized audiovisual capture. This process is evident within elite sports that have resisted and adopted video review, as I demonstrate in a series of brief historical samples.

National Football League (NFL)

The National Football League (NFL) is the organization most associated with instant replay, including in international coverage, where football is cited as evidence that replay will "Americanize" a given sport. The NFL first experimented with replay after a controversial call on a fumble in the 1978 AFC Championship Game between the Oakland Raiders and Denver Broncos before officially installing limited replay in 1986; only officials could initiate a review, and they had very few camera images to work from.[81]

The version of replay implemented in 1986 was renewed on an annual basis until NFL owners decided to end it in 1992. The reasons they gave would be associated more with baseball or soccer today: replay interrupted the flow of play, made games too long for a growing TV audience, and did not deliver on the promise to correct human error, which, after all, was just part of the sport.[82] Recognizing that replay would continue as an entertainment feature in broadcasts, Tex Schramm (considered the father of instant replay in professional football), warned that the league was making a mistake: "With the TV coverage, you'll continue to have instant replay," just without the possibility of formal action; bad calls "will still be seen at home and you'll have a strong reaction from the public when they see plays they know are wrong."[83] Washington coach Joe Gibbs argued similarly that if "everybody in America sees the wrong team win a game" because of an obvious, uncorrected error, the league would face a credibility crisis.[84]

Instant replay was absent in the NFL until 1999. Several high-profile officiating errors during the 1998 season provided the necessary momentum for its return. League leaders emphasized that the new replay system would focus on correcting "major . . . human errors, game-changing errors."[85] The system installed in 1999 was more extensive than previous iterations, allowing coaches to initiate two challenges per game at the potential cost of timeouts. That system has remained essentially in place up to the present day, with changes including an expansion of reviewable plays and additional responsibilities for on-field and specialized replay officials.

National Rugby League (NRL) and Rugby Union

The National Rugby League (NRL) first used video evidence for judiciary purposes after a 1978 brawl during a Wests-Norths game. League general manager John Quayle recalled concerns that "video would bring League to its knees. It'd be the death of the game." But by 1990 NRL officials widely associated video review with protecting fair play.[86] The NRL first adopted in-game replay for Super League competition in 1996 after Rupert Murdoch won a court victory in the so-called "Super League War." The system installed a designated "video referee" who could reference television replays to assist the on-ground referee in judging whether a try was accurately scored.[87]

After initial implementation in 1996, a series of crises dictated changes to the system: several controversial calls in 2000 led the NRL to expand video review to goal-kicking situations, in 2003 the NRL empowered video referees to police time-wasting (e.g., players faking injuries to trigger replay reviews), and in 2008 the NRL removed previous, controversial expansions of the video referee's powers—specifically for ruling on stripping incidents during scrums, and on foul play—and added a second on-field referee, which was seen as one of the biggest changes to the sport in a century.[88] From 2014 to the time of this writing, the NRL started to move toward a "video referee bunker" system with a Central Command Center where in-game reviews could be made faster and where decisions could be communicated to fans through social media. The bunker system was proposed by the NRL as a measure designed to address ongoing controversies over referee decisions, and testing was announced for the 2015 season.[89]

After a number of officiating controversies, and following the NRL's adoption of a video replay system, Rugby Union debuted its own video replay system—called the Television Match Official (TMO)—in a 2000 match between New Zealand and Tonga.[90] Agreeing with the common rationale that television coverage was already displaying mistakes, critics argued that Rugby Union's decision was overdue. As Stephen Jones of the *Sunday Times* asked, if Sky Sports's "all-seeing" coverage made it so that "every household in Britain" could "know the correct decision, why on earth not tell the referee and players?"[91] Initially the TMO was limited to adjudicating the legality of tries, penalties, conversions, and drop goals and not allowed (due to pace-of-play concerns) for any calls that would involve scrolling back in time to review a play. Due to continuing controversies, Rugby Union expanded the scope of reviewable calls over time, even as officials' worries over a "stop-start" brand of rugby persisted.[92]

International Cricket Council (ICC)

To address long-standing accusations about home biases in umpiring, cricket officials began in 1986 to invite neutral umpires to stand in Test matches (the longest form of the sport, and often considered the highest standard of play). In 1992 the ICC first experimented with one neutral umpire per Test, and eventually expanded to two neutral umpires starting in 2002.[93] Cricket was growing into a high-stakes sport in 1992, around the same time when television and slow-motion replay were emerging as vital to mediated sport. Cricket officials felt that some kind of backup TV replay system was necessary as umpires' mistakes were increasingly exposed on television. So, in 1992 the ICC added a "third umpire" (or TV umpire) who sat away from the cricket ground, had access to TV replays, and advised the on-ground umpires on disputed calls (e.g., catches, line decisions). Hawk-Eye, now an essential replay technology in several sports, debuted in cricket during television coverage of the 2001 Ashes series.[94]

Hawk-Eye employs several cameras to track the flight of a ball and feed data into a computer model. In cricket, the path of the ball is tracked from the moment it leaves the bowler's hand to the point when it is dead, and in tennis the ball is tracked through its flight path to its landing spot on the court. The computer model, developed by inventor Paul Hawkins (who has a PhD in artificial intelligence), compiles thousands of measurements of the playing surface (contours, lines, changes in size as the surface heats up on warm days) and reproduces an image of the ball's flight and landing spot that is accurate, his company claims, to within 3.6 millimeters.[95] Hawk-Eye is among the more popular replay systems among fans and players because it produces an instantaneous and precise image that viewers at home or at an event can see onscreen (often alongside exasperated or elated players). It was used initially in cricket as an entertainment-based feature for broadcasts before making its way into official review due to pressure from television companies. Seth Stevenson of *Slate* notes that "the driving demand" for Hawk-Eye "came from cricket broadcasters, not cricket officials," as its precise images "could instantly settle barstool debates as people watched matches on the telly."[96]

The ICC began trials in 2002 for Hawk-Eye-assisted referee calls on leg-before-wicket (LBW) decisions, historically among the most controversial calls in cricket. In 2008 Hawk-Eye became part of cricket's larger Decision Review System (DRS). The DRS was first implemented by the Board of Control for Cricket in India (BCCI) for a Test cricket match between India and Sri Lanka in 2008, and allowed a player to request a review of on-field umpire decisions concerning dismissals. It also allowed a TV umpire to review slow-motion replays from multiple angles, sound from stump microphones, and Hawk-Eye ball-tracking data. The ICC adopted a DRS for the first time in 2009 and made it mandatory for all international matches, but decided in 2011 to make it optional after controversies concerning the accuracy of one of the system's technologies, called Hot Spot, which uses infrared cameras to mark the ball's point of contact.[97]

In addition to providing an important site for video and computer modeling systems, cricket has also fostered developments in sound-based replay technologies, particularly the Snick-O-Meter (or "Snicko"). The Snick-O-Meter debuted during television coverage of England's home Tests in 1999 and, like several other technologies eventually adopted for replay officiating, was implemented to add entertainment value to television broadcasts. Snicko was designed to pick up the faintest sounds through stump and pitch microphones and to translate the data to a sound graph superimposed on the screen. Snicko, like Hot Spot, has been primarily applied to questions of whether a ball made contact with a bat, and these technologies—the thermal image provided by Hot Spot and the sound image provided by Snicko—represent the key pieces for judging ball-to-bat contact. Hot Spot has been controversial since its implementation by the ICC in 2006 because the thermal image it produces from the friction of ball meeting bat has worked better for spinners who deliver the ball with more rotation than for faster bowlers, and its images can be obscured in the late afternoon because of reflections thrown by the setting sun. Snicko has raised questions of whether a source other than ball-to-bat contact (e.g., ball on pad, bat on pad) might trigger a sound tremor.[98]

Once again, technology companies worked their way toward appellate implementation first through television networks, capitalizing on their systems as both sources of and solutions for emerging visual problems. Snicko had been used solely for the edification of television audiences until 2013, when BGG Sports, the company that developed Hot Spot, started pushing for the simultaneous implementation of Hot Spot and Snicko in the Decision Review System. Resistance to pairing Snicko sound capture with Hot Spot images was based on the length of time it would take for a technician to synchronize the sound with the infrared image. But BGG Sports introduced new infrared cameras in 2011 that reduced motion blur (which, the company promised, would address controversies over "fine edge" measurements), and developed a "Real Time Snicko" system that paired the images captured from twelve different cameras with the sound capture of two stump microphones in real time. This provided an automated synchronization of infrared image and sound capture. After BGG Sports addressed the sound-image synchronization issue, Snick-O-Meter was approved as part of the DRS for the 2013–2014 Ashes Test series.[99]

Professional Tennis

Hawk-Eye has also been credited for changing the way professional tennis is viewed and officiated; as with the other sports I am discussing, it began as an entertainment feature here as well. Hawk-Eye replays were first used in tennis as part of the BBC's Davis Cup coverage in 2002, and the technology won an Emmy in 2003 for Outstanding Innovative Technical Achievement.[100] But its current status in professional tennis can be traced back primarily to a single event: a quarterfinal match between Serena Williams and Jennifer Capriati at the 2004 U.S. Open. Capriati defeated Williams after the chair umpire overruled a line judge during the final set, calling a backhand shot out even though the line judge had (accurately) called it in. Hawk-Eye television replays used by USA Network clearly showed the ball was in, and Hawk-Eye also revealed three other bad calls that went against Williams.[101] At the time the U.S. Tennis Association (USTA) used a machine called Cyclops to help judges with calls (in or out) on serves, but tennis had not adopted instant replay as an aid to officials.

Two weeks before the Williams-Capriati match, International Tennis Federation (ITF) and USTA officials were testing a system called Auto-Ref—a competitor to Hawk-Eye that similarly used an ultra-high-speed camera to capture the ball—and the match served as a catalyst for continued testing through 2005. The ITF approved Hawk-Eye and tested it successfully at the Champions Tour's season-ending event at Royal Albert Hall in London, and Hawk-Eye was adopted at various levels of professional tennis before being implemented, along with a player challenge system, by the USTA at the 2006 U.S. Open.[102] Within that system, Hawk-Eye replay images were displayed on two large video screens at the court so fans and chair umpires could see the images simultaneously. USTA's challenge system granted each player two challenges per set to review line calls; challenges could be retained or lost based on whether the player's objection was verified by replay. Commentators noted that "for such a tradition-rich sport, replay [was] radical—the most dramatic rules change since the tiebreaker was adopted in 1970."[103] Referencing the truth value of "modern" technologies, Association of Tennis Professionals (ATP) chairman Etienne de Villiers argued that the change was overdue: "To me, it was always crazy that with modern GPS technology we could tell where a person is to within a yard or meter on the planet earth, and yet we can't tell whether a tennis ball is in or out."[104] And Paul Hawkins made the equally common case that "if the person at home has a better view than the person in the chair," then replay becomes a necessary correction.[105]

Since 2008 four major governing bodies—the ITF, the Women's Tennis Association (WTA), the ATP, and the Grand Slam Committee—have operated under a unified set of rules for challenges at professional tournaments, allowing players three unsuccessful challenges per set and one extra challenge if the set reaches a tie break. Today Hawk-Eye is employed, along with the unified challenge rules, at all Grand Slam events with the exception of the French Open (where the clay courts show the ball's point of impact), and Hawk-Eye is installed on most courts where high-profile matches are played. Hawk-Eye was also used at the 2008 and 2012 Olympics, and has been more common at smaller tournament venues as well.[106]

National Hockey League (NHL)

After years of debate over cost the NHL decided to implement instant replay for the 1991–1992 season in order to address controversial goal calls, some of which had determined game outcomes. The league provided a video judge in every arena to assist on-ice referees, particularly on questions of whether the puck crossed the goal line, was kicked or thrown into the net, ricocheted off an official, or went in after the net was dislodged.[107]

Beginning in 2003 the NHL moved to a centralized video review system that shifted control over replays to a "Situation Room" in Toronto staffed by NHL employees who monitor games on banks of television screens.[108] The NHL's centralized system represents an important shift among leagues and governing bodies from a primarily reactive stance regarding television-based replay to a more proactive one. In its current form the system begins with video judges stationed in every arena who have the authority to stop play, order a review, and correspond with employees in the Situation Room (who make the final call). The same staff work in the Situation Room for 1,230 games, which the NHL cites as a source of consistency and accuracy. The NHL's system is widely regarded as a model in contemporary sport. Officials from MLB and the NFL have visited the NHL's facilities in order to consider designs for their own centralized systems, and the NRL "bunker" system is similarly inspired.[109] Centralized replay hubs represent a formal and highly organized adoption of the logic of mechanical witnessing, a significant change from the incremental and reactive implementations of replay that characterized the earlier histories of most elite televised sports.

A particularly important component of the NHL's centralization is league-produced video. The NHL has high-definition cameras operated by league personnel inside every arena, positioned high above the goal line and inside the goal. Situation Room staff can reference video from these cameras to make goal decisions, and the NHL provides these same images to broadcasters. Crucially, the NHL can capture video that the networks miss.[110] As more sports adopt centralized video replay systems, the locus of control for producing video evidence, which has historically been situated with broadcast companies, could shift toward an increasingly cooperative exchange. This would only integrate replay further into the media's sport content economy.

Even as the NHL's system is considered a model, the league runs into the same homeopathic problems faced in other sports as its multiplication of video evidence (both network-produced and league-produced) and its centralized efficiencies create increasing expectations among fans, journalists, coaches, and players for inerrancy. Take goal calls, for example, which have been of central concern for NHL replay. Overhead and in-net cameras can capture decisive images that assist officials, but their viewpoints are often obscured by the haphazard pile of bodies and activity that occurs around the net. Insufficient video evidence for overturning erroneous on-ice goal calls has led to continuing controversy over a problem that the league has tried to address via replay since 1991, a problem typically complicated by additional cameras.[111]

The NHL has also struggled with decisions over whether to expand replay to penalties, which are even more subjective than goal calls. Indeed, the approval of instant replay in 1991 coincided with several rule changes aimed at decreasing violent play. The NHL's system is a model here as well, as applications of replay to player safety have only more recently characterized replay systems in other sports. Instant replay adjudication of fouls has historically been inconsistent in the NHL, however, and ongoing problems, including high-profile errors in playoff games, have motivated the league to reduce the scope of replay judgments on penalties. Indeed, the NHL has resisted recent calls by players and journalists to add penalties like high sticking and goalie interference to its video review system, arguing that the subjective nature of these calls would require absolute certainty of the criteria for judging video evidence.[112]

Major League Baseball (MLB)

MLB first adopted replay in 2008 after a series of high-profile blown calls made the sport's traditional resistance to video review less sustainable. Replay was limited initially to boundary calls, but MLB discussed expanding the scope of video review as early as 2009, after television replays exposed several significant umpiring errors during postseason play.[113] Then came Joyce's call, and the loss of Galarraga's perfect game, in 2010.

Although Commissioner Selig did not reverse Joyce's call, there was a widespread sentiment that major changes were inevitable. For all intents and purposes MLB already had an informal instant replay system: every stadium had giant screens showing constant replays, fans could see the same images on TV, and YouTube extended the life of the most controversial clips.[114] Even Selig, who had resisted the encroachment of replay throughout his tenure, said after Joyce's error that he would need to examine "the expanded use of instant replay."[115] Through MLB's successive expansions of replay, the Galarraga incident remained in the foreground. In 2012 MLB extended replay beyond home run decisions alone to trapped balls and line drives down the foul lines. In 2014 MLB added a system for managers' challenges, outfitting every ballpark with twelve cameras and providing each team with a video replay coordinator who could review images as well as phone managers to advise them on whether to challenge a call. In response to these expansions, Jim Leyland, who managed the Detroit Tigers in 2010, said, "All of a sudden, everything is fair and square . . . [n]ot that it wasn't before, because the human element was there for all the teams. But nobody wants a Galarraga to lose a perfect game."[116] By the start of the 2014 season, the only decisions not available for review were those regarding balls and strikes, check swings, calls on obstruction or interference, and the infield fly rule.[117]

Historically among the leagues most resistant to replay, MLB now maintains one of the more elaborate systems in sport. In 2014 MLB built a Replay Operations Center (ROC) partly modeled after the NHL's centralized video review system. The ROC has thirty-seven high-definition televisions and is staffed by up to eight umpires at a time. Video technicians have access to between seven and twelve cameras at each game, and can cue up replays from multiple angles in order to assist the umpires, who make a final decision on whether to overturn an on-field call.[118] League leaders who viewed replay as an affront to baseball's human element have become vocal supporters in recent years, articulating the most common lines of argument for extended video review. New York Yankees manager Joe Girardi warned in 2010 that expanded replay could lead to the game being run though "videotape or a robot."[119] By 2013, after being on the wrong end of several bad calls, he argued that "in this day and age" the technologies were available and there was no excuse for not using them.[120] In 2012 Vice President of Baseball Operations Joe Torre wondered "why we want everything to be perfect" when baseball "just isn't a perfect game," but a decisive error in the 2012 American League Championship Series (ALCS) that helped the Detroit Tigers to defeat the Yankees served as a "tipping point" for Torre: "The one thing I didn't want to have happen was something like that really take center stage over the game itself. . . . That's when I realized that we certainly can't ignore the technology."[121] MLB's sea change testifies to the ideological claims to reality and historical judgment embodied in the mechanical witness and mechanical referee, claims to which even the most tradition-oriented sport organizations seem to inevitably succumb.

Fédération Internationale de Football Association (FIFA)

In 1995 FIFA considered adding a "second referee" who could, much like the third umpire in cricket, reference a video monitor to judge disputed goals and penalties. As in other major sports, FIFA was responding to pressure from European and U.S. television companies. As Glenn Moore of *The Independent* explained, soccer had "long been unpopular with some television executives because its constant flow prevents advertisements being shown during play." A system that allowed timeouts for reviews would create delays long enough to insert commercials. In a move typical of much of the historical debate on replay in soccer, he related the implications of video review to two of the game's most controversial moments: Diego Maradona's "Hand of God" goal against England in 1986 and Geoff Hurst's second goal against West Germany in the 1966 World Cup.[122] Maradona scored his "Hand of God" goal (so named after he made postgame comments implying divine intervention) in a 2–1 quarterfinal victory over England. Slow-motion television replays clearly showed that Maradona scored the goal illegally off his left hand, but since there was no formal review system, the goal stood both in the live moment and in the years since as one of soccer's most infamous plays. As I cover above, the footage of Hurst's goal has been subject to colorization, high-definition enhancement, and computer modeling in attempts to resolve the controversy surrounding it, remaining a constant reference point in soccer replay debates.[123]

In 2005, after continuing controversies over replays of questionable goal calls, FIFA president Sepp Blatter said, "Not a day goes by without technology making progress, and we, therefore, have a duty to at least examine whether new technology can be used for the good of the game."[124] FIFA announced it would experiment with a chip-enabled soccer ball in the 2005 World Under-17 tournament and possibly implement the technology for the 2006 World Cup. Journalist Rob Hughes noted that this would "neatly round a circle of everlasting controversy" since the 2006 World Cup was in Germany, exactly forty years from the date of Hurst's goal.[125] The chip, developed by Adidas, Cairos Technologies, and the Fraunhofer Institute, was suspended in the middle of the ball in response to early concerns over its durability against hard kicks and its accuracy during high-velocity flight. Whenever the ball touched the goal line, the chip transmitted a radio signal to multiple antennas positioned around the stadium, which routed data through a high-speed fiber-optic ring to a bank of computer servers, and then to the referee's watch, all in real time. Despite initial confidence, officials worried about accuracy and efficiency issues after testing in 2005 and again in 2007, and decided that goal-line replay technologies were not ready for major tournaments.[126]

In 2009 French striker Thierry Henry committed a clear handball while setting up a game-winning goal against the Republic of Ireland in the World Cup finals playoff. The goal brought back memories of Maradona (it was dubbed the "Hand of Gaul") and eliminated Ireland, allowing France to advance. Calls for replay were renewed, but as FIFA prepared for the 2010 World Cup, it was apparent that the organization had no active programs for video review or goal-line technologies.[127]

The moment that finally broke FIFA's resistance came in the 2010 World Cup, when officials missed a goal by England's Frank Lampard against Germany in a Round of 16 match. Much like the Galarraga-Joyce crisis in MLB (which happened in the same year), the clarity of the error, and the high stakes of the moment, signaled the inevitable expansion of video review. Television replays showed that Lampard's shot hit the crossbar and bounced inside the goal line by around two feet. George Vecsey of the *New York Times* wrote that Lampard's goal was "so clear, so available, that any FIFA monitor in the stadium could have seen it on first view, clicked for an instant replay and stopped play to reverse the noncall."[128] *Courier Mail* journalist Michael Hiestand argued: "2010 might go down as the year of instant replay, when the last opposition finally gave up fighting the use of technology to correct human error in big time games." Indeed, after initial resistance Blatter conceded: "It's obvious that after the experiences so far at this World Cup it would be nonsense not to reopen the file. . . . Something has to be changed."[129] In a 2012 FIFA report on implementing goal-line technology, Blatter referenced the 2010 World Cup again, writing that he had supported replay "ever since Frank Lampard's goal against Germany at the 2010 World Cup was not given." Blatter also argued that it was time for FIFA to catch up with the progress of bodily and audiovisual technologies: "In this age where the game has evolved so much technically and tactically and players' athleticism is ever greater, goals are at a premium and it is more important than ever to be able to determine whether one has been scored."[130]

FIFA tested goal-line technology from 2010 to 2012 and used it for the first time at the 2012 Club World Cup in Japan. The International Football Association Board (IFAB), an organization within FIFA responsible for serving as "the eternal guardian of the laws," officially approved in 2012 systems made by Hawk-Eye and Danish-German company GoalRef (which uses magnetic fields to determine whether the ball crosses the goal line), to be used first in December of that year at the FIFA Club World Cup and eventually at the 2014 World Cup in Brazil. The decision, according to Adam Elder at *Wired*, would "all but end flubbed calls that have decided games as monumental as the World Cup final and made the sport look embarrassingly Jurassic in a hyper-connected age of instant replay and instant communication."[131] The introduction of goal-line technologies at the 2014 World Cup did mostly address historical problems with goal calls. Predictably, however, fans and sportswriters turned their attention next to calls that FIFA's review system did *not* cover (e.g., diving, fouls). U.S. journalists covering the 2014 World Cup argued that these non-calls were damaging the commercial appeal of soccer for U.S. viewers and would need to be addressed by expanded review.[132] Following a path of replay expansion common to other sports, Blatter announced in late 2014 that FIFA would test video replays and a coach's challenge system at the 2015 Under-20 World Cup in New Zealand.[133]

National Basketball Association (NBA)

The NBA first discussed instant replay in 2002 after controversy in a playoff game between the Charlotte Hornets and Orlando Magic. Charlotte's Baron Davis made what should have been a game-winning shot with .7 seconds left in the game, but officials discounted the basket. Television replays showed that Davis's shot clearly beat the final buzzer, but there was tacit agreement among NBA officials at the time that it was not humanly possible to catch, turn, and shoot a ball in less than one second. The fact that TV replays established this *was* possible signaled the beginning of replay discussions from the league's front office.[134] Over the summer of 2002 the NBA's Board of Governors approved the use of replay by a large majority. Vice President of Operations Stu Jackson explained that the availability of technologies that could assist in call corrections was the "driving force" behind the change.[135]

The NBA publicized its interest in moving toward a centralized video review system after Adam Silver succeeded David Stern as commissioner in 2014. Silver was concerned about replay interrupting the game's flow and believed that a central system would create more efficiency. The centralized system was further justified by several controversial calls during the 2014 playoffs, which led to arguments for expanding the scope of reviewable plays and granting referees more power to initiate reviews. Silver announced finalized plans for the NBA's centralized review system in May 2014, noting that the NHL would serve as a model for their own "command center" where, they hoped, reviews could be faster and more consistent. Under the system used at the time, referees consulted video replays on small television monitors in the arena, and there were questions of whether they had access to every possible angle.[136]

The NBA's Replay Center, which launched for the 2014–2015 season, has ninety-four HD monitors, direct connections to all twenty-nine NBA arenas, twenty work stations for replay staff, and, according to the league's official site, enough bandwidth capacity to download the entire Library of Congress digital archive in "just over 30 minutes."[137] While the NBA does not (like the NHL) capture replay video through its own cameras, Center staff do contribute league-produced content to live coverage of games: a social media editor communicates the results of each review through Twitter and a blog archive, and the NBA's senior vice president of replay and referee operations explains rulings to local and national television commentators through a live camera feed. On-court officials initiate reviews and refer questions to the Replay Center staff, who support the officials in making a final judgment. In addition, Center staff closely monitor every game so that in cases of possible violations or questionable calls, they can cue up a section of video and display it on a courtside monitor for the head referee. Under the system that preceded centralization, NBA review officials had to request video from the networks. Under the new centralized system, the Replay Center receives a constant stream of video from every game broadcast (thus the bandwidth boasting). Moreover, staffers actively edit the video clips they flag for review, using touch-screen editing software to crop and enlarge images or to break a video clip into a mosaic of synchronized boxes before sending their edited version instantaneously to on-court officials.[138]

The result of all this innovation? The NBA's increased capacity to display and evaluate more video has revealed more officiating errors and led to calls for detailed public reports on the league's officiating processes for the sake of further transparency and scrutiny.[139] Again, replay begets replay.

"Perfection, Soulless Perfection"

Each of the preceding histories maps out a process wherein instant replay serves as both cause and solution to a growing crisis in officiating authority, aligns with concurrent advances in human-athletic potential and extrahuman sight, and permeates even those sports that have historically resisted video review. Journalists rarely cover the competitive practices of technology companies until a league decides to test or implement some specific replay system to address a controversy. Replay's colonization of sport might be imagined as an inevitable outgrowth of technological progress (the agency for which is often nebulous, per the common refrain that "the technologies exist") more than as a product of the coordinated, interdependent actions of technology companies, broadcasters, and leagues. Yet replay has not been uncritically accepted in any of the leagues or governing bodies examined above. In fact, the expansion of replay throughout elite sport is remarkable because video review so directly conflicts with idealizations of sport as a sacred, *human* activity—one that embraces chance, unresolvable debate, and magic in contrast to quotidian preoccupations with calculation and perfection. Thus Sepp Blatter's oft-cited plea against replay in soccer: "Let it be as it is and let's leave [soccer] with errors. . . . The television companies will have the right to say [the referee] was right or wrong, but still the referee makes the decision—a man, not a machine."[140] Yet Blatter gave in to video review, and his conversion, like that of other replay critics, speaks to a seemingly inevitable predicament based on the ideological power of mechanical witnessing: either maintain a principled stance on the value of human fallibility or concede to the perceptual superiority of cameras and computers. Replay brings this human-machine dialectic to the surface as a characteristically religious problem, expressed most clearly around the theme of *perfection*.

The most vocal critics of replay often see themselves as spokespersons for a lost cause, recognizing that those few people left who prize human imperfection and unsettled historical debates will be increasingly "doomed to the scientific evidence."[141] Forecasts of an inevitable, mechanized future are common. William C. Rhoden of the *New York Times* wrote, for example:

> We're heading in a direction that may one day see games being officiated by cameras and computers, with human officials little more than water boys for technology, relegated to marking down and distance. No need for challenges; the games will be perfectly officiated. Never a blown call again. Perfection, soulless perfection.[142]

In projected futures like Rhoden's, human beings are the engineers of sport's demise. Replay's unconscious optics tempt us with images of perfect judgment, fostering a dream that is misguided and fundamentally antithetical to sport. The resulting loss of sport's human element is imagined in at least two related forms.

First, there is a sense that human, bodily presence is being lost. The ritual through which an on-field referee defers judgment to a replay official in a stadium sky box or at a central command center constitutes a bodily displacement: the continuity stops, the referee leaves the field of play, and hidden deliberations are relayed through fiber-optic cables, antennae, computers, and editing stations, all while viewers and commentators carry out a parallel discussion of the video evidence. Critics condemn this process as "distant . . . technical . . . bloodless"; they complain that it puts decisions into the hands of "constables . . . ruling as in a star chamber" and subjects viewers to the deflating experience of having important decisions in big games "handed down to us from a dark upstairs room" by a person nobody ever sees.[143] Sport loses the fun of those "occasional injustices" once delivered by "the natural eyes of . . . highly trained gym teachers" moonlighting as professional referees.[144] The decision that comes back to the referee from a replay official is distant from the performative drama of the live call, the tangle of bodies, the obscured vantage points of field-level experience, and the raw affective energies of pumping blood and adrenaline. Even Verna came to worry about the "overuse" of replay as a body problem: "The game has lost some of its sensuality. . . . It's become all about angles now."[145] Our overdeveloped concern with getting calls right, according to Posnanski, means "we are willing to sacrifice time . . . the power of the moment."[146]

Thus, the perceived loss of sport's human element takes shape in a second sense as an intolerance of fallibility. That intolerance is blamed on television and its role in the commercial growth of sport. For example, the author of a 2003 Australian Rugby Union officiating manual cited faster and stronger players, specialized coaching, and increased live television coverage as forces that were changing the "fabric" of rugby. Replays, in particular, were affecting "the referee's presence on the field," as fans could scrutinize calls through unprecedented access to the decision-making process. While technology added "value to the spectacle" of rugby, the manual's author worried that "the 'human effect'" was "slowly being taken from the game as the hunger for perfection [became] greater."[147] Malcolm Knox of Australia's *The Age* wondered similarly about rugby's future, suggesting that officials were creating an unrealistic and self-destructive expectation that technology could "eradicate human error."[148] By both creating and feeding fans' appetite for infallibility, officials were allowing the profane corruptions of a technology-crazed culture to colonize sport. An increasingly "unhealthy dependence" on video review reflected a larger "tendency in all walks of life to devolve responsibility . . . to inanimate devices." That same dependency signaled the loss of sport as an "exclusive" preserve for human frailty as modern technologies chipped away at all "the realness and raw vulnerability" left in the world.[149] The "effort to make umpiring decisions as close to perfect as possible" spelled the end of days when "tough decisions were left to human judgment"; sport fans were now replay addicts, dependent on machines to make evaluations that they no longer trusted humans to perform.[150]

What makes sport "human," then, is fidelity to chance, irrationality, imperfection, and the contingency of history (the balancing-out of injustices over time, the eternal reward coming to suffering fan bases)—in short, to sport's protections against an increasingly desacralized world. Peter McKnight summed this up in a *Vancouver Sun* article: "Sports aren't exact and inerrant, neat and tidy; they're about making mistakes and mending them, about guts and glory—they are, in short, the very essence of the human condition."[151] Replay critics contrast that essence with the "soullessness" of perfection, which some regard as an irreligious image projected by machines. As Mark Kiszla of the *Denver Post* argued, instant replay is "the single worst invention by modern [humans]. . . . Only God is perfect. Instant replay is the devil's device to remind us how we constantly mess up."[152] In a guest article for the blog site *Soccerlens*, exercise physiologist Ricardo Guerra maintains that both daily life and soccer are "characterized by a continuous stream of potentially fateful events that cannot be turned back," and that disrupting "this essential philosophical dynamic of the game is unnatural, nonhuman and defies the omnipotence of God." Neither in life nor in sport should humans be tempted to believe they can appropriate divine authority over time and redemption through machines.[153]

In 1989, before most major commercial sports had adopted replay systems, journalist Ira Berkow warned that handing over officiating control to "video cops" would impoverish our imagination, snuffing out at birth the endless debates and apocryphal stories that animate sport history.[154] That theme persisted as more sports installed replay systems. Alan Schwartz complained, for example, that "as fans are spoon-fed every angle, their imagination withers"; because of replay, "there are no secrets, nothing left unseen or unexplained."[155] And Bob Halloran claimed that instant replay had "stolen a magnificent part of sport—its eternity . . . our ability to argue forever about whether a tennis ball hit the line, or if a receiver got two feet in bounds."[156] Critics often imagine these costs retrospectively. Replay would, for example, have robbed us of the mystery behind legendary figures and events for which there is no visual record (Wilt Chamberlain's 100-point game in 1962, Satchel Paige's pitching career).[157] If tennis had had Hawk-Eye when John McEnroe played, we would have been deprived of his famous line "You cannot be serious!"[158] Debates over video review often involve imagining whether in-game replays would have prevented decades of controversy surrounding notorious plays, and whether such prevention would be good or bad for sport.[159]

What of these implied and explicit religious warnings against replay as an affront to the human essence of sport, to God's providence over history and redemption? Has elite sport sold its soul to replay and the dream of perfect judgment? On the surface it would seem that sport producers concede to the inevitable governance of cameras for the same reason a Luddite buys an iPhone or a Catholic church installs large video screens in its sanctuary: it is simply the way the world is headed. This sense of inevitable progress is problematic, however, because it ignores how replay comes into sport through the same imperatives for televisual spectacle and liveness that make sport programming content such a valuable commodity. These imperatives made it sensible for leagues and governing bodies to move away from their early reactive posture and figure out a way to appropriate the video review systems pushed by broadcast companies (as has happened with centralized replay hubs, for example).

Mechanical witnessing does, however, fundamentally shift the grounds for vision, judgment, and experiences of live time. Replay makes that shift *legible* in the form of a conflict that troubles most contemporary religious institutions: in order to increase their scope and influence, religions depend on media technologies to bring people scattered across geographical and temporal distances into immediate contact with sacred or transcendent experiences (e.g., sermons, pilgrimages, or, in the case of sport, live games); yet religious leaders must *disavow* the importance of technology in order to maintain ideals of locality, community, and purity in the face of so much conspicuous commodification and global expansion.[160] Jacques Derrida identifies this condition of dependency and disavowal as part of an "autoimmune" relationship between religion and media: when religious leaders critique the evils of technology, they essentially attack *themselves*, their own means of growth and prosperity. Yet they must do so in order to offer reconnection with the kinds of "sacrosanct" experiences that preceded machines and founded religion (as when leaders in soccer or baseball resist replay to market their sports as rare sanctuaries for preindustrial values).[161] As much as leaders attempt to "dissociate" religion from the contaminating effects of technology, their "drive to remain unscathed" is always problematic, as religion and technology are "indissociable." The result is the autoimmune response, which continuously "haunts the community" as its members search for a return to religious experiences untainted by technology.[162]

That haunting is given expression when critics and supporters of replay alike recognize that the crises presented by mechanical witnessing are now built into sport media production, that there is no going back to a time before the optical revelations of slow motion, or freeze-frame capture, or computer simulation. When critics of replay call for a return to an authentically human version of sport, they imagine an outside threat against which the community must immunize itself when, in fact, those religious experiences presumably under attack—revelation, witnessing, liveness, flow—are themselves media creations. Yet *someone* must speak up against mechanical witnessing and its fostering of intolerance for those human and religious qualities (imperfection, mystery) that make sport meaningful. There is, then, a constant push for recovery in elite televised sport, a constant enlivening of dialectical tensions (between human and machine, mystery and positivism) aimed at preserving sacredness in a principled, if self-consciously futile, effort against the camera's promise of perfectibility. Why futile? Because, as supporters of replay argue, "the technologies already exist": replay's development as a homeopathic or autoimmune response to problems of revelation and historical authority inescapably alters the experience of witnessing.

What are the practical implications of that change? Are the shifts in historical authority from the eye to the camera, and from governing bodies to fans, really as impactful as the above debates suggest? I want to conclude by examining these questions through the theme of empowerment, which emerges in replay debates as an active struggle over historical production among fans, referees, governing bodies, and sport media producers.

Implications: Officiating Authority and the Power of Forensic Witnessing

Contemporary replay systems position viewers, Mulvin writes, as arbiters of truth within "an epistemological architecture constituted in and through the circulation of broadcasting texts as pieces of evidence."[163] Thomas Oates argues similarly that "televised replay constructs an environment where viewers can carefully examine procedures and techniques and are encouraged to adopt a perspective that polices both." In this environment, "bodies are offered up as objects of knowledge" and fans are invited to accompany officials, both as fellow judges and as critics of the referees' interpretations and verdicts. During a live game, fans join officials "in policing the game in a real-time scenario," and after a controversial decision, they participate alongside sportswriters and commentators "poring over the minutiae of replay evidence" for weeks on end.[164]

Fans' access to officiating texts and processes might bring to mind what Henry Jenkins has notably called "participatory culture," a condition under which fans actively struggle over textual meanings with corporate media producers.[165] New media technologies play a significant role in this struggle, as fans' ability to produce and distribute video through the "web's robust system of circulation" has increased the "speed and scale" at which consumer responses and demands can influence the larger culture and put pressure on powerful institutions like networks and leagues. Do any of these changes constitute a meaningful shift in power toward viewers?

For Lawrence Grossberg, fan "empowerment" does not equate to resistance that evades "existing structures of power." Rather, empowerment "refers to the generation of energy and passion" that creates conditions under which resistance might be possible. Fans are empowered in the sense that their investments (of time, energy, affect) make them "capable of going on, of continuing to struggle to make a difference." This sense of empowerment is especially important, Grossberg argues, in a condition where "pessimism has become common sense" and people feel there is no way to make a meaning-ful difference in the world.[166] It is in this sense that I think replay empowers fans: it provides the basic conditions for struggling over historical produc-tion by fostering obsessive patterns of looking at, doubling back toward, reexamining, and turning over publicly shared visual evidence. In short, replay transforms witnessing into a forensic practice. This transformation may or may not contribute to specific, concrete changes to policies or orga-nizational structures. But defining empowerment only as the enactment of such changes would make us miss the bigger picture: replay fundamentally changes the way we see elite televised sport by posing alterations in legibility, flow, and cessation that may or may not facilitate action and change. The main limitation to these struggles over historical authority is the distrust that video review promotes. I want to account for that limitation before of-fering final thoughts on what I see as the more promising habits of stoppage and examination fostered by replay. Jenkins views fans as "textual poachers" motivated by a mixture of devotion and frustration to actively appropriate the very "mass-produced texts which provide the raw materials" for their fandom. The poaching of texts can represent (among other possibilities) fans' dissatisfaction with the meanings proffered by dominant media and, perhaps most importantly, the circulation of that dissatisfaction through new media channels.[167] Jenkins recognizes that poaching is circumscribed by the continuing hegemony of corporate media, although he has been criti-cized for insufficiently addressing how large media companies appropriate fan participation as free labor.[168] Putting that critique aside for the moment, it is clear that the participatory culture of sport fandom is at least *perceived* as a threat to officiating, and thus to the broader authority of leagues and governing bodies.

From its earliest appearance in elite sport, replay has been regarded as a problematic invitation to fan participation in the officiating process. *Washington Post* sportswriter Norman Chad warned in 1986 that by installing replay, the NFL "could impugn its officials' and its own credibility with the cameras"; by inserting a delay in the game, Chad argued, "you're in-viting the fan to doubt the whole process."[169] His words were prescient, as officiating is viewed today as an impossible, onerous job given new media technologies and online fan cultures. Sport media commentators complain that HD television, super-slow-motion replay, and multiple camera angles give "every couch potato a better view than the umps," so that there "are more whisker-thin margins to discern and more scrutinizing eyes to cope with than ever."[170] Controversial calls circulate "everywhere" online and are "replayed relentlessly on TV's growing ranks of highlight shows—giving a simple human error an audience of millions" and creating an "echo chamber" within which fans demand justice.[171] Consistent with concerns over the declining human element in sport, journalists complain that replay fosters a corrosive desire for perfection; fans today "expect a level of precision that once would have seemed obnoxious" and apply their imagined expertise to analyzing "replays as if they were the Zapruder film."[172] The resulting illusion of perfectibility is not only irreligious but also indicative of a threatening change in fans' self-concept. The visual evidence that forms the basis for officiating decisions is now too public; its accessibility decentralizes the referee's authority and distributes interpretive power to anyone with a television, smartphone, or tablet.

Such challenges to officials' authority predate contemporary replay technologies. In his book *The Man in Black*, Gordon Thomson traces attacks on the referee back to the mid-1500s.[173] Instant replay does, however, raise unique and more recent problems related to the interpretive work of officiating. Refereeing is a hermeneutical practice that requires the official to make a judgment call based on an often subjective set of criteria and according to a defensible interpretation of a sport's rules.[174] To protect the flow and creativity of game play, the referee must also balance between enforcing an overly rigid interpretation of the rules (the letter of the law rather than its spirit) and being too lenient (thus risking unfairness or injuries).[175] These interpretive judgments have been controversial as long as there has been officiating, but instant replay brought meaningful changes. Both the technological means of enhanced capture and the sheer number of replay texts expand the interpretive range of witnessing exponentially. There is time set aside to examine the smallest details of the moving image. And the televised review process provides both a deliberative model and the requisite textual evidence for fans to take up an interpretive, policing role alongside officials, commentators, and sportswriters.

Demonstrating Jenkins's notion of participatory culture, fans have more access to meticulous visual evidence and more means of participating in the production and circulation of meaning and doubt. One noteworthy result has been what *Slate* magazine's Josh Levin identified as the "YouTube Zapruder film . . . [for] sports junkies." YouTube, according to Levin, has provided a means for producing and distributing discontent over refereeing decisions that far surpasses angry message-board posts or ranting phone calls: "A video reel of the [referees'] treachery . . . has the potential to win the hearts and minds of your fellow sports fans." This is because fans can appropriate video evidence to invent more persuasive arguments about corruption or injustice than they could have through (presumably biased) words alone: "People lie. The camera doesn't."[176] Fans who produce these videos employ replay-based production techniques like slow motion (ripping replay clips produced in the live broadcast, or altering clips with video-editing software) and rely on video-hosting services to distribute their messages.

Fan-produced videos vary in form and length, but the most clearly "Zapruder"-like films focus on a single call or provide a highlight reel of questionable calls from a specific game. The typical approach is to edit together relevant pieces of video evidence with inserted text panels in order to tell a story that challenges referees' official decisions as well as the authority and integrity of governing bodies. In one video, for example, fans question the officiating during Super Bowl XL (which featured several controversial calls that favored the Pittsburgh Steelers against the Seattle Seahawks) by juxtaposing text-panel commentaries with relevant video evidence that they have edited through freeze-frame, slow motion, and graphics. As in most fan-produced replay videos, their efforts to retell the story of the game involve altering the chronological sequence of key events during the live broadcast. Here, instances of similar types of calls against the Steelers and Seahawks (e.g., pass interference) are placed side by side in order to demonstrate an inconsistent application of the rules.[177] To cite some similar examples: a fan claims that the referees stole Super Bowl XLIII from the Arizona Cardinals by juxtaposing a sequence of direct quotes from the NFL rule book with offending video evidence; a video claiming that Italy was robbed during the 2002 World Cup begins with text panels complaining that "Italy Had 5 Good Goals Called Off in 3 Straight Games" and then prompts doubtful viewers to "Just Look" at the proceeding evidence; a highlight video claiming that the NBA rigged the 2002 playoff series between the Sacramento Kings and Los Angeles Lakers in favor of Los Angeles begins with a presumably damning quote from Commissioner David Stern, professing his "special fascination" with the Lakers.[178]

Given their oppositional stances and appropriations of broadcast television imagery, YouTube fan videos might seem to be clear examples of "poached" texts. Yet caution is required. As Mark Andrejevic warns, the assumption that interactive media are inherently progressive and empowering goes unexamined too often in scholarly and popular thought when, in fact, fan production is often appropriated as free labor by large media companies.[179] By expressing their discontent through publicly produced and circulated videos, fans provide a profitable form of participation that previously—in the form of, say, an angry phone call to a friend or an unanswered e-mail to league executives—had little economic value. When such expressions of discontent are publicized online, they circulate as texts for sport highlight and debate shows and intensify fans' affective investments in teams, rivalries, and the *next* chance at evening the score. Most sport news and highlight shows now regularly feature tweets, Facebook postings, and YouTube videos to incorporate the voice of the fan into elongated controversies or to promote upcoming games.

Publicized discontent also loops constantly back to the television broadcast, reinforcing the value of being there live to witness an offense. As Markus Stauff notes, within the "constellation of media sports, YouTube works above all as a secondary resource," an accessible archive of events defined by, and made relevant by, live television. Fan videos are largely "referential," responding to meanings and problems that originate with the live broadcast.[180] The questions fans raise about officiating will often parallel the commentaries of announcers and journalists, fans' editing techniques will often mimic those used by corporate producers, and most of the evidentiary value in a fan video will be derived from broadcasters' control over capture and enhancement. As Levin argues, "In the end, the YouTube Zapruder film can't possibly live up to its promise"; it will not end debates over competing interpretations of a call, and it mostly adds yet another layer to those postgame wrangles that have made sport so profitable.[181] When fan videos do operate outside the ordinary bounds of corporate sport media, it is often to experiment with conspiracy theories or (most troublingly) to employ or provoke explicitly racist, sexist, nationalistic, or homophobic responses.

This is not to say that fan participation is inherently paranoid or unproductive. There are, in fact, instances where social media contribute to meaningful, material changes in sport. In 2012, for example, YouTube replay videos (and other online expressions of outrage) contributed to the resolution of a labor dispute in favor of the NFL Referees Association after replacement officials made an egregious, game-deciding error in a nationally televised game.[182] In cases like this, however, fan productivity is just one contributor (and a somewhat indirect one) to a larger process of change that still runs through corporate sport media and league decision-making structures. In terms of creating change (to outcomes, policies, or dominant cultural and economic power), we have good reasons to question whether fan-produced critiques of officiating really *do* anything meaningfully oppositional.[183]

The practical limitations of fans' distrust relate to what Slavoj Žižek calls a "demise of symbolic efficiency." Symbolic efficiency turns on the question "What do you believe, your eyes or my words?" The symbolic order functions when we believe the truth of an authority's words over what we see.[184] In sport, for example, a referee's spoken judgment (the announcement of a replay decision, the explanation of a rule application) represents the truth of what happened because of prior arrangement between the participants: a sport's governing body writes the rules, provides guidelines for interpreting them, empowers the referee as an arbiter, and requires that competitors accept the referee's judgments as final; teams and athletes agree to these terms in order to compete in highly publicized and profitable elite sport organizations. When a referee speaks, then, it is the authority of a governing body speaking *through* her or him that makes a decision final.[185] The referee's individuality matters less than her or his representation of a greater, binding power (the league, the laws of the game). There is an efficient symbolic fiction at work here: we assume that this higher power transcends the direct reality of the person who represents it. I can *see* that behind their uniforms referees are fallible, corruptible, perhaps too old. In the case of some sports (the NFL, FIFA) the referee may be a part-time employee, exercising greater expertise in some other field (e.g., teaching, pharmaceutical sales). Yet I am still willing to concede, even if begrudgingly or angrily, that this person is trained and backed by an institution that makes her words authoritative.[186] Fans buy into this fiction not because they are dupes but because they realize that *some* form of authority is required to hold sport together and make outcomes meaningful.

The efficiency of symbolic authority breaks down when I am willing to trust only what I see.[187] And what I see through replay, according to many commentators, is the official being *exposed* as incompetent. During a stoppage, referees "stand around like dummies," on the field, trying to deliberate "above the noise of 75,000 people"; satellite TV coverage, banks of cameras, and looping replays "make most officials look like Mr. Magoo on a foggy day" or "like victims as the global village sifts through their decisions frame by frame after the fact"; losing control to replay leaves the referee "bereft, a paper tiger in the middle of a jungle, prey to all manner of pressure."[188] *Atlantic Monthly* journalist Ashley Fetters describes replay enacting a "quiet revolution" that weakens "the officials' authority by making their blunders clearly visible to everyone."[189] The result, as Henry Winter of the *Daily Telegraph* writes, is that officiating is more difficult than ever, as referees "must live with the perfect storm of quick, often cynical players racing from end to end in a game covered by 30-odd camera angles, instant replays for the commentators, and an unruly jury on the terraces and on Twitter."[190] As Selena Roberts summarizes in the *New York Times*, "In essence, video killed the referee star."[191]

For the purposes of empowerment these problems of symbolic authority might seem like good news. Perhaps such pervasive distrust means new possibilities for activism and change.[192] In a context of symbolic decline, however, criticism can be too indiscriminate. It produces what Andrejevic refers to as a "facile postmodernism" wherein the ability to debunk every claim and deconstruct every reality becomes enjoyable for its own sake rather than for some specific political end. This supposedly "savvy" stance toward authority does not meaningfully challenge entrenched power. Rather, it forecloses "access to useful knowledge" by relying only on opinion and direct experience. Every fact is a product of bias. Every contradictory or abrasive opinion represents intellectual courage.[193] The result is an inert form of "empowered" participation that is easily appropriated by sport media producers.[194] YouTube Zapruder videos extend the value of live broadcasts by elongating controversies over key plays and outcomes.

Fans' distrust of officiating authority is not inherently empowering if we conceive of empowerment as a rejection of the underlying logics or processes of sport media production. Yet that distrust does point to a broader, fundamental change in the quality of witnessing. Peters describes witnessing as "an attitude cultivated by live television" that potentially burdens the viewer as an accomplice to what is seen. This is because "audiovisual media . . . are able to catch contingent details of events that would previously have been either imperceptible or lost to memory." As cameras freeze motion and microphones capture hidden sounds, we "find ourselves endowed with a much amplified and nuanced record of events, a 'superabundance of details' rich with evidentiary value." We come into a condition where we cannot say that we did not see.[195] The fact we see and hear so much does not, of course, guarantee progressive action. Appreciating the implications of this overabundance of visual evidence involves, to borrow from Andrejevic, an "attempt to understand . . . the ways in which creative activity and exploitation coexist and interpenetrate one another within the context of the emerging online economy." To get to that understanding, we have to resist binary characterizations of audience participation: the active versus passive viewer, the "manipulated dupe" versus the "subversive textual poacher."[196] These problems have long characterized arguments over fan resistance in sport studies. Going back to Ian Taylor's seminal work in the early 1970s on hooliganism as working-class resistance to the "bourgeoisification" of soccer, studies on sport fans have been occupied with efforts to define standards for active and passive, authentic and inauthentic, or resistive and co-opted fandom.[197] Scholars have more recently critiqued these typologies, conceptualizing fandom, resistance, and authenticity not as ontological objects but as social constructs situated in contexts where power is fluid and contingent.[198] Given such fluidity, the disruptive potential of interactive media can be neither uncritically celebrated nor dismissed outright.

To play on the analogy of the Zapruder film (which is commonly invoked in sport replay debates), the potential of replay resides less in its documentation of a specific event than within the circulatory patterns through which participants learn to see, attend to, and interpret visual evidence. In this way the Zapruder analogy is remarkably apt.[199] In the cultural vernacular, "Zapruder" refers both to the actual film that contained Abraham

Zapruder's recording of the Kennedy assassination and to the status of that film's images as some of the most widely circulated and analyzed visual artifacts in history.[200] Art Simon writes that as its images "circulated through government commissions and investigative agencies, the print and televised press, museums of high culture and strange collections of camp, the research of assassination critics and the products of commercial filmmaking," the Zapruder film sparked dissent and debate across "an ever-widening discursive field . . . dominated by visual representation and characterized by a complex struggle over access to and interpretation of" visual imagery and historical authorship.[201] The Zapruder film's cultural value is not based in any resolution of conflict or specific political change; competing visual interpretations and conspiracy theories remain endless. Rather, the film influenced a growing visual culture wherein suspicions against powerful authorities (the government, the press) developed around the widespread availability of film and photographic imagery and the opportunities for interpretive work that this availability provided. The images captured by Zapruder's camera were (as with later developments in video capture) presumably "unimpeachable" and at the same time "highly suspect . . . constantly open to multiple interpretations."[202] Editing techniques, enhancements, and reproductions—most notably optics technician Robert Groden's enlargement of frames depicting Kennedy's head wound—enlivened suspicion and conspiracy theories.[203] The problems of symbolic efficiency are clearly revisited here: all government statements are suspicious; every image can be manipulated. Yet these broader patterns of attentive looking and circulation may still prove valuable, especially if we appreciate those visual-cultural problems unique to sport replay.

Replay critics' complaints about cultural decline may be overblown, but their underlying argument is largely correct: more and more, live sport texts are becoming forensic documents, mixing together the religious value of witnessing with a prosecutorial sense of mission, a vigilance against historical injustices that it will soon be too late to correct. One important result, as I have argued above, is that several inherent dialectical tensions come to the surface: the status of replay as both revelatory and dehumanizing, the autoimmune relationship between religion and media, the combination of wonderment and positivism that attends the concurrent progress of athletic bodies and audiovisual technologies. The fact that replay is viewed by both its supporters and its critics as an inevitable element of that progress is important, as this presumption has motivated and will likely continue to motivate further investments in the production systems and practices that intensify these dialectical problems. In addition, the fact that this turn toward forensic witnessing is often perceived as irreligious likely means that sport media production will be continuously haunted by an autoimmune response to replay as fans, journalists, officiating organizations, and leagues search for an impossible return to religious experiences untainted by technology.[204]

Finally, replay represents a broader way of seeing sport that might address the problems of memory and continuity that I analyze in the previous chapter. Recall that for Benjamin, disrupting historical progress requires altering the speed at which images flit through the present.[205] In that light, it matters a great deal that replay stops time, reverses it, and fosters an obsessive reexamination of historical evidence. Appellate systems create a pattern of historical production wherein the flow of the live game comes to a halt, and it is *within that standstill* that "a constellation saturated with tensions" might take shape.[206] Consider that in each of the case studies and timelines I analyze above, the live moment is a constant reference point for connecting past injustices to the potential future of a tainted historical record. These problems of past and future take shape as a disruptive recollection of past events (related errors, unresolved controversies) that call into question the authority of governing bodies and officials and, most importantly, justify a fundamental reorientation toward present time and historical recording. No single replay image or event that I cover in this chapter could be said to constitute a dialectical break between ideal and actual history. Rather, those tensions that do emerge (e.g., between transcendence and positivism, religion and technology) come out of replay *systems* and their alterations of witnessing through stoppage, display, and examination. As Benjamin writes: "Where thinking comes to standstill . . . there the dialectical image appears."[207] Replay matters most of all because it crystallizes a desire for historical truth *and* the technological means for pursuing that truth, both of which justify stoppage as a necessary component of the broadcast and as a basic condition for memory.

The more replay shapes sport programming, the more producers invite the possibilities of "involuntary recollection" through audiovisual capture.[208] As Miriam Hansen argues, that recollection enters "through the back door of the optical unconscious" as the camera explores space and movement and teaches the viewer to see something unexpected, disruptive, revealing.[209] Benjamin associates this potential for "involuntary" insight with both photography and film, arguing that each technology exceeds the designs and intentions of its producers. In "A Short History of Photography," he writes: "All of the artistic preparations of the photographer and all the design in the positioning of his model to the contrary, the viewer feels an irresistible compulsion to seek the tiny spark of an accident, the here and now." That spark registers through the camera, beyond the limits of the naked eye, uncovering the "physiognomic" secrets of movement and space formerly sheltered in "daydreams" but now available for empirical observation.[210] Benjamin argues that both photography and film technologies "subjected the human sensorium to a complex kind of training," and that film in particular relies on "perception conditioned by shock . . . as a formal principle."[211] In this way the camera could disrupt the "continuity of experience" just as "fragments of the past . . . destroy the continuity of history," so that those details of the past lost to memory might surge back into present-day consciousness.[212] This is, in sum, replay's influence over witnessing: it conditions this "irresistible compulsion" to see something inconsistent and discontinuous, and to perceive that the *now* (the live moment) is the only time for meaningful action.

4

TRANSCENDENCE AFTER
TECHNOLOGICAL DOPING

IN CHAPTER 2 I ARGUED that athletic bodies are constituted as ahistorical and immutable objects of religious adoration insofar as the various institutional interventions they are subject to remain secondary to an apparently essential truth: elite competition reveals an ever-evolving capacity for human achievement that is never reducible to politics or technology.[1] That image of progress could come apart, I suggested, if the work of production that sustains it were to become a recognizable and continuous challenge to its most powerful fundaments: humanness, naturalness, and transcendence. In this chapter I argue that such a challenge is emerging through contemporary developments in performance enhancement and technological intervention.

Performance technologies pose a particularly significant threat to idealized notions of human-athletic transcendence because they relate directly to questions of agency in elite competition: is it the athlete's natural body or the machine that performs so spectacularly? This brings into focus broader questions about the value of transcendence as a sign of *human* excellence. As Tara Magdalinski argues, technologies shift the meanings of sport from a "naturalistic activity that allows for freedom of movement and the bodily expression of physical potential" to "a highly disciplined, rationalised endeavour that rewards performances for their measurable outcomes." Athletes and regulatory agencies find themselves having to constantly reclaim sport's intrinsic worth by arguing that no level of technological intervention can affect the fundamental integrity of human performance. Given the visibility of performance technologies at the highest levels of competition, this is an increasingly difficult case to make.[2]

This chapter focuses on controversies surrounding "technological doping," a relatively recent construct in ongoing debates over enhancement and antidoping regulation. In the most basic sense, technological doping refers to the use of a technological aid (for example, a wearable or prosthetic device) to gain a competitive advantage. In a more complex sense, technological doping represents, I argue, a specific stage in a series of ongoing social agreements on performance enhancement, a moment when the qualities of secrecy and visibility associated with doping are undergoing changes that point toward the challenges and possibilities of transhumanist sport. I understand the implications of this moment through Martha C. Nussbaum's distinction between internal and external transcendence and through broader academic and popular debates on transhuman and cyborg athletes.

My argument tracks a succession of stages in the institutional and popular agreements surrounding doping as they lead up to and through technological doping. Each stage represents changing problems of human-technological integration in sport as follows: from human bodies and technological aids as separate systems (through the example of cycling), to wearable technologies as integrated with the body but removable (through the example of swimming), to prosthetics as more fully integrated with organic body parts (through the example of disability sport and cyborg athletes), and finally to the integration of transhuman and cyborg athletes into mainstream (e.g., categorically gendered, able-bodied) competition. I conclude by considering how this process creates shifts in the meanings of human-athletic transcendence, as well as the limits and possibilities of the political and religious change those shifts represent.

Athletics and the Problem of External Transcendence

There is not a single meaning for "transcendence" in sport, but we can identify some thematic elements. As Jim Parry summarizes, from a formally theological (or organized religious) perspective, transcendence "carries at least two meanings: firstly, going beyond certain limits, surpassing or exceeding; and secondly, superior or supreme." Both of these meanings relate to spiritual experiences derived from witnessing athletic movement.[3] In an analogous though more commonly secular sense, commentators consistently argue that sport transcends political divisions and limitations (such as those surrounding race, gender, sexuality, ethnicity, nationality, religion, or disability) when people of diverse cultural backgrounds gather around important games, or when marginalized athletes struggle for inclusion, or when meritocratic values win out over prejudice. Finally, transcendence often relates to the idea that record-breaking performances constitute a break with previously held limitations, the discovery of a new horizon for human possibility. I focus to some extent on all of these meanings, but it is this final sense that occupies the majority of my time. The ideal of surpassing species limitations relates most directly to Martha Nussbaum's influential treatment of external transcendence.

Nussbaum's critique begins with a scene from Homer's *Odyssey*, where Calypso offers Odysseus immortality if he will stay on the island of Ogygia as her husband. Odysseus is faced, Nussbaum argues, with a choice that reflects a "widely shared human belief" about transcendence: "transcend the condition of humanity" and become liberated from pain, aging, and death, or face each of these as the fate proper to a human life. In choosing to leave Ogygia, Odysseus chooses "the form of a human life and the possibilities of excellence, love, and achievement that inhabit that form." Despite the temptation to transcend human limits, he understands that the alternative Calypso offers is incomprehensible as a life of human experience and value.[4] Thus the representative nature of Odysseus's choice: as the means to achieve a *radical* escape from human limitations become available, upon what terms do we say "yes" or "no" to that opportunity? Contemporary elite sport is faced with this decision, and is in the process of providing an answer.

For Nussbaum the form of transcendence appropriate to human life is internal transcendence, wherein the limitations of "human finitude" and the "human body"—the inevitability of pain, loss, aging, and death—provide the backdrop against which human excellences can be pursued intelligibly. This transcendence is "internal" because its meaningfulness is not derived from an extrahuman standard; one transcends "by *descent*, delving more deeply into oneself and one's humanity" within the context of lived experience. By contrast, Nussbaum calls for us "to reject as incoherent . . . the aspiration to leave behind altogether the constitutive conditions of our humanity, and to seek for a life that is really the life of another sort of being," a desire that she associates with external transcendence.[5]

The line between internal and external transcendence is not absolute. Our desire to overcome human constraints is both reasonable and potentially fruitful, and there is no final way to determine when the pursuit of excellence tempts us toward extrahuman desires.[6] Yet there are cases where transcendence undermines the meaningfulness of a certain activity, and this is particularly clear, Nussbaum argues, in the case of athletics:

> The Greeks, no less than contemporary Americans, praise outstanding athletic performance as a wonderful instance of human excellence. . . . But clearly, such achievement has a point and value only

relatively to the context of the human body, which imposes certain species-specific limits and creates certain possibilities of movement rather than others. To excel is to use those abilities especially fully, to struggle against those limits especially successfully. But if this means that even races or contests between different animal species will usually seem pointless and odd, it means all the more that there will be no athletic excellence at all, and no meaningful concept of athletic excellence, in the life of a being that is, by nature, capable of anything and physically unlimited—able, for instance, to change its shape at will and to transport itself from here to there without effort. What would such achievement be, in a being for whom it is all easy? What would be the rules of the game?[7]

These are, as I show, the very questions raised against performance enhancement in contemporary sport. Nussbaum does not argue against all forms of enhancement or improvement. Neither does she advocate for hampering athletes' development (by, for example, starving them, beating them, or limiting their training). Rather, she offers a basic distinction that makes sense not only for Greek athletes but also for contemporary ones: species-related limitations are natural and constitute meaningful achievement, while unlimited capacity for movement is extrahuman and destructive of the very point of competition. This distinction is not absolute. The boundary for appropriately transcending the body's athletic limits "seems to be set by a vague and yet powerful notion of the possibilities of the human species as such." Perhaps we can know where the dividing line is after we cross it, when we reach the point where transcendent athletic achievements are no longer recognizably human.[8]

The main difficulty comes in referencing the body as a context for identifying species-specific limitations. Nussbaum recognizes that fairness and naturalness are contingent standards relative to particular historical and cultural contexts. Yet "there are certain ways athletes have of . . . getting past the body's boundaries, that seem to us to remove the whole point of the activity," and our sense that a boundary has been violated has much to do with the norms of a particular time. Nussbaum takes contemporary anxieties over performance-enhancing drugs as case in point.[9]

Here is the problem: if internal transcendence is transcendence "by descent" into the grounded, material realities of the human body and the human lifeworld, what we find by delving more deeply into the history of elite athletic bodies is the lack of any origin point at which the body was natural in the sense of being untouched, pure, or limited by born capacity. Nussbaum's argument is nuanced enough to make room for this problem. She notes that there is no clear line between transcendence internal to inherent human limits and that external to them and suggests "a delicate and always flexible balancing act between the claims of excellence, which lead us to push outward, and the necessity of the human context, which pushes us back in."[10] This is very close to what happens in contemporary sport: performance enhancement is pushed to boundaries considered to be extrahuman, and certain objectors—governing officials, doctors, coaches, athletes—push back in the name of human or natural sport. This struggle plays out in practical terms as a test of institutional and popular tolerances. If we can think of "internal transcendence" as an idealization of species-specific limitations that frame appropriate human achievement, and "external transcendence" as a desire to break free from those limits, then the practical, public challenge of performance enhancement becomes clear: to pursue the desire for external transcendence as far as possible while still providing a competitive context that remains recognizably human—a test of bodily capacity and the attending virtues of hard work, determination, sweat, blood. This has been the characteristic public challenge ever since "doping" was invented as a construct.

With *technological* doping, we have the latest, and perhaps furthest, extension toward external transcendence in athletics in the form of ever more conspicuous human-technology interfaces. With the growing prominence of wearable and prosthetic technologies it is now fairly common, as I demonstrate below, to read about the hopes and fears attached to transhuman and cyborg athletes in popular sport commentaries. Increased attention to *trans*human sport is especially important insofar as it suggests awareness of a transformational moment charged with possibility and danger.

As Michael Atkinson summarizes, a "transhuman" is a person "who is on the path to becoming more intensively merged with biotechnology." Transhumanism is a transitional phase in a longer progression toward a posthuman state wherein enhancement of humans' physical and cognitive capacities liberates the species "from the trappings and limitations of the natural body via a complete interface with technology" (e.g., the creation of fully cybernetic bodies or the capacity to upload consciousness and preserve it after bodily death).[11] Transhumanist philosophy has developed in part within an identifiable social movement that advocates the overcoming of human limits via technology. According to the "Transhumanist Declaration" of Humanity+ (formerly the World Transhumanist Association), for example, "humanity's potential is still mostly unrealized"; we can "envision the possibility of broadening human potential by overcoming aging, cognitive shortcomings, involuntary suffering."[12] Transhumanism has also been a subject of intense debate among sport ethicists (especially in the areas of biotechnology and medicine) over the political, economic, and moral implications of altering athletic bodies. Finally, transhumanism has become a more recent concern for sociology of sport and related fields, as the logics of transhumanist philosophy migrate across the boundaries of movement politics and academic debate and into the popular spaces of sport culture.[13]

As Atkinson argues, "Elite sport culture is a zone pregnant with transhuman significance and possibility because of its diffuse emphasis on performance, perfection, science, and physical manipulation."[14] Transhuman ideology is so consistent with elite sport that it has easily penetrated and substantially shaped approaches to performance at every level: training, injury treatment, performance-enhancing drugs, assistive and prosthetic technologies, and competitive regulation. There has, however, been significant academic debate (among, for example, bioethicists, theologians, and disability studies scholars) over how and whether to regulate new sport technologies for competition, and over the influence of transhumanist trends in improving or deepening existing economic and political inequities. Because specific aspects of these debates overlap with and inform technological doping controversies, I sketch them out briefly here.

Critics of transhumanism argue that transhumanist pursuits in sport—and transhumanist imaginings more generally—represent a drive for mastery and perfection that exceeds the context of meaningfully human accomplishments. This is, again, the basic concern summarized in external transcendence. Michael J. Sandel argues, for example, that enhancement diminishes the agency of the human athlete. In fact, a "bionic athlete" is not "an agent at all"; credit for that athlete's accomplishments belongs to a pharmacist or inventor. That shift in agency destroys an appreciation for the "gifted" nature of athletic ability and corrupts "competition as a human activity that honors the cultivation and display of natural talents."[15] Michael McNamee rejects similarly "the idea of the transhuman athlete," describing it as "a form of pathological perfectionism" that devalues the "institutionalised rule governed nature" of sport and circumvents the relationship between human improvement and natural, evolutionary time.[16] Rather than pursue the dream of transcending humanity, McNamee argues, we should set the "moral limits" of sport and other endeavors according to a realization of our mortality.[17]

Critics have also pointed to problems of distributive justice in transhumanist projects. Elaine Graham questions whether transhumanism could truly "usher in egalitarian and inclusive forms of political agency" or whether the access to technology and capital necessary for expanding "selfhood beyond the limits imposed by finite bodies" will simply increase the power of wealthy Western nations.[18] Tracy J. Trothen detects a naïve hopefulness among transhumanists, who too often ignore the relationship between the desire to enhance certain qualities and dominant ideological notions of ability, masculinity, and human supremacy over nature. She argues that this desire is actualized only when one has access to disproportionately allocated resources.[19] This is a critique that I emphasize throughout my analysis of technological doping, as it imposes an important reality check on the claims of transcending the limits not only of the human body but of political inequities as well.

Finally, critics of transhumanist sport warn against the conflation of transcendence with neoliberal politics. Atkinson argues, for example, that "contemporary body enhancement processes in sport" advance "late modernist techno-capitalist agendas"—namely, the development of athletic bodies through an alignment of corporate, scientific, regulatory, and state institutions, all subject to the rationality of the free market and all aiming at the production of subjects presumably free to pursue their unbounded, limitless potential. According to these ideals, elite performance becomes subject to quantitative, empirical, and market-based calculation: "Any athletic deficiency . . . is probed, mapped, evidenced, re-sourced, and conquered much like a new market problem."[20] This is a concern related closely to issues of distributive justice, as wealthy, Western nations disproportionately possess the technological and economic means to address issues of bodily limitation. I focus on this problem throughout my analysis, considering especially the roles that corporations and national sporting bodies play in technological doping.

Advocates for transhumanist sport argue that technological enhancement is completely consistent with the nature or spirit of elite athletics. This claim is often directed against the concerns of external transcendence: elite sport has always been defined by a desire to exceed the natural limits of the species, so why all the hand wringing? According to Andy Miah, transhumanism is "already realised" in sport, which perpetuates an "ambiguous concept of humanness" that permits technological enhancement as a valid means of transcending the body's limitations. Despite the antidoping sentiments expressed by governments, sport federations, and athletes, the ongoing pursuit of performance enhancement implies an endorsement of technology-driven transcendence throughout elite sport.[21] Challenging the assumption that "human nature" is defined by species-specific limitations (the assumption that underwrites the distinction between internal and external transcendence), Miah argues that sport reveals a fundamental consistency between humanness and technological enhancement. Embracing enhancement, Miah writes, "entails making a statement about what is valuable about being human, which might be little more than acknowledging that humans are a kind of being that seeks to transcend the limitations of biology."[22] Claudio Tamburrini and Torbjörn Tännsjö argue similarly that the ethos of sport medicine has been historically consistent with the aim of "transcending limitations" in sport, an arena where elite athletes in particular represent humans' desire "to surpass the limits of what hitherto has been considered as possible for the species."[23] Tamburrini maintains that "the eventual creation of a new transhuman species" would not be the ruin of sport; it would simply meet elite sport's demands for performative capacity, public entertainment, and the transcendence of bodily limitations.[24] As I show below, critics of antidoping programs argue similarly that enhancement (and, by implicit extension, external transcendence) is consistent with the essence of elite sport.

Advocates for transhumanist sport pay attention to issues of distributive justice but believe transhumanism could address, rather than deepen, inequities. Tamburrini, for example, argues that such concerns are not sufficient for limiting the development of transhuman athletes. Enhancements could, in fact, level out differences in born (e.g., genetic) capability. Even if technologies pushed beyond leveling differences, the creation of a greater gap between enhanced athletes and "common people" would be consistent with the values of elite sport. "The larger the gap," Tamburrini writes, "the greater the fascination we feel for those who extend the boundaries of human nature."[25]

Advocates emphasize frequently the inequities of the genetic lottery. Born, genetic endowments are distributed (or gifted) arbitrarily, and arguments on behalf of human nature too often ignore this as an inherent problem of fairness. As Eric Juengst writes, "The spirit of sport is in part a celebration of differential genetic endowments, distributed through the 'natural lottery' of genealogy." What is truly unsettling about performance enhancement, Juengst argues, is that it challenges a segregated, hierarchical system that elevates "genetically advantaged athletes from their disadvantaged competitors."[26] Transhuman and cyborg athletes could then challenge inequitable body hierarchies, such as those related to gender or disability. Kutte Jönsson argues, for example, that the moralism surrounding performance technologies relates less to competitive advantage than to the threat those technologies represent to "conservative ideas regarding gender." If sporting bodies allowed the development of new, potentially "non-gendered" cyborg athletes, then this could undermine the very foundations of gender-segregated categories for ability.[27] Disability sport scholars argue similarly that regulatory efforts to prohibit athletes with disabilities from competing in able-bodied sport have to do with the threat that prosthetic and assistive technologies represent to idealizations of natural (human) performance.[28] Such emancipatory visions of gender or disability politics have come under criticism as overly idealistic, and I consider those debates especially in my conclusion.

Whether or not transhumanism is named in sport, it is constantly implied in the blurring of boundaries between nature, humanity, and technology represented by enhanced athletic bodies.[29] It is, in fact, only through attention to technology that we can fully comprehend contemporary athletic bodies as contexts for species-specific limits. Magdalinski writes that "the interface between the body and technology" presents "a perilous moment where the integrity of the former and the validity of the latter might be compromised," where athletes and their performances become potentially "contaminated" by technologies that exceed the "limits of the body's physical capacity."[30] In terms of the distinction between internal and external transcendence, the natural body serves as the appropriate context for pursuing intelligibly human excellences, while technology represents a potentially extrahuman corruption. But this distinction holds up only if technology is truly antithetical to the "spirit" of elite sport.[31] The history behind technological doping reveals that it is not. Advocates for transhumanist sport make an important point about the fundamental, if disavowed, consistencies between performance technologies and transcendence in elite athletics. So do critics, whose warnings regarding problems of distributive justice and neoliberal ideology are borne out in the institutional agreements behind technological doping.

Defining Technological Doping

Doping as Tacit Agreement

Again, "technological doping" refers to the use of a technological aid to gain a competitive advantage. The presence of the word "doping" within this construct is curious. Doping is popularly synonymous with cheating, which makes perfect sense here. But "doping" also typically connotes the use of drugs and other performance-enhancing substances to alter the body at a cellular level, whereas "technology" more often suggests something external to the body and inorganic. One way to grasp what technological doping means is to understand how this adjective modifies the more frequently solo term "doping." Thus I begin with a brief overview of what doping has meant historically in sport before moving into a treatment of the more recent problems that technological doping represents. My aim is not to present a full history of doping, which has been done more thoroughly elsewhere.[32] Rather, I want to characterize the moralism surrounding doping as, in John Hoberman's words, part of a "tacit agreement" between officials, medical professionals, and athletes that is designed to reap the social and economic benefits of elite performance while also attending to popular idealisms surrounding the purity of sport.[33] I also want to trace the changing nature of that agreement as the framework within which technological doping makes sense.

While there is not a clear, unifying definition of doping, the term most commonly refers to an alteration of the body through the ingestion or injection of a substance designed to provide a competitive advantage. As the editors of the book *Performance-Enhancing Technologies in Sports* summarize, for example, doping involves "the use of means such as drugs, infusions of red blood cells, or, perhaps in the near future, genetic manipulation to enhance athletes' performance" in a way that constitutes "cheating" according to particular cultural, institutional, or philosophical standards.[34] Similarly, Verner Møller notes that there is basic agreement among sport practitioners "that athletes' use of potent substances such as amphetamine, anabolic steroids, growth hormones, and EPO [Erythropoietin, a hormone that improves endurance by increasing red blood cell count] are to be regarded as doping." Yet the boundaries defining banned versus permitted substances seem to be set (as Nussbaum suggests) according to vague yet powerful notions of species-specific limitations. Many banned substances (like EPO or testosterone) are produced naturally by the body. The levels of these substances can be boosted, however, from *without* (as in the case of a drug produced in a lab and administered by injection), and it is this process that sets the apparent boundaries for doping: the increase of a substance through methods external to the body's natural functioning and the practical effects of that increase on performance within the idealized context of a "level playing field."[35]

The definitional and regulatory practices of sport organizations are only part of what constitutes doping, however. As John Hoberman suggests, doping is also a broader cultural concept that refers not only to "the boosting of human performance by artificial means" but also to the social and institutional norms by which some forms of performance enhancement are deemed illegitimate or unnatural; to a scientific game of cat and mouse between doping athletes, laboratory technicians, and the regulatory officials tasked with policing their sport; and finally to "a profound cultural ambivalence toward athletic performance that has emerged over the past century," whereby pharmacological enhancements (stimulants, painkillers, antidepressants) are widely embraced while athletes are uniquely required to offer "an untainted, and therefore accurate, measure of human potential."[36] Hoberman views this ambivalence as part of a basic "internal contradiction between achievement and sportsmanship" underlying antidoping policies in elite sport, where "the inevitable demands for higher performance create new forms of 'legitimate' doping, even as officially sponsored doping controls are strictly enforced."[37]

Rob Beamish and Ian Ritchie complain that most histories of performance enhancement retrospectively trace doping as a problem of cheating that dates back to the Greeks and Romans, who used stimulants, hallucinogens, opioids, and "even testicular extracts" to gain an advantage, and then continues through similar practices in the nineteenth and twentieth centuries (e.g., the consumption of strychnine, cocaine, chloroform). The problem with such accounts is that they transpose "contemporary sensibilities" about cheating onto sport's past in a way that is anachronistic.[38] Maxwell Mehlman argues, "There is no record of any objection to athletes' use of biomedical enhancements before the second decade of the twentieth century." Before then, the common assumption was that athletes should take advantage of whatever might improve their performance. From the late 1920s to the mid-1960s, resistance to performance enhancement amounted to largely inconsequential "stirrings." Concerns around amphetamine and steroid use and the "spirit" of sport were raised, for example, within governing bodies like the International Association of Athletics Federations (IAAF) and International Olympic Committee (IOC), but these bodies took no substantial regulatory actions.[39]

The IOC was especially lax until 1967, when amphetamines were implicated in the death of British cyclist Tom Simpson during the Tour de France. Convinced that "anti-doping platitudes" would not be enough anymore, the IOC decided to test for a list of banned substances for the first time at the 1968 Summer Games in Mexico City.[40] Yet the Olympic testing program was "widely regarded as a sham" designed to reassure sporting publics that measures were being taken against drugs. IOC president Juan Antonio Samaranch stated that doping made "a mockery of the very essence of sport, the soul of what we, like our predecessors, consider sacrosanct ideals" and called doped athletes "the thieves of performance." Yet the IOC leaned on a policy of decentralization to deflect responsibility for regulating performance-enhancing substances to individual sports' governing bodies. The result was a notoriously ineffective system. Between 1968 and 1996, only around "one in every thousand Olympic athletes tested positive for a banned substance at the Games."[41] As Hoberman argues, the IOC's failures were by design. Samaranch oversaw "an almost total commercialization of the Olympic Games that . . . converted the [Olympic] 'Movement' into an advertising vehicle" for multinational corporations and U.S. television networks. Antidoping platitudes "concealed the IOC's longtime underfunding and delay in implementing drug testing that might really work," as effective control would expose star athletes, alienate corporate sponsors, and threaten the commercial spectacle of record-breaking performances.[42]

The presumed failure to police doping actually represents, in Hoberman's words, a "tacit agreement" between federations, athletes, medical personnel, and coaches consistent with the demands for ever greater levels of performance that are inherent to elite sport.[43] This agreement "has been less a conspiracy than a loose arrangement entered into by international sports bodies and the national federations that operate under their authority," a fact that is largely ignored by sport journalists, who commonly portray athletes, trainers, or lab technicians as corrupt individuals, and regulators as "beleaguered but honest" people who cannot keep up with ever-evolving methods for outmaneuvering testing.[44] Thus, as Beamish and Ritchie argue, the "unwritten code" between officials, doctors, and athletes that historically "affirmed the use of scientific expertise in the pursuit of victory" is consistently ignored by commentators who project a "transhistorical image" of "sport's 'purity'" and "the so-called 'level playing field.'"[45] This idealized image of sport is, to Hoberman, "curiously naïve," not only because it ignores the implicit consensus that has historically upheld doping practices but also because the concept of doping itself "represents an unprecedented kind of self-inhibition imposed on the development of human potential."[46] Beamish and Ritchie note that the use of steroids and blood boosting from the 1950s through the 1980s was not regarded by athletes, officials, or doctors as "cheating" because it did not break any formal or informal rules. It was consistent then (and remains consistent today) with the inescapable relationship between elite sport and the development of instrumental, scientific interventions in human performance.[47] "Doping" is a projection of contemporary moralism onto a past that it does not fit.

But where does this moralism come from? As Bryan Denham suggests, much of it is "event-driven," as doping scandals mobilize struggles for control between legislators, corporate leaders, sporting bodies, medical organizations, media companies, and other stakeholders whose interests are variously served and undermined by the regulation of performance-enhancing substances.[48]

In the United States, for example, the "war on drugs" has historically afforded politicians a chance to sermonize against drug abuse and the government's responsibility to protect young people.[49] Legislators have opportunistically staged public hearings and called on witnesses to tell stories about the harms of steroid abuse after major sport scandals, while their colleagues with ties to supplement companies have worked with industry leaders and lobbyists to insulate certain substances from government regulation. As a result, U.S. antisteroid policies have categorized several performance-enhancing substances (including some steroid precursors) as "dietary supplements" and allowed for their sale over the counter.[50]

Similar negotiations for control have characterized the relationships between governments and international sport medical commissions. Physicians employed on the medical commissions of federations like the IOC and IAAF, for example, have been historically complicit in the passivity and ineffectiveness of antidoping programs, actively thwarting colleagues' efforts to ban certain substances and testifying before government bodies (especially after public crises) that the extent of doping in sport, or the danger of a specific substance, was overblown.[51] These physicians' efforts represent what Hoberman calls "sportive nationalism": the "use of elite athletes by governments or other national bodies to demonstrate national fitness and vitality for the purpose of enhancing national prestige." As far back as the 1970s, for example, prominent West German physicians who regarded anabolic steroids as essential to their athletes' performance actively thwarted bans. They had the complicit support of government officials until doping scandals at the 1988 Seoul Olympics made support for "medically supervised steroid use" politically unsustainable.[52]

The event most often credited with forcing a renegotiation of the tacit agreements behind doping was the 1998 scandal at the Tour de France surrounding the cycling team sponsored by watch manufacturer Festina Lotus AV. The scandal became known as the "Festina affair" after officials discovered EPO, steroids, syringes, and other doping products in a Festina team employee's car. Festina's doctor confessed that the team ran a systematic doping program, and police raids of other teams brought attention to widespread, organized doping throughout the sport. The raids angered several racers, many of whom staged on-course protests and withdrew from the event.[53] Doping had been "an omnipresent seamy underside of the Tour since its first days," but it became all too public through the spectacle of raids, confessions, protests, and criminal charges.[54]

The Festina affair especially revealed the unwillingness of the Union Cycliste Internationale (UCI, the governing body for professional cycling) to confront drug use. In addition, the French government's intervention through customs and police, plus its decision to bring criminal charges against team doctors, represented a shift in control over regulating drugs from sporting bodies to the judicial system. This threatened the authority of sport's governing bodies, particularly the IOC, "to deal with problems 'in house,' without recourse to the law." It was within this context that the IOC called a conference in 1999 with the intention of reestablishing its authority over antidoping programs.[55] The conference served, however, as an occasion for delegates from various governments to batter IOC officials on their history of corruption and the ineffectiveness of their antidoping efforts.[56] Thus began the IOC's withdrawal from the front lines of global antidoping campaigns, and its decision to support the formation of an independent agency—the World Anti-Doping Agency (WADA)—governed by a committee of IOC and government representatives. WADA enforcement began with the 2000 Sydney Olympics, and its first World Anti-Doping Code was instated in 2003.[57]

U.S. antidoping regulations underwent similar changes, and for similar reasons. Until 2000, antidoping regulation was run by the U.S. Olympic Committee (USOC), which, like the IOC, had a reputation for not being serious about policing banned substances. The USOC recommended an independent agency, and the U.S. Anti-Doping Agency (USADA) was formed in 2000. Like WADA, it is responsible for testing, research, adjudication, and penalties.[58] According to the USADA's official website, the USOC recognized the need to "externalize the anti-doping program" in order "to remove the inherent conflict of interest that results from an organization being charged with both promoting and growing a sport, and handling anti-doping rule violations potentially involving the sport's elite athletes."[59] The USADA is one of several National Anti-Doping Organizations (NADOs) that comply with the World Anti-Doping Code, each of which attempts to work with the organizing bodies of individual sports, creating a proverbial alphabet soup of regulatory agencies often engaged in incommensurable promotional and regulatory pursuits. These pursuits include host nations' interests in projecting "nationalist values and ideologies" around high-profile international sporting events, contests between self-regulation and state regulation of sporting federations, and struggles for control between government agencies, global and national antidoping organizations, and the governing bodies of individual sports, which have for the past decade publicly accused one another of incompetence, corruption, and defamation.[60]

The eventfulness of a specific scandal often reveals cracks in the tacit agreements around doping, activating not a radical break or movement for total reform but a subtle readjustment in the terms of agreement. If we are to speak of breaking points or ruptures leading to changes in the doping consensus, we have to do so in a qualified sense.

First of all, the doping consensus is held together by both tight associations (as with coordinated efforts between legislators and lobbyists) and loose associations (as in the unspoken agreements between physicians and government officials), creating different mechanisms for change at disparate locations in the larger agreement. The actors do not necessarily need to know about each other or consciously coordinate their maneuvers; this is not across-the-board conspiracy. They need only pursue their share of the spoils of high performance—nationalist pride, protective moralism, televisual spectacle, supplement sales—to end up aligned with the transhumanist, externally transcendent ideology inherent to elite sport.

Second, event-based changes in the doping consensus have historically been incremental. What we perceive as a rupture has more to do with the public spectacles of hearings, resignations, arrests, bans, accusations, and so on than with changes in the actual institutional arrangements that led to a given scandal.

Yet fundamental change is not the only measure of cultural importance for antidoping politics. Certainly it matters that there are striking and increasingly conspicuous inconsistencies between antidoping moralism and the realities of policy reform, as these inconsistencies throw light on the pretenses of "pure" sport. Yet even as those pretenses are exposed, the doping consensus endlessly adjusts. Although media coverage emphasizes that policy changes emerge from public mandates, this is not at all clear. In fact, by most measures sporting publics are ambivalent about doping. Public opinion polls point in multiple, inconsistent directions (as always), but there is some evidence that concern over steroids and other performance-enhancing drugs is declining, especially among younger respondents, who express more liberal attitudes toward doping, penalization, and credit for athletic accomplishments.[61] In addition, the sport organizations most closely associated with doping rarely suffer financial losses. Major League Baseball (MLB) is coming through its so-called "steroid era" with record profits, including a reported $9 billion in gross revenues for 2014.[62] After a number of major scandals, anyone who pays attention to sport knows that the IOC is corrupt, yet the organization still commands multibillion-dollar television contracts as networks continue to gamble on the popularity of live Olympic broadcasts years into the future.[63] The 2012 Games in London constituted the most watched television event in U.S. history.[64] In 2014, NBC Universal (which has been the main carrier of the Games in the United States since 1992) agreed to pay $7.75 billion for exclusive broadcast rights to the Olympics from 2022 to 2032.[65] In 2015 the BBC—which has broadcast the Olympics since 1948—lost European broadcast rights to Eurosport (and its U.S. parent company Discovery Communications) in a €1.3 billion deal.[66] After the Festina affair consumers actually bought *more* of the watches made by Festina, which benefited for years from the publicity and name recognition brought by the scandal.[67]

Paul Dimeo has called for "a new vision of sport" in which we "accept that sport is a technological process" aimed at reinventing bodies, and where we come to terms with the fact that we "cannot have great moments of physical transcendence, of pushing forward the boundaries of human perfection, of idealising the athletic body, and have clean, pure, upright competitors."[68] There is plenty of evidence to suggest that we are approaching this point, if we have not already arrived.

The "Drift in Technical Incompliance"

While the Festina affair was focused on enhanced cyclists rather than enhanced bicycles, cycling has served as a formative site for the concerns that became articulated eventually as "technological doping." Hoberman marks the popularity of the bicycle during the 1890s as a moment when the hyperbolic promises of enhancement (especially represented at the time in claims surrounding Charles Brown-Séquard's testicular extracts) translated to "the actual stimulants that would boost athletic performance": "The merging of man [sic] and bicycle offered history's first opportunity to pharmacologize the man-machine relationship" through experiments with kola nuts, caffeine, and theobromine.[69] The mechanical end of that merger came into crisis with the dominance of "superbikes" in professional cycling competition, as the aerospace and military industries infiltrated the sport.[70] New materials and designs—including disc wheels, carbon fiber, and "aero-bars" (which allowed cyclists to ride in an aerodynamic "forward-stretched 'Superman' stance")—were instrumental in victories at the 1984 Los Angeles Olympics as well as the 1992 Games in Barcelona.[71] By the 1996 Atlanta Olympics, almost all the top competitors had carbon-fiber monocoque bicycles (a design that essentially removes joints from the bicycle frame to more evenly distribute stress), high-tech wheels, and aerodynamic helmets, shoes, and clothing.[72]

The Atlanta Games became a breaking point for the UCI. The organization's technical advisor, Jean Wauthier, pointed to 1996 as "the culmination of a drift in technical incompliance that had been moving since the 1980s." After Atlanta the UCI directed its technical commission to draw up new regulatory guidelines by the 2000 Sydney Olympics, and the result was the Lugano Charter.[73] The charter reasserted boundaries between the cyclist as performer and the bicycle as implement, consistent with what the UCI considered the cultural and historical essence of cycling:

> The bicycle serves to express the effort of the cyclist. . . . If we forget that the technology used is subordinate to the project itself, and not the reverse, we cross the line beyond which technology takes hold of the system and seeks to impose its own logic. That is the situation facing us today. . . . Priority is increasingly given to form. The performance achieved depends more on the form of the man-machine [*sic*] ensemble than the physical qualities of the rider, and this goes against the very meaning of cycle sport.[74]

The Lugano Charter is often regarded as a philosophical document with principles that are difficult to enforce, but it quite effectively banned many of the technologies that had been developed and implemented in the sport since the 1980s. Its limits continue to upset sport engineers and cycling manufacturers, who have viewed the document as a reactionary barrier to innovation.[75] As with many ideological boundaries, one discerns the line between human- and machine-based performance only after it has been crossed. It matters, then, that the superbikes the UCI sought to regulate *looked* wrong. Their technological form marked a presumably new human-machine assemblage in which the bicycle had actually overtaken the rider as the locus of performance, thus replacing the rider's body as the object to be developed, conditioned, and tested. This raised the pivotal question related to technological doping: is it the athlete's or the machine's performance that is measured in competition? That question presumes that one can separate athletes' bodies from their technological aids and, even more fundamentally, that there are dividing lines between technologized and nontechnologized bodies in elite sport.

The challenge of maintaining such lines in a sport like cycling makes *attempts* to pull apart physiology and machine—to use the plain, visible fact of their interdependency as a platform for reasserting the essential agency of the human performer—all the more important. Accordingly, per the Lugano Charter, the bicycle must "express" the talents of the rider, not the other way around. Consider, for example, Wauthier's explanation of the goal behind implementing the UCI's technical rules: "Cycling is a techno-sport. The technical object—the bicycle—is used as a device that manifests the abilities of the rider. We want to glorify the rider's abilities to the exclusion of all other factors."[76] For the UCI, technical aspects of the bicycle—materials, frame design, wheels, the riding posture it fixes—became variables to control in a constant effort to redraw boundaries between rider and bicycle as new technologies emerged within the cycling industry.[77]

The UCI's firm stance on bicycle technologies is curious when compared with its lax approach to performance-enhancing drugs. According to a damning 2015 report (commissioned by the UCI), between 1992 and 2006 UCI officials knew about the "endemic" nature of doping in cycling, yet publicly characterized the problem as limited to individual bad actors. Moreover, the UCI's testing procedures—announcing sample collections ahead of time, leaving riders unattended—provided easy opportunities "to evade testing positive through medical supervision, whilst at the same time giving the impression to the public that . . . UCI was tough on doping." The UCI's top priority was to promote cycling, and officials viewed antidoping measures as detrimental to the sport's image. Its leadership actively undermined the development of effective policies by giving preferential treatment to star athletes (especially Lance Armstrong, whom officials saw as a savior for the sport after the Festina affair), publicly criticizing whistleblowers, and creating an environment in which people vocal about reform were threatened and marginalized.[78]

Through its different approaches to riders and bicycles, the UCI demonstrated how human bodies and performance technologies can be compartmentalized for regulatory purposes. When bodies and technologies interface, they do not *necessarily* constitute a crisis for one another; much depends on whether they can be imagined as separate operating systems with distinct inorganic and organic functions.[79] That separability depends, in part, on the kinds of visual problems that human-technology interfaces represent for regulators. Consider again the Festina affair. EPO, a substance found in the Festina investigations and one that is central to doping crises in cycling, does not register on the body's surface (for example, in the form of increased muscularity). Suspicion might arise from competitive measurements—cycling's one-hour record is especially important—but the substance's presence in the body is largely concealed.[80] In fact, "blood doping" has been practiced since the 1970s, but a credible test for EPO (based on blood and urine sampling) was not developed until 2000.[81] Thus the "drift in technical incompliance" that resulted in the Lugano Charter related more to the visual problems represented by bicycles than to riders. As the authors of a report from the London-based Institution of Mechanical Engineers (IMechE) suggest, the 1996 Olympics became the breaking point for the UCI because "the velodrome was filled with carbon fibre-monocoque superbikes worth tens of thousands of pounds, their riders contorted into a 'superman' position to minimise drag."[82] The UCI's solution to bikes "contorting" riders was simple: regulate the bikes. The two systems—rider and superbike—could be treated as nonintegrated, the bike serving as a locus of control that bent the body into a presumably unnatural posture. The actual performances of cyclists are not so easy to explain away; the riders' bodies are potentially altered at a cellular level as well as by their interface with frames and aero-bars, and for practical purposes a cyclist's movement makes sense only in relation to a bicycle. Yet the capacity to separate mechanical and organic causes leaves regulatory bodies like the UCI with an option to control for technology alone, allowing the (presumably nontechnologized) body to slip by. As I show next, technological doping arrives as a construct when it becomes increasingly difficult to imagine human bodies and performance technologies as separated systems.

Technological Doping and High-Tech Swimsuits

"Technological doping" (or "technology doping") started to circulate as an explicit construct during controversies surrounding swimwear company Speedo's LZR swimsuit in 2008.[83] Italian swimming coach Alberto Castagnetti is most often credited with coining the phrase, "which became a rallying cry for opponents to the suits."[84] Since then technological doping has become a commonplace summary of concerns over the merging of athletic bodies and performance-enhancing technologies, especially in sports where wearable, prosthetic, or assistive technologies are conspicuous (e.g., bobsledding, speed skating, track and field, cycling, the Paralympics).[85] Technological doping relates specifically to what Ted Butryn calls "self technologies," which "consist of innovations which alter the physical and/or psychological makeup of athletes who employ them, and which therefore ultimately confound traditional definitions of 'human performance.'"[86] What we find in technological doping's emergence is less a wholly different mindset about the problems of technology and external transcendence than a subtle reorganization of the terms behind the doping agreement, especially in response to the growing externalization of self technologies.

The LZR, designed in partnership with NASA, had a full-body, seamless design that compressed swimmers' bodies (especially around the groin and abdomen) in order to stabilize an ideal swimming posture, reduce drag, and trap air for greater buoyancy.[87] During 2008 a total of 108 world records were broken, mostly by swimmers wearing LZR suits, and swimmers wearing the suits won 94 percent of all races at the 2008 Summer Olympics in Beijing.[88] The LZR was initially approved by the Fédération Internationale de Natation (FINA), the governing body for aquatic sports, but following controversies around so many broken records, FINA decided during a 2009 meeting in Dubai to ban all high-tech, full-body suits, setting strict standards for design (waist-to-knee coverage for men and shoulder-to-knee coverage for women), materials (limited to textiles), and buoyancy.[89] Much like the UCI's Lugano Charter, FINA's Dubai Charter sought to protect the "integrity" of its sport by reaffirming the performative agency of the swimmers' bodies over and above emerging technologies:

> In the context of the discussion in connection with swimsuits development and their alleged impact on sport, FINA reaffirms that it will continue monitoring the evolution of the sport equipment with the main objective of keeping the integrity of the sport. . . . In doing so, FINA wishes to recall that the main and core principle is that swimming is a sport essentially based on the physical performance of the athlete. This is the fundament which FINA has and will continue to preserve as its main objective and priority. FINA brings together athletes from around the world to compete on equal conditions and thereby decides the winner by the athlete who is physically the best.[90]

Like the Lugano Charter, the Dubai Charter treats technological aids as variables that must be controlled for in order to determine which athletes win fairly, and in both documents the material and philosophical reference point (the "fundament") for such control is the "physical performance of the athlete"—the agency of a body separated as much as possible from its technological enhancements. Like cycling, swimming features obvious technological aids (especially with the development of full-body suits), making it important to reaffirm continuously the essential agency of the human body within a conspicuously technological assemblage. Yet there are significant differences between the assemblage of rider and bicycle and that of swimmer and suit, which throw light on the emergence of technological doping as a construct.

In her analysis of high-tech swimsuit controversies, Magdalinski suggests that wearable technologies often provoke "fewer concerns that the boundary between nature and artifice is being obscured." While banned substances "corrupt the body internally," a suit is a prosthetic device that can be worn for competition, then removed, never integrating with or altering the body at a "cellular level."[91] Certainly the problems of enhanced performance and competitive advantage remain, but they are qualitatively different: suits "help the body to perform more efficiently," just as drugs do, but "they do so from outside the body"; in contrast, drugs threaten to enact a more fundamental—molecular, permanent—alteration of the body's limits.[92] When the fundamental question of technological doping came up during the 2008 LZR controversy—as Christine Brennan of *USA Today* put it, "Is it the swimmers? Or is it the suit?"—many commentators held that a swimsuit could not replace years of dedicated training or conjure elite athletic ability.[93] Speedo's head of global research and development emphasized that the LZR should not get too much credit or blame for broken records: "The last time I dropped a suit into the pool, it didn't get very far."[94] And retired swimming great Mark Spitz said: "If it was the swimming suit [breaking world records], then I'm buying Tiger Woods' golf clubs, because it doesn't matter who the swinger is."[95] These images of *removal* were important, as they emphasized the means by which the swimmer's agency could be claimed apart from the suit. Different from drug-based doping, the suits represented, as commentators put it, "doping by wardrobe" or "drugs on a hanger."[96] It was the suits' externality that made it possible to distinguish the swimmers' bodies as "discrete" objects within the human-technology interface, objects manipulated from without rather than from within.[97]

With removable, prosthetic enhancements, the ability to distinguish between athlete and technology depends on the material and symbolic boundaries between natural (organic) bodies and separable (mechanical) parts. The skin serves as one such boundary, and was especially important to the LZR swimsuit controversy. Magdalinski writes that skin constitutes a physical and symbolic boundary "between the inner and outer," a potential defense against exterior technologies becoming too fully integrated with the body. Whatever effect the LZR suits had on swimmers' performances, one could make the case that the effect was temporary—that the suit was a synthetic layer that never fully integrated with the natural skin underneath or with the bodily functions that the natural skin encased.[98]

This argument was difficult to sustain, however, with the LZR. The suit so significantly altered swimmers' bodies that it revealed the skin as an ultimately "porous, insecure margin" that allows even removable technologies to traverse borders between human and mechanical agency.[99] Karen Crouse of the *New York Times* noted how high-tech suits both enhanced and standardized competitors' bodies: "Squeezed into a corset-like suit, a muscled and stocky body is as streamlined as a long and lean one; a soft abdomen as effective as six-pack abs." University of Southern California swim coach Dave Salo said similarly, "A lot of kids who aren't in very good shape can put on one of these suits and be streamlined like seals." Retired German swimmer Franziska Van Almsick intimated that the LZR's design was a precursor to a "full-body condom, where all you see is the swimmer's face."[100] The molded, seamless, full-body design of the LZR was, in fact, so skin-tight that swimmers needed around fifteen minutes to put it on.[101] Speedo posted a five-minute instructional video online, which went through the necessity of wearing a plastic bag on each foot to help slide the suit onto the legs, positioning a core stabilizer above the hip bones, and having two people help to zip the wearer in. *New Yorker* writer Patricia Marx tried on a LZR suit and described the effort as "equivalent to fitting a rhinoceros into a party balloon."[102] The constrictive quality of the suit mattered a great deal, as it went beyond merely covering or compressing the skin to altering the body's shape. This was less a second skin than an alternative skin, a casing that smoothed and tightened small natural deviations from ideal physique into a standardized, mechanized form perfectly suited to sport-specific production.

The effects of that standardization *looked* nonhuman. A reporter for the *Guardian Unlimited*, for example, described the pool at the Beijing Olympics as populated by "shoals of rubber-clad flying fish."[103] This visual problem extended to the apparently substantial effect high-tech suits had on competitive advantage. Swimmers reported feeling superhuman when wearing the LZR. Several said it made them feel like they were swimming "downhill." U.S. swimmer Michael Phelps said he felt like a "rocket"; his teammate Ryan Lochte said, "When I put that suit on, I'm like an action hero. I feel like I can do anything: fly across water, lift up a car."[104] Swimmers who signed contracts with other equipment companies worried about keeping up competitively. After watching Speedo-sponsored athletes breaking world records, German swimmer Thomas Rupprath (under contract with Adidas) said, "The German swim federation has to seriously consider [the LZR]. Otherwise we will sink completely into mediocrity."[105]

The breaking point for high-tech suits came at the 2009 world championships, when German swimmer Paul Biedermann upset Michael Phelps in the 200-meter freestyle race. Biedermann was wearing an Arena X-Glide suit, a full-body polyurethane product from Adidas that was a successor to Speedo's design, while Phelps was wearing the (already outdated) LZR. Biedermann had until that point never won a world championship or Olympic medal, yet he broke Phelps's record in the 200 meters by .96 seconds. Karen Crouse reported a "consensus" at the world championships "that it is the suits—and not the swimmers—that have gotten faster," and Biedermann actually confirmed this in accounting for his surprise win by saying, "I hope there will be a time when I can beat Michael Phelps without the suit." Phelps's coach, Bob Bowman, threatened to hold Phelps out of international competition until high-tech suits were banned, and FINA's ban (already under development at the time) would be implemented in 2010. Bowman warned, "We've lost all the history of the sport," and even Biedermann identified this as a moment of risk: "We're in a dangerous situation of what comes next. It's really important to go back to the real swimming."[106]

The greatest perceived threat to "real swimming" and legitimate history came from equipment companies. According to an article in the *Toronto Star*, it was the responsibility of FINA and the regulating bodies of other sports "to keep technological changes under control so that athletic competition is truly a contest between athletes, not designers."[107] Writing for the blog site *Reach for the Wall*, Sally Jenkins described Biedermann's win similarly as a contest between natural and technologized athletes:

> Score one for laminates. The human got crushed. The nature of the confrontation was clear: Michael Phelps, the amphibious freak of nature, against the Arena X-Glide body suit, an artificial swim shell with a science fiction title worn by German Paul Biedermann. It was man against thermoplastic, basically a case of Phelps trying to swim faster than a guy wearing the hull of a spacecraft. We all know who won. . . . The suitmakers, of course.[108]

Jenkins's depiction summarizes nicely the vague boundaries that characterize antidoping moralism in elite sport, especially in light of advancing technologies. Only one year earlier, Speedo's LZR constituted technological doping, but with the next-generation Arena X-Glide, Phelps could be posed as a "freak of nature" ("freak" implying, as it often does in sport, a *genetic* deviation from the norm) in an outdated suit, doing his best against a technology that was transforming "middle-of-the-pack swimmers into Aquaman superheroes."[109] Before the championship race, reporters had asked Phelps whether he was concerned that the X-Glide gave Biedermann an unfair advantage, so this was the framework—Phelps versus technology—heading into the 200-meter final. Both Phelps and Biedermann were wearing full-body suits; neither was competing unenhanced. But within the context of competitive advantage Phelps was presumably *closer* to nature in an outmoded technology, more reliant on the physiology underneath than on the exterior shell. Consistent with the broader social agreements behind doping and antidoping efforts, the boundary lines separating technological interventions that transcend *within* species-specific limitations from those that transcend *beyond* them are drawn contingently. This makes them no less real or powerful, however, especially because they emerge within concrete competitive contexts. It mattered that Phelps was a multiple Olympic and world championship medalist, while Biedermann was not, and that Biedermann both improved his own previous times and broke world records by significant margins while wearing the X-Glide. Both swimmers technologically doped according to conventional senses of that construct (it is important to note that Phelps wore the LZR in seven of his eight events at Beijing in 2008), but Biedermann represented more dramatically a transfer in agency from human body to performance technology.[110] That is what constituted a breaking point in the developing controversy over high-tech suits: the crossing of a boundary past which Biedermann's transcendence of previous limits could not be explained within the context of his (human) body.

The Shifting Agreements behind Technological Doping

From the controversies surrounding high-tech swimsuits onward, technological doping has represented a specific stage in the ever-developing social agreements on performance enhancement in which the politics of secrecy and visibility associated with substance-based doping have undergone change due to the externality of wearable and prosthetic technologies. I do not want to oversimplify the distinction between substance-based doping and technological doping by implying that the former is internalized (inside the body, behind closed doors) and thus easier to hide while the latter is externalized and thus carried out in plain view. Both technological and substance-based doping involve an interplay of exterior signs (increased musculature, record-breaking performance) and interior problems (cellular change, psychological vulnerability). These problems are relatively obscured or conspicuous depending on the nature of a particular doping controversy. Neither is this simply a change in techniques. As Hoberman argues, the fundamental question surrounding doping has never been "about specific substances or techniques" but about "whether we should impose limits on athletic ambition and certain methods that might serve it."[111] What technological doping represents is a more outward response to the question of limiting enhancement, one that exposes more than ever the long-standing contradictions between antidoping moralism and real institutional practices.

Substance-based doping is often called "the worst-kept secret" in sport, but there is still room for a consensual illusion that every news report or commission investigation is a revelation, the uncovering of a scandal that could shake sport to its foundations.[112] Sometimes those revelations are identified as systemic (as with the Festina affair, for example), but even in such cases popular reports establish scenes where nefarious actors operate in relative secrecy: the doctors work at the fringes of mainstream medicine; the labs are hidden until discovered and raided by police; the athletes inject one another in bathroom stalls; the testing technicians turn the other way while samples are switched. Notions of secrecy and revelation are especially advanced through the endless cat-and-mouse game behind developments in performance enhancement. As Mehlman writes, ever since the IOC started testing for banned substances in 1968, a familiar process has played out: a new substance is detected, but there is not a test for it; an antidoping agency develops a test and adds the substance to its banned list; and "before long, a new substance turns up, and the process starts over." There is usually a substantial gap between initial detection and the development of reliable testing (as, for example, with EPO).[113] As a result, regulators always seem several steps behind the development of the latest drug or masking agent; the full depth and breadth of the problem appear inescapably concealed, hinted at only by exterior signs of trouble like bodily transformations or falling records. This may be a troubling reality for people invested in the ideals of pure sport, but it also marks a certain decorum. The behind-the-scenes nature of the doping consensus retains for sporting publics the option to *not know completely* what is going on. Otherwise there would be no doping scandals, only reminders.

With technological doping the exterior of an athlete's body becomes more conspicuous as a site for interventions and enhancements. Many of the moral tenets behind antidoping efforts—like naturalness, purity, or the level playing field—remain powerful, but it becomes more difficult to imagine the doping as either an act of individual weakness or a contest between corrupted athletes and outmatched regulators that plays out mostly behind closed doors. Familiar, major companies like Speedo, Adidas, and Nike move to the center of performance enhancement in elite sport, as do the interdependent relationships these companies have forged with athletes, coaches, governments, and regulators. There is constant attention to which company's products competitors are wearing or riding, and whether sponsors will allow their athletes out of exclusive contracts so they can use the latest breakthrough from a competing manufacturer.[114] The conspicuousness of branded products in the human-technology interface invites this kind of attention, especially as companies and sponsored athletes speak to the influence of a new technology over performance (always careful to push as far toward the technology's transformative effects as possible without discounting human agency). The institutionalized agreements behind performance enhancement are more obviously inscribed on athletic bodies, changing the decorum surrounding sport's "worst-kept secret."

For example, in 2012 Neils De Vos, the chief executive of UK Athletics (the governing body for sport in the United Kingdom), spoke in a private lecture at Oxford University of a "philosophy that flowed through" the development of British sport after the nation's poor showing at the 1996 Olympic Games in Atlanta. The United Kingdom realized that it could leverage its "inbuilt" economic advantage over other nations by investing in performance technologies that provided a competitive edge. De Vos admitted he "didn't buy" the notion that Britain's success since the low point of 1996 could be explained as a product of small, cumulative gains. "It's actually technological doping," he said, "but nonetheless it works and we've won a vast number of medals as a result of it." After his lecture was publicized, De Vos described technological doping as an "ill-chosen phrase."[115] The retraction was understandable given popular associations between doping and cheating, but what De Vos described was a perfectly public, state-sanctioned investment in sportive nationalism. In fact, the United Kingdom has been at the forefront of sport engineering since the development of UK Sport in 1997. UK Sport is an organization funded by the National Lottery and the British government that invests around £100 million a year in athletes identified as potential medalists in the Olympic and Paralympic Games, particularly through the areas of coaching, training, medical support, and technology.[116] According to a report from the IMechE, £7.5 million of UK Sport's funding was allocated to research and development between 2009 and 2013. The organization partnered with more than one hundred companies and twenty-five academic groups to develop new performance technologies during this period.[117]

Such partnerships between governments, corporations, and universities are common within nations looking to improve their prospects in international competition. In 2012, for example, the Australian government launched the Australian Sports Technologies Network, a partnership between universities, the Commonwealth Scientific and Industrial Research Organisation (CSIRO), sport technology companies, venture capitalists, and information technology experts that was designed to advance the manufacture of Australian-made performance technologies.[118] Similar partnerships are often formed in the aftermath of poor Olympic showings. South Korea, for example, experienced a peak in Olympic success at the 1988 Summer Games in Seoul, but the country's medal counts declined until after the 2000 Games, when the government decided to create policies to improve its athletes' performances. Like UK Sport, the Korean Sports Council (KSC) allocated resources to sports and athletes with the greatest perceived medal potential, and the Korean government significantly increased investments in elite sport (by nearly ₩90 million between 2002 and 2007). In addition, Korea's Chaebol (business conglomerate structure) has become a prominent partner in elite sport funding and leadership for sport science, with major companies like Samsung and Hyundai serving as sponsors. The government of Japan also decided, after poor showings at the 1988 and 1996 Olympic Games, to increase investments in elite sport, with a one-time distribution of ¥25 billion in 1990 and longer-term funding through a national sport lottery established in 2001. Japan's Ministry of Education, Culture, Sports, Science, and Technology (MEXT, developed in 2000) established a plan that included increased investments in sport science and medicine. These investments led to the establishment of the Japan Institute of Sport Sciences (JISS) in 2001 and the National Training Centre (NTC) in 2007, both sites for science and training development for Olympic athletes. In these and other cases, public-private partnerships pay off. Barrie Houlihan, Jae-Woo Park, and Mayumi Ya-Ya Yamamoto report that there is "unequivocal evidence" of a correlation between "public expenditure on elite sport policy objectives" and winning medals.[119] As Chris Hables Gray writes, "Great athletes cannot win alone now. They must have infrastructure."[120]

Within these private-public partnerships major corporations play a central role and are often the most visible players in technological doping. In the United States, for example, where there is no federal funding for Olympic sports, corporate sponsorship of technology development is instrumental to competitive success.[121] Team USA won its first medal in two-man bobsledding since 1952 at the 2014 Sochi Winter Olympics thanks, in large part, to a sponsorship with BMW North America, which spent $24 million on research and development for a carbon-fiber bobsled design.[122] Also at the Sochi Olympics, McLaren Applied Technologies (with funding from UK Sport) developed a bobsled for the U.K. team; Ferrari designed a bobsled for the Italian team; Columbia Sportswear designed uniforms for the Canadian, Russian, and U.S. freestyle ski teams with a "snow camouflage" pattern designed to disguise body movement (an important factor in judging); and Lockheed Martin and Under Armour collaborated on a molded suit for U.S. speed skaters that underwent both three hundred hours of wind tunnel testing and computational fluid dynamics analysis.[123] These relationships between national sport and private industry are based in mutual interest, as the technologies developed have overlapping uses in athletic, military, industry, and consumer contexts (UK Sport has partnered in recent years, for example, with BAE Systems, a major military technology engineering company, to develop training and performance technologies for Olympic and Paralympic competition).[124] Also, Olympic sport provides valuable brand-development opportunities for technology and apparel companies, as news media cover the impact of their products in elite competition and their sponsorship campaigns reach billions of viewers.

One important concern with state and private funding for national sport is that it adds to the already systemic inequalities in international competition that favor wealthy nations with highly developed technological and industrial infrastructures. The influence of this funding on the pervasive presence of performance technologies in elite sport, and the near certainty that this presence will only increase as wealthy nations continue to leverage their technological and economic advantages in the name of sportive nationalism, means a likely reconfiguration of elite performance around proliferating human-technology interfaces. Those partnerships between military, engineering, state, and corporate institutions that have shaped Olympic competition now pervade the development of performance and safety technologies in professional sports like rugby, auto racing, and football.[125]

The primary hope for retaining the *human* performer—the physical body of the athlete—through the proliferation of human-technology interfaces is, as analyzed above, the remaining capacity to disarticulate body and machine. That capacity comes under perhaps its greatest challenge through disability sport, which represents the latest stage in technological doping.

Prosthetics, Cyborg Athletes, and the Problem of Over-Ability: The Case of Oscar Pistorius

Technological doping comes up often within the context of disability sport, especially in regard to the integration of prosthetics with natural (organic) bodies and the problems that prosthetic technologies raise for competitive balance both within and beyond disability sport contexts. These problems emerge primarily around advances in prosthetic technologies that go beyond therapeutic or restorative functions in increasing the performance capacities of athletes with disabilities, raising the specter of overly able cyborg bodies. Robert Rawdon Wilson defines a prosthetic as "an artificial body part that supplements the body, but a part that carries an operating system different from the body's organic processes." As prostheses refine human capacity, they "blur the edges" of "technological and organic" systems and produce cyborg bodies.[126] This is how Donna Haraway famously conceived of cyborgs—products of a "border war" between "organism and machine." In a simple sense a cyborg is a subject that is part human, part machine (with the prosthetically enhanced athlete being a prominent example). More subtly, a cyborg is an embodied, performative transgression of essentialized distinctions "between natural and artificial, mind and body, self-developing and externally designed."[127] It is, in short, an assemblage that potentially collapses the boundaries between internal and external transcendence by integrating technologies with the most foundational conceptions of humanness and species limits.

When South African runner Oscar Pistorius applied for Olympic eligibility leading up to the 2008 Beijing Games, he threatened to cross what seemed a clear and necessary dividing line between disability and able-bodied sport, setting into motion an IAAF effort to bar him from competition. At issue were Pistorius's Cheetah Flex-Foot prosthetic legs, a carbon-fiber design created by Iceland-based orthopedics manufacturer Össur. Pistorius was born without fibulas and had both his legs amputated below the knee at eleven months old, so he competed on two prosthetics. Regulators worried that the Cheetahs transformed Pistorius from disabled to over-abled, granting him a mechanical advantage over his able-bodied counterparts.[128]

Traditionally, prosthetics have "signified the body was *deficient*, rather than *unfairly enhanced*," and that presumably deficient body could be relegated to the separate competitive and regulatory context of disability sport.[129] In Paralympic sport, for example, there are complex (and controversial) classification systems for determining competitive eligibility. Regulators emphasize that success should be determined by factors common to nondisabled sport (skill, fitness, strategy, mental strength). The main difference is that athletes compete against one another according to type and degree of impairment (Ian Brittain suggests a "crude analogy" to weight classes in boxing, though the standards in Paralympic sport are much more nuanced).[130] As long as *impairment* remains the characteristic distinguishing disabled from able-bodied competition, the impact of prosthetic technologies is contained. As Brittain explains, however, with "massive improvements" in performance technologies, some Paralympic athletes are performing at Olympic-level standards. The role that technology plays in these improvements has raised questions about competitive advantage over able-bodied athletes, a concern that has become related to technological doping.[131] This is the context within which Pistorius's effort to compete in the 2012 Olympic Games triggered a crisis for the IAAF.

Pistorius was not the first athlete with a disability to compete in the Olympics. In the 1904 Saint Louis Games, German American gymnast George Eyser won three gold medals competing on a wooden leg. Hungary's Olivér Halassy (whose left lower leg had been amputated after a traffic accident when he was eight years old) won a silver medal in water polo at the 1928 Olympics in Amsterdam and gold medals at the 1932 Los Angeles and 1936 Berlin Games. Hungarian pistol shooter Károly Takács—who competed with his left hand after his right (shooting) hand had been injured by a grenade—won gold medals at the 1948 London Olympics and the 1952 Helsinki Olympics. Lis

Hartel, a Danish athlete who was paralyzed in both legs from polio, won silver medals in individual dressage at the 1952 Helsinki Games and the 1956 Melbourne/Stockholm Games. Hartel is additionally noteworthy because 1952 was the first time women won the right to compete in Olympic dressage, and against men. New Zealand's Neroli Fairhall, who competed in archery at the 1984 Olympics, was the first paraplegic athlete in the Olympic Games. In the 2000 Sydney Games, U.S. runner Marla Runyon became the first legally blind competitor at the Olympics when she ran in the 1,500-meter final in track. South African Natalie du Toit swam the 10-kilometer marathon with one leg at the 2008 Beijing Olympics. And Natalia Partyka, a Polish table tennis player whose right arm is severed below the elbow, competed at the 2008 Beijing and 2012 London Olympics. In none of these cases, however, did advanced technologies pose a problem of over-ability.[132]

What made the Pistorius case different was the presence of prosthetics that threatened—in terms of both form and function—to unbalance the supposedly level playing field of (able-bodied) sport. P. David Howe suggests that what produces a cyborg is the "synergy" between athletes' bodily frames and their performance of sport-specific techniques. The basic difference between an able-bodied athlete wearing technologically advanced clothing and shoes in a track event and an athlete with a disability wearing prosthetic legs is that the clothing and shoes presumably enhance the movement functionality of a natural body, while the prosthetics seem to define the possibilities and limits of mobility *in total*.[133] As we know from the controversy around high-tech swimsuits, this boundary between human and technological agency can certainly be crossed in able-bodied sport, and on similar grounds: the enhancement could be nonhuman or extrahuman in both look and functionality. But the threat of body-technology integration is different in disability sport. A swimsuit can be banned and removed, leaving behind a body that is presumably natural (returned to normal mobility). A prosthetic like the Cheetah, on the other hand, seems to encapsulate the very possibilities of movement; its visibility signals an "artificial," extrahuman source of agency that potentially *exceeds* the capacity of the organic part it replaces. It produces, in short, a cyborg.[134] As Moss Norman and Fiona Moola argue, "Disabled athletes bear a disproportionate burden of cyborg embodiment because of the hypervisibility and spectacle of their cybernetic sporting selves (i.e. prosthetics, wheelchairs, etc.)." The potential crossover of athletes with disabilities into able-bodied competition is viewed among regulators and commentators as the first step toward a "cyborgification" of elite sport.[135]

Pistorius began to compete against able-bodied runners in IAAF-sanctioned events in 2004, when he won a 100-meter race in Pretoria. He then placed sixth in the 400-meter at the 2005 South African Championship and, after taking time away from competition to focus on his education, finished second in the 2007 South African Championship 400-meter race. In March 2007, however, the IAAF introduced an amendment to Rule 144.2 that prohibited "use of any technical device that incorporates springs, wheels or any other element that provides the user with an advantage over another athlete not using such a device."[136] Pistorius's eligibility for able-bodied competition was thrown into doubt. He had received an invitation to compete in the Norwich Union Glasgow Grand Prix (to be held on June 3, 2007), but the IAAF withdrew the invitation. On June 15, 2007, the IAAF reversed course, stating that Pistorius would be considered eligible unless the organization obtained scientific evidence that his prosthetics gave him an unfair advantage. Pistorius was allowed to race at the July 2007 Golden Gala event in Rome, where the IAAF coordinated with an Italian sport laboratory to record Pistorius's gait using multiple high-definition cameras. The results were inconclusive, so the IAAF commissioned a study by Professor Peter Brüggemann of the German Sport University in Cologne. After two days of study Brüggemann and his colleagues determined that Pistorius's prosthetics provided an advantage in energy return at the ankle, knee, and hip joints as compared against the "natural legs" of able-bodied test subjects, and that "fast running with the dedicated Cheetah prosthetics is a different kind of locomotion than sprinting with natural human legs" that could result in a "lower metabolic cost." Based on these findings the IAAF ruled that the Cheetahs violated Rule 144.2 and that Pistorius was ineligible to compete in IAAF-sanctioned events.[137] This confirmed many commentators' suspicions that the amendment to the rule was designed to deny Pistorius Olympic eligibility, even as IAAF officials denied this.[138]

Pistorius appealed to the Court of Arbitration for Sport (CAS), which overturned the IAAF ruling. In the decision to uphold Pistorius's appeal, the CAS panel cited several concerns: it seemed "likely" that the IAAF had amended Rule 144.2 "with [Pistorius] in mind"; the testing was conducted with an apparently prejudicial view of Pistorius's advantages and disadvantages, as it did not consider "the effect of the device over the entire race"; and the CAS panel found no compelling evidence that Pistorius gained any metabolic or biomechanical advantages from his prosthetics as compared to able-bodied competitors. The CAS decision was based on an analysis of the Brüggemann study as well as on test results that Pistorius provided from a Houston laboratory.[139] The decision was considered a "watershed," as Pistorius became the first amputee to successfully challenge rules barring competitive eligibility based on technological advantage. Pistorius was left with only sixty-four days to attempt a qualifying time for the 2008 South African Olympic team. He failed to qualify in 2008, but he did in 2012, competing in the 2012

London Olympics and advancing to the semifinal of the 400-meter before being eliminated.[140]

According to Magdalinski, the IAAF's efforts to exclude Pistorius illustrated how the "interface between the organic body and inorganic prosthetic [had] caused increasing disquiet about the 'humanity' of performance."[141] This evaluation was widely shared among scholars in the years during and after Pistorius's fight for entry into Olympic competition. Silvia Camporesi argued in 2008 that Pistorius's case was a "snap-shot into the future of sport" when our conception of "'natural,' able-bodied athletes" would "appear anachronistic."[142] C. L. Cole read the CAS ruling as a challenge to the presumed stability of able and disabled bodies that had upheld the "imaginary of fairness" in sport.[143] Norman and Moola maintained similarly that by transgressing the "boundary between ability/disability, nature/machine," Pistorius revealed "the margins of ability as porous, leaky, and unstable" and threatened "to collapse the very ontological and corporeal security of the humanist subject."[144] If so, Pistorius was the latest and perhaps most pronounced sign of sport's transhuman moment. His eligibility seemed an especially important step in the process of giving over to the temptations of external transcendence, whereby athletes "surpassing biological boundaries by unchecked transformations" would serve as the realization of "posthumanist currents" in elite sport.[145]

One of the most important features of the Pistorius case was that discussion of these potential reconfigurations of humanness, ability, and advantage migrated from their typical confines within academic, bioethical, and medical circles into popular discourse. Coverage of Pistorius commonly emphasized the problems of technological doping in light of broader concerns over "transhumans" and "cyborgs."[146] Jeré Longman summarized in a 2007 *New York Times* article the question that Pistorius had popularized: "Would the nature of sport be altered if athletes using artificial limbs could run faster or jump higher than the best athletes using their natural limbs?"[147] In an opinion piece for CNN, bioethicist Paul Root Wolpe considered sport's potential future after Pistorius's Olympic eligibility. If prosthetic technologies allowed athletes with disabilities to eventually exceed their able-bodied counterparts (again, Pistorius did *not* seem to have such an advantage), it would be difficult to imagine a regulatory response that decelerated bodily modifications. Requiring athletes with disabilities to use less advanced technologies to level the playing field would create an "untenable" standard since there was no way to determine "the degree to which technology mimics true physiological function." Given the challenges with defining disability, and the artificial conditions that competition is built around, what would be the baseline for measurement? Pistorius's eligibility was, then, the beginning of a "conundrum": "More and more, our powerful technological achievements will butt heads with our sense of naturalness and fairness. A lot of the debate and controversy around biotechnology will be played out in athletic competitions."[148] Writing for *New Scientist*, Anders Sandberg, a researcher at the University of Oxford Future of Humanity Institute, argued similarly that Pistorius represented "a deep shift in our view of what it means to be disabled, enhanced—or even human" as his case opened a likely cycle of bodily modifications that would make it difficult "for sport to maintain its fairly puritan views."[149]

Slippery-slope arguments indicated the seeming inevitability of these changes to athletic bodies. Commentators wondered if able-bodied athletes would eventually choose self-mutilation, exchanging "healthy natural limbs" for "artificial ones."[150] A *New York Daily News* journalist predicted the decline of track and field into a technological "era of darkness": "If a runner thrives on his Cheetahs, if his times fall from solid 46 seconds to world-championship caliber 44s, then somebody somewhere—perhaps 10, 20 years from now—will at least ponder swapping bone for carbon fiber."[151] Though especially dystopian, these visions summarized basic anxieties about technological doping and external transcendence: what happens when we move from a natural body registering a "solid" time to a prosthetically altered body registering an elite time that cannot be explained within the context of that body's supposedly natural limits?

As I have argued throughout my analysis, the ethical and political questions surrounding performance enhancement are being resolved in the direction of transhumanist sport, with antidoping sentiment serving in some cases as necessary publicity, in other cases as principled but institutionally marginalized dissent. Transhumanist trends do not, however, necessarily portend a reinvention of human-athletic transcendence. The main reason, emphasized above, is that doping is consistent with the political, economic, and cultural aspirations of elite sport. At the same time, the interventions of governments, technology companies, and medical laboratories are so conspicuously inscribed on athletic bodies that popular and regulatory options for reclaiming, or clinging to, a transcendence internal to the body and its natural limits are shrinking. I want to conclude by taking up a final question: if the image of immutable human-athletic transcendence is, in fact, coming apart, to what extent does this constitute a meaningful political and religious shift in elite sport?

Implications: The Future of Externally Transcendent Sport?

As Tracy Trothen argues, "The religious-like dimensions of both transhumanism and sport add potency to the meeting of enhancements and elite sport, given that aspects of both can be regarded as sacred by followers." Thus, the transhumanist trends represented by performance technologies affect several "sacred aspects of sport," including physicality, effort, and perfection.[152] Transhumanism comes into sport across the same porous boundaries between formal and civil religion as well as between sacred and profane that, as I have argued throughout this book, broadly characterize sport cultural production. Its influence over these "sacred aspects" of sport might be understood across broadly denominational and/or secularized conceptions of transcendence.[153]

Consider the basic senses of transcendence that began this chapter. If one thinks about human-athletic transcendence in formally theological terms, then performance technologies might affect the quality of spiritual experience derived from witnessing elite sport achievements. More specifically, technologies might call into question what those achievements *prove* about transcendence—as, for example, the revelation of abilities gifted by God. As Patrick Hopkins notes, formally religious traditions and transhumanism are likely to "antagonize [each other] . . . over the method of transcendence pursued, and the overall attitude toward given nature that motivates the pursuit."[154] Gerald McKenny argues, for example, that external transcendence is in some ways consistent with Christian theological aspirations for "human fulfillment" beyond the limits of "natural human capacities." The difference between Christian and transhuman transcendence is that the former is achieved from within the human condition (from humans' inborn capacity to commune with God), while the latter relies on technological interventions that fundamentally change human nature.[155] In terms of the continuum between internal and external transcendence, the question of whether transcendence occurs *within* the context of the human body comes down to whether technological interventions can be reconciled with the (natural, divine) plan of creation.[156]

If one thinks about human-athletic transcendence in secular terms—as, for example, the act of rising above politics and economics, or as evolutionary progress—the question over techniques of transcendence remains, but technological interventions may not necessarily violate the plan of creation as much as disrupt the fantasy of a noninstitutionalized, ahistorical essence behind elite accomplishment. Even in these cases, we are likely to see analogues connecting the religious and secular or the sacred and profane (as in the relationship between a divine creator and lab technicians figuratively playing God). This brings us back to the argument from Chapter 2, that an athletic body stands as an immutable object of adoration only insofar as the work of institutional production behind its creation is hidden from view. Once institutional interventions become apparent, as they do with technological doping, this compromises elite athletes' representations of the ahistorical essence.[157] The more elite athletes represent assemblages wherein the technological appears to subordinate the human as the primary source of agency, the more elite sport moves toward a transcendence external to the presumably inborn limits of the species.

These trends toward external transcendence are, as I argued above, emergent from the tacit agreements behind performance enhancement, and they are likely to increase in scope and visibility given public-private investments in elite televised sport and the potential integration of transhuman and cyborg athletes into so-called normal competition. It does seem, as many academic and popular commentators suggest, that performance enhancement will increasingly destabilize notions of naturalness, ability, the level playing field, and human agency. By no means does that destabilization guarantee progressive political change. At the same time, it matters that questions about humanness, technology, and transcendence now circulate commonly throughout sport culture, and that these questions are raised by the very institutional sources proclaiming the sanctity of natural sport. I want to close, then, with two overarching statements on the limits and possibilities of transcendence after technological doping.

First, *a transhuman or cyborg athlete "transcends" only under specific, contingent ideological conditions.* Commentators assume that performance technologies inherently threaten sport's human element, but external transcendence is not a possibility intrinsic to technologized bodies. It is imagined, made, and unmade through the cultural and institutional processes that produce human-machine assemblages. To understand where, how, and why athletes transcend we have to pay attention to context. The Pistorius case is particularly illustrative.

The potential for integration between disability sport and able-bodied sport represents something of a late stage in the developing challenges surrounding technological doping. The "drift in technical incompliance" represented by superbikes seemed easy enough to regulate because rider and bicycle could be imagined as separate systems—organic and inorganic. High-tech swimsuits were removable (and thus could be banned from competition) but they also reshaped swimmers' bodies, hinting at a different kind of trouble: the potential influence of apparel and technology companies over altering human-athletic form. Athletes with disabilities represented a unique regulatory challenge, as prosthetics seemed to define their very possibilities for movement; thus these athletes brought a categorically different, potentially super-endowed body into competition, one that threatened the natural performance of their able-bodied counterparts. In each of these stages, regulators could claim the fundamental or irreducible value of human performance as long as they could make a credible, *public* case for disarticulating body and technology—banning devices or imposing rigid technical rules on the assumption that a natural body could be verified scientifically and sanctioned for competition.

It is tempting to view the integration of cyborg athletes into able-bodied sport as a tipping point; perhaps it will prove to be. This is the view implied in responses from both transhumanist enthusiasts and resistant regulators, who perceived in the Pistorius case the crossing of a decisive boundary: either allow him to compete in able-bodied sport and concede the coming age of posthuman athletes or protect the remaining humanness of sport by banning him on technological grounds. The problem with this view is that it does not sufficiently acknowledge the limits of Pistorius's disruptiveness.

Pistorius became the representative of a new technological age not only because of his legal case against the IAAF or his legitimately elite athletic ability but also because he fit within normative boundaries of what an athlete with disabilities could or ought to be. As Ivo Van Hilvoorde and Laurens Landeweerd argue, Pistorius stimulated transhumanist imaginings of progress beyond the boundaries of human limitation, but scientific and technological debates over his "normalcy" and "super-ability" disguised a thoroughly "ideological project" wherein those athletes who represent a "normalization of dis-abilities" also likely represent an affirmation of neoliberal ideals.[158] In fact, Pistorius fit perfectly into the mold of the "supercrip," a common media stereotype for persons with disabilities who presumably transcend the obstacles of their impairment through virtues like individualism, perseverance, and hard work.[159] Pistorius was also appealing as a conventionally attractive, white, heterosexual male. He modeled for French fashion company Thierry Mugler and was sponsored by Nike. A *New York Times* writer described Pistorius's physique in a fragrance ad: "his thick slab of a chest and powerful forearms in motion"; his blades, "stylized to evoke the legs of a superhero, dipped in liquid chrome and wrapped in metallic foil, now resembling something like the shiny body of a motorcycle crossed with a dental pick."[160] This was a common way of reconciling Pistorius's human and machine parts: from the mid-leg down he was technologically sleek, and the rest of the way up he was alluring flesh, musculature, chiseled facial features. Before his first race in the 2012 Olympics a spectator shouted to Pistorius, "You sexy beauty," a widely circulated sign of his popular reputation as inspirational athlete and international sex symbol.[161]

Pistorius's prosthetics represented different questions about ability and disability after he went on trial for the murder of his girlfriend, Reeva Steenkamp. On February 14, 2013, Pistorius shot and killed Steenkamp through a locked bathroom door in his home. He pled innocent to murder, claiming that he had mistaken Steenkamp for a burglar. Pistorius was initially found guilty of culpable homicide in 2014, before South Africa's Supreme Court overturned the conviction and found him guilty of murder in 2015.[162] From his breakout performance in 2004 through his 2014 murder trial, Pistorius insisted in multiple interviews that he did not view himself as disabled. Writing for South Africa's *Daily Maverick*, Rebecca Davis noted that whether or not these denials were sincere or necessary to his case against the IAAF, they created the image of an athlete "transcending disability," an image that had been "largely shattered" during his murder trial.[163] Certainly that shattering had to do with the disturbing details of the shooting, as well as with reports and testimony during the trial that Pistorius had a history of anger problems, gun obsession, alcohol abuse, and violence against women.[164] But Pistorius's transcendence was also revoked by his defense team, which strategically divested his body of its prosthetic super-abilities.

Pistorius's murder defense was built around the premise that as a person with a disability, he reasonably feared for his life more than an able-bodied person would. Wayne Derman, the chief medical officer for the South African Paralympic team, described Pistorius as "hyper-vigilant," constantly "scanning" for threats, suffering from an "exaggerated fight or flight" response that, Derman argued, was common among persons with disabilities. Defense lawyer Barry Roux described Pistorius's experiences with disability as traumatic, leading to an "exaggerated response to danger." Mental health professionals suggested that Pistorius's early experience with amputation and his family upbringing had left him with profound anxieties and insecurities.[165]

For their approach to work, defense lawyers had to draw lines between an on-track image of super-ability and an off-track image of *dis*ability, and this effort came down to the presence or absence of Pistorius's prosthetics. As Peter Bansel and Browyn Davies summarize: with his prosthetics on, Pistorius was depicted "as a strong and powerful sportsman who [had] heroically overcome his disability"; without them, he was "re/assembled as fearful and vulnerable, needing to shoot to protect himself and his girlfriend precisely *because* of his disability."[166] Defense arguments and media coverage connected Pistorius's fear about an intruder with the fears of wealthy white South Africans who, in a supposed state of siege by black criminals, were purchasing guns and locking themselves into gated communities.[167] Within this context of disability- and culturally induced fear, Pistorius fired out of reflex and understood his actions only after the fact. News reports emphasized how he was uncontrollably retching in the courtroom, unable to bear the tragedy in retrospect. Commentators sympathetic to his case insisted that Pistorius could not be faking these emotions.[168] One clinical psychologist who took the stand went as far as to reinvent Pistorius's Olympic dream as a quest to please his mother: "It's interesting that his biggest dream was to race against able-bodied athletes, perhaps an attempt to give psychological credence to his mother's position that he was not disabled."[169] The defense crafted, then, a fundamental shift in context. On the track, the challenge of mastering interactions between prosthetic and organic parts defined Pistorius's transcendence. In his home, in the courtroom, his mastery over that assemblage came apart.

What the Pistorius murder trial illustrates is that human-machine assemblages do not embody any kind of inherent capacity for external transcendence. If Pistorius had formerly represented a foundational shift in our conceptions of ability and humanness, his body was now relocated to the thoroughly human, immanent plane of race, class, gender, and disability politics, all configured around the plan of a high-dollar defense strategy. At the same time, transcendence implies a permanence that, even if ideologically upheld, cannot be so easily revoked. Disability advocacy groups and disability studies scholars, for example, responded skeptically to the Pistorius defense strategy. Some viewed it as exploitative, advancing stereotyped notions of disabled persons as helpless, traumatized, and resentful. Pistorius's former disavowals of disability also contrasted problematically with the image of vulnerability shaped in the trial. As Carol Glazer, president of the National Organization on Disability, insisted, "Anyone who can figure out how to win able-boded [world championship and Olympic competitions] . . . has figured out how to adapt to his disability. It's highly unlikely that the same disability would trigger hyper-vigilance or other stress reactions." Pistorius had clearly demonstrated a capacity for elite physicality. He could not simply take it all back, especially not to justify murder.[170]

Neither could Pistorius's defense team control for the complex associations between mobility and able-bodiedness on which their case for psychological and physical vulnerability rested. During pretrial preparation, Pistorius's team hired a U.S. company called The Evidence Room to make a video reenactment of the shooting. In the video Pistorius walks across his uncle's living-room floor and toward the bathroom on his stumps, his right arm extended as if holding a gun. Then, from a bird's-eye view, Pistorius is shown on all fours, still without his prosthetics, struggling to drag a motionless woman (his sister Aimee, playing the part of Steenkamp) out of the bathroom and down the stairs. The video was never used in trial, but it was leaked to and broadcast by an Australian TV station.[171] The defense team did not comment on why the footage was not used in court, only that it was obtained and aired "illegally," in breach of a nondisclosure agreement with The Evidence Room. One reason for keeping the video out of the courtroom, according to some legal experts, was that it undermined the defense's case. Johannesburg-based criminal lawyer Martin Hood argued, "What we can take from the video is that Oscar is a lot more mobile on his stumps than his defence team has tried to make out."[172] Again, the defense's separation between on-track super-ability and off-track vulnerability depended on the meanings of Pistorius's body with and without his prosthetics. Here we see the limits to assuming that prosthetic endowment defines the entire spectrum of mobility for persons with disabilities. This applies not only to the Pistorius defense but also, perhaps, to the more broadly protean possibilities of transhuman and cyborg athletes. To say that transcendence is conditioned ideologically is not to say that it is wholly constrained. Even under the highly controlled conditions involved in producing a defense video, Pistorius's body caused trouble.

Any claims regarding transhuman or cyborg athletes and social change must be considered within a context where these athletes are produced by the investments and interventions of powerful institutions (governments, corporations, sporting federations). At the same time, these bodies throw light on the means of production behind athletic transcendence, potentially shifting the ways in which categories like the "natural" or the "human" are popularly understood. As Haraway argues, cyborgs are "the illegitimate offspring of militarism and patriarchal capitalism," but "illegitimate offspring are often exceedingly unfaithful to their origins."[173] The transhuman or cyborg athlete does not come into elite sport as an outsider but as a product of institutionalized economic and political priorities. Most of the present evidence suggests that elite sport institutions will produce increasing numbers of technologically enhanced athletes. The question is whether current strategies for containing and appropriating those athletes' contradictions (regarding, for example, ability, advantage, and humanness) can keep pace with increased rates of production. More transhuman athletes will likely mean more reactionary and insufficient regulations, more legal battles, and more struggles for resources and competitive eligibility. Elite sport institutions appear poised to produce an ever greater number of athletes who threaten the natural and human tenets of top competition.

This brings me to my second statement of limitations: *The gendered assumptions that uphold humanness and naturalness in sport may continue to thrive beneath the problems of technological doping.* In elite sport, conceptions of natural ability have been historically gendered, especially through the presumed naturalness of sex-segregated competition. As Claire Sullivan notes, presumptions that "all males (born or 'made')" have natural physical advantages "over all females (born or 'made')" have predominated discussions about "female, intersex, and transsexual athletes' rights to compete" in sex-segregated sports. Much as with antidoping policies or efforts to segregate able-bodied and disability sport, sporting federations have sought scientific and popular verification of gender identity in the name of protecting standards for fair play, which governing institutions, athletes, and fans worry would be violated by bodies that confound gender binaries (e.g., females born with male chromosomal patterns, transgender female athletes, and female athletes who have undergone sex reassignment).[174]

The threats that transhuman and cyborg bodies pose to notions of humanness and the level playing field are both technologized *and* gendered, as prosthetics and performance-enhancing substances extend the body beyond its presumably natural (male, biologically determined) limits.[175] As scholars in queer theory have argued, the same cultural and economic systems that uphold the normalcy of able-bodiedness by contrasting it against disability often uphold the normalcy of heterosexuality in contrast with queerness. In that sense cyborg, disabled, transgender, or intersex bodies potentially violate interwoven gendered and technologized systems of power, undermining the mythos of natural sport.[176] Transhuman cyborgs might then queer essentialized identity categories associated with gender, sexuality, disability, or race, as well as the human-technology binaries that underwrite them.[177] This is a common image of transcendence in transhumanist sport, and it is worth evaluating in light of the trends surrounding technological doping.

Haraway writes that "the cyborg is a contested and heterogeneous construct . . . [that is] capable of sustaining oppositional and liberatory projects at the levels of research practice, cultural productions, and political intervention" but also becomes available for appropriation "in terms of master control principles, articulated within a rationalist paradigm of language and embodiment."[178] Technological doping calls to mind this latter concern about appropriation, as the institutionalized agreements that enable it shape the possibilities of transhuman, cyborg athletes at the highest levels of sport. Technological doping represents the collective economic and political investments of corporations and governments interested in supporting those athletes who best advance these institutions' competitive, nationalistic, and commercial priorities. Athletes who do not fit the profile of idealized nationalist or marketable figures are likely to be excluded. When that exclusion focuses disproportionately on athletes who confound fixed gender and sexual categorizations, we need to count it as a containment strategy curtailing transhuman and cyborg athletes' fuller potential to disrupt the ideological underpinnings of natural, human sport.

National sporting bodies commonly seek exemption from international nondiscrimination laws that force federations like the IAAF and IOC to change their policies related to transgender, transsexual, and intersex athletes.[179] In such cases, politicians and administrations often weave together gendered, sexualized, and technologized conceptions of competitive advantage and ability, suggesting how each of these represents a continuum of threats to natural sport. For example, in 2004 the U.K. government introduced the Gender Recognition Bill in order to comply with an antidiscrimination ruling by the European Court of Human Rights. The bill was to provide "full legal status for people in their acquired gender." U.K. sporting bodies sought exemption immediately.[180] Discussions between UK Sport, the IOC, and the British government produced an amendment that would allow U.K. sporting bodies continued leeway in making decisions over competitive eligibility for transsexual athletes. Lord Filkin, the parliamentary undersecretary of state, justified the necessity of the amendment by conflating sexuality with performance-enhancing drugs:

> This amendment is designed to ensure sporting bodies can uphold safe and fair competition. . . . In the same way as a sporting body is perfectly entitled to exclude a person taking performance enhancing drugs, for reasons of competitive parity, they would be entitled to exclude a male-to-female transsexual person if competitive parity or the safety of other competitors was at stake.[181]

This is a common-sense and unfortunately predictable connection given how long regulators have relied on overlapping presumptions about gender and technology to distinguish between normal and illegally enhanced bodies.[182] Examples include the now-infamous "naked parades" conducted by the IAAF in the 1960s, where women athletes were stripped so that gynecologists could examine their genitalia to make sure they were not men attempting to pass as women; presumably more scientific efforts to affirm a male-female binary by testing women, transgender, transsexual, and intersex athletes for chromosomal sex, testosterone levels, or hyperandrogenism; and (as in the Pistorius case) parallel efforts to scientifically verify a natural, nontechnologized body by quantifying differences between organic and machine-based mobility.[183] Filkin's conflation of transsexuality with performance-enhancing drugs hints, then, at a persistently gendered consciousness regarding technology and competitive advantage, a need to guard against the deviations from natural (male *or* female, nontechnologized) bodies that threaten competitive balance.

My concern is that as long as the institutions behind technological doping select conventionally gendered representatives, the political promise of transhuman and cyborg athletes will be circumscribed by the very agreements that produce their bodies. Governments, national sporting bodies, and corporations cannot create *all* the cyborgs, but they do disproportionately control the financial and research infrastructures required to make technologically doped athletes. This means that at least for now, the transhuman athletes populating elite sport are more likely than not to portray ideal bodies deployed for rationalist purposes.[184]

As Heather Walton suggests, it is important to impose a "reality check" on optimistic projections about a progressive, disruptive cyborg politics based on the material struggles of "flesh and blood" persons. What we find is that "the boundary territory . . . where identity is contested is not always a happy place of delightful confusion"; it is also a space where powerful institutions react *against* the indeterminacy of nonconforming bodies. Yet there is room for cautious optimism.[185] Sullivan points out that whenever regulators attempt to redraw the boundaries for determining natural bodies, they "open a floodgate for potential opposition" to other types of variation that presumably threaten the level playing field. The ensuing debates throw light on inconsistencies inherent to scientific, gendered, and technological systems for competitive classification.[186] This does not, as John Sloop warns, constitute a "revolutionary" rethinking of naturalness in sport. But increasingly popular recognition of the body's indeterminacy may matter a great deal, even as conceptions of natural athleticism are constantly reclaimed. In the not-too-distant past, questions concerning the body's gendered or nontechnological integrity would have been raised almost exclusively by academics and activists. Now these questions show up everywhere in coverage of elite sport.[187]

Nikki Sullivan claims that "what has begun to emerge in and through critiques of popular commonsense understandings of the body, technology, [and their interrelationships] . . . is the notion of a chiasmic interdependence of soma and techné": an understanding of the body as fundamentally "technologized" and of technologies as fundamentally "enfleshed."[188] In elite sport the blurring of edges between mechanical and organic systems—swimsuits and skin, prosthetics and stumps—extends the physiological and functional ways in which athletic bodies have long been imagined, spurring regulators' constant efforts to detect the *male* machinery (genitalia, hyperandrogenism) presumably central to performance. There are no guarantees for a progressive politics here. It does, however, seem likely that as public-private institutions produce increasing numbers of technologically doped athletes, sporting bodies and regulators will find less room for reclaiming those athletes' performances as *essentially* human.

To borrow, finally, from Heather Graham (whose argument rests on a more formally theological foundation than mine), cyborgs and transhumans make it difficult to think about "transcendence" as a term that separates the human and the divine, or technological invention and "other-worldly" creation. Cyborgs mobilize reconceived notions of how "the human, the technological, the natural," and the divine interrelate; they block our ability to "drift" back toward nostalgic notions of purity.[189] Even as categories like transcendence undergo change, we must be aware, as Walton warns, that religious traditions are "intransigent" and often renewed "painfully." "We are working," she writes, "within theological and cultural forms that fight back against our attempts to reform them." At the same time, the "intractability" of these forms also provides a "means of preserving some resources we may need for social transformation."[190] In the end, this is where I would place my greatest hope for political change surrounding transcendence in sport culture. As regulatory agencies and government officials attempt to reclaim natural sport from the aftermath of their own interventions, it seems they will continue to supply the resources needed for legal, activist, and popular challenges to existing policies of exclusion and containment.

5

THE BIRTH AND DEATH

OF THE NATIONAL

FOOTBALL LEAGUE

THE NATIONAL FOOTBALL LEAGUE (NFL) is, at the time of this writing, in the midst of a crisis over traumatic brain injury that has many commentators contemplating the death of professional football as the top sport in the United States. Given the sport's current popularity, this might seem absurd. According to the Nielsen consumer research company, television ratings for regular-season NFL games rose more than one percentage point from 2006 to 2010, "accounting for more than 3.5 million additional viewers per game."[1] Starting in 2010 the league's Sunday and Monday night broadcasts consistently outperformed *all* forms of television programming, including top network dramas, comedies, and reality TV shows.[2] For three consecutive years the Super Bowl was the most watched television program in U.S. history, beginning with Super Bowl XLIV in 2010 (106.5 million viewers), then Super Bowl XLV in 2011 (111 million viewers), and finally Super Bowl XLVI in 2012 (111.3 million viewers). Super Bowl XLVII in 2013 broke the streak, with an average audience of 108.7 million, making it the third most watched television program in U.S. history.[3] In 2014 the league confirmed for the first time in federal court that its retired players were at an increased risk for complications related to head trauma. During that same year the NFL reached 202.3 million unique viewers; with an average of 17.6 million viewers watching each game telecast, 2014 ranked just behind 2010 with the second highest total of viewers in league history.[4] Before the start of the 2015 season the NFL settled a $1 billion class-action lawsuit brought by more than five thousand former players, who accused the league of concealing evidence about the dangers of head injury. Even so, week one of the 2015 season was the highest rated in league history, with an average audience of 19.9 million viewers for Thursday night, Sunday, and Monday night games.[5]

Yet ratings snapshots, as *Atlantic* writer Derek Thompson points out, may not be attuned to larger cultural shifts, and by no means indicate invincibility.[6] The head-trauma crisis has been decades in the making, but has intensified over the same timespan as the league's rising ratings dominance. In recent years multiple retired players have committed suicide—including Philadelphia Eagles safety Andre Waters in 2006, Chicago Bears safety Dave Duerson in 2011, and Atlanta Falcons safety Ray Easterling and San Diego Chargers linebacker Junior Seau in 2012—potentially due to chronic traumatic encephalopathy (CTE), a degenerative brain disease increasingly found in athletes with a history of repetitive head trauma.[7] Before Easterling committed suicide, he and six other former players had brought a lawsuit against the NFL that, after being consolidated with eighty other lawsuits in 2012, grew into the class-action case that was settled in 2015.[8]

Public concern surrounding these developments has trickled down through all levels of football. According to a widely cited report from ESPN, Pop Warner, the largest youth football organization in the United States, saw a 9.5 percent drop in participation between 2010 and 2012. This has been taken widely as a "sign that the concussion crisis that began in the NFL is having a dramatic impact at the lowest rungs of the sport."[9] Likely concerned about the youth/high school/college pipeline that supplies talent to the league, in 2012 the NFL launched a "Heads Up Football" program in partnership with USA Football, a youth football governing body funded and staffed by the league.[10] As part of the Heads Up program, USA Football runs clinics aimed at teaching parents and coaches tackling techniques that (they argue) take the head out of harm's way. The organization runs television advertisements that especially target mothers, reassuring them that youth tackle football can be made safe with proper technique. Many commentators, including former NFL players and coaches, have criticized the campaign as propaganda, calling into question the very idea of "safe tackling."[11]

Dissent over NFL safety and publicity programs is now common among retired players. Former Dallas Cowboys quarterback Troy Aikman said in a 2011 interview with HBO that the league was "at a crossroads" and would possibly look back on this "period of greed" and its "missteps" regarding head injury as the beginning of its demise as the United States' most popular sport.[12] Aikman's voice carried considerable weight. He was a Hall of Fame inductee and a longtime color commentator for the Fox network's NFL broadcasts who had suffered multiple concussions during his playing career. Aikman is also one of several retired players who have argued against youth participation in recent years, stating that he would not "encourage [his own son] to go play football, in light of what we are learning about head injuries."[13] President Barack Obama expressed the same sentiment in a 2013 interview with the *New Republic*, saying that if he had a son he would "have to think long and hard before I let him play football." Former Baltimore Ravens safety Ed Reed applauded the president's comments, which hinted at the national status of the debate over football safety. Reed added, "I am not forcing football on my son. . . . All I can say is, 'Son, I played football so you don't have to.'"[14] The question "Would you allow your son to play football?" is now routinely asked of current and former players and coaches in news stories. Many say no.

Predictions about the NFL's death vary, but there are a few consistent themes. First and most generally, commentators suggest that publicity surrounding the active cover-up of evidence about football-related brain trauma (more on this below) will be too much for even the league's formidable public-relations machinery to handle. This prediction relates to both the cover-up *and* the evidence. As Fred Nance, an adviser to the Cleveland Browns put it, the controversy over head injury is a "cultural IED [improvised explosive device] . . . exploding in the middle of the business of the NFL."[15] Michael Kaplan, a lawyer who represents clients with brain trauma, argued that no amount of marketing could deflect attention from the NFL's past or convince parents that the game could be made safe: "Simply put . . . [f]ootball is a concussion delivery system."[16]

Second, commentators predict that the NFL's talent-supply pipeline could dwindle as parents learn more about the dangers of football and decide that the sport is too risky for their children. *Grantland* writer Jonah Lehrer argues, for example: "If the sport of football ever dies, it will die from the outside in," beginning with "unpaid high school athletes playing on Friday nights . . . with nervous parents reading about brain trauma, with doctors warning about the physics of soft tissue smashing into hard bone."[17] Sport news is now full of anecdotal reports of youth and high school football coaches worried that parents' fears might shut down the "feeder system" that sustains their programs.[18] Some localities have decided to shut down their youth tackle football programs, even in conservative states where the sport is especially popular.[19] Many observers see parents' concerns as leading football down the same road as boxing, where the sport becomes so associated with brain injury (e.g., punch drunkenness, dementia) that the well-to-do withdraw and leave football to socioeconomically marginalized players brutalizing one another for the entertainment of privileged spectators.[20]

Third, some commentators argue that lawsuits will be the NFL's undoing. *Grantland* writers Kevin Grier and Tyler Cowen maintain, for example, that the "most plausible route to the death of football starts with liability suits." Concussions are being reported increasingly at the college and high school levels; if ex-players win judgments, according to Grier and Cowen, college and high school programs may not be able to retain liability coverage, and coaches and team physicians may have to worry about their own financial exposure.[21] Lawsuits have also exposed, and may continue to reveal, the NFL's denial of a link between football and traumatic brain injury, a strategy that has drawn frequent comparisons to Big Tobacco. Perhaps the NFL will, like the tobacco industry, have to fight for economic, legal, and popular survival as decades of cover-ups and misdirection come to light.[22]

The NFL has a tendency to recreate its past in such moments of crisis, to revisit origins as a reservoir for idealized memory. In 1963 Commissioner Pete Rozelle established NFL Properties to gain internal control over licensing, merchandising, and community outreach. Travis Vogan notes that NFL Properties' primary mission was "not to generate revenue, but to shape the league's image and broaden its circulation."[23] Rozelle incorporated NFL Films as the league's in-house production company in 1964 for similar reasons: to serve as "a promotional vehicle to glamorize the game and present it in its best light."[24] In addition to employing in-house resources, the NFL has worked with entertainment industry directors, producers, and production companies in an ongoing effort to craft and control a mythic account of the league's history. As Vogan argues, the NFL's rise as "the most visible and profitable sports organization" in the United States was marked by "racial tensions, labor discord, violence, and other unsavory elements" that the league has since worked to sanitize in official accounts of its past.[25]

What the NFL offers through mythic versions of its past is a historical template that it can refresh as a resource for regular brand maintenance and as a vehicle for responding to publicity crises. Historical and audiovisual evidence that does not fit either of these missions can be either ignored or appropriated in order to authenticate a nostalgic version of the past.[26] This means that commemorative texts produced by the NFL (like those by other powerful sport organizations) tend to discourage critical reflection on how present injustices are rooted in long-standing political and economic structures.[27] Yet even for an institution like the NFL, which has invested heavily in maintaining its telling of events as the official version, the traces and residues left by historical conflicts threaten to exceed ideological control.[28]

This is, I believe, the problem that the NFL faces regarding traumatic brain injury. Accordingly, I argue in this chapter that the possibilities of the NFL's death can be understood in light of the league's tendency to revisit its beginnings. In more general terms, I view the NFL as an example of how sacred origins might serve not only as reservoirs for idealized memory but also as scenes of foundational injustice. Origins uniquely authenticate the past in the present by creating essential meaning around the genesis of a culture or institution. To revisit origins is to elevate fundamental matters of collective identity. This comes with an inherent risk: perpetual return to idealized beginnings might expose the discontinuities and corruptions of an institution's rise, resulting in a gradual and condemning retelling of its official history.

I am not interested in building a forecast model for whether the NFL will die or survive. The more intriguing question, in my estimation, is whether the league can any longer reinvent its past without the risk of dredging up yet more evidence of an essential violence that not only tinges the visual spectacle of colliding bodies but also brings into visibility *around head injury* a larger constellation of unjust policies regarding labor, health, and safety. To address this question I turn to the NFL's official origin story, the famous 1958 championship game between the Baltimore Colts and New York Giants. My primary textual focus is ESPN's fiftieth-anniversary commemorative special *The Greatest Game Ever Played*, which aired for the first time on December 13, 2008. I read this and other fiftieth-anniversary commemorations in the context of the political and economic tensions that shaped league policies proximate to 1958 and 2008. Combining an understanding of how television shapes attitudes toward the present with a critical perspective on origins, I demonstrate how textual conflicts in commemorations of the 1958 championship game point to the reinforcement of present-day labor injustices, especially retired players' struggles for long-term pension, health-care, and disability benefits. These struggles reveal deep divides between retired players and the NFL and NFL Players Association (NFLPA, the league players' union) that the league has historically sublimated into images of generational indebtedness and harmony. Some of the players who participated in the 1958 championship game have been the victims of these policies, revealing how the league's original moment of commercial ascendance was simultaneous with its undermining of players' collective bargaining rights. My hope is that by bracketing the story of the traumatic brain injury crisis around the 1958 origin point and the 2008 fiftieth-anniversary commemoration, I can locate two moments of particularly concentrated historical, economic, and political production as well as the important labor and publicity practices that bridged these moments.

I support my argument in four parts. First, I outline a critical approach to understanding the 1958 championship game as an origin story. Second, I analyze the historical antagonisms that emerge out of fiftieth-anniversary commemorations of the 1958 championship game as a way of contemplating the NFL's death in light of its birth. Third, I take leave of ESPN's commemorative special to consider how the practices of NFL disability and scientific committees shaped the brain injury crisis. Finally, I consider how the problems of memory and representation that condensed around the league's origins might define its future.

The Greatest Game Ever Played
and the Problem of Origins

Journalist Phil Patton begins his book *Razzle-Dazzle: The Curious Marriage of Television and Professional Football* with a representative vision of the modern NFL being born on television:

> John Unitas dropped back quickly with the ball, held it poised at his ear for a brief, scanning moment, and then, with the quick flicking motion so familiar to his watchers, released the pass. Unitas's hand turned over in his characteristic sweeping follow-through and Raymond Berry took the pass twenty yards downfield.
>
> This was the moment when pro football began its reign as the country's favorite television sport; it can be defined that exactly.[29]

Here Patton describes a dramatic moment in the 1958 NFL Championship Game between the Baltimore Colts and the New York Giants, during the first sudden-death overtime period in the history of professional football. The Colts would score the game-winning touchdown on this drive. Soon after, *Sports Illustrated* called the 1958 championship "the best football game ever played," a label that would eventually be fixed as "The Greatest Game Ever Played" and imagined almost universally by sport historians and journalists as the moment the NFL was born as a commercial empire.[30]

Players participating in the 1958 championship game included present and future greats like Roosevelt Brown, Rosey Grier, Frank Gifford, Sam Huff, Emlen Tunnell, Mel Triplett, Andy Robustelli, and Pat Summerall for the Giants and Johnny Unitas, Raymond Berry, Jim Mutscheller, Lenny Moore, Alan Ameche, Art Donovan, Jim Parker, Ordell Braase, Bill Pellington, and Gino Marchetti for the Colts.[31] The Giants offense was coached by Vince Lombardi, who a few years later would build one of the greatest dynasties in NFL history as head coach of the Green Bay Packers. Eventually the Super Bowl trophy would be named after Lombardi, and he would become an icon of masculine leadership in nearly every sector of U.S. society. Tom Landry coached the Giants defense and would himself build a legendary dynasty as the head coach of the Dallas Cowboys. The Colts head coach, Weeb Ewbank, would win the 1958 championship game and later coach the New York Jets to one of the greatest upsets in championship history as they defeated the Baltimore Colts in Super Bowl III. Super Bowl III would encourage an eventual merger between the NFL and the American Football League (AFL), a defining moment in the NFL's economic rise.

The 1958 championship game was broadcast to around forty-five million people, at that point the largest audience to ever watch a televised professional football game. The capture of the game's dramatic turns by television cameras shaped what many football fans and writers perceive as a moment of fateful historical timing, an *original* revelation in the U.S. sport cultural experience. As journalist Mark Bowden writes in his 2008 commemoration *The Best Game Ever*, "Given the game's inherent appeal and its neat fit with TV, pro football was bound to click at some point with the American public. This was that moment."[32] Patton summarizes: "Never did medium and message operate more closely together" than in football and television's conjoined historical rise as forms of entertainment.[33]

As I argued in Chapter 3, televisual capture imbues live sporting events with metaphysical weight, focusing the ideological and social value of bearing witness to a moment of revelation. The idea that the 1958 championship game brought an audience of millions and the heroics of the game together at *precisely the right time* (both at the apex of a rising television culture and during a prime-time slot) is a fundamentally televisual fantasy, conflating the image of a fateful historical opening with the capture of television cameras. The NFL's origin event is thus a story about televisual witnessing that arranges elements of fate, timing, and skill in ways that depict the league's rise as both engineered and ordained. Bowden, for example, depicts the afternoon of the 1958 championship game as teetering on a historical edge between eternity and irrelevance in a moment of great risk:

> Today's kickoff at two o'clock meant that the game's finish might spill into early evening, into the promised land of prime time, the sweet spot of TV programming, when more ears and eyes were focused on the same thing than in the entire history of humankind. If the game were close, and exciting, it might creep into this national hearth, when the multitudes switched on their TVs for Sunday night viewing, the most valuable time slot of the week. If even a small portion of those who tuned in liked what they saw . . . interest could soar. A blowout, one of those games that peaked early and then ground to a predictable finish, would have the opposite effect. It could be a disaster.
>
> But this game would be no disaster. It was about to ignite.[34]

Bowden's image of television creating an opening full of historical potential testifies to its privileged access to live ruptures in ordinary time.[35] The NFL has persistently defined its present and selectively forgotten its past in terms of these ruptures, with the 1958 championship game serving as a representative model. Particularly important for the NFL is the capacity to dissociate the two-dimensional celluloid heroes the league routinely recalls from the past, in film and televisual imagery, from the present-day, material, and broken bodies of these same players who have been affected by unjust league policies. It is television's selective capacity for capture, recovery, and replay that allows us to fantasize a straight line from the live energies of an origin event to the needs and desires of our own moment. As intense concentrations of essential historical meaning, origin stories represent especially powerful resources from which institutional leaders can invent an imagined purity. But origins might also contain an institution's founding sins, a taint of barbarism that transmits through all of its succeeding history.[36]

As Joanne Wright suggests, origin stories "serve a heuristic purpose" by authorizing possibilities for future political action, legitimating hierarchical relations, and shaping contexts for citizenship and identity, all functions deeply implicated with power and "the politics of the present."[37] Origins represent the desire for an essentially pure beginning that can be revisited and refreshed to cleanse the sins of succeeding history. Edward Said argues that origin stories reveal how humans have a powerful, even "primordial . . . need for unity, a need to apprehend an otherwise dispersed number of circumstances and to put them in some sort of telling order, sequential, moral, or logical," that makes sense of the present in terms of a beginning.[38]

To reiterate the question I pose in this chapter: Can this cycle of crisis and original return continue without the occurrence of a fundamental shift for the NFL, from a long period of effective brand protection to a dredging-up of founding sins? Michel Foucault argues that "what is found at the historical beginning of things is not the inviolable identity of their origin; it is the dissension of other things. It is disparity."[39] In promising a recovery of pure beginnings, origins rhetoric points to "the excesses of its own speech," revealing how an origin moment always "lies at a place of inevitable loss," a starting point for assured disappointment.[40] Certainly origin stories can be cleansed of their contradictory details, and they frequently are. Yet audiovisual capture records traces of suppressed conflict that can break through even the most carefully edited surfaces, and this is especially relevant for the NFL's approach to historical production. In *The Greatest Game Ever Played* ESPN directs critical awareness away from long-term health and retiree issues, and from related issues of labor struggle, by depicting affectionate cross-generational connections between past and present players and coaches. Yet there are important moments in the commemoration that hint at a deeper, more fractured context for both the original 1958 game and its fiftieth-anniversary celebration in 2008. My analysis focuses first on ESPN's carefully designed version of the league's rise before identifying fissures in its story of generational debt and sacrifice.

ESPN's The Greatest Game Ever Played: *1958/2008*

ESPN's fiftieth-anniversary commemoration of "The Greatest Game Ever Played" brings players from the Baltimore Colts and New York Giants who participated in the 1958 championship game together with present-day players and coaches from the Indianapolis Colts and New York Giants. The players and coaches watch clips of the 1958 championship in sets arranged to look like casual, domestic settings (e.g., home libraries, living rooms). The special is formatted around a repetitive pattern in which a clip of the game is shown, usually with audio of original radio broadcasts explaining the action, and then the former and present coaches and players discuss matters of cultural context or strategy in the clip. ESPN's primary emphasis is on cross-generational connection and the debt owed to the heroes of the 1958 championship game by current players, coaches, league officials, and fans.

In most commemorations of the 1958 championship game, televisuality and audiovisual capture serve as themes for imagining the possible historical loss of the game. This possibility is highlighted in moments of danger and contingency in which only by means of seemingly fated alignments of events does the game survive for replay in the present. The 1958 championship is elevated to the status of an origin moment in part because a number of disparate circumstances seem to fall into a logical order, forming a solid foundation for the entire history that proceeds. These same images of fate direct attention away from disparities in the NFL's origins by suggesting that the league rose due to forces that transcend base economics and politics.

The first step in understanding how the 1958 origin story suppresses historical conflict is to analyze how it conflates providence and visual capture. ESPN opens with a narration by anchor Chris Berman, who walks across the field in Yankee Stadium, the site of the 1958 championship game. Here at the beginning of the commemoration Berman connects the NFL's rise to televisuality. Against shots of film rolling through old projectors, Berman narrates the tribute's basic theme: the generation of great men who played in the 1958 championship game built a bridge to the current generation, who owe a debt of gratitude. In addition to this sense of cross-generational obligation, ESPN's documentary offers time as a continuous and linear progression within which present-day players act as surrogates for their forebears. Berman says:

The motion picture. It is how memories have been captured for more than a hundred years. It is how examples of true excellence are passed down from generation to generation. . . . To see the heights the NFL has reached, we see its path in the frames of history, a fifty-year-old title game like no other before or since. . . . Now for the first time, the legends who played in the game that put the NFL on the road to greatness watch the game with champions of today. And they'll see it as they've never seen it before. In color.[41]

Such an emphasis on television as a technology of historical capture and generational transport is vital to imagining the importance of the 1958 championship game in almost every commemoration. During Berman's opening narration, ESPN juxtaposes film images of modern-day Indianapolis Colts quarterback Peyton Manning with clips of legendary Baltimore Colts quarterback Johnny Unitas, and clips of the 2008 New York Giants defense with clips of New York Giants Hall of Fame linebacker Sam Huff. Here and throughout the special, ESPN emphasizes the historical coincidence that, in the two years leading into the fiftieth anniversary of the 1958 championship game, the very two franchises that had competed in The Greatest Game Ever Played won the Super Bowl: the Colts in 2007 and the Giants in 2008. The Colts franchise was infamously moved under cover of night in 1984 from Baltimore to Indianapolis (thus the name change), but ESPN does not concern itself with this, choosing instead to smooth the generational link by pairing Baltimore Colts players from 1958 with Indianapolis Colts players and coaches from 2008.

The coincidence of the 2007 and 2008 Super Bowls is one of several cross-generational alignments ESPN uses to craft a fated history. Berman notes that the original television broadcast was "lost to history" but that ESPN has "pieced together the game from various film archives." The idea that with the original television broadcast unavailable the game could have been permanently lost emphasizes the imagined stakes for present generations, who presumably need the 1958 championship game as a source of renewal and memory.[42]

Through a kind of archeological adventure, ESPN cobbled together film fragments discovered on dusty shelves, pulled radio broadcast fragments from the ether, and reconstituted the pieces as an authentic replay of the past. For years the only full recording that existed of the 1958 championship game was coaches' film in the NFL Films archive, which showed every play but from a distance.[43] Then, while John Dahl, the producer of ESPN's *The Greatest Game Ever Played*, was conducting an interview with Weeb Ewbank, he noticed in Ewbank's basement some old film canisters, one of which contained game film with thirty plays recorded by the Colts coaching staff.[44] The film, which was marred by dust and scratches, would be colorized by Legend Films for ESPN's commemoration. Against the possibility of permanent historical loss one is discouraged from considering how these found fragments might provide an incomplete or problematic rendering of the league's past: the very rarity of the film, discovered only by serendipity, suggests the sacredness of a nearly unrecoverable origin point.

Colorization was consistent with ESPN's focus on *updating* the game for present viewers through cross-generational connections. Dahl said he was motivated to do this after watching a special in which Legend Films colorized the 1960 Masters golf tournament. He noted, "It was important to me that it look authentic. . . . I believe it looks truly like it was shot in color in 1958."[45] Here Dahl grounds a fantasy of authentic recovery in contemporary televisual standards, inviting viewers to peek through the spectral veil of old and obscured black-and-white film to see the game in its original, "true" color. That this version of the game was unavailable to live television audiences in 1958 puts the contemporary viewer in a privileged position relative to the original game, situated somewhere between the live witnessing of people in the stands and the experience of viewers who saw the game through a glass darkly on black-and-white television sets.[46] As Neil Best of *Newsday* put it, colorization made the game "seem more tangible and less like a historic relic"—in other words, more authentic in present time.[47]

Throughout ESPN's special, and in most commemorations of the game, these recoveries are made all the more precious by reference to momentary contingencies of visual capture. For example, ESPN emphasizes at some length how Colts running back Alan Ameche's game-winning touchdown run in overtime was almost not recorded. Legendary photographer Neil Leifer, a participant in ESPN's special, captured Ameche's score in what became one of the most iconic photographs in U.S. sport history. Leifer was sixteen years old in 1958, an amateur photographer who by chance was in precisely the right place at the right time. In ESPN's special, Leifer describes a series of fortunate alignments of time and place. Ameche's score happened in the perfect light of dusk, providing "what in the film world you would call 'magic hour.'" On the previous play, Colts tight end Jim Mutscheller had nearly scored but instead went out of bounds at the one-yard-line. Looking back, Leifer understands this as the fateful origin of his own legacy: "Thank God [Mutscheller's catch] didn't go touchdown. Might have been the end of a career that hadn't begun." The Colts just happened to be headed in the direction of the end zone where Leifer was positioned. "Had it gone the other way," Leifer says, "I would've never . . . gotten the picture." Later, Leifer would build his legend photographing sport stars like

Muhammad Ali, but he understood the beginning of his career to be in this chance moment.

Ameche's winning touchdown run was itself almost lost to live television audiences. With the Colts at the Giants' eight-yard line in overtime, driving for the winning score, the power cable for NBC's broadcast was disconnected by a drunk fan who, according to a witness, swung on the cable "like Tarzan on his grapevine."[48] The plug was pulled right as the broadcast was going into a time-out, giving director Harry Coyle enough time to order an NBC employee on the field to delay the game by any means necessary. The employee (mistaken at the time by radio broadcasters as a fan) grabbed the ball and ran around for long enough to allow NBC's crew to restore the broadcast.[49]

These themes of risk, capture, and timing also defined players' personal ways of assigning meaning to the game. ESPN's commemoration focuses on several pass completions in overtime from Unitas to wide receiver Raymond Berry that put the Colts in position to win, and especially on the close relationship between Berry and Unitas, who would spend countless hours after practice throwing, catching, and discussing strategy down to the most minor detail. Berry would come to understand the Colts' victory as payoff for his obsessive work habits. Bowden writes that as Berry rushed off the field after the winning score, "he had no words yet for the feeling that overcame him in that moment," and he knew only that "he had been touched by something powerful and other. Maybe destiny, although the term was hackneyed." Later, Bowden explains, Berry had come to understand this as the fulfillment of years of hard work in "a moment that rewarded everything":

> Fate had delivered a moment that provided its worth, and not just in any game at any random point. It had come in the pivotal moment of the ultimate game of their careers. It had come on what was the most important play of his professional life. It was hard not to feel how spooky that was, and how wonderful. The timing . . . well, it went beyond just being good, or being lucky. He would come to see it eventually as the hand of God.[50]

Bowden's account perfectly summarizes the idea that the 1958 championship game was an origin moment constituted by fated temporal alignments. It is not just that Berry's hard work paid off but that it paid off at *precisely the right time.* To contest such a seemingly destined set of occurrences—the accidental discovery of coaches' lost film, a boy photographer in exactly the right place at the right time, a television producer running around like a madman to delay a broadcast—is to deny a representative joyfulness in sport histories, where apparent accidents seem revealed in present time as part of a larger plan. At the same time, accident and circumstance are dramatic antitheses to the planned, purposeful, and strategic decisions made by league officials proximate to The Greatest Game Ever Played. These decisions are part of a fuller history of labor inequity that is becoming more and more irrepressible in contemporary commemorations.

Rewriting the NFL's Origin Story

Hannah Arendt argues that origins "must be intimately connected with violence," that "no beginning could be made without violence, without violating."[51] René Girard maintains similarly in his book *Violence and the Sacred* that all religious communities are founded on an original violence, designed to suppress or purge the community's own "internal violence"—the "dissensions, rivalries, jealousies, and quarrels" that threaten its "social fabric."[52] For Girard, much as for Kenneth Burke, this purgation is achieved through the sacrifice of a surrogate victim, a scapegoat, upon whom the community's ills are ritually loaded and eliminated.[53] Whatever form founding violence takes, it relates, as Wright argues, to "the desire to *make political use* of origins" in order to suppress formative injustices "or evade politics altogether," even as origin stories "are, themselves, deeply political." When a commemorative special seeks to idealize origins or a critical theorist seeks to deconstruct them, these are both political maneuvers related to "the politics of the present"; the power of origins thinking can be leveraged in multiple directions.[54]

The NFL's violence is not primarily built around scapegoating, but it does advance sacrificial notions in at least a few senses: in the form of an original humility, an altar upon which now-retired players paved the way for present-day stars by playing their part at the beginning of an evolutionary arc; in the form of league efforts to undermine players' rights to collectively bargain for greater health, safety, and retirement protections; and finally, in a newly emergent linkage between football-related head trauma, degenerative brain disease, and the NFL's cover-up of related scientific evidence. To borrow loosely from Girard, then, the NFL's present-day relations "emanate" from its violent beginnings, and it is to these beginnings that the league returns in times of "discord." The problem the NFL faces is that while the details of its founding violence have been largely invisible to contemporary generations, an "actual break" from that violence never occurred. For this reason, the league's transgressions "can always stage a stunning, catastrophic comeback," and this possibility is highlighted in contemplations of the NFL's death.[55] To borrow from Arendt, the league cannot suppress the truth of any origin story: "In the beginning was a crime."[56]

By giving a voice to retirees from the 1958 championship game, ESPN also grants viewers at least partial access to historical tensions that hint at an alternative version of the NFL's origins. Within the boundaries set by ESPN's commemoration, these moments are primarily critical prompts, temporary cracks in a carefully edited façade. Yet the fiftieth anniversary of The Greatest Game Ever Played also marks an important alteration to league history, as events leading up to and through 2008—including congressional hearings in 2007 and a mounting publicity crisis surrounding the scientific evidence on football-related head trauma—would in 2009 lead the NFL to confirm publicly for the first time that there was a relationship between football and brain disease.

The fiftieth-anniversary commemoration provides, then, an opportune moment for revising the NFL's origin story. I begin this section by pointing to problems in ESPN's depiction of salary disparities between players from 1958 and 2008 as a product of cross-generational sacrifice. I highlight, by way of contrast, the context of the late 1950s NFL as an origin point for labor struggles that have ever since positioned league owners in a superior bargaining position to the NFLPA and retired players on issues that have shaped the head trauma crisis, including long-term health-care, retirement, and disability benefits.

Then, I take leave of ESPN's commemoration to establish the labor struggles of the late 1950s as the foundation for present-day divisions between active and retired players. The ESPN special provides only limited hints at this context, as salary discrepancies between 1958 and 2008 are but one factor. Less conspicuous is the fact that as the NFL and NFLPA negotiated more favorable shares of rising television revenues, retiree issues were actively marginalized. This was especially true when it came to long-term health-care and disability compensation, issues related directly to traumatic brain injury since former players typically become symptomatic in their retirement years.

We Had Nothing, and We Are Not Happy

ESPN's efforts to connect past and present generations of players, coaches, and journalists as they view the 1958 championship game both idealize and call attention to economic disparities between current and retired NFL players. While these disparities are mostly sublimated into images of generational sacrifice, ESPN's special is also patterned with economic contrasts that point to the NFL's history of labor inequities during both the original context of the late 1950s and the fiftieth-anniversary celebration in 2008. While in no way does ESPN's presentation encourage viewers to look further into these inequities, the conversational format does introduce tensions between past and present interlocutors that hint at suppressed resentments and unspoken conflicts. Some viewers might recognize here the traces of decades of bitter and well-publicized labor disputes. These moments of tension demonstrate how televisuality captures multiple and contradictory historical currents as they run through a commemorative text, providing the means for both pursuing and subverting progressive memory practices.[57]

From the beginning of ESPN's *The Greatest Game Ever Played*, participants discuss the gap in players' and coaches' salaries from 1958 to 2008. For example, in a conversation with current Indianapolis Colts defensive lineman Dwight Freeney, Baltimore Colts defensive lineman Alex Sandusky tells him that in his first year as a "regular" player he made $5,000. Freeney asks how much a house was back then, and Sandusky says gratefully, "You could have bought one of them row houses in Baltimore for forty-five-hundred, I mean a nice row house." ESPN cuts to old, grainy film depictions of middle-class citizens washing the steps and sidewalks of their row houses, inviting the viewer to consider the economic, cultural, and physical proximity of fans and players in the late 1950s. Later, retired Colts running back Lenny Moore tells current Giants running back Brandon Jacobs: "If you made eleven, twelve thousand a year, we were happy. If you were all pro, you could count on a thousand-dollar raise, and man, we thought we were rich." Sandusky tells Freeney about holding down a job and having to go to work the day after playing a game: "On Monday morning I was on the production floor, seven o'clock. I didn't get much work done, but I was there. They expected to see me." Retired Giants kicker Pat Summerall tells current Colts kicker Adam Vinatieri that he "taught school in the off season" and "had a watermelon farm in Florida." All of these scenes depict a familiar story grounded in the mythos of the American Dream, in which current players are afforded an opportunity to thank their forebears for doing their part in the natural arc of generational sacrifice.

Through its conversational format ESPN advances a history of cross-generational debt, wherein athletes and coaches from the 2008 Colts and Giants teams trace the genesis of their own wealth and fame back to the humble origins of their 1958 counterparts. In an exchange between Jacobs and Moore, for example, Jacobs says, "We're playing this game the way we're playing it now because of you guys starting for us back then," and Moore nods in agreement. Similarly, Freeney says to Sandusky in one segment: "This is where it all started, you guys paved the way for us." At the end of ESPN's special, Sandusky turns to Freeney and, grinning, talks about how the 1958 game made Freeney rich. Both laugh, and Freeney says, "[I] appreciate that." An exchange between 1958 Giants defensive lineman Rosey Grier and current Giants offensive tackle Chris Snee humorously and harmlessly hints at the tensions related to salary gaps: Grier puts Snee on the spot by asking, "Aren't you embarrassed at the money you guys make and the money we made?" He then laughs. Snee smiles and says, "Embarrassed? No. I'm thankful for you guys paving the way."

ESPN's image of the NFL as a fraternity that transcends generational boundaries covers over labor disputes that originated proximate to the 1958 championship game and continued to raise bitter tensions between retired players' groups and the NFL and NFLPA around the time of the 2008 fiftieth-anniversary commemoration. It is worth pausing here to take a closer look at the labor struggles that shaped the NFL of the 1950s, in order to establish the historical problems that ESPN's commemoration only hints at.

Commissioner Pete Rozelle, whose tenure began in 1960, is credited as the visionary who brought profit sharing and other parity measures to the NFL, creating a game with ideal competitive balance and shared wealth from television contracts. In his history of the NFL's commercial rise, journalist Mark Yost writes: "Rozelle, perhaps better than anyone, read the omens of the 1958 championship game; and he understood that television, more than being a mere adjunct to ticket sales, represented the key to future financial riches for the NFL and its owners."[58] The 1961 NFL owners' meetings paved the way for sharing the profits of television revenues between franchises, and a succession of lucrative television contracts followed. On January 10, 1962, CBS and the NFL signed a national contract for $4.65 million over two years. After the NFL merged fully with the AFL in 1970, earnings for national broadcasting rights grew exponentially, from $63 million in 1974 to a 2005 deal that secured about $3.75 billion a year in broadcasting rights through 2011.[59] In 2011, the NFL extended its contracts with Fox, NBC, and CBS through 2022 for an estimated average of $3 billion a year (a 60 percent increase over the previous agreement).[60]

From the standpoint of the early 2000s to the present, one can easily imagine the 1958 championship game as an embryonic origin point for the conjoined and cumulative rise of football and television in U.S. culture. Certainly this is the official narrative advanced by NFL productions and popular commemorative specials. In fact, it was during the 1950s—when players first began to organize for improved salary, pension, and health-care benefits—that the league developed strategies for undermining players' collective bargaining power. Resulting labor disputes reveal that low player salaries in the late 1950s were the product not of necessary generational sacrifice but of the contrivances of league officials. The moment of the NFL's emergence as the United States' most popular televised sport drama was simultaneous with the initiation of a decades-long strategy for limiting revenue sharing, safe labor protections, and health and retirement benefits.

The NFL has been successful throughout its history in limiting players' bargaining power by reducing and controlling competition for their services.

In 1950 the All-America Football Conference (AAFC) and NFL merged, and nearly one-third of players lost their jobs as leadership reduced the league from eighteen to twelve teams. Salaries dropped and then stagnated as a large group of players competed for fewer spots. By the late 1950s NFL salaries were lagging behind owners' revenue increases and, as Craig Coenen writes, "[after] accounting for inflation, players' real wages were actually less in 1959 than they had been ten years earlier."[61] Players formed the NFLPA in 1956 in an effort to gain leverage. But for the next few years, owners refused to formally recognize the union and gave in only to minimal demands, primarily with the hope of quelling collective bargaining efforts.[62]

The NFLPA succeeded in gaining minor concessions in 1957, but these related to a publicity effort by the league, which was participating at the time in congressional hearings on antitrust issues pertaining to sport. The Supreme Court had ruled in 1957 that the NFL was subject to antitrust law. The decision prompted congressional hearings on antitrust law and sport in July 1957, at which NFL owners were criticized for refusing to recognize or negotiate with the players' union. During his second round of testimony in front of the judiciary committee, Commissioner Bert Bell (whose tenure lasted from 1945 to 1959) announced recognition of the NFLPA in order to address damage to the league's image. He also announced that the league would meet NFLPA demands for a $5,000 minimum salary, an injury clause guaranteeing pay to players hurt on the field, and pay for preseason games.[63] None of these concessions substantially improved players' work conditions. In addition, Bell recognized the NFLPA without prior approval from the owners and could not secure enough votes to make the recognition official. Bell's actions did, however, prove instrumental in the NFL's antitrust efforts.[64]

In response to the NFL's concession to NFLPA demands, the House Judiciary Antitrust Subcommittee put forward in January 1958 a bill that would grant professional sport leagues limited antitrust exemptions.[65] Sport antitrust legislation failed to gain support several times until finally, in 1961, President Kennedy signed into law the Sports Broadcasting Act, which created an exemption from antitrust law that allowed NFL teams to package their TV rights into a single contract and to sell that package to networks.[66]

Given the importance of television to the NFL's cultural and economic rise, the Sports Broadcasting Act is often viewed as the most important legal victory in league history. The legislation has provided owners a consistently dominant bargaining position, as the collective power to dictate terms for television contracts means control over the league's primary source of revenue. That power has helped the league to fend off and absorb competing leagues (thus limiting players' options for employment), to dictate terms for revenue sharing, and to build up substantial monetary reserves to cushion against losses from player strikes.[67] Thus, immediately before and immediately follow-ing The Greatest Game Ever Played, the NFL established the foundation for delimiting players' collective bargaining power. As Coenen writes, from 1958 to 1968 "NFL owners satisfied just one NFLPA demand: a pension plan"— and only after the threat of a lawsuit. At the time, "unionization . . . provided little more than a nuisance."[68] During this same time period, the NFL's tele-vision value grew substantially. The $4.65 million contract that the league signed with CBS for the 1962–1963 season increased to $28.2 million for 1964–1965, and to $75.2 million for 1966–1969. Player salaries did not keep pace. For 1962–1963 the average player salary was $20,000, and this increased only to $21,000 for 1964–1965 and $22,000 for 1966–1969. By the end of the 1960s, as Michael Schiavone notes, "annual television income per team increased by $1.27 million" while "player salaries increased by only $2,000."[69]

This gap between television revenue and salary increases punctures the veneer of generational debt advanced in *The Greatest Game Ever Played*. At one point in the tribute ESPN uses a radio replay to tell the audience that the winners of the 1958 championship game would receive about $5,000 per player while the losers would receive slightly under $3,000. Immediately after, Brandon Jacobs begins to tell Lenny Moore about per-game playoff bonuses for current players; as Jacobs is about to reveal the figure, Moore says, "Don't tell me." Former Giants running back Frank Gifford asks current Giants head coach Tom Coughlin what the Giants received for winning the 2008 Super Bowl. Coughlin tells him, after a knowing hesitation, that players earned a $175,000 postseason bonus. Gifford responds irritably, "Our whole team didn't make that."

In his book commemorating the fiftieth anniversary, *The Glory Game*, Gifford addresses the connection between television and the rise of the league at the core of the 1958 championship origin story and its real meaning for player salaries at the time: "That game began to convince sports editors to start assigning writers to football teams. . . . Once we had actual beat writers, and extensive TV coverage, the true exposure began. . . . Not that it mattered much to us. Salaries didn't explode; they still crawled upward, by a thousand or so each season."[70] Gifford's open frustrations suggest that the resentments of retirees from the late 1950s toward the current generation of NFL and NFLPA leadership are intense enough to break the normal decorum associ-ated with commemorative specials. Those players who translated their role in the 1958 championship game into financial success did so *after* their playing days were over. Gifford and Summerall, for example, became famous broad-casters as the NFL grew commercially. Gifford was one of Howard Cosell's partners through the heyday of *Monday Night Football*, which lasted until the early 1980s.[71] Summerall paired with former Oakland Raiders head coach

John Madden for twenty-one years, forming one of the most popular commentating partnerships in the history of televised sport.

In the context of late 1950s labor relations, the players from the 1958 Colts and Giants teams, as well as their peers from other clubs, had no real chance at a significant share of growing television revenues. One especially important reason was the so-called "Rozelle Rule." Named informally after Commissioner Rozelle, the rule was designed to stop the creation of an informal free agency system, implemented after San Francisco 49ers wide receiver R. C. Owens played out his option year in 1962 and then signed with the Baltimore Colts for the next season.[72] In a long-standing practice comparable to Major League Baseball's infamous reserve clause, the NFL allowed teams to invoke a final option year in a player's contract when they wanted to retain rights to that player for an additional season. In principle any player who completed his option year would be free the next year to sign with another team, but the owners regarded the option as automatically and continuously renewable.[73] Owens's move was a threat to this convention. In response, the commissioner required franchises acquiring a player to compensate (in the form of players, draft picks, or money) that player's former team. The commissioner had unilateral control over the form and amount of compensation, and uncertainty over the severity of costs dissuaded most owners from signing away players from other teams. The Rozelle Rule was in place from 1963 to 1976; during that period, 174 players completed their option year but only 34 signed with a different team the following season. With so much control over players' mobility, owners were able to depress salaries and maximize profits.[74]

Relations between active players and owners would, however, change over the coming years. Through a series of strikes and renegotiated collective bargaining agreements (CBAs) between 1968 and 1992, the NFLPA repeatedly failed to secure a full-fledged free agency system, in part because of the consolidation of owners' financial and legal power but also because of a lack of unity and coordination among the players. In 1993 the NFL and NFLPA finally negotiated terms for a free agency system on the grounds that the players would also accept a salary cap tied to revenues. From 1993 to 2006 player salaries and league revenues increased substantially. Even though negotiations over a new collective bargaining agreement in 2006 were at times hostile, neither the NFL nor the NFLPA wanted a publicized labor fight to disrupt the league's rising popularity and profitability. The fact that active players and owners alike were making more money than ever held together a period of relative labor peace.[75]

Retirees and retiree advocates often trace denials of long-term healthcare and disability benefits back to this achievement of labor peace, when the increasing convergence of interests between active players (represented by the NFLPA) and the NFL led to the marginalization of retired players' needs. Tensions between retired and active players were especially publicized during the 2011 NFL lockout. In May 2008 (roughly seven months before the broadcast debut of ESPN's *The Greatest Game Ever Played*), NFL owners voted unanimously to opt out of the CBA negotiated in 2006, even though the agreement was not set to expire until 2011. The owners likely perceived that they could get the NFLPA to accept a lesser share of revenues and decreased labor costs.[76] The 2010 season was played without a salary cap, and in 2011 the NFLPA decertified itself as a union so that individual players could sue the NFL on antitrust grounds. The league responded by imposing a work stoppage. The 2011 lockout was resolved with a new ten-year CBA that guaranteed no work stoppages until 2021. In addition to agreements on revenue sharing, the new CBA emphasized health and safety through several measures, including lifetime eligibility for the NFL's health plan, reductions in full-contact practice periods, reductions in the length of offseason training programs, and greater financial protection for injured players.[77]

On the surface, these would seem positive changes for retirees. During the 2011 CBA negotiations, however, retired players struggled to gain access to talks and accused active players and league officials of negotiating with no consciousness of their obligations to the past.[78] The 2011 CBA did include between $900 million and $1 billion of additional funds for retirement benefits, including a new "Legacy Fund" of $620 million dedicated to pensions for retirees who had played before 1993.[79] But retiree advocates insisted that the agreement changed nothing and that the NFL and NFLPA had sold them out. Shortly before the NFL and NFLPA signed the new CBA, a group of retired players filed a class-action lawsuit against the NFLPA, claiming that the players, along with the NFL, were "conspiring to depress the amounts of pension and disability benefits to be paid for former NFL players in order to maximize the salaries and benefits to current NFL players." Judy Battista wrote in the *New York Times* that the complaint underscored "the fissures between retired and current players, some of which have simmered for years."[80] Relations between active and retired players were especially strained in the years preceding the 2011 CBA due to controversies over the league's disability claims compensation system.

"Delay, Deny, and Hope We Die": The Disability Initial Claims Committee and Retirement Board

Contemporary news stories about retired players struggling with chronic pain, mobility issues, mental illness, and dementia elevate disability as a particularly powerful, embodied inscription of NFL labor, safety, and health-care injustices. As I emphasize below, scientific evidence of a link between football and degenerative conditions has become so popularized that retirees' struggles project a reimagined future for anyone who plays the game. That is the view from the present state of affairs, but it is a relatively recent perspective: the fact that retirees' health problems are not merely the products of impersonal, apolitical forces (e.g., the ravages of time) was covered over for a long period.[81] As revealed during 2007 congressional hearings, the NFL had designed its disability compensation system, from the earliest days of its rise to power, primarily to reject retirees' claims. The system was built around two committees: the Disability Initial Claims Committee (DICC) and the Retirement Board (RB). The activities of these committees complemented those of the Mild Traumatic Brain Injury committee (MTBI) to structure the NFL's larger machinery for denying any connection between football and long-term degenerative conditions: the DICC and RB fought retirees seeking compensation for permanent disability, while the MTBI issued industry-based scientific claims about the risks of football-related head trauma. Together, these committees represented a comprehensive strategy to contest connections between football and degenerative health problems on legal, scientific, and popular fronts. The MTBI is the subject of the next section. Here, I focus on the DICC and RB.

The NFL's retirement plan has existed since 1962. Initially it was called the Bert Bell NFL Player Retirement Plan, but after a series of CBA renegotiations, it merged in 1993 with the Pete Rozelle NFL Player Retirement Plan. In 1998 the Bell/Rozelle Plan was amended to include benefits for "total and permanent disability as a result of psychological/psychiatric disorder," including when a disorder "is caused by or relates to a head injury (or injuries) sustained by a Player arising out of League football activities (e.g., repetitive concussions)."[82] Until the DICC and RB became the subject of congressional hearings in 2007, however, their existence and function were relatively unknown. Alan Schwartz at the *New York Times* began reporting on head injury in football in 2006, after Andre Waters committed suicide. Credited often as the "gadfly" who first publicized the emerging crisis, Schwartz has since outlined the interconnected activities of the DICC, RB, and MTBI.[83] These activities were especially condensed and popularized by ESPN investigative reporters Mark Fainaru-Wada (who broke the Barry Bonds steroid scandal story) and Steve Fainaru (who won a Pulitzer Prize for his reporting on the war in Iraq) in their book *League of Denial* in 2013, and in a PBS *Frontline* special based on the book in the same year.[84] Prior to such coverage, the NFL had rehearsed its legal and medical approaches to denying the existence of football-related brain disease largely within the insulated confines of the disability claims process.

As detailed in 2007 hearings before the House Judiciary Subcommittee on Commercial and Administrative Law, disability applications first went to the two-person DICC (staffed by one representative each from the NFLPA and NFL), then moved on to the RB (staffed by three members appointed by the NFL and three by the NFLPA).[85] In 2007 the RB was composed of two team owners, one team president, a sport agent, two retired players, and no medical doctors or disability experts. The RB did not talk directly to players applying for disability benefits or their physicians, and while the board could request medical reports, it also had full discretion to accept or reject medical evidence. The hearings revealed that out of 7,900 retired players, only 317 were receiving disability payments, and that neither the NFL nor the NFLPA was keeping records on players who retired because of injury. As former Minnesota Vikings offensive lineman Brent Boyd summarized in his testimony, the RB's approach was "delay, deny and hope we die."[86] When asked about including doctors in the review process, Commissioner Roger Goodell said he was "not opposed" to the idea, but congressional pressure produced relatively small changes: the NFL added a medical doctor to advise the initial claims committee, doctor panels in major metropolitan areas so players could see a specialist more easily, and a claims specialist to help players through the application process.[87]

Many players have suffered, and continue to suffer, under the NFL's disability claims system, but perhaps the most telling representative of league priorities is former Baltimore Colts quarterback Johnny Unitas, who died in 2002 barely able to use his right hand. Throughout ESPN's *The Greatest Game Ever Played* and in almost any tribute to that championship game, Unitas is the main character, a one-person summary of the presumably more humble cultural and economic context of football in 1958. For example, immediately after the 1958 championship, Unitas turned down an opportunity to appear on the *Ed Sullivan Show* so he could "go home with the guys." A few days later *SPORT* magazine recognized him as the game's most valuable player by giving him a Corvette, which he promptly sold for a station wagon.[88] A 2008 *Baltimore Sun* story recounted how New York Giants general manager Ernie Acorsi, who was sixteen years old when the 1958 championship was played, would call "his old friend" Unitas every year on the anniversary of the game as he drove past Yankee Stadium. Acorsi would ask, "You know what today is?" Unitas would respond, "No, I don't know." Acorsi would then say, "Come on, John. It's December 28," and Unitas would ask, "What's that?"[89] Unitas's habit of shrugging off all references to his legacy has often been taken as an open invitation to craft a usable, nostalgic past out of his accomplishments. It seems Unitas wanted nothing in return for his role in history; his reported forgetting of the meaning of December 28 suggests that his past is an unconditional gift, a burden-free offering of memory preserved in the two-dimensional heroics of televisual replay.

In fact, in his retirement years Unitas suffered from a disability caused by his years in football, and he was angered by the NFL's rejection of a claim he filed. As recounted in a 2001 *Sports Illustrated* article, "Johnny Unitas once owned the most dangerous right arm in the NFL. . . . Now Unitas cannot close the hand that made Raymond Berry famous."[90] Unitas took a hit to his elbow in a 1968 game against the Dallas Cowboys, and by the mid-1990s damage to the nerves that controlled his right hand and fingers made it impossible for him to grasp objects. Unitas's condition worsened into his retirement years. He said of his hand: "I have no strength in the fingers. I can't use a hammer or saw around the house. I can't button buttons. I can't use zippers. Very difficult to tie shoes. I can't brush my teeth with it, because I can't hold a brush. I can't hold a fork with the right hand. I can't pick this phone up. . . . You give me [a] full cup of coffee, and I can't hold it. I can't comb my hair."[91] Unitas applied to the league for disability compensation but was turned down because he did not apply by age fifty-five (his condition did not manifest until age sixty), the league was already paying him a pension of $4,000 a month, and, in the league's opinion, Unitas was not "totally and permanently disabled."[92] During the 2007 congressional hearings Sandy Unitas, Johnny Unitas's widow, testified to her husband's disability, remarking, "My husband made the NFL what it is today, and when he went to the NFL for disability benefits, he was rejected." Former Miami Dolphins running back Mercury Morris suggested that by denying Unitas's disability claim, the league was trying to send a message to retirees: "They were saying, 'If we can do that to Johnny Unitas, we can do it to anybody.'"[93] Retiree advocacy groups have responded by pointing to cases like Unitas's as evidence that greed and callousness motivate the NFL and NLPA in their dealings with retirees.[94] One of these groups, Fourth and Goal Unites, was founded by retired Baltimore Colts players in part to extend the advocacy efforts of 1958 championship game participants, like Unitas and Mutscheller, as well as other Colts alumni who were told by the NFL and NFLPA in 2005 that they had no position from which to bargain for pension and disability rights because they were not union members.[95]

The organizing struggles of players from the 1958 championship game are only one indication of long-standing and often bitter divisions between retirees from the 1940s and 1950s and present-day NFL and NFLPA leadership. In the years leading up to the fiftieth anniversary of The Greatest Game Ever Played, those divisions were coming to a head. NFLPA executive director Gene Upshaw was especially being criticized for failing to help retired players struggling with severe health and financial troubles. Upshaw was the longest-serving executive director of the NFLPA in league history (from 1983 until his death in 2008), and in the latter part of his tenure the NFL made some meaningful improvements in retirement benefits. Of particular note, the league increased pension pay for pre-1977 players in 2002. The increase was $110 million in total, and went to around fourteen hundred retirees who played before 1977 (around eight hundred of whom played before 1959). Among those eight hundred, the minimum pension credit was doubled, from $100 to $200 a month for each year played. Pension experts claimed that this kind of retroactive increase—going back so many years—was unprecedented in U.S. labor history. Raymond Berry, who starred in The Greatest Game Ever Played, wrote to the NFL and praised the league for remembering and appreciating players from his era.[96] Also noteworthy, in 2007 the NFL started a $10 million program to pay for joint replacements, cardiovascular screenings, and assisted-living costs for retired players struggling financially and physically, an apparent acknowledgment of advocacy groups' complaints about insufficient health-care support for retirees who had played for low salaries during an era when medical care—especially for traumatic head injury—was unsophisticated.[97]

For many retirees however, these and similar measures have failed to address considerable salary, pension, and health-care discrepancies affecting players who founded the league's current popularity. The 2002 agreement, for example, made it so recent retirees and players likely to retire after 2002 would receive substantially greater pensions than players from the 1940s and 1950s. The NFL and NFLPA reasoned that the active and recently retired players around this time had created the greatest profit and salary increases, and so should receive the greater share of benefits. As Mike Freeman of the *New York Times* reported, players from the 1940s and 1950s saw this approach as yet another example of how the league "promotes and markets its heritage, but has traditionally done little to improve pension plans for its oldest retirees." Chuck Bednarik, a Hall of Fame linebacker and center for the Philadelphia Eagles who played from 1949 to 1962 (and who is commonly featured in NFL-produced commemorative specials), claimed that the pension increase amounted to "chump change"; before the revision in 2002 his monthly benefit was $1,200.[98]

Retiree complaints typically angered Upshaw, who pointed out in 2007 that $60 million a year in benefits were being paid out to retirees and that the NFLPA could not afford to pay benefits to former players that equaled those of current players. This was, and remains, a constant point of contention: when present-day NFLPA leaders say they cannot afford to distribute more profits to retiree funds, retirees read this as a greedy abdication of responsibility to the very people who made the original sacrifices that founded present-day players' salaries.[99] Hall of Fame tight end Mike Ditka summarized this perfectly in 2007 when speaking at an event on behalf of the retiree advocacy group Gridiron Greats: "These guys today who play the game of football . . . they are not the makers of the game. . . . They are the keepers of the game, period. They are doing what was laid down by a lot of other guys before them, who didn't make money, who played hurt all the time, who didn't have the sports medicine."[100] Ditka's direct contradiction of the league's official line— that retiree sacrifices "paved the way" for the current age of prosperity—is now commonplace among retirees and retiree advocacy groups, including among former players who, like Ditka, are major figures in the league's past and present history. In an oft-cited 2006 report by the *Charlotte Observer*, for example, thirteen Hall of Fame players went on the record with concerns about the NFL's and NFLPA's failures in addressing the health and financial problems of the sport's earliest players. Howie Long, a former Oakland Raiders defensive lineman and a prominent analyst for Fox Sports' NFL coverage, described his experience of being inducted into the Hall of Fame in 2000: "It was a travesty the kind of carnage I saw out of these guys who were in their 50s and 60s, who had defined and in many ways laid the foundation for the NFL being what it is today. . . . Many of them couldn't afford to have their knee replaced or had fallen through" the league's "imaginary" safety net. Lenny Moore, the Colts star running back from the 1958 championship game, complained that Upshaw had failed to negotiate on behalf of retired players. John Elway, who played quarterback for the Denver Broncos and is now the organization's general manager, said there was "plenty of money" being made and that rather than distributing most of it to current players, the league needed to "take care of the pioneers who came before us and made it possible for us to make all the money we do today." In the same article Upshaw made a now-infamous defense of his record on retirement issues, summarizing for many former players the NFL's and NFLPA's real attitudes toward its founding figures:

> For these [retirees] to say what they get is peanuts, they're being ungrateful. . . . The bottom line is I don't work for [the retired players]. They don't hire me and they can't fire me. They can complain about me all day long. . . . But the active players have the vote. That's who pays my salary. . . . They [retirees] say they don't have anybody in the [bargaining] room. Well, they don't and they never will. I'm the only one in that room. They're not in the bargaining unit. They don't even have a vote.[101]

Legally speaking, Upshaw was correct. Morally, he established himself as a spokesperson for the league's callous stance toward retirees, who, as an increasing number of news reports revealed, were systematically being denied disability benefits.

News of the DICC and RB process emerged in tandem with increasing popular concern over traumatic head injury.[102] Upshaw makes an easy enough scapegoat, but his role in disability and pension inequities is best understood as part of a structural problem related to the labor peace achieved between the NFL and NFLPA in 2006. After decades of publicly damaging strikes and CBA negotiations, the "peace" represented a convergence of interests between active players and owners, each relatively satisfied with their shares of ever-expanding revenues. The NFLPA remained a weak union, but its players were making a lot of money. Writing for the *New York Times* in 2006, William Rhoden argued that "in exchange for so-called peace, Upshaw's union has become so entangled with owners that it can't effectively lead the players into a confrontation." This was especially problematic given the pressing need for long-term health-care protections, as retirees' "emotional and physical problems" were surfacing a decade or more after their playing days were over.[103]

The disability claims process, and the labor inequities that underwrote it, are an important part of the context for the head trauma crisis proximate to the 2008 anniversary of The Greatest Game Ever Played, even if ESPN's commemoration only hints at that context through momentary attention to salary divides. To get to the related activities of the MTBI, we have to depart even further from the ESPN special and, in fact, from most commemorations of the league's origins.

The MTBI and NFL Science

In a 2012 report related to their work for *League of Denial*, Fainaru and Fainaru-Wada revealed that the RB paid disability benefits to players suffering from chronic brain disease in at least three documented cases—in 1997, 1999, and 2005—even as the league was publicly denying a link between football and degenerative conditions. In two cases the RB confirmed, and in the third implied, a link between head injury and chronic conditions, in part on the basis of the findings of neutral physicians. During approximately the same time period—from 2003 to 2009—the MTBI published a series of sixteen scientific papers in the journal *Neurosurgery* that called into question the relationships between football-related trauma, brain injury, and long-term health risks. Bob Fitzsimmons, the lawyer for one of the documented disability cases, called this contradiction between behind-the-scenes confirmation and public denial "the proverbial smoking gun"—"devastating evidence" that the NFL had confirmed legally and in consultation with independent physicians a link between football and brain disease, even as it publicized MTBI scientific reports denying that such a link existed.[104]

The Mild Traumatic Brain Injury committee was formed in 1994 by Commissioner Paul Tagliabue, ostensibly to provide scientific assessments of brain injury that could inform player safety policies. Writers called 1994 "the season of the concussion" as several high-profile players suffered head injuries over the course of the year.[105] Tagliabue wrote off concussions as a "pack journalism issue," but forming the MTBI made sense from a public-relations standpoint.[106] In 1994 there was an especially intense focus in the news and sport media on neurologists' warnings about the long-term effects of multiple concussions, and reporters commonly argued that glorifying violence and ignoring safety issues could imperil the NFL.[107] New York Jets wide receiver Al Toon retired early in 1992, and Chicago Bears running back Merrill Hoge retired early in 1994, both citing doctors' warnings that repeated head trauma put them at risk of long-term degenerative conditions.[108] Connections between football-related head trauma and health problems had also been building in medical literature.[109]

The MTBI was composed mostly by NFL insiders, about half of them team doctors (among whom it was common practice to send concussed players back onto the field). There were only three people on the initial MTBI with expertise in neurology: neuropsychologist Mark Lovell, neurologist Ira Casson, and neurosurgeon Hank Feuer. Lovell was the only expert on sport and head injury included on the committee. Commissioner Tagliabue selected as the committee's chair Elliott Pellman, a rheumatologist and the team physician for the New York Jets. With the appointment Pellman became one of the most influential head injury researchers in the country, even though he had no expertise in neurology.[110] Fainaru-Wada and Fainaru report that Pellman was regarded by one league executive as a "concierge" physician, someone who mostly gave flu shots and recommended specialists. In the earliest years of the MTBI, Pellman spoke at coaching clinics with colleagues in neuropsychology, who were troubled by his complete lack of knowledge regarding the existing research on brain injury and sport.[111]

The full extent of Pellman's faults would be revealed in later years. In 2003, in his role as the Jets team physician, Pellman sent wide receiver Wayne Chrebet back into a game one quarter after Chrebet had been knocked unconscious. Before sending Chrebet back in, Pellman told him, "There's going to be some controversy about you going back to play," but added that returning to the field was "very important" for Chrebet's career.[112] In 2005 the *New York Times* revealed that Pellman had falsified his résumé. He claimed to have a medical degree from the State University of New York (SUNY) at Stony Brook, when in fact he had a certificate of completion from Universidad Autónoma de Guadalajara in Mexico. He also claimed to be an associate clinical professor at the Albert Einstein College of Medicine when he was actually an assistant clinical professor, an honorary and lower-ranking position. The program in Guadalajara was relatively well regarded by U.S. medical associations, but Pellman had clearly falsified his credentials.[113]

From its inception the MTBI functioned as a crisis management committee with a scientific front. The articles that the committee published not only called into question the relationship between football and brain injury but also positioned NFL-supported research in active opposition to findings in sport medicine scholarship. The MTBI published its studies in *Neurosurgery* under the editorship of Michael Apuzzo. Apuzzo was an accomplished professor of neurosurgery at the University of Southern California. He was also a consultant to the NFL, and according to Fainaru-Wada and Fainaru, some league insiders considered him to be a bit of a "jock sniffer" and "a sports guy wannabe." Apuzzo regularly flew from Los Angeles to New York to attend Giants games on the sideline, checking on players with injuries outside his area of expertise primarily to feel like he was part of the team. He compared his experience at the 2001 Super Bowl between the New York Giants and Baltimore Ravens to the powerful camaraderie he felt during military service. He made it a point to tell colleagues that he had meals with Commissioner Tagliabue.[114]

It would be unfair to call Apuzzo a stooge, but his relationship with the NFL did have an apparent influence over his editorship. Michael Kirk, the director for PBS's *Frontline* special *League of Denial* noted that in addition to publishing MTBI research in *Neurosurgery*, Apuzzo also published two papers by Dr. Bennet Omalu, who in 2002 discovered chronic traumatic encephalopathy. This is to Apuzzo's credit, considering the potential damage CTE could (and eventually would) have on the league.[115] Apuzzo also appointed Dr. Robert Cantu as editor for a special section in *Neurosurgery* on head injury in sport. Cantu was at the time the foremost researcher on sport-related head injury and return-to-play guidelines. While he had reservations about Pellman and the MTBI, Cantu also hoped that NFL research might prove valuable, especially given the league's resources and access to players.[116] When Cantu approached Apuzzo with concerns that MTBI papers were designed to serve the interests of the NFL, however, Apuzzo overruled him on their publication. Cantu said in an interview that he stayed on as section editor only because he hoped to make his voice heard, but he saw that "it was pretty clear that all of those papers were going to see publication in that journal."[117] Thus, the special sports section of *Neurosurgery* served as a controlled stage for the emerging scientific and public debate over football and head trauma.

An important staple of MTBI science from the very beginning was the idea that NFL players were somehow invulnerable to the effects of head trauma. In 1994, Pellman told *Sports Illustrated* that "veterans clear [concussion symptoms] more quickly than rookies. . . . They can unscramble their brains a little faster" since they expect to get "dinged," while rookies tend to panic when they feel symptoms.[118] Similar claims grounded the MTBI's fourth paper, published in 2004. In that paper Pellman and his coauthors argued: "Despite public and media perceptions, repeat [trauma] affects only a relatively small number of NFL players." In direct opposition to existing research, they insisted that players rarely suffer repeat concussions within the same season and that players with a history of concussions show no signs of slower neurological recovery. They suggested that the existing research exaggerated the risk for multiple or repeat head trauma and that, on this basis, current treatment and return-to-play guidelines were "arbitrary" and "too conservative for professional football."[119] This specification—too conservative *for professional football*—was important, as Pellman and his MTBI colleagues took great care to distinguish NFL players from high school and college football players, elevating them as a class of athlete that, reviewers worried, was being depicted as "impervious to brain damage, as if they were superhuman."[120] The MTBI repeated this claim in its next (fifth) paper: NFL players had since youth football gone through a "winnowing process"; their ascent to the professional ranks demonstrated that they had been "selected out" as uniquely more resistant to "prolonged postconcussion syndrome than the general population."[121]

MTBI papers varied in methodology and focus, but they built a thematic case that positioned league-sponsored research in direct contrast to the existing and developing scholarly record on football-related brain injury: NFL players were a special breed of athlete who could quickly "clear" postconcussion symptoms and safely return to play (even in the same game); other researchers were exaggerating the risks of repeated head trauma (subsequent injury, slower recovery time, chronic degenerative conditions) as there was no evidence of these problems among NFL players; CTE was a condition unique to boxing and did not exist in the NFL; postconcussion symptoms could linger for high school and college football players but, again, not for NFL players; researchers had created systems for grading and managing concussions that were too arbitrary and conservative for the NFL, a fact proven by NFL players' immediate postinjury return to the field.[122]

The special sports section of *Neurosurgery* was not, however, a forum wholly controlled by the league. In addition to serving as a publication outlet for industry science, it also staged debates that would eventually migrate from academic confines into popular forums. Particularly important to this process were two papers, published by Bennet Omalu and his colleagues, that first connected football and CTE. Omalu was a Nigerian-born forensic pathologist who knew little about football. He had recently graduated from the University of Pittsburgh Medical Center and, as the most junior pathologist at the Allegheny County coroner's office, was on call on a Saturday in 2002 when former Pittsburgh Steelers center Mike Webster was brought in for an autopsy.[123]

Webster was a Hall of Fame center for the Steelers and a beloved local legend. When he died at fifty years old, some of his postcareer troubles were known to fans: he was struggling with mental illness, financially ruined, and falling apart physically. The full extent of Webster's decline would be revealed only in later years. He was addicted to Ritalin. The bottoms of his feet were so badly cracked that it hurt to walk, so he wrapped them in duct tape. Because he could not afford a dentist, he super-glued his teeth back into place. Due to constant pain he had trouble sleeping, so he used a stun gun to knock himself unconscious. He collected several guns and spoke about killing NFL officials, including members of the NFL disability committee, whom he blamed for his troubles.[124] He suffered from a depressive disorder, memory loss, and Parkinsonian symptoms.[125]

Omalu removed Webster's brain and eventually discovered Alzheimer's-like markers in his brain tissue, though the pathology was inconsistent with Alzheimer's. In 2003, Omalu brought Webster's brain to his mentor, Ronald Hamilton, who, after examining it, guessed that he was looking at a former boxer.[126] Believing that they had discovered a unique disorder, Omalu and Hamilton contacted Steve DeKosky, a renowned expert in Alzheimer's and neurological disease. DeKosky confirmed that this did, in fact, appear to be a new syndrome, the discovery of which, he believed, would "change everything" by linking repetitive head trauma to degenerative processes.[127] Omalu labeled the syndrome CTE.

Apuzzo accepted Omalu and his coauthors' paper—titled "Chronic Traumatic Encephalopathy in a National League Football Player"—for publication in *Neurosurgery* in 2005. Apuzzo was still approving NFL-sponsored studies over the growing objections of reviewers, but at least in this case he was willing to insert a major challenge to the NFL's position on long-term brain injury in the same journal. Omalu was, however, required during the review process to remove a historical account of the MTBI as well as an assertion that the committee should have addressed long-term brain injury years before. In their 2005 paper Omalu and his coauthors announced "the first documented case of long-term neurodegenerative changes in a retired professional NFL player consistent with chronic traumatic encephalopathy" and suggested that "true prevalence rates" for the disease remained unknown, as autopsy was the only way to confirm a diagnosis. Their findings built on the existing scientific case for frequency of head trauma in football by suggesting that impacts sustained over a player's career could have long-term consequences in retirement.[128] After the paper was published, members of the MTBI called for its retraction. The editorial staff did not oblige, but the MTBI was allowed to publish its objections in a commentary section in *Neurosurgery*.[129]

Even as the sports section of *Neurosurgery* remained a peer-reviewed outlet for sanctioning NFL industry science, it also developed as an important site for direct, increasing conflict between MTBI researchers and academic researchers, who argued on opposite sides of a debate that was beginning to dovetail with popular news reports about retirees struggling with mental health problems and committing suicide. A particularly good example of this convergence came in 2005, when former Steelers offensive lineman Terry Long committed suicide by drinking antifreeze.

Long's body was delivered, like Webster's, to the Allegheny County coroner's office. Omalu was not on call when the body arrived, but the doctor who performed the autopsy preserved Long's brain for Omalu so he could examine it later. The Allegheny County coroner was Cyril Wecht, who, as Fainaru-Wada and Fainaru note, was known as a "celebrity pathologist" due to his "uncanny ability to insinuate himself into every major crime and fatality of the day," including the cases of O. J. Simpson and JonBenét Ramsey as well as the Kennedy assassination (he was particularly famous for his conspiratorial criticisms of the Warren Commission). Consistent with his record of seeking the public spotlight, Wecht did not wait for Omalu to study Long's brain, or for the results of toxicology reports.[130] He announced immediately after the coroner's office released the autopsy report that Long had died from inflammatory meningitis and CTE resulting from football-related head trauma. Wecht noted that football helmets could not protect completely against "all the measured force produced when some 300-pound player with a hand the size of a Christmas ham whacks you in the head dozens of times a game, season after season." In an apparent effort to teach the public about football-related CTE, Wecht compared it to the more familiar colloquialism "punch drunk," associated with boxing.[131] In 2006, after the results of toxicology reports came to light, the coroner's office changed the cause of death to suicide, while retaining the diagnosis of long-term brain damage.[132]

Long had played beside Webster on the Steelers offensive line in the mid-1980s, and as with Webster, his postcareer struggles were known by fans in Pittsburgh. He had attempted suicide in 1991, the day after head coach

Chuck Noll informed him that he had tested positive for steroids. In that case he attempted to overdose on sleeping pills and also ingested rat poison. Shortly before his death in 2005, Long was charged with setting fire to a chicken- and vegetable-processing plant that he owned in order to collect $1.1 million in insurance money, and he was accused of fraudulently collecting $1.2 million of state loan money in a separate case. Afterward he tried again to commit suicide, this time by drinking a bottle of Drano.[133]

Omalu repeated the process he had used to analyze Webster and found similar evidence of CTE in Long's brain; he and his coauthors published their findings in the November 2006 issue of *Neurosurgery*.[134] By the time the paper went to print the Long case had already become a subject of public dispute among Wecht, Omalu, and the NFL. Joseph Maroon, a respected doctor who served as the Steelers' neurosurgeon during Long's career, criticized Wecht and the coroner's office the day after they announced Long had died from the cumulative effects of head trauma. Maroon told the *Pittsburgh Post-Gazette* that Wecht's argument about Long being "killed by football" was "preposterous and a misinterpretation of facts," as Long had "a history of no significant head injuries" (a claim that proved to be false).[135] Omalu was resolute, confident that his tests had uncovered evidence of CTE, just as they had with Webster. He argued that people with CTE suffer from depression, memory loss, and loss of executive function, symptoms which lead eventually to attempted suicide. He concluded that "Terry Long committed suicide" due to CTE sustained from "his long-term play. . . . The NFL is in denial."[136]

The possible connection between football-related head injury and suicide was, and remains today, a subject of controversy in the medical literature (as do related diagnostic criteria for CTE).[137] There can be little doubt, however, about the power of player suicide stories in mobilizing medical debates across academic borders and into popular awareness. For example, Omalu examined in 2007 the brain of former Philadelphia Eagles and Arizona Cardinals safety Andre Waters, who shot himself in the head at the age of forty-four. Omalu reported that Waters had the brain tissue of an eighty-five-year-old man and early stages of Alzheimer's disease, then claimed that his suicide was ultimately the result of football-related brain damage and depression.[138] Waters's suicide motivated former New England Patriots linebacker Ted Johnson to discuss publicly his struggles with postconcussion depression and cognitive impairment. In 2002 Johnson suffered two concussions within four days, and head coach Bill Belichick returned him to full-contact practices and play while he was still symptomatic.[139] Former Chicago Bears safety Dave Duerson's suicide in 2011 was especially chilling. Duerson was a member of the NFLPA whose experience reviewing disability cases made him aware of CTE. Concerned that he was suffering from the condition, Duerson wrote a letter to family members asking that his brain be examined after his death. Then in order to preserve his brain he shot himself in the chest.[140] By 2011 around twenty NFL veterans had been diagnosed with CTE, and several had committed suicide.[141] Mike Lopresti at *USA Today* characterized this as a moment when chronic brain injury debates had become fully public: "This is not just a story for medical journals anymore. The alarm is going off. Feel the ominous, chilling wind that just blew through football? Dave Duerson's suicide message. . . . There seems no unanimous medical verdict on the details, but suspected victims are piling up."[142]

In fact, the fight over MTBI committee science and the NFL's record of disability claims denial had been trickling into the consciousness of sporting publics for years, notably through the work of journalists like Alan Schwartz. In 2007 the NFL's case on traumatic brain injury started to truly unravel, in large part as a result of negative publicity surrounding the MTBI.

Under public pressure Commissioner Goodell decided in 2007 to remove Pellman as the MTBI chair. In addition to the 2005 *New York Times* report on Pellman's false résumé, a damning 2006 *ESPN: The Magazine* report revealed that the MTBI had, under Pellman's leadership, excluded hundreds of baseline neurological test results of NFL players from its published research articles.[143] The NFL replaced Pellman with Dr. Ira Casson and Dr. David Viano, both neurologists who had been on the committee since 1994.[144] Casson earned the nickname "Dr. No" after he tersely shot down a link between football and brain injury in a 2007 interview with HBO's *Real Sports*; this unflinching denial of medical evidence by a trained neurologist was considered by some observers to be one of the most damaging moments in the MTBI's history.[145] Viano and Casson were also criticized by their coauthors for altering the conclusion of a 2005 article in *Neurosurgery*—the seventh paper in the series published by the MTBI. The article evaluated as safe the NFL's record of returning around half of concussed players to the same game, a point the authors (remarkably) all agreed on. Yet Viano and Casson changed the conclusion to argue that it "might be safe" to apply similar return-to-play approaches for high school and college players, a suggestion that defied credibility even for their MTBI colleagues.[146]

The NFL started to modify its popular position on head trauma, but in 2007 the in-house message remained the same: as argued in a pamphlet distributed to all teams, there was no scientific evidence that multiple head injuries posed a risk for future injuries, for return to the field, or for long-term conditions.[147] The NFL would not acknowledge until 2009 that medical research confirmed a relationship between football, head injury, and long-term complications.[148] In between was the 2008 season, a moment of relative respite from explosive news stories about head injury and retiree struggles, within which ESPN's *The Greatest Game Ever Played* could craft an idealized version of the league's past. The 2008 season is also frequently viewed, in retrospect, as a tipping point. Starting in 2009 the NFL would incrementally concede, in public and in court, the evidence on football-related head injury. After years of coverage, debate, and exposure, the crisis was building toward a point of rupture.

In 2009 NFL television coverage started to change. Announcers spoke less of "warriors" and more about dementia. Networks removed highlights of devastating hits from their promotions.[149] It was already too late. Those moments of audiovisual capture that had served to market football in the past—violent collisions, raw power, speed—now projected a disturbing new image for the future of the game. As one reporter suggested rather unsettlingly, an entire generation of retirees was going to systematically decline in health and cognitive function on television, over a prolonged period, and in front of millions of viewers.[150]

ESPN's fragile control over cross-generational conflict in *The Greatest Game Ever Played* marks an inherent dialectical tension between *beginnings* and postcareer *futures* that may shape NFL commemorative practices moving forward. We can pose again the fundamental question of this chapter: Can the NFL attempt recovery of an idealized past without risking yet another reminder of its violent origins?

Conclusion: NFL History, 2009 and Beyond

In the lead-up to Super Bowl XLVI in 2012, the NFL invested millions of dollars in a publicity campaign called "NFL Evolution," which mixed idealizations of the league's past with promotions of new safety programs and measures. As part of this effort, the league developed a sixty-second advertisement that aired during the Super Bowl. This was an opportunity for the NFL to promote its stance on player safety through a revisionist account of its past, in front of a projected audience of more than 100 million viewers. As the NFL's chief marketing officer noted, the Super Bowl was the league's "biggest stage," providing an opportunity to address the concerns of "a massive casual audience . . . particularly mothers."[151]

The ad began with an origin moment, featuring in black and white a kickoff return on a rain-soaked field in Canton, Ohio, in 1906, the players wearing no helmets and running in lightly padded shirts and pants. After this opening, actors depicting legendary NFL players ran through a succession of simulated game sequences depicting a chronology of the league's "evolution" regarding player safety. Each player streaked across a field and broke tackles before morphing into a historical successor, each transformation representing concurrent changes in protective equipment, eras, playing surfaces, and audiovisual quality. Through each scene Baltimore Ravens linebacker Ray Lewis narrated a version of NFL history in which the league responded progressively to player safety issues with new equipment and rules, until the final figure—Chicago Bears punt returner Devin Hester—made his way into the end zone. Lewis concluded: "Here's to making the next century safer, and more exciting, than ever. Forever forward. Forever football."[152] Here again (as I argued in Chapter 2) was the relationship between continuity, succession, and forgetting that so often structures official histories in elite televised sport.

The NFL ran the commercial again in 2013, during Super Bowl XLVII. After it aired in 2013, Matt Crossman of the *Sporting News* noted on Twitter that three players depicted in the ad—Ollie Matson, Rick Upchurch, and Mel Gray—were among the more than five thousand former players involved in the class-action head injury lawsuit against the NFL.[153] As coverage of the ad suggested, the presence of these players illustrated an inescapable problem for the NFL: the league's "evolution" has been built out of an essential violence that it cannot help but display, even in the most carefully crafted campaigns.[154]

It would be naïve to suggest that the league is out of options as far as its commemorative practices go. The NFL will produce more slick, effective, multimillion-dollar media campaigns touting its new religion on player safety and brain injury science. As long as its television ratings remain at their current levels, the league will also retain its hegemony within the larger U.S. media sport content economy.[155] As Kevin Clark of the *Wall Street Journal* writes, the NFL "runs the television industry, the advertising industry, and nearly anything else that requires a lot of eyeballs."[156] This is not an overstatement, at least not in the United States. As I argued in Chapter 3, live sport content shapes distribution rights negotiations and cable and satellite subscription packages, and NFL content is far and away the most valuable commodity in U.S. television.

It is also difficult to imagine, however, how the NFL can any longer return to its beginnings without potentially dredging up evidence of founding crimes. Once origins are rewritten they bring a *revised* narrative unity to the story of an institution's growth. Origins also uniquely transmit the founding sins of a community through successive history, and repeated returns risk the excavation of yet more details. NFL Evolution is but one example. There is hardly, at present, a news story about player safety or league policy that does not further crystallize (in pieces or in total) the various historical fragments shaping the brain injury crisis. The year 2008 marked not only the anniversary of The Greatest Game Ever Played but also a dividing line past which an unproblematic recovery of origins was no longer possible. The cross-generational conflicts patterned throughout ESPN's special only hinted at greater ruptures that would open from 2009 forward.

In 2007 the NFL was criticized in congressional hearings for its disability claims system. Two years later the league was back in front of Congress, this time to answer questions about the MTBI and the league's history of promoting contrarian science. The 2009 hearings brought into focus the broader crises that were coalescing around brain injury: disability policies, labor inequities, active and retired player disputes, television revenues, and MTBI activities. Representatives threatened the NFL's partial antitrust exemption. They criticized the NFLPA for refusing to acknowledge until recently the long-term risks of head injury and for failing to negotiate safe working conditions for its members. Cantu, the series editor at *Neurosurgery* who had taken issue with the MTBI studies, testified that there was "ongoing and convincing evidence" of a connection between head injury and degenerative conditions. Witnesses called into question the independence of team doctors, noting that they worked for the owners and coaches and were primarily tasked with returning injured players to the field.[157] The 2009 hearings represented an ongoing revision of NFL history in concentrated, dramatized form. The league had to change its approach.

In contrast to all previous statements from NFL officials and MTBI researchers, NFL spokesperson Greg Aiello said in December 2009, "It's quite obvious from the medical research that's been done that concussions can lead to long-term problems." Schwartz wrote that the statement was "tacit acknowledgement" by the NFL that it "was no longer able to defend a position that conflicted with nearly all scientific understanding of head trauma." When Aiello was asked about the contradiction between his statement and the league's previous stance on the medical evidence, he said: "We all share the same interest. That's as much as I'm going to say."[158] This was the beginning of a new approach for the NFL: offer a qualified confirmation of the science, and deny the cover-up. This approach was instantiated legally by the 2015 settlement of the class-action lawsuit, which (consistent with precedent in other class-action settlements) allowed the NFL to avoid disclosing publicly what it knew about football-related brain injury and to avoid any admission of wrongdoing.[159] The league's confessions of guilt have been characteristically unspoken, implied through rules and organizational changes.

After years of insisting through the MTBI that there was no risk in returning to the field after a concussion, the NFL adopted a stricter return-to-play policy beginning in 2009, and included independent physicians in player evaluations (play-by-play commentators now commonly say during NFL games that a player is being evaluated by "the independent neurologist," a strange combination of public relations and confession). The league also made several changes to on-field safety rules, including moving kickoffs in order to reduce high-speed collisions, banning helmet-to-helmet hits, and, most recently, adding spotters who can stop a game if they suspect a player has sustained a head injury.[160]

Whether these changes have made a difference is a matter of controversy. Football is an inescapably violent sport, and much of the medical evidence points to its inherent risks. Also, head injury reports are not standardized. NFL teams use different terms and metrics in gathering data, and it is usually unclear whether increases or decreases in reported incidents are due to players' and teams' increased willingness to acknowledge head injuries or the impact of new rules.[161] There were 115 concussions reported by the NFL from the start of the 2008 preseason through week eight, a number that would increase by 21 percent in 2009 and 34 percent in 2010.[162] The recent trend has been more positive. According to data collected by PBS's *Frontline*, the number of concussions in the NFL has dropped from 171 (in 2012) to 152 (in 2013) to 123 (in 2014). *Frontline* credits the league's acknowledgment of dangers related to head trauma and its institution of new safety measures, though continuing problems with return-to-play protocols mean that concussed players are still sometimes going back into games.[163]

Congressional scrutiny of the MTBI motivated more changes to the committee. Commissioner Goodell removed Casson and Viano in 2009.[164] In 2010 Goodell rebranded the MTBI as the "Head, Neck, and Spine Committee" and appointed Dr. H. Hunt Batjer and Dr. Richard G. Ellenbogen as co-chairs. The appointments of Batjer and Ellenbogen, both respected neurologists, represented a potentially meaningful break with the MTBI's previous history.[165]

Through all of these changes, however, the NFL has maintained an aggressively defensive stance, moving little (if at all) on the basic connection between football and degenerative conditions like CTE. For example, the league commissioned a study from the University of Michigan but then attacked the study's methodology after researchers reported in 2009 that NFL retirees experienced higher rates of memory problems (including Alzheimer's, dementia, and other memory-related diseases) than men in the general U.S. population, with retirees ages thirty to forty-nine reporting dementia-related diagnoses at rates nineteen times higher than the national average.[166] In another example, the NFL donated $1 million in 2010 to the Boston University Center for the Study of Traumatic Encephalopathy and made the Center the preferred brain bank for the NFL. Researchers at the Center reported in 2014 that seventy-six out of seventy-nine brains of deceased NFL players showed signs of CTE, to date the most alarming study on the disorder as it relates to football.[167] The NFL responded in 2014 by threatening to attack in court the connection between head injury and neurodegenerative disease if retirees did not settle their class-action lawsuit (settlement being a public-relations victory that might bring a sense of closure to the controversy). Dusting off the MTBI's pre-2009 argument, a league lawyer insisted that "recent research . . . demonstrates considerable uncertainty about the role that concussions play in later-life impairment" as well as the actual incidence and severity of injuries among former athletes. Chris Seeger, the lead attorney for the retired players, worried that if the NFL litigated the case its lawyers would resort to "scorched earth" tactics (e.g., shaming former players on the stand by asking them to disclose personal information about depression or their sexuality).[168]

The NFL got its wish with the 2015 class-action settlement, but its continuing denial of culpability all but guarantees future publicity crises. The 2015 settlement, for example, will not provide rewards for future deaths related to CTE, a condition that at present can be diagnosed only postmortem. Per the agreement, the families of players who died and were diagnosed with CTE between 2006 and 2014 can seek up to $4 million in compensation, but future deaths will not be covered, ostensibly to keep from "incentivizing" suicide. A small group of players opted out of the settlement and filed an objection over the coverage limit. Dr. Robert Stern from the Boston University School of Medicine said in the objection that a reliable test for CTE in a living person would be available within the next five to ten years; such a test would, under the current settlement, be used to deny coverage in the future. The NFL will be released effectively from liability for players beyond 2014, but Stern suggested it could face a much worse publicity crisis once it starts denying compensation for living persons with CTE.[169]

In addition, the tally of deceased players' brains examined for CTE at the Boston University brain bank continues to grow. At the beginning of the 2015 season researchers there had studied 165 brains of people who played football in high school, in college, or professionally. There was evidence of CTE in 131 of the brains (79 percent). A total of 91 brains from the bank belonged to NFL players, and 87 of those (96 percent) showed signs of CTE.[170] The MTBI's claim that NFL players had evolved to clear trauma more quickly did not pass the smell test before, but here is proof of its speciousness. If the postcareer forensic evidence of CTE upholds these percentages, how does this affect the decisions of active players, or of parents? Per Stern's warning, what happens if or when CTE can be detected in living players?

This is the specter that now hangs over NFL memory practices: the habit of perpetual return to idealized origins is being replaced, or at least amended, by a seemingly inevitable projection toward postcareer degeneration. San Francisco 49ers linebacker Chris Borland retired in 2015, at the age of twenty-four and after only one season in the NFL, because of concerns over long-term brain damage. He was the team's leading tackler as a rookie and had a promising career ahead of him. Borland's announcement was taken as a watershed moment for the NFL, a sign of how aware contemporary players are about the long-term health risks of football. Although Borland stood out because of his youth, several other productive, young NFL players had also retired before his announcement over similar concerns. In what is becoming a generic series of connections, reporters conflated Borland's story with declining youth football numbers, former players' suicides, and popular awareness of football-related brain injury. Many commentators argued that the NFL's high TV ratings and revenues would only conceal the league's fate in the short term; this was the beginning of the end.[171]

The ultimate question of the NFL's death can only be deferred. We cannot know whether it might happen or what form it might take; nor can we be certain whether the years following the 2015 class-action settlement will be viewed in retrospect as a tipping point toward economic and cultural decline or as a moment of effective crisis management and recovery. What we can say is that "death" is emerging as a new commemorative genre for the NFL, one that necessitates a revised relationship to the league's origins.

Consider a final example. In a 2015 segment for the HBO program *Real Sports*, Bryant Gumbel interviews members of the 1985 Chicago Bears Super Bowl team, upheld as one of the greatest teams in league history. Once called "The Monsters of the Midway," the segment title tells us, they are "monsters no more." The team's former quarterback Jim McMahon reveals that just like other retirees he has had suicidal thoughts; if he owned a gun, he insists, he would have already killed himself. McMahon has early-onset dementia. He reports lying in his bed for days or weeks on end, staring up at the ceiling fan. He has short-term memory loss and cannot find his way home when he goes out. HBO profiles Dave Duerson, who had been a member of the 1985 Bears. Duerson's son recounts the contents of his father's suicide letter: he suffered from depression and short-term memory loss and wanted his brain preserved for study at the NFL's brain bank. Gumbel notes that twenty-three players from the 1985 Bears team are plaintiffs in the class-action lawsuit (to be settled later that year); this is about half of the team. After a series of profiles on former players suffering from physical and cognitive disabilities, Gumbel emphasizes that even for asymptomatic retirees a future of decline lingers as a "haunting possibility." Former Bears defensive lineman Steve McMichael tells Gumbel, "I don't have brain damage yet . . . *yet.*" Then he pauses, and repeats: "*Yet.*" Former defensive lineman Richard Dent assumes that brain damage symptoms are "on the horizon" for him. Looking back on this revised understanding of one of the league's most iconic teams, Gumbel asks the head coach for the 1985 Bears, Mike Ditka, "Is this going to wind up being the cross on which football is nailed?"[172] What of this crucifixion metaphor? Perhaps it is sensationalistic, but it also summarizes the dramatic center of NFL death narratives, the image of a sacrifice *necessitated* by original sin.

6

ED O'BANNON

CHANGES EVERYTHING?

*Some Closing Theses on Sport
and Negative Theology*

ED O'BANNON, a former star basketball player at the University of California at Los Angeles (UCLA), served as lead plaintiff on a class-action lawsuit filed against the National Collegiate Athletic Association (NCAA) in 2009. The suit claimed that former college athletes should be compensated for the use of their likenesses on television, on apparel, and in video games. When the O'Bannon case was filed, the NCAA's various licensing deals had an estimated worth of $4 billion. None of that money went to players. Professor Andrew Zimbalist, a well-known economist and critic of the NCAA, said at the time that the O'Bannon case would expose "the phony and false way" in which the organization employs a "hybrid model" to define amateurism.[1] Under this model, the NCAA has long worked various legal and publicity angles within two conjoined but contradictory systems: a *free-market* system, wherein the organization negotiates lucrative media contracts and licensing deals, and a nonprofit *educational* system, wherein the organization bars "student-athletes" from compensation, due process, and collective bargaining rights by emphasizing their amateurism.[2]

The amateur ideal is coming apart in light of revenue generation and spending in men's college basketball and football. Often summarized as an "arms race," such spending represents an effort to compete for top players, coaches, and shares of media and licensing agreements that has changed the face of elite college sport in the United States, leading to palatial athletics buildings, state-of-the-art practice facilities, stadium and arena expansions, and multimillion-dollar contracts for coaches. As Joe Nocera of the *New York Times* writes, "[The] hypocrisy that permeates big-money college sports takes your breath away." There is, as he maintains, a "glaring, and increasingly untenable, discrepancy between what football and basketball players get and what everyone else in their food chain reaps" that has "bred a deep cynicism among the athletes themselves" and led to "increasingly loud calls for reform" among players, fans, academics, and sport journalists.[3]

The O'Bannon case is the centerpiece in a series of legal challenges to the amateur ethos that holds together elite college sport's entire economic system. These challenges come at a time when college athletes are mobilizing against administrators, fans are ambivalent about the hybrid free-market/amateur model, and a series of high-profile academic scandals are exposing the often impossible reconciliation of academic and for-profit sport missions. As of now, the NCAA has fragile legal and popular backing for the current arrangement, but amateurism is, as one journalist put it, "on life support."[4]

Here is one last story about the "death" of something sacred, from which I want to extrapolate, with an eye to the preceding chapters, a set of theses regarding sport and negative theology. These theses are particular to the historical and cultural moment captured in this book, but I am confident that they map out a trajectory for understanding, critiquing, and perhaps acting on significant changes underway in elite televised sport.

O'Bannon versus the Amateur Ideal

In 2014 federal judge Claudia Wilken ruled in favor of the plaintiffs in the O'Bannon case, finding that the NCAA was in violation of antitrust law. The organization would no longer be able to prohibit athletes from earning money from the use of their likenesses and images. Football players in the top conferences and all Division I men's basketball players could now receive a share in the revenues they generated.[5]

The O'Bannon decision coincided with other legal threats to the NCAA's hegemony. The day before the decision, the NCAA voted to grant the five most powerful Division I conferences—the Football Bowl Series or FBS conferences, formerly called Division I-A, which include the Southeastern Conference (SEC), the Atlantic Coast Conference (ACC), the Pacific-12 (PAC 12), the Big Ten, and the Big 12—autonomy to increase the value of scholarships, improve players' benefits, and relax some NCAA restrictions related to amateurism. The decision, in part a response to legal and public pressure, further separated the college sport haves from the have-nots based on revenue generation, highlighting the market-based leverage of the so-called "Big 5" or "Power 5" conferences. As SEC commissioner Mike Slive put it, these conferences could now "provide student-athletes with things that meet the 21st-century model of how we think about intercollegiate athletes."[6] To translate: this was a market adjustment that anticipated the deteriorating legal and public standing of amateurism.

Around the same time, football players at Northwestern University were organizing to form a union, a move that would potentially allow college athletes to collectively bargain for market-rate pay and benefits.[7] Northwestern quarterback Kain Colter had long been concerned about college athletes' rights and was inspired to unionize his football team while taking a course about the social and political history of labor in the United States.[8] In the spring of 2014 Peter Ohr, a regional director of the National Labor Relations Board (NLRB), ruled that Northwestern's football players were eligible to unionize based on the amount of time per week they spent on football (as many as fifty hours) and the control exerted on them through scholarships, which functioned as contracts for compensation. In a direct rebuttal of the student-athlete ideal, Ohr wrote: "It cannot be said the employer's scholarship players are 'primarily students.'"[9] Colter had been making the same case publicly. The NCAA was, he said, "like a dictatorship" where no one represented the players in negotiations. He also noted, "Everything we do is scheduled around football," including course scheduling. "We're brought to the university to play football."[10]

The NCAA appealed to the full NLRB in Washington, DC. In a unanimous decision the board declined jurisdiction over the case. The decision did not determine whether Northwestern's football players were employees— the most important question at hand—or preclude consideration of future unionization cases in college sport, but it did dismiss the Northwestern players' petition.[11] Some labor leaders saw the decision as a "nail in the coffin" for organizing college athletes, while others saw it as a "bump in the road."[12] The NCAA was clearly pleased, since the NLRB had blocked a challenge to the foundational construct of the student-athlete. The Northwestern players' actions did, however, represent a growing threat of athlete activism and the legal fragility of the amateur ideal. The NCAA decided to grant autonomy to the Power 5 conferences after Colter started to organize his teammates, an apparently preemptive response to the future possibility of expanded players' rights.[13]

The NCAA was also successful in appealing Judge Wilken's decision in the O'Bannon case, winning a partial but important victory in 2015. According to the Court of Appeals for the Ninth Circuit, the NCAA was, in fact, in violation of antitrust law, but the NCAA was not required to allow universities to compensate athletes beyond the cost of attending school.[14] Once again, amateurism held together the hybrid for-profit/educational model. One judge wrote: "The difference between offering student-athletes education-related compensation and offering them cash sums untethered to education expenses is . . . a quantum leap. Once that line is crossed, we see no basis for returning to a rule of amateurism and no defined stopping point."[15] Here was legal affirmation of the persistent refrain articulated by NCAA officials, athletic directors, university presidents, and other power brokers with vested interests in the current arrangement: yes, college sport has become a big business, but if you pay the players, it will be the end of the amateur ideal. This is, of course, the entire point of legal and activist challenges: to kill a powerful fiction. However, much like other sacrosanct ideals (e.g., tradition), amateurism is self-justifying. It remains a remarkably durable point of retreat, even as every practice and object it attaches to comes under the control of conspicuous market forces.

The NCAA's appeal victory in the O'Bannon case marks the uncertain legal future of the amateur ideal. Some legal experts read the decision as "a huge victory for the NCAA" as it upheld the basic definition of amateurism (restriction of payments to the costs of attending school). O'Bannon's lawyers focused on the court's ruling that the NCAA was not exempt from antitrust laws, which they saw as an opening for their basic case: that college athletes have a right to participate in the licensing market. This was, they announced, the opening they would pursue going forward.[16]

Fans (at least according to opinion polls) are still largely resistant to the idea of paying college athletes. At some level, however, they recognize that in big-time programs the student-athlete is a fabrication. According to a Monmouth University poll in 2015, 67 percent of respondents believed that elite programs placed too much emphasis on athletics, and only 24 percent believed that these programs achieved an appropriate balance with education.[17] A 2013 Marist University poll found that 67 percent of fans assumed college athletic programs commonly broke NCAA rules when recruiting and training players; that was up from 55 percent in 2012. The same poll had 95 percent of fans saying that education should be a student-athlete's top priority, per the amateur ideal. These respondents wanted athletes going to classes, training part time, and not being paid beyond a scholarship, just like regular students.[18] Pay-for-play remains, then, the ultimate taboo. For now, when officials argue that moving to a "pay-for-play model . . . would be the death of college athletics," they can redraw a powerful boundary, even as fans already know that the losses in such a death—a decline in concern for educational integrity, a deterioration of the amateur ethos in intercollegiate competition—are already apparent under the current system.[19]

The amateur ideal has historically reconciled inconsistencies between market-based and educational practices in elite college sport, representing an enduring yet increasingly strained negotiation of legal and moralistic principles between the NCAA, its member institutions, the state, and the courts. This negotiation was exemplified in the 1984 Supreme Court decision *NCAA v. Board of Regents of the University of Oklahoma*, which related to an antitrust lawsuit filed by the University of Oklahoma and the University of Georgia, two college football powers. At the time the NCAA controlled negotiations of national television contracts for college football and limited how many times individual teams could appear on air. The court ruled 7–2 that this restrained trade in violation of antitrust law, commenting that the NCAA was operating as a "classic cartel." The decision allowed individual conferences to negotiate their own television deals, and in doing so affirmed elite college sport as a commercial enterprise. That affirmation was attenuated, however, by restatements of the amateur ideal. Justice Byron R. White wrote in his dissent that the NCAA provided "a public good—a viable system of amateur athletics . . . the very existence of which might be threatened by unbridled competition in the economic sphere." The majority differed mainly on the question of whether a free-market system and the amateur ideal could coexist. They could, according to Justice John Paul Stevens: the court affirmed the "freedom to compete" while also acknowledging that the NCAA needed "ample latitude" to maintain "the revered tradition of amateurism in college sports."[20]

Thus the free-market/amateur structure for revenue-generating college athletics—specifically football and men's basketball—was established. The powerful football conferences set out to negotiate their own TV contracts. The NCAA, threatened by the loss of control over football revenues, still retained exclusive rights to negotiate television deals for the highly valuable Division I men's basketball tournament (known commonly as "March Madness"). The NCAA's financial health is now tied almost entirely to the tournament.[21]

The arms race that followed led eventually to the current state of big-money programs. According to a *Forbes* magazine report in 2015, the top college basketball teams in the country were worth more than $30 million each. *Forbes* reported in 2014 that the top football programs were worth more than $100 million.[22] Between 2006 and 2012, coaches' salaries in Division I-FBS football increased by 70 percent alongside increasingly lucrative media rights deals.[23] In 2015 the top college football coach (Nick Saban at the University of Alabama) made nearly $7.1 million per year, and the top men's basketball coach (John Calipari at the University of Kentucky) made around $6.3 million per year.[24]

Contrary to popular belief, most college athletic programs lose money, and most (including some among the small handful of profitable programs) rely on subsidies from their affiliated universities—especially in the form of student fees—in order to keep up in the arms race.[25] Profitable or not, however, the biggest programs make select coaches, administrators, and officials rich.

By contrast, the players, whose labor is sold to networks and fans, are compensated under an amateur model. When the question of paying players a fair-market share of revenues comes up—often under the rubric "pay for play"—administrators and officials fall back on the figure of the student-athlete, a chimera assembled out of disjointed amateur and free-market parts that by any empirical or practical measure does not exist in the top programs. The NCAA reported in 2011 that athletes in Division I men's and women's sports spent the equivalent of a full-time work week on athletic activities during the season in their sports (for men's basketball players and football players more than forty hours a week, and for women's basketball players almost thirty-eight hours a week).[26] The PAC 12 conference reported in 2015 that its athletes spent an average of fifty hours a week during the season on athletics and raised concerns about missing classes, not having enough time to study, and being too sleep-deprived to perform academically.[27]

A common objection to pay-for-play is that college athletes are already compensated through full scholarships, but there are important details to consider. Until the NCAA granted autonomy to the Power 5 conferences, scholarships were limited to tuition, room and board, and course textbooks and did not cover the full costs of attending school (including nonrequired books, transportation, and basic necessities). This shortfall relates to the NCAA's attempts—starting with the "Sanity Code" in 1948 (a policy that permitted scholarship awards, but only in cases of financial need)—to uphold the guise of amateurism by paying *some* compensation to athletes based on their skills but prohibiting payment equal to the full costs of attending school.[28] Under the new regulations, top programs now have the option to grant scholarships that cover these additional expenses, though this change raises persisting questions about inequitable distribution to individual athletes as well as competitive imbalances that favor the richest athletic programs and conferences.[29]

As Zimbalist notes, the best athletes at the biggest programs receive full scholarships and are treated like royalty (special dormitories and dining halls, celebrity status, tutoring services). The issue for reformers, however, is that the discrepancy between the revenues these athletes generate and the value of an athletic scholarship constitutes an exploitative labor relationship.[30] According to a widely reported study from the National College Players Association (NCPA, an advocacy group) and the department of sport management at Drexel University, between 2011 and 2015 a full athletic scholarship was worth an average of around $23,000 per year. The study estimated fair market value for elite football players' services at $137,357 per year and for elite men's basketball players' services at $289,031 per year.[31] These numbers are consistent with previous research on gaps between revenue generation and scholarship compensation.[32]

As civil rights historian Taylor Branch writes in an influential essay for *The Atlantic*, the "whole edifice" of the amateur/free-market system "depends on the players' willingness to perform what is effectively volunteer work," an arrangement that athletes and officials are both "acutely aware of." Amateurism and the student-athlete are, Branch argues, "cynical hoaxes, legal confections propagated by the universities so they can exploit the skills and fame of young athletes." The only way to change elite college sport, he suggests, is to desacralize the amateur ideal.[33]

As with every example I have analyzed in this book, the O'Bannon case and the legal and activist challenges proximate to it offer no final guarantees for radical change, but they project alternative possibilities for one of the most durable, powerful, and inequitable institutions in the history of U.S. sport. This is what I attempt to capture in each of the theses that follow: the importance of operating under a "logic of no guarantees" while still imagining the potential for a meaningfully alternative future through religious conflicts in elite televised sport.[34]

Theses on Sport and Negative Theology

Each thesis below builds from the definitions of "theology" and "religion" offered in Chapter 1 and applied throughout this book. Before proceeding I want to briefly review each of these definitions. I have conceived of theology as a framework for imagining a "wholly other" alternative to the political, economic, and social conditions of the present.[35] Critical theorists borrow this idea of a radically alternative world from more conventional notions of theology (the study of the nature of God and religious belief), but their commitments are largely materialist, secular, and atheistic. I conceive of religion, through Eduardo Mendieta's work, as a summary of the institutional and symbolic contexts that theology gives expression to. Thus I have used these two terms somewhat interchangeably: theology is, as Mendieta argues, the "medium in which religion is able to speak and disclose its truth content."[36]

Critical theorists advance a "negative" theology in at least two senses that I have found important for elite televised sport. First, a negative theology is, as Adorno argues, "directed against natural and supernatural interpretation alike."[37] Consistent with religious studies scholars' calls to read *across* the porous border between sacred and profane or immanent and transcendent constituted by commercial media production, a negative theology opposes interpretations of social experience or economic production that are *either* metaphysical *or* materialist.[38] It allows, instead, a back-and-forth migration between religious images, terms, and ideals and their secular, economic, and politicized analogues.[39] Second, a negative theology calls on theorists to detach theological images from their institutional appropriations in order to recover their suppressed political potential and mobilize them against the very notions of historical progress they have upheld.[40] This approach to negative theology as both a critique of history and a practice of interpretation is, I have maintained throughout this book, ideally suited to understanding the problems and possibilities of political and economic change in contemporary elite sport.

1. Elite Sport Is at a Moment of Historically Significant Conjuncture Surrounding Its Most Foundational "Religious" Ideals; This Is an Opportune Time for Critical and Activist Work

Throughout this book I have relied on Stuart Hall's conception of conjuncture as "a period in which the contradictions and problems and antagonisms, which are always present in different domains in a society, begin to . . . accumulate" or "fuse" around a point of rupture.[41] To cite Walter Benjamin's parallel (but more explicitly theological) terminology, in moments of "recognizability" tensions between an idealized religious image or trope and its political and economic mobilizations can become popularly legible, crystallizing into "a constellation saturated with tensions."[42] Conjuncture includes the aftermath of the resulting ruptures, relevant processes of social change, and "challenges to the existing historical project or social order."[43]

I have maintained in each of the preceding chapters that meaningful social, political, and economic change might occur within and through elite sport via challenges to certain foundational religious or theological ideals. Amateurism is a perfect example. It holds together the entire economic system of elite college athletics, and its status as a sacrosanct ideal allows—in fact *forces*—strained legal and moral arguments, such as when administrators acknowledge that college sport is big business while paternalistically guarding so-called student-athletes from the stain of commercialism. Even if, as I argued in Chapter 1, the boundary between sacred and profane is porous, it remains within the power of administrators and officials to redraw that boundary and to have it legally sanctioned. Relating this idea to college sport, judges uphold the formal protections of antitrust and labor laws (as in the 2015 appeals decision on the O'Bannon case, or the 1984 *NCAA v. Board of*

Regents decision) while also protecting as "revered" the amateur ideal, sealing it off as a question of *higher law*. This is clearly discernable as a religious problem. Seeding apostasy and winning in courts of law and public opinion alike are thus interdependent projects.

In Chapter 1 I raised the concern that sport is commonly perceived as fundamentally incompatible with politics, a form of activity that is not just "apolitical" (as many fans, players, coaches, or commentators might argue) but "actively *anti*-political" (a charge more common among academics).[44] As David Andrews and Michael Giardina note, academics interested in a critical study of sport have established it "as the labyrinthine and multifaceted social, cultural, political, and economic institution that it is," an institution interrelated with, operating through, and influencing a larger structure of social forces.[45] Yet academics (especially those outside sport culture studies) still tend to totalize sport as inherently repressive, an institution for which critical work can expose corruptions but hardly locate alternative futures. If this is the predominant view, then we can have only very limited critical studies of sport, failing to sufficiently appreciate those conjunctures within and through which sport exerts unique force.

This is, in my estimation, *the* barrier to critical and cultural work on sport-related conjunctures. The problem cannot be addressed by justifying sport as yet another site that stages ideological struggles that are timely in a particular discipline. If that is the strategy, then sport scholars lose by way of comparison: if I can learn everything I need to know about these problems by researching a context with more status, why bother with sport? Why not just leave engagements with sport to the "sport" people? Instead, I think it is important to advance sport as a context within, through, and around which certain fusions or constellations take unique shape, so that gerrymandering sport from a cultural configuration within which it is ideologically central stands as an analytical failure. It seems to me that this case can be made especially strongly around religious antagonisms formed uniquely within and through elite sport.

2. Religious Tropes and Images Constitute Particularly Critical Antagonisms in Elite Sport Culture

The legal and activist efforts represented in the O'Bannon case, in the Northwestern unionization attempt, and in similar interventions demonstrate that fundamental change in elite college sport requires direct attacks against the sanctity of amateurism. This was how Walter Byers, the architect of the contemporary NCAA, understood the pathway to change. Byers coined the term "student-athlete" and from 1951 to the early 1980s built the NCAA into a commercial empire that he came to regret. In his 1995 book *Unsportsman-like Conduct*, Byers writes: "Prosecutors and the courts, with the support of the public, should use antitrust laws to break up the collegiate cartel—not just in athletics, but in other aspects of collegiate life as well."[46] This is essentially what is happening now. The resulting changes are incremental and keep in place the most important inequities, and public support is only just beginning to shift. At the same time, it is increasingly difficult to imagine amateurism remaining a stable, organizing ideal for elite college sport moving forward.

In each of the preceding chapters, I have made a similar point: the dissolution of a religious ideal by no means guarantees radical change. Yet many of the religious ideals I have examined—for example, eternity, witnessing, transcendence—can no longer be recovered or deployed in the same terms, can no longer underwrite the same narrative of continuous historical progress in elite sport. In this sense *inevitability* is itself an important theological trope. It supports, as I argued in Chapter 2, problematic evolutionary notions of human-athletic advance that constitute eternity through the forgetting of obsolete bodies. It can also, however, work against the maintenance of religious idealism, projecting an image of inescapable desacralization: instant replay fosters an irreligious desire for perfection; new biotechnologies shift the locus of transcendence from body to machine; origins transmit foundational sins that prove impossible to purge. What can be done to turn back the tide of technological advance, market expansion, or body modification? Nothing. Soccer and Major League Baseball have instant replay. Cyborgs are running in the Olympics. Retired football players are about to degenerate en masse, on television.

These shifts call to mind a clinical understanding of the word "critical," related to decisive turning points (as in the medical phrase "critical condition") and an attunement to coming historical and cultural changes.[47] Contemporary sport is at the center of any number of such critical turning points, as religious tropes like witnessing, eternity, or transcendence foster a compulsion to discern problems of historical production in the smallest details of movement and space; create a hyperawareness about time, labor, and the planned obsolescence of bodies; raise foundational questions about advances in human physiological and cognitive potential; and call into question the categorical naturalness of bodies. These and other theological tropes provide important starting points from which we can map out lines of force unique to sport and trace their influence throughout a broader constellation of cultural and historical problems.

3. Athletic Bodies Are Theological Objects that Inscribe Cultural Tensions Both Unique to and Expansive beyond Sport

As I noted in Chapter 1, reading an image, object, or trope "theologically" involves the following: interpreting the meanings of that image across the porous boundary between sacred and profane constituted in commercial media production, juxtaposing the heights of that image's idealistic promises (e.g., progress, transcendence, revelation) against the betrayal of those promises in actual history, and recovering the suppressed political potential of that image in order to read it back "against the grain" of history.[48] This is the approach to understanding athletic bodies as theological objects that I have advanced throughout this book.

To follow from Benjamin, a theological object has no inherent meaning (though belief in its essential qualities constitutes much of its cultural power). Rather, as Susan Buck-Morss writes, an object takes on theological meaning through its construction within a particular cultural context. When idealized conceptions of that object's history come together with its present-day instantiations, the result is a "double focus" that illuminates simultaneously the object's "utopian potential" and the "betrayal of that potential."[49]

The figure of the student-athlete is a good example. It reflects an ancient Western cultural ideal—the training of a body-mind complex ideally suited to civic life—that becomes profaned when inserted into the highly professionalized and commercialized context of contemporary elite college sport.[50] Controversy surrounding the "student-athlete" has much to do, then, with the double focus that Buck-Morss identifies. The configuration promises and promotes an ideal balance of intellectual and physiological development within a benevolent institutional structure *and* at the same time signifies the betrayal of that ideal within the context of corporatized universities and athletic programs. By constantly restating "student-athlete" or "amateurism" as defenses for the current system, administrators and officials might still appeal to fans who want these ideals retained as symbolic reserves and points of nostalgic return, but they also further illuminate a discontinuity between expressed faith and actual practice. The construct "student-athlete" condenses a history of its own betrayals.

The student-athlete construct also illustrates how conjuncture involves the rupturing of contradictions and antagonisms that are "always present" but become uniquely legible under particular cultural and historical conditions.[51] From the NCAA's founding in 1905, its authority has been based more on the fragile moralism of amateurism than on material (legislative, political, economic) force.[52] Amateurism was itself always misfit to U.S. ideals regarding class and individualism. The concept had its roots in nineteenth-century Britain, where it was used to separate elites from competition with the working class. As Ronald Smith notes, U.S. society "had rejected the British concept of a fixed status system based on heredity, position, education, and wealth," so amateurism had to be modified. It retained, however, the feel of a "borrowed affectation," especially when the NCAA invoked it in attempts to bar collegians from competing for money.[53] Still, the NCAA has leveraged the amateur ideal throughout its history—sometimes feebly, sometimes quite powerfully—to promote and govern college athletics. The big-business imagery that today throws light on the NCAA's hypocrisy has been building since the organization was founded. Harvard constructed the first palatial college football stadium in 1905, with Princeton and Yale following about a decade later. The die was cast, and by 1930 U.S. universities had constructed seventy-four large stadiums, seven of which could seat more than seventy thousand spectators each. In an effort to fill these stadiums, college teams started to hire professional coaches and increase coaching salaries, which in some cases approached pay rates for top academic administrators.[54]

The NCAA and its member institutions have, from the beginning, struggled to negotiate conflicting interests, and academic groups, fans, journalists, and players have long recognized the corruptions of the amateur/for-profit model. How is our current moment of recognizability different, then? Why have the tensions present at the NCAA's founding fused to the point where amateurism is "on life support"? Perhaps the most straightforward answer relates to the (qualified) success of recent legal challenges. More qualitatively, there is a feeling among many commentators that there is now simply *too much* accumulation of capital and *too much* mediated exposure for the amateur ideal—which has always had fragile legal standing—to hold together as a popular justification.

This can be profitably viewed as a body problem. As the O'Bannon case highlights, audiovisual capture of collegiate athletes provides evidence for the inherent hypocrisy of the amateur/for-profit model and grounds athletes' claims to fair compensation in the obvious constitution of their bodies as products (as likenesses, performers, marketable ideals). This was the arrangement established in *NCAA v. Board of Regents*. As Justice Stevens wrote in the majority opinion: "In order to preserve the character and quality of the 'product,' athletes must not be paid, must be required to attend class, and the like."[55] When the NCAA polices college athlete behavior, it exposes its own protective investments surrounding amateurism as a commodity. Most college athletics scandals now reflect this hypocrisy. For example, in 2010, Auburn University quarterback Cam Newton was under investigation because his father had allegedly accepted illegal payments while Newton was deciding at which school to play football. During the investigation, Newton was wearing, in compliance with Auburn University's $10.6 million contract with apparel company Under Armour, fifteen of the company's logos.[56] In 2013 the NCAA investigated star Texas A&M quarterback Johnny Manziel for allegedly selling his autograph. At the time, Texas A&M sold Manziel's jersey at the official team store, Electronic Arts (EA) Sports used his likeness in its NCAA football video game, and major networks used his image to promote broadcasts. Most damning, the NCAA was selling Manziel's jersey, as well as other team apparel, on its official website, a practice that it ended only after considerable public pressure.[57] Through such controversies, offending college athletes become increasingly sympathetic characters, representatives of an economic system within which they generate revenues for institutions that own both their image and their labor.

To be clear, I have identified athletic bodies as theological *objects* not as an attempt to isolate and "read power" off of them. Rather, my aim has been to reference athletic bodies as conspicuous, moving, fleshly intersections of the complex social relations that "surround, interpenetrate, and shape" them.[58] In Chapter 1 I set out to understand elite sport in much the same way as Jean-Marie Brohm: athletics serve as a "fundamental way" of relating to the body in capitalist society, a collective fantasizing of the body as "object, and instrument, a technical means to an end, a reified factor of output and productivity." Brohm recognized that the capacity to idealize the body's potential through competition was entering into *"a period of continuous crisis,"* and this is a basic thread running through each of the preceding chapters.[59] As he argues, athletic bodies both "refract" and "aggravate" the political, economic, and social conflicts of which they are a part.[60] They are sites for the most acute religious crises in elite televised sport.

4. Audiovisual Capture Incorporates into Sport Media Production the Means for Both Reinforcing and Subverting Religious Ideals

For Benjamin, media technologies relate structurally to the process by which a historical object can be blasted out of "the continuum of historical succession" to force a "confrontation" between that object's past idealizations and its present reality.[61] Dialectical images create a "lightning flash" of recognition that is much "like illumination from a camera flashbulb." Photography, film, and electricity provide metaphorical understandings for the "shock" experience of recognition.[62] This relationship is especially summarized in Benjamin's conception of an "unconscious optics," which he developed based on the camera's capacity to capture and reveal previously unseen secrets of movement.[63] Through the optical unconscious, memory and recognition can sneak in "through the back door" to operate against powerful producers' constructions of official history. Most important, an unconscious optics suggests how the very means of mediated production through which powerful institutions create histories of their own progress might also contain the materials for those institutions' undoing.[64]

Underlying each of the controversies covered in this book is a structural relationship between sport historical production and audiovisual capture. As I argued in Chapter 3, sport serves as a primary training ground for conditioning forensic habits of seeing and judging and for raising "questions of truth . . . experience . . . and the trustworthiness of perception" bound up in witnessing history through audiovisual production.[65] Whether in the context of instant replay, "technological doping," or origin stories, sport media production supplies content and develops habits of witnessing that potentially subvert the idealized histories produced by leagues and governing bodies. To borrow from Benjamin, elite televised sport is a primary institution through which we develop "an irresistible compulsion to seek the tiny spark of an accident," to slow down the historical continuum and judge history in the very moment of its production, to perceive the intense stakes in forgetting, and to appreciate the present as a fleeting, urgent opening for intervention.[66]

The O'Bannon case began with just such a spark when O'Bannon first saw himself in an EA Sports video game. As reported in the *New York Times*: "O'Bannon, who played on UCLA's 1995 national championship team, watched as a friend's son queued up a video game in 2008. O'Bannon saw himself on the screen: the left hand, the slim frame, the No. 31 jersey. O'Bannon enjoyed the tribute, but then realized he was not being paid for his likeness."[67] In order to comply with NCAA rules, EA Sports excluded the names of the active and former college athletes featured in their games, but included other indicators—including jersey number, height, weight, race, hair color, position, and athletic attributes—of the avatar's real-life representee. The issues surrounding rights to likeness extended eventually to television broadcasts, posing a fundamental challenge to the NCAA's and its corporate partners' ability to produce programming under the legal and economic protections of an amateur model. It is one thing to acknowledge (as Justice Stevens did in *NCAA v. Board of Regents*) amateurism as a "product" alongside a restatement of idealized principles, but here was a visual referent that made the contradictions between amateur and for-profit systems dangerously recognizable. The likenesses represented an open secret, not only about who the avatars *really* represented but, more importantly, about a larger system of production wherein profitability was based on denying student-athletes legal rights to their own images. This is but one example of how antagonisms over sacrosanct ideals can become embedded within media content itself, through the very means of production that have historically suppressed those ideals' core contradictions.

5. Theological Ideals Can, under Certain Circumstances, Constitute Conjunctures, but This Does Not Guarantee Progressive Change

What if the amateur ideal was truly blasted apart, and college athletes were paid based on the fair market value of their labor? This would address some inequities while potentially creating or intensifying others. The overarching problem is that pay-for-play is at its core an affirmation of the very market logic that created an unjust system in the first place. Citing this as a justi-fication for *not* paying players, however, plays into the specious arguments of administrators and officials, who claim that they are protecting college athletes from the taint of runaway capitalism. Elite college sport is already an established free-market system with an amateur labor component that relates directly to brand management and revenue generation. Short of reversing more than a century of development behind the current amateur/for-profit system—for example, fully professionalizing elite college sport (departing from the amateur ethos to follow the model of the contemporary Olympics) or, in the opposite direction, regulating television and apparel contracts—reform is likely to be invented from the logics and materials of the current structure. This is not to say that the current system is inevitable, only that it exerts tremendous power.

The present argument for more equitable economic relations is tied to rev-enue generation in football and men's college basketball. As I argued above, the fact that football players and men's basketball players generate millions of dollars for administrators, athletic directors, coaches, apparel company ex-ecutives, and other powerful officials while receiving comparatively minimal compensation for their labor is at the heart of current calls for reform. This problem is further complicated by the fact that money flows up to a hege-monically white, male power structure. As the University of Central Flori-da Institute for Diversity and Ethics in Sport's "Racial and Gender Report Card" for 2014 indicated, white men occupy an overwhelming percentage of power positions at every level of Division I athletics (university presidents, athletic directors, head coaching positions in men's and women's sports, and conference commissioners).[68] This is especially problematic considering that the two most profitable college sports in the United States (football and men's basketball) are built around the spectacle of mostly African American play-ers overseen by coaches and administrators who are predominantly wealthy, white, and male. This problem is slightly more pronounced in basketball, where in 2014 around 58 percent of athletes were African American, while in FBS football around 53 percent of players were African American, 42 percent were white, 2 percent were Latino, and 2 percent were Asian/Pacific Islander.[69]

The basic moral justifications behind pay-for-play arguments are grounded in these economic and racial inequities. Although the question of compensation is often generalized ("Should *college athletes* be paid?") it applies almost exclusively to the top revenue-generating men's sports. Even as pay-for-play might address unjust labor relations specific to men's basketball and college football, then, it could also deepen existing inequities of funding and resources between these and all other Division I-FBS sports. This is especially true for women's sports and related protections under Title IX, the law that forbids sex discrimination in federally funded education programs and activities.[70] The most recent available data from the NCAA suggests substantial gaps in median expenditures for Division I-FBS men's and women's athletics, including a median gap (per team) of roughly $1 million for athletic student aid, $2 million for head coaches' compensation, $600,000 for administrators' compensation, $280,000 for recruiting, $1 million for travel, and $360,000 for equipment, uniforms, and supplies.[71]

At present the Title IX implications of pay-for-play are unclear. This is mainly because the current hybrid for-profit/nonprofit system potentially subjects athletic programs to federal laws regarding both workplace equity *and* educational equity—namely, the Equal Pay Act of 1963, the National Labor Relations Act of 1935 (per the Northwestern case), and Title IX.[72]

A program can meet equal-accommodation requirements by addressing any one of three tests contained within Title IX: provide participation opportunities proportionate to male and female student enrollments, demonstrate a record of program expansion responsive to developing interests in sports among the underrepresented sex (usually women), and demonstrate that the current program fully meets the interests and abilities of the underrepresented sex.[73] Deborah Brake writes that the three-part test "has proven to be strong medicine for expanding women's sports opportunities" as it took the "radical" step of insisting on equal participation "rather than merely espousing the ideal of a gender-neutral process." As effective as the test has been, a "far more radical measure . . . would have required equal sums of money for men's and women's athletics," but due to political opposition this was never considered.[74] The result allows (predominantly male) administrators and officials to claim the moral high ground in rejecting pay-for-play (here in the name of participatory equity in women's sports) even as they are shielded from laws requiring pay equity. Whether changing to a pay-for-play system would better address existing inequalities in men's and women's sports is unclear. This would depend in part on how Title IX rules on athletic scholarship equity are interpreted and in part on whether shifting player compensation from an educational context (scholarships) to a free-market context (salaries) would subject men's and women's compensation to pay equity laws.[75]

Just as with the other cases I examined in the previous chapters, college sport seems to be on the brink of a substantial change that by no means guarantees a radical break with the current structure. In his influential essay "The Problem of Ideology," Hall cites a passage from Antonio Gramsci that summarizes perfectly the point of analyzing historical change absent final guarantees. It is worth quoting in full here:

> What matters is the criticism to which . . . an ideological complex is subjected by the first representatives of the new historical phase. This criticism makes possible a process of differentiation and change in the relative weight that the elements of the old ideologies used to possess. What was previously secondary and subordinate, or even incidental, is now taken to be primary—becomes the nucleus of a new ideological and theoretical complex.[76]

Even if (or when) ideological struggle does not result in the realization of a wholly other system, shifts in the "relative weight" of existing elements can constitute the foundation for a new, alternative, and potentially more just arrangement of social forces. At the same time, elements of the older system might initially break apart but then resolidify in the shape of practices or appropriations invented to conform to the new reality. The dissolution of amateurism and its replacement by pay-for-play, for example, might address some race and class injustices while at the same time strengthening market-based justifications for gender inequities; technological doping might call into question naturalized assumptions about gender, sexuality, and ability while also opening new markets for technology companies and reinforcing the power of nations with advanced medical and technological infrastructures. In fact, such simultaneously progressive and inequitable outcomes are very likely.

Perhaps this distinguishes my approach to theology from other projects inspired by the so-called theological turn in critical and cultural theory. I am not assuming that a wholly other present can be theorized or realized within or through sport. What intrigues me, per Gramsci's insights, is the following: (1) the extent to which theological images and tropes contain resources for change toward a "new historical phase" in elite sport culture and (2) the practical, political possibility that critiquing and reimagining these tropes and images might found an alternative structure of social relations. For me the importance of theology relates, as Lawrence Grossberg argues, to the theoretical and political task of gaining a "better understanding of where we are so that we can get somewhere else (some place, we hope, that is better—based on more just principles of equality and the distribution of wealth and power), so that we can have a little more control over the history that we are already making." This is not to give up on big questions about equity, justice, or radical change. It is to "politicize" and "historicize" those questions, to measure theoretical and activist interventions according to "the political positions and trajectories" that they enable within specific contexts of power.[77]

NOTES

CHAPTER 1

1. Karl Marx, "Toward a Critique of Hegel's *Philosophy of Right*: Introduction," in *Karl Marx: Selected Writings*, 2nd ed., ed. David McClellan (New York: Oxford University Press, 2000), 71–72. For critiques of common readings of Marx's statement that religion was the "opium of the people," see Andrew McKinnon, "Reading 'Opium of the People': Expression, Protest, and the Dialectics of Religion," *Critical Sociology* 31, nos. 1–2 (2005): 15–38; and Roland Boer, "Opium, Idols and Revolution: Marx and Engels on Religion," *Religion Compass* 5, no. 11 (2011): 698–707.

2. Marx, "Toward a Critique," 71–72.

3. Terry Eagleton, "Football: A Dear Friend to Capitalism," *The Guardian*, June 15, 2010, http://www.theguardian.com/commentisfree/2010/jun/15/football-socialism-crack-cocaine-people.

4. Ben Carrington, "Sport without Final Guarantees: Cultural Studies/Marxism/Sport," in *Marxism, Cultural Studies and Sport*, ed. Ben Carrington and Ian McDonald (New York: Routledge, 2009), 20.

5. Ibid., 22.

6. James Hay, Stuart Hall, and Lawrence Grossberg, "Interview with Stuart Hall, June 12, 2012," *Communication and Critical/Cultural Studies* 10, no. 1 (2013): 16–17.

7. Carrington, "Sport without Final Guarantees," 22.

8. Lawrence Grossberg, *Cultural Studies in the Future Tense* (Durham, NC: Duke University Press, 2010), 20.

9. McKinnon, "Reading 'Opium of the People,'" 15–16, 19–20; Boer, "Opium, Idols and Revolution," 703; Marx, "Toward a Critique," 72.

10. McKinnon, "Reading 'Opium of the People,'" 24–25. McKinnon also cites and translates on these pages Sergio Rojo's argument about the dialectics in Marx's opium metaphor. See Sergio Vuscovic Rojo, "La religion, opium du people et protestation contre

la misère réele: Les positions de Marx et de Lénine," *Social Compass* 35, nos. 2–3 (1988): 210, 214.

11. McKinnon, "Reading 'Opium of the People,'" 25–27.

12. Max Horkheimer, "Thoughts on Religion," in *Critical Theory: Selected Essays*, trans. Matthew J. O'Connell (New York: Herder and Herder, 1972), 129. Also see McKinnon, "Reading 'Opium of the People,'" 27.

13. Horkheimer, "Thoughts on Religion," 129–131.

14. Charles S. Prebish, *Religion and Sport: The Meeting of Sacred and Profane* (Westport, CT: Greenwood Press, 1993), 13; Michael Novak, *The Joy of Sports: Endzones, Bases, Baskets, Balls, and the Consecration of the American Spirit*, rev. ed. (Lanham, MD: Madison Books, 1994), 30–31; Joseph L. Price, ed., *From Season to Season: Sports as American Religion* (Macon, GA: Mercer University Press, 2001), 57; Eric Bain-Selbo, *Game Day and God: Football, Faith, and Politics in the American South* (Macon, GA: Mercer University Press, 2009), 23–26.

15. Prebish, *Religion and Sport*, 13.

16. Harry Edwards, *Sociology of Sport* (Homewood, IL: The Dorsey Press, 1973), 90. For a review of the idea in the sport culture scholarship that sport might supplant religion, see Michael L. Butterworth, "Ritual in the 'Church of Baseball': Suppressing the Discourse of Democracy after 9/11," *Communication and Critical/Cultural Studies* 2, no. 2 (2005): 111–112. Also see Brad Schultz and Mary Lou Sheffer, eds., *Sport and Religion in the Twenty-First Century* (Lanham, MD: Lexington Books, 2016); Varda Burstyn, *The Rites of Men: Manhood, Politics, and the Culture of Sport* (Toronto: University of Toronto Press, 1999), 19; and Steven J. Overman, *The Influence of the Protestant Ethic on Sport and Recreation* (Aldershot, UK: Avebury, 1997), 7. For examples of popular concern over sport displacing religion, see, for example, *Agence France-Presse*, "Football: The Soothing Role of World Cup Fever," May 28, 2014; Chris Beneke and Arthur Remillard, "Is Religion Losing Ground to Sports?" *Washington Post*, January 31, 2014, https://www.washingtonpost.com/opinions/is-religion-losing-ground-to-sports/2014/01/31/6faa4d64-82bd-11e3-9dd4-e7278db80d86_story.html; and Michael Serazio, "Just How Much Is Sports Fandom like Religion?" *The Atlantic*, January 29, 2013, http://www.theatlantic.com/entertainment/archive/2013/01/just-how-much-is-sports-fandom-like-religion/272631/.

17. Jeffrey Scholes and Raphael Sassower, *Religion and Sports in American Culture* (New York: Routledge, 2014), 4.

18. Robert J. Higgs and Michael C. Braswell, *An Unholy Alliance: The Sacred and Modern Sports* (Macon, GA: Mercer University Press, 2004), 27.

19. Higgs and Braswell, *An Unholy Alliance*, 14.

20. William J. Baker, *Playing with God: Religion and Modern Sport* (Cambridge, MA: Harvard University Press, 2007), 3–5. For more on cultural and historical navigations between formal religious principles and sport, see Jim Parry, Mark Nesti, and Nick Watson, eds., *Theology, Ethics and Transcendence in Sports* (New York: Routledge, 2011); Craig A. Forney, *The Holy Trinity of American Sports: Civil Religion in Football, Baseball, and Basketball* (Macon, GA: Mercer University Press, 2007); and Robert J. Higgs, *God in the Stadium: Sports and Religion in America* (Lexington: University Press of Kentucky, 1995).

21. Michael L. Butterworth, "Saved at Home: Christian Branding and Faith Nights in the 'Church of Baseball,'" *Quarterly Journal of Speech* 97, no. 3 (2011): 309–333. Also see Michael L. Butterworth, "The Passion of the Tebow: Sports Media and Heroic Language in the Tragic Frame," *Critical Studies in Media Communication* 30, no. 1 (2013): 17–33. As Butterworth notes, sport has become one of many sites for the "Christotainment" industry. For more on the popular branding of Christianity, see Shirley R. Steinberg and Joe L. Kincheloe, eds., *Christotainment: Selling Jesus through Popular Culture* (Boulder, CO: Westview Press,

2009); and James B. Twitchell, *Shopping for God: How Christianity Went from In Your Heart to In Your Face* (New York: Simon and Schuster, 2007).

22. Clifford Putney, *Muscular Christianity: Manhood and Sports in Protestant America, 1880–1920* (Cambridge, MA: Harvard University Press, 2001), 11. For an examination of sport, religion, and masculinity specific to the Mormon faith, see Richard Ian Kimball, *Sports in Zion: Mormon Recreation, 1890–1940* (Urbana: University of Illinois Press, 2003).

23. Tony Ladd and James A. Mathisen, *Muscular Christianity: Evangelical Protestants and the Development of American Sport* (Grand Rapids, MI: Baker Books, 1999), 11–13.

24. For an excellent analysis of these debates, see Shirl Hoffman, "Prayer Out of Bounds," in Parry, Nesti, and Watson, *Theology, Ethics, and Transcendence in Sports*, 35–63.

25. "Civil religion" is a prominent coinage in sport culture studies that derives from Robert Bellah's influential work. See Robert N. Bellah, "Civil Religion in America," *Daedalus* 96, no. 1 (1967): 1–21.

26. Sean McCloud, "Popular Culture Fandoms, the Boundaries of Religious Studies, and the Project of the Self," *Culture and Religion* 4, no. 2 (2003): 193–195. McCloud summarizes this tendency as "parallelomania," a term that he borrows from Samuel Samdel, the former president of the Society of Biblical Literature and Exegesis.

27. James Carey, *Communication as Culture: Essays on Media and Society* (New York: Routledge, 1992), 48.

28. For more on Apophatic theology, see, for example, Chris Boesel and Catherine Keller, eds., *Apophatic Bodies: Negative Theology, Incarnation, and Relationality* (New York: Fordham University Press, 2010); William Franke, ed., *On What Cannot Be Said: Apophatic Discourses in Philosophy, Religion, Literature, and the Arts* (Notre Dame, IN: Notre Dame University Press, 2007).

29. David Kaufmann, "Beyond Use, within Reason: Adorno, Benjamin, and the Question of Theology," *New German Critique* 83 (Spring/Summer 2001): 151, 168–169; Rudolf J. Siebert, "The Critical Theory of Society: The Longing for the Totally Other," *Critical Sociology* 31, nos. 1–2 (2005): 62.

30. Eduardo Mendieta, "Introduction: Religion as Critique, Theology as Social Critique and Enlightened Reason," in *The Frankfurt School on Religion: Key Writings by the Major Thinkers*, ed. Eduardo Mendieta (New York: Routledge, 2005), 10–11; Horkheimer, "Thoughts on Religion," 129–131; Walter Benjamin, "Theses on the Philosophy of History," in *Illuminations*, ed. Hannah Arendt and trans. Harry Zohn (New York: Harcourt, Brace and World, 1955), 259.

31. For an overview of debates over the term "theology" in religious studies, see Linell E. Cady and Delwin Brown, eds., *Religious Studies, Theology, and the University: Conflicting Maps, Changing Terrain* (Albany: State University of New York Press, 2002).

32. "Wholly other" is a phrase often associated with Max Horkheimer. See Rudolf Siebert, "Horkheimer's Sociology of Religion," *Telos* 30 (Winter 1976): 127. For general overviews of the relationship between contemporary philosophy, theology, and capitalism, see John Milbank, Slavoj Žižek, and Creston Davis, "Introduction," in *Paul's New Moment: Continental Philosophy and the Future of Christian Theology* (Grand Rapids, MI: Brazos Press, 2010), 1–4; and Creston Davis, "Introduction: Holy Saturday or Resurrection Sunday? Staging an Unlikely Debate," in Slavoj Žižek and John Milbank, *The Monstrosity of Christ: Paradox or Dialectic?* ed. Creston Davis (Cambridge, MA: MIT Press, 2009), 3–7.

33. I say "largely" because of the notable exception of Christian theologian John Milbank's work. In addition to Milbank's writings in *Paul's New Moment* and *The Monstrosity of Christ*, see John Milbank, *Theology and Social Theory: Beyond Secular Reason*, 2nd ed. (Malden, MA: Wiley-Blackwell, 2006).

34. As Eduardo Mendieta summarizes, "The Frankfurt School's critique of religion turns religion into a source of social critique that traverses the traditional disciplinary boundaries that have been used to gerrymander religion." While it is "not denominational, or confessional . . . its sources can be traced to the atheistic Messianic Judaism, crisis theology, and Christian Socialism of the early part of the twentieth century" (Mendieta, "Introduction: Religion as Critique," 11). For more on the relationship between Western Marxism and liberation theology, see Roland Boer, "The Perpetual Allure of the Bible for Marxism," *Historical Materialism* 15, no. 4 (2007): 53–77.

35. See Milbank, Žižek, and Davis, "Introduction," in *Paul's New Moment*; and Davis, "Introduction," in *The Monstrosity of Christ*.

36. Boer, "The Perpetual Allure," 62.

37. Ibid.; Giorgio Agamben, *The Time that Remains: A Commentary on the Letter to the Romans*, trans. Patricia Dailey (Stanford, CA: Stanford University Press, 2005). In addition to Žižek's contributions to *Paul's New Moment* and *The Monstrosity of Christ*, see Slavoj Žižek, *The Fragile Absolute: Or, Why Is the Christian Legacy Worth Fighting For?* (New York: Verso, 2009); Slavoj Žižek, *The Sublime Object of Ideology* (New York: Verso, 2009); and Slavoj Žižek, *The Puppet and the Dwarf: The Perverse Core of Christianity* (Cambridge, MA: MIT Press, 2003). Among Derrida's most cited connections with Benjamin is a long note in *Specters of Marx*, where Derrida identifies consistencies on the themes of messianism and his own work's inheritance from Benjamin's "Theses." Regarding Benjamin's first thesis, Derrida writes: "Let us quote this passage for what is consonant there, despite many differences and keeping relative proportions in mind, with what we are trying to say here about a certain messianic destitution, in a spectral logic of inheritance and generations, but a logic turned toward the future no less than the past, a heterogeneous and disjointed time. What Benjamin calls *Anspruch* (claim, appeal, interpellation, address) is not far from what we are suggesting with the word *injunction*." Jacques Derrida, *The Specters of Marx: The State of the Debt, the Work of Mourning, and the New International*, trans. Peggy Kamuf (New York: Routledge, 1994), 180–181n2.

38. For a more detailed account of the disconnect between earlier Western Marxists and contemporary thinkers of the theological turn, see Boer, "The Perpetual Allure."

39. My thinking is influenced by approaches to method and theory in cultural studies, where choices over each are based on what might work given the problems of a particular context. See, for example, Cary Nelson, Paula Treichler, and Lawrence Grossberg, "Cultural Studies: An Introduction," in *Cultural Studies*, ed. Lawrence Grossberg, Cary Nelson, and Paula Treichler (New York: Routledge, 1992), 2; and Stuart Hall, "Politics, Contingency, Strategy," *Small Axe* 1 (March 1997): 152.

40. Grossberg, *Cultural Studies in the Future Tense*, 27.

41. This problem involves the "immanentist" character of postmodern or poststructuralist contemporary critical theory, the idea that critics cannot do criticism from a position outside the very ideological structures they challenge. For an excellent summary of this problem, see Dana L. Cloud and Joshua Gunn, "W(h)ither Ideology?" *Western Journal of Communication* 75, no. 4 (2011): 414–417.

42. Boer, "The Perpetual Allure," 62.

43. Max Horkheimer, "Theism and Atheism," in *Critique of Instrumental Reason*, trans. Matthew J. O'Connell (New York: Seabury Press, 1974), 50.

44. Mendieta, "Introduction: Religion as Critique," 6–11.

45. Carrington, "Sport without Final Guarantees," 20–21. William J. Morgan argues that this is the legacy of neo-Marxist and New Left approaches to sport: the contention "that there is nothing about the social makeup of sport that suggests it possesses any eman-

cipatory potential. . . . [T]here is no place to turn in the world of sport, no current practice or institution of sport" where anything but repression can be found. See William J. Morgan, *Leftist Theories of Sport: A Critique and Reconstruction* (Urbana, IL: University of Illinois Press, 1994), 25.

46. Carrington, "Sport without Final Guarantees," 22.

47. Hay, Hall, and Grossberg, "Interview with Stuart Hall," 16.

48. Stuart Hall, "The Problem of Ideology—Marxism without Guarantees," *Journal of Communication Inquiry* 10, no. 2 (1986): 28–44.

49. Hay, Hall, and Grossberg, "Interview with Stuart Hall," 17. Also see Grossberg, *Cultural Studies in the Future Tense*, 40–43.

50. Walter Benjamin, *The Arcades Project*, trans. Howard Eiland and Kevin McLaughlin (Cambridge, MA: Harvard University Press, 1999), 462–463.

51. Benjamin, *Arcades*, 462.

52. Samuel McCormick, "Neighbors and Citizens: Local Speakers in the Now of Their Recognizability," *Philosophy and Rhetoric* 44, no. 4 (2011): 432; Susan Buck-Morss, *The Dialectics of Seeing: Walter Benjamin and the Arcades Project* (Cambridge, MA: MIT Press, 1989), 218–219.

53. McCormick, "Neighbors," 433; Buck-Morss, *The Dialectics of Seeing*, 219; Benjamin, *Arcades*, 464.

54. McCormick, "Neighbors," 432–443; Buck-Morss, *The Dialectics of Seeing*, 219; Benjamin, "Theses," 263.

55. Benjamin, *Arcades*, 475.

56. Ibid., 463, 475; Benjamin, "Theses," 257.

57. Hay, Hall, and Grossberg, "Interview with Stuart Hall," 16–18.

58. Benjamin, "Theses," 255.

59. McCormick, "Neighbors," 439.

60. Ibid., 435. Also see Žižek, *The Puppet and the Dwarf*, 133–143.

61. McCormick, "Neighbors," 440–441.

62. Grossberg, *Cultural Studies in the Future Tense*, 22–23. For work that frames critical and cultural studies of sport under a logic of "no guarantees," see Carrington, "Sport without Final Guarantees"; David L. Andrews and Michael D. Giardina, "Sport without Guarantees: Toward a Cultural Studies that Matters," *Cultural Studies* ↔ *Critical Methodologies* 8, no. 4 (2008): 395–422.

63. Grossberg, *Cultural Studies in the Future Tense*, 22–23.

64. Lawrence Grossberg, "The Circulation of Cultural Studies," *Critical Studies in Mass Communication* 6, no. 4 (1989): 415.

65. Hall, "The Problem of Ideology," 40–43.

66. Jean-Marie Brohm, *Sport—a Prison of Measured Time*, trans. Ian Fraser (Worcester, UK: Pluto Press, 1989), 1–2.

67. Brohm, *Sport*, 5–6, emphasis original.

68. Milbank, Žižek, and Davis, "Introduction," 1. Also see Davis, "Introduction: Holy Saturday."

69. Ibid., 5.

70. David Held, *Introduction to Critical Theory: Horkheimer to Habermas* (Berkeley: University of California Press, 1980), 184–185.

71. See Susan Buck-Morss, *The Origin of Negative Dialectics: Theodor W. Adorno, Walter Benjamin, and the Frankfurt Institute* (New York: Free Press, 1977), 6.

72. Theodor W. Adorno and Walter Benjamin, *The Complete Correspondence 1928–1940*, ed. Henri Lonitz and trans. Nicholas Walker (Cambridge, MA: Harvard University

Press, 1999), 66–67. For an analysis of Adorno's and Benjamin's disagreements over theology, see Buck-Morss, *The Origin of Negative Dialectics*, 143–146.

73. Quoted in Kaufmann, "Beyond Use, within Reason," 151.

74. Siebert, "The Critical Theory of Society," 62.

75. Kaufmann, "Beyond Use, within Reason," 168–169.

76. Richard Gruneau, *Class, Sports, and Social Development* (Amherst: University of Massachusetts Press, 1983), 32–34.

77. See, for example, Ivo Jirasek, "Pilgrimage as a Form of Physical and Movement Spirituality," in Parry, Nesti, and Watson, *Theology, Ethics and Transcendence in Sports*, 223–232; Bain-Selbo, *Game Day and God*, 1–26; Forney, *The Holy Trinity*, 4n12; Joseph L. Price, *Rounding the Bases: Baseball and Religion in America* (Macon, GA: Mercer University Press, 2006), 71–92; Bonnie Miller-McLemore, "Through the Eyes of Mircea Eliade: United States Football as a Religious Rite de Passage," in *From Season to Season: Sports as American Religion*, ed. Joseph L. Price (Macon, GA: Mercer University Press, 2001), 115–135; Joseph L. Price, "An American Apotheosis: Sports as Popular Religion," in *From Season to Season*, 215–231; and Prebish, *Religion and Sport*, 3–17.

78. Mircea Eliade, *The Sacred and the Profane: The Nature of Religion*, trans. Willard R. Trask (New York: Harper and Row, 1961), 70.

79. See Gordon Lynch, *The Sacred in the Modern World: A Cultural Sociological Approach* (New York: Oxford University Press, 2012), 15.

80. Jeffrey H. Mahan, "Reflections on the Past and Future of the Study of Religion and Popular Culture," in *Between Sacred and Profane: Researching Religion and Popular Culture*, ed. Gordon Lynch (New York: I. B. Taurus, 2007), 52; Gordon Lynch, "What Is This 'Religion' in the Study of Religion and Popular Culture?" in Lynch, *Between Sacred and Profane*, 136–138.

81. Lynch, "What Is This 'Religion,'" 136–138. While my interests in sacred/profane binaries are specific to sport, my thinking is also influenced by similar challenges issued through studies on media and ritual. See, for example, Stewart M. Hoover and Shalini Venturelli, "The Category of the Religious: The Blindspot of Contemporary Media Theory?" *Critical Studies in Mass Communication* 13, no. 3 (1996): 251–265; Nick Couldry, *Media Rituals: A Critical Approach* (New York: Routledge, 2003); Mihai Coman, "Cultural Anthropology and Mass Media: A Processual Approach," in *Media Anthropology*, ed. Eric W. Rothenbuhler and Mihai Coman (Thousand Oaks, CA: Sage, 2005), 46–55; Johanna Sumiala-Seppänen and Matteo Stocchetti, "Mediated Sacralization and the Construction of Postmodern *Communio Sanctorum*: The Case of the Swedish Foreign Minister Anna Lindh," *Material Religion* 1, no. 2 (2005): 228–248; Johanna Sumiala-Seppänen, "Implications of the Sacred in Media Studies," in *Implications of the Sacred in (Post)Modern Media*, ed. Johanna Sumiala-Seppänen, Knut Lundby, and Raimo Salokangas (Gothenburg: Nordicom, 2006), 11–29; Simon Cottle, "Mediatized Rituals: Beyond Manufacturing Consent," *Media, Culture and Society* 28, no. 3 (2006): 411–432; and Mervi Pantti and Johanna Sumiala, "Till Death Do Us Join: Media, Mourning Rituals and the Sacred Centre of the Society," *Media, Culture and Society* 31, no. 1 (2009): 120–122.

82. Scholes and Sassower, *Religion and Sports*, 4.

83. Kenneth Burke, *The Rhetoric of Religion: Studies in Logology* (Berkeley: University of California Press, 1970), 2.

84. Ibid., 13.

85. Ibid., 15.

86. Joshua Gunn, *Modern Occult Rhetoric: Mass Media and the Drama of Secrecy in the Twentieth Century* (Tuscaloosa: University of Alabama Press, 2005), xxii.

87. Edwards, *Sociology of Sport,* 261–262.

88. McCloud, "Popular Culture Fandoms," 191–194.

89. Buck-Morss, *The Dialectics of Seeing,* 248–249.

90. Ibid., 249

91. Ibid., 13–14.

92. James Martell, "Taking Benjamin Seriously as a Political Thinker," *Philosophy and Rhetoric* 44, no. 4 (2011): 298. Buck-Morss captures this particularly well in *The Origin of Negative Dialectics* by detailing distinct responses to Benjamin's work by his friends Gershom Scholem and Bertolt Brecht. Both criticized Benjamin's attempts to move between and reconcile theological and materialist thought, but for different reasons: Scholem wanted Benjamin to remain grounded principally in theology, while Brecht saw him as too mystical. As famous as Adorno was for claiming that Benjamin's thinking was not dialectical enough, he was alone among Benjamin's friends in supporting the effort to incorporate theology and materialist thought. See Buck-Morss, *The Origin of Negative Dialectics,* 140–146.

93. See Mendieta, "Introduction: Religion as Critique," 10–11; Horkheimer, "Thoughts on Religion," 129–131.

94. Milbank, Žižek, and Davis, "Introduction," *Paul's New Moment,* 1–2.

95. Benjamin, "Theses," 259–260. Rolf Tiedemann warns against reading the Angel of History and other figures in the "Theses" (e.g., the Messiah) as literal religious images. He writes, "The angel in the ninth thesis by no means represents the Messiah. This is unmistakably audible in the sentence, 'The angel would *like to stay,* awaken the dead, and make whole what has been smashed'" and suggests that the sentence "supports the conclusion that Benjamin intended the angel to stand for the historical materialist." Rolf Tiedemann, "Historical Materialism or Political Messianism? An Interpretation of the Theses 'On the Concept of History,'" in *Benjamin: Philosophy, History, Aesthetics,* ed. Gary Smith (Chicago: University of Chicago Press, 1989), 181. Commentators on the "Theses" often read the Angel as representing Benjamin's concerns over the "weak Messianic power" possessed by historical materialists. In the most basic sense, Messianism provides an image of time ceasing or slowing so that all of history is contemplated in an "enormous abridgement" of past, present, and future (Benjamin, "Theses," 265). That abridgement is "Messianic" in the sense that it *burdens* the present generation not only to recognize but also to respond to past events in a time of unique awareness. For Benjamin our generation, like those before it, has "been endowed with a *weak* Messianic power" through which to settle the claims of the past (ibid., 256). Like the Angel, we are capable of experiencing the claims of the dead and forgotten, but, as Jill Petersen Adams writes, "unlike a true Messiah, we have no power to raise the dead, and we cannot undo the wrongs done to them" (Jill Petersen Adams, "Mourning, the Messianic, and the Specter: Derrida's Appropriation of Benjamin in 'Specters of Marx,'" *Philosophy Today* 51, no. 5 [2007]: 140–147). Even so, the historical materialist is uniquely aware that the past makes a continuing claim that "cannot be settled cheaply," and that every generation inherits responsibility for its unsettled burdens (Benjamin, "Theses," 256). For more on the roots of Jewish Messianism as they relate to Benjamin's thinking, see Anson Rabinach, "Between Enlightenment and Apocalypse: Benjamin, Bloch and Modern German Jewish Messianism," *New German Critique* 34 (Winter, 1985): 78–124; Buck-Morss, *The Dialectics of Seeing,* 231–245; and Richard A. Lee, "The Negative History of the Moment of Possibility: Walter Benjamin and the Coming of the Messiah," in *Rethinking the Frankfurt School: Alternative Legacies of Cultural Critique,* ed. Jeffrey T. Nealon and Caren Irr (Albany: State University of New York Press, 2002), 151. For more on Messianic themes in the contemporary theological turn, see Derrida, *The Specters of Marx,* 180–181n2; Žižek, *The Puppet and the Dwarf,* 3–9, 130–143; Agamben, *The Time that Remains*; and Arthur Bradley and

Paul Fletcher, "Introduction: On a Newly Arisen Messianic Tone in Philosophy," *Journal for Cultural Research* 13, nos. 3–4 (2009): 183–189.

96. Michael Bowman, "Cultural Critique as Performance: The Example of Walter Benjamin," *Literature in Performance* 8, no. 1 (1988): 6.

97. Benjamin, "Theses," 257–258. As Matthias Fritsch notes in his book *The Promise of Memory*, Benjamin's critique of historicism is aimed primarily at objectivist views of history, as they were represented in the German Historical School of the late nineteenth and early twentieth century and in Enlightenment philosophy. But Benjamin also detects, Fritsch writes, historicist tendencies in a "vulgar" Marxist conception of history, which "projects the classless society as the *telos* of an infinite progress." Despite this critique of "vulgar Marxism," Fritsch cautions against reading Benjamin's turn toward theology as an attempt to "'save' or even eschew a leftist . . . or a Marxist [agenda]." Benjamin was "fully aware," Fritsch argues, "of the theological, prophetic background to Marx that later commentaries uncovered. . . . Furthermore, Benjamin not only recognizes this background, but unmistakably affirms the translation of religious semantic potentials into a materialist view of history in which the messianic dimension is associated with, and discovered in, a this-worldly politics" (Matthias Fritsch, *The Promise of Memory: History and Politics in Marx, Benjamin, and Derrida* [Albany: State University of New York Press, 2005], 35–37, 159).

98. Benjamin, "Theses," 255, 262.

99. Ibid., 253. This partnership between historical materialism and theology is represented in the first thesis through the famous anecdote of the chess-playing puppet. The puppet sits at a table and, through a clever illusion, appears to play independently, answering his opponent's every move with a countermove. But in reality "a little hunchback who was an expert chess player" sits beneath and uses strings to guide the puppet's hands. Benjamin imagines a "philosophical counterpart" to this arrangement. The puppet represents "historical materialism" and can "win all the time" (in the class struggle and against historicism) "if it enlists the services of theology" (ibid.). When Benjamin writes about "historical materialism" in the remaining theses, he is advancing a "corrective," as Tiedemann puts it, to what the historical materialism referenced in the first thesis "does *not* do": it does not enlist the services of theology, it no longer affirms the unity of theory and praxis that "has been espoused by historical materialism since Marx," and this puts the outcome of historical struggle in doubt. To restore that unity, Benjamin "invokes anew the theological origin of Marxian concepts" while maintaining their "secularized content" (Tiedemann, "Historical Materialism," 188, 190–191). Benjamin looked to unify theology and historical materialism as a way to distinguish his approach from the historical materialism traditionally associated with Marx, which had, as Tiedemann writes, been "annexed and corrupted by the politics of the Soviet Union" (Tiedemann, "Historical Materialism," 191; also see Žižek, *The Sublime Object*, 161). Benjamin maintained that if historical materialism was to be revitalized after that annexation, an alliance would need to be formed with theology. As Gershom Scholem argues, the "Theses" represent "the completion of Benjamin's awakening from the shock of the Hitler-Stalin Pact," a political moment that, Tiedemann writes, "had to seem increasingly hopeless" (Tiedemann, "Historical Materialism," 192; Scholem is cited from this page in Tiedemann's essay; also see Gershom Scholem, *Walter Benjamin: The Story of a Friendship*, trans. Harry Zohn [Philadelphia, PA: The Jewish Publication Society of America, 1981], 221). Tiedemann emphasizes that the "Theses" clearly prioritize a materialist understanding of cultural change: historical materialism is to win by enlisting the services of theology and bringing them under its control; this is not an equal merger, and materialism is in charge. But theology also brings a transformative potential back into historical materialism as a lingering structure of thought and experience (Tiedemann, "Historical Materialism," 189–190).

100. Joshua Gunn, "Benjamin's Magic," *Telos* 119 (Spring 2001): 68–69.

101. Tiedemann, "Historical Materialism," 184; Benjamin, "Theses," 256. Benjamin's position that the past is unfinished is a key theological assumption in his larger critique of historical progress. In a letter reprinted in *The Arcades Project*, Horkheimer writes to Benjamin on the subject of whether history is incomplete and whether the past can still be redeemed: "The determination of incompleteness is idealistic. . . . Past injustice has occurred and is completed. The slain are really slain. . . . If one takes the lack of closure entirely seriously, one must believe in the Last Judgment." Benjamin responds that the "corrective to this line of thinking" is to consider history as "a form of remembrance" where what seems "determined" can be modified, a "mindfulness" that is for him fundamentally theological (Benjamin, *Arcades*, 471). As Gunn argues, Benjamin is not denying Horkheimer's materialist view that the dead are actually dead, and Horkheimer understands the practical aim of Benjamin's theological "corrective": that "an overly empirical 'dead' past forecloses any promise of change" and "plays into historicist renderings of the past" (Gunn, "Benjamin's Magic," 70). Horkheimer's letter in *The Arcades Project* is dated March 16, 1937. His later writings on theology cite the uniquely religious potential to imagine a "wholly other" alternative to the present, as I have noted. As Rudolf Siebert writes, Horkheimer stated in 1966 "that he could not support any philosophy lacking a theological moment, i.e., awareness of the Infinite or the wholly other" (Siebert, "Horkheimer's Sociology of Religion," 127).

102. Žižek, *The Sublime Object*, 161; Benjamin, "Theses," 257.

103. Michel Foucault, "Nietzsche, Genealogy, History," in *Michel Foucault: Aesthetics, Method, and Epistemology*, ed. James D. Faubion and trans. Robert Hurley (New York: New Press, 1998), 375–376.

104. Buck-Morss, *The Dialectics of Seeing*, 245.

105. Benjamin, *Arcades*, 470; McCormick, "Neighbors," 434; Buck-Morss, *The Dialectics of Seeing*, 218–219.

106. Benjamin, *Arcades*, 463.

107. Ibid., 475; McCormick, "Neighbors," 434. Also see Samuel Weber, *Benjamin's -abilities* (Cambridge, MA: Harvard University Press, 2008), 50–51.

108. McCormick, "Neighbors," 434.

109. Brohm, *Sport*, 5–6.

110. Ibid., 15.

111. Ibid., 5, emphasis original.

112. Ibid., 7.

113. Gunn, "Benjamin's Magic," 71.

114. Peter Gilgen, "History after Film," in *Mapping Benjamin: The Work of Art in the Digital Age*, ed. Hans Ulrich Gumbrecht and Michael Marrinan (Stanford, CA: Stanford University Press, 2003), 60.

115. Buck-Morss, *The Dialectics of Seeing*, 250. In *The Arcades Project* Benjamin cites French historian Andre Monglond: "The past has left images of itself in literary texts, images comparable to those which are imprinted by light on a photosensitive plate. The future alone possesses developers active enough to scan such surfaces perfectly" (Andre Monglond, *Le Preromantisme français* [Paris: Librairie Jose Corti, 1966], quoted in Benjamin, *Arcades*, 482).

116. Buck-Morss, *The Dialectics of Seeing*, 250.

117. Walter Benjamin, "The Work of Art in the Age of Mechanical Reproduction," in *Illuminations*, 238–239.

118. Miriam Hansen, *Babel and Babylon: Spectatorship in American Silent Film* (Cambridge, MA: Harvard University Press, 1991), 110–111.

119. Benjamin, "The Work of Art," 238–239.

120. See John Fiske, *Television Culture* (New York: Methuen, 1987), 219, 246; and Thomas P. Oates, "The Erotic Gaze in the NFL Draft," *Communication and Critical/Cultural Studies* 4, no. 1 (2007): 85.

121. Jennifer Hargreaves and Patricia Vertinsky, "Introduction," in *Physical Culture, Power and the Body*, ed. Jennifer Hargreaves and Patricia Vertinsky (New York: Routledge, 2007), 1.

122. As Brian Massumi argues, "[Emphasizing] positionality begins by subtracting movement from the picture" and "catches the body in a cultural freeze-frame." Accordingly, Debra Hawhee warns against the tendency in contemporary theory to "freeze bodies" by focusing primarily on signification and ignoring the importance of their movement "through time." See Brian Massumi, *Parables for the Virtual: Movement, Affect, Sensation* (Durham, NC: Duke University Press, 2002), 3; and Debra Hawhee, *Moving Bodies: Kenneth Burke at the Edges of Language* (Columbia: University of South Carolina Press, 2009), 7.

123. Jaime Schultz, *Qualifying Times: Points of Change in U.S. Women's Sport* (Urbana: University of Illinois Press, 2014), 8–9.

124. For an overview of these debates, see McCloud, "Popular Culture Fandoms," 189–199.

125. Mendieta, "Introduction: Religion as Critique," 8, 11.

126. Ibid., 11.

127. Dominic Erdozain, *The Problem of Pleasure: Sport, Recreation, and the Crisis of Victorian Religion* (Rochester, NY: Boydell Press, 2010), 1.

128. Brett Hutchins and David Rowe, *Sport beyond Television: The Internet, Digital Media and the Rise of Networked Media Sport* (New York: Routledge, 2012), 22.

129. Bill Carter, "The Top Attraction on TV? No Script, but Plenty of Action," *New York Times*, December 20, 2010; Derek Thompson, "The Fragile Dominance of the NFL," *The Atlantic*, September 22, 2014, http://www.theatlantic.com/business/archive/2014/09/nfl-scandals-could-destroy-football-and-pay-tv/380568/.

130. Cheryl Cooky, Michael A. Messner, and Michela Musto, "'It's Dude Time!' A Quarter Century of Excluding Women's Sports in Televised News and Highlight Shows," *Communication and Sport* 3, no. 3 (2015): 261.

131. Richard Deitsch, "USA-Japan Women's World Cup Final Shatters American TV Ratings Record," *Sports Illustrated*, July 6, 2015, http://www.si.com/planet-futbol/2015/07/06/usa-japan-womens-world-cup-tv-ratings-record.

132. ESPN, "Even in the Wake of a Record-Setting Women's World Cup, Myths Still Surround Women's Sports," ESPNW, July 7, 2015, http://espn.go.com/espnw/news-commentary/article/13215042/even-wake-record-setting-women-world-cup-myths-surround-women-sports. For more on the most recent coverage trends regarding gender and the Olympics, see Andrew C. Billings et al., "(Re)calling London: The Gender Frame Agenda within NBC's Primetime Broadcast of the 2012 Olympiad," *Journalism and Mass Communication Quarterly* 91, no. 1 (2014): 38–58.

133. Erin Whiteside and Marie Hardin, "Women (Not) Watching Women: Leisure Time, Television, and Implications for Televised Coverage of Women's Sports," *Communication, Culture and Critique* 4, no. 2 (2011): 124. Also see Susan Tyler Eastman and Andrew C. Billings, "Biased Voices of Sports: Racial and Gender Stereotyping in College Basketball Announcing," *Howard Journal of Communications* 12, no. 4 (2001): 183–201; and Jennifer D. Greer, Marie Hardin, and Casey Homan, "'Naturally' Less Exciting? Visual Production of Men's and Women's Track and Field Coverage during the 2004 Olympics," *Journal of Broad-*

casting and Electronic Media 53, no. 2 (2009): 173–189. On the normalization of masculine assumptions, see, for example, Marie Hardin and Stacie Shain, "Strength in Numbers? The Experiences and Attitudes of Women in Sports Media Careers," *Journalism and Mass Communication Quarterly* 82, no. 4 (2005): 804–819; and Marie Hardin and Stacie Shain, "'Feeling Much Smaller than You Know You Are': The Fragmented Professional Identity of Female Sports Journalists," *Critical Studies in Media Communication* 23, no. 4 (2006): 322–338.

134. Paul Connerton, "Seven Types of Forgetting," *Memory Studies* 1, no. 1 (2008): 67.

135. John Durham Peters, "Witnessing," *Media, Culture and Society* 23, no. 6 (2001): 707.

136. Benjamin, "Theses," 255, 264; Benjamin, *Arcades*, 475.

137. Martha C. Nussbaum, "Transcendence and Human Values," *Philosophy and Phenomenological Research* 64, no. 2 (2002): 446–447; Martha C. Nussbaum, *Love's Knowledge: Essays on Philosophy and Literature* (New York: Oxford University Press, 1992), 378–379.

138. Nussbaum, "Transcendence and Human Values," 372.

139. John Hoberman, *Testosterone Dreams: Rejuvenation, Aphrodisia, Doping* (Berkeley: University of California Press, 2006), 194–195.

140. Michael Atkinson, "Heidegger, Parkour, Post-sport, and the Essence of Being," in *A Companion to Sport*, ed. David L. Andrews and Ben Carrington (Malden, MA: Blackwell, 2013), 360–361.

141. Benjamin, "Theses," 256.

142. Michael McCann, "What the Appeals Court Ruling Means for O'Bannon's Ongoing NCAA Lawsuit," *Sports Illustrated*, September 30, 2015, http://www.si.com/college-basketball/2015/09/30/ed-obannon-ncaa-lawsuit-appeals-court-ruling.

143. Joe Nocera, "Let's Start Paying College Athletes," *New York Times*, January 1, 2012.

CHAPTER 2

1. Phil Sheridan, "Great Wall and Even Greater Olympians," *Philadelphia Inquirer*, August 25, 2008.

2. Gary Kamiya, "Running into History: Usain Bolt's Performance Was the Greatest Individual Athletic Feat of Our Time," *Salon*, August 21, 2008, http://www.salon.com/2008/08/21/historic/.

3. Andrew Gilligan, "Bolt Can Become Greatest Ever; in the Space of Two Incredible Finals, the Jamaican Gave Hope that He Can Foster a New Era of Glory for Sprinting," *Evening Standard* (London), August 21, 2008.

4. John Fiske, *Television Culture* (New York: Methuen, 1987), 219.

5. David Walsh, "Running into History; Usain Bolt Remains the Fastest Man in the World and Is Hoping to Return to Jamaica from London as a 'Living Legend' but, after a Dip in Form, Victory in the 100m Final Is No Forgone Conclusion," *Sunday Times* (London), July 22, 2012.

6. Oliver Holt, "In a Flash Bolt Won; Usain Clicks and It's THE Image of 2012," *Daily Mirror* (Ireland), August 10, 2012.

7. Allon Sinai, "Bolt Makes Us Marvel at the Joy of Seeing the Unbelievable," *Jerusalem Post*, August 7, 2012; Kevin Garside, "Brilliant Usain Bolt Flies to Golden Double at London 2012 Olympics; Jamaican Sprints into History with 200m Win that Confirms Status as World's Iconic Athlete," *The Independent* (UK), August 10, 2012.

8. Oliver Brown, "London 2012 Olympics: Glory Days Showed Great Britain at Its Best; London's Original Promise to 'Inspire a Generation' Sounded Grandiose, Even Glib,

and Yet the Substance of That Pledge Has Been Realised This Past Fortnight in the Most Stirring, Moving Fashion," *The Telegraph* (UK), August 12, 2012.

9. Quoted in Paul Waldie, "Untouchable; Jamaican Sprinter Invokes Legends of Ali, Jordan with Unprecedented Defence of Dual Olympic Titles and a Personality that Transcends His Sport," *Globe and Mail* (Canada), August 10, 2012.

10. Edwin Moses, "Bolt Should Retire Now to Protect His Legacy; Jamaican Has Achieved Greatness and Needs to Quit at the Top or Risk Being Caught by Rivals," *Daily Telegraph* (London), August 13, 2012.

11. Andy Bull, "Usain Bolt Joins the Immortals Just as the Cracks Begin to Appear," *The Guardian*," August 19, 2016, https://www.theguardian.com/sport/2016/aug/19/usain-bolt-retiring-immortality-200m-olympics, quoting Bolt.

12. Walter Benjamin, "Theses on the Philosophy of History," in *Illuminations*, ed. Hannah Arendt and trans. Harry Zohn (New York: Harcourt, Brace and World, 1955), 255–266.

13. Carole Blair, Marsha S. Jeppeson, and Enrico Pucci Jr., "Public Memorializing in Postmodernity: The Vietnam Veterans Memorial as Prototype," *Quarterly Journal of Speech* 77, no. 3 (1991): 263–288.

14. Paul Connerton, "Seven Types of Forgetting," *Memory Studies* 1, no. 1 (2008): 67.

15. Fredric Jameson, "Postmodernism and Consumer Society," in *The Anti-aesthetic: Essays on Postmodern Culture*, ed. Hal Foster (Port Townsend, WA: Bay Press, 1983), 124–125.

16. William Balthrop, Carole Blair, and Neil Michel, "The Presence of the Present: Hijacking the 'Good War'?" *Western Journal of Communication* 74, no. 2 (2010): 194–196. Also see Connerton, "Seven Types of Forgetting," 59.

17. In attributing the concept of "circulation" to Latour I am taking a cue from Cara A. Finnegan and Jiyeon Kang, who note: "Latour's key term is 'mediation;' however, given Latour's interest in mediation as movement, what he describes as mediation can, in our estimation, be termed 'circulation.'" See Cara A. Finnegan and Jiyeon Kang, "'Sighting' the Public: Iconoclasm and Public Sphere Theory," *Quarterly Journal of Speech* 90, no. 4 (2004): 401n114.

18. All references to these TV series, including cited content, are to *The Top 100: NFL's Greatest Players* (Mt. Laurel, NJ: NFL Films, 2010) and to *The Top 100 Players of 2013* (Mt. Laurel, NJ: NFL Films, 2013), respectively.

19. Frank Deford, "Better than Ever?" *National Public Radio*, January 23, 2008.

20. Michael Cowley, "There's No Winner, but Past versus Present Is Still Sport's Greatest Contest," *Sydney Morning Herald* (Australia), January 19, 2008.

21. Deford, "Better than Ever?"

22. Hank Gola, "A Giant Upset for Ages. Road Warriors' Run Decimates Patriots' Dynasty," *Daily News* (New York), February 5, 2008.

23. ESPN, "Tiger Woods Apologizes for 'Selfish' Behavior," ESPN, February 20, 2010, http://sports.espn.go.com/golf/news/story?id=4927694; Mark Seal, "The Temptation of Tiger Woods," *Vanity Fair*, May 2010, http://www.vanityfair.com/culture/features/2010/05/tiger-woods-article-full-201005; Golf Channel, "Faldo: Woods Is 'Mere Mortal,' Struggling Mentally," Golf Channel Digital, June 25, 2013, http://www.golfchannel.com/news/golftalkcentral/faldo-woods-is-mere-mortal-struggling-mentally.

24. Brian O'Connor, "Roger Federer's Legacy Assured despite the Fall from Grace," *Irish Times*, July 1, 2013, http://www.irishtimes.com/sport/other-sports/roger-federer-s-legacy-assured-despite-the-fall-from-grace-1.1448452; Benjamin Klein, "Roger Federer Must Consider Retirement to Maintain Legacy," *Bleacher Report*, July 7, 2013, http://bleacherreport.com/articles/1696115-roger-federer-must-consider-retirement-to-maintain-legacy.

25. Leaping Larry, "Sporting Life," *The Age* (Melbourne, Australia), August 21, 2008.

26. Charles Soukup, "I Love the 80s: The Pleasures of a Postmodern History," *Southern Communication Journal* 75, no. 1 (2010): 76–93.

27. Kenneth Burke, *The Rhetoric of Religion: Studies in Logology* (Berkeley: University of California Press, 1970), 27.

28. Ibid., 142.

29. Ibid., 278; Barbara A. Biesecker, *Addressing Postmodernity: Kenneth Burke, Rhetoric, and a Theory of Social Change* (Tuscaloosa: University of Alabama Press, 1997), 101–102.

30. Cara A. Finnegan, *Picturing Poverty: Print Culture and FSA Photographs* (Washington, DC: Smithsonian Books, 2003), xii, 222–223.

31. Bruno Latour, "How to Be Iconophilic in Art, Science, and Religion?" in *Picturing Science, Producing Art*, ed. Caroline A. Jones and Peter Galison (New York: Routledge, 2013), 424, 426, 427.

32. Finnegan and Kang, "'Sighting' the Public," 395.

33. Ibid.

34. Dave Zirin, *Welcome to the Terrordome: The Pain, Politics and Promise of Sport* (Chicago: Haymarket Books, 2007), 152–156.

35. Frank Deford, "Finding Phelps' Place in History," National Public Radio (NPR), August 20, 2008.

36. Jim McCabe, "Great Unknown." This debate carried into 2009, as the NFL postseason extended into the new year.

37. Deford, "Better than Ever?"

38. Deford, "Finding Phelps' Place."

39. Ibid.

40. *Agence France-Presse*, "Tennis: 'Greatest Final Ever' at Wimbledon Hailed by British Press," July 7, 2008; Valentine Low, "Nothing Will Ever Match This; (Says John McEnroe Who Was in the Second Best Final of All Time)," *Evening Standard* (London), July 7, 2008.

41. Will Swanton, "Federer Losing His Shine," *Sunday Age* (Melbourne, Australia), April 6, 2008.

42. Bruce Jenkins, "Federer-Nadal Rivalry Running on Its Last Legs," *Sports Illustrated*, May 21, 2013, http://sportsillustrated.cnn.com/tennis/news/20130521/roger-federer-rafael-nadal-rivalry/. At the time of this writing, Federer is in the midst of a "late-career renaissance," his renewed successes having "erased" doubts raised in 2013. Oliver Brown, "Wimbledon 2015: Roger Federer Destroys Andy Murray with Devilish Serve," *The Telegraph* (UK), July 10, 2015, http://www.telegraph.co.uk/sport/tennis/wimbledon/11733002/Wimbledon-2015-Roger-Federer-destroys-Andy-Murray-with-devilish-serve.html; Douglas Robson, "Roger Federer Nears the Top, Erases Doubts of 2013," *USA Today*, November 10, 2014, http://www.usatoday.com/story/sports/tennis/2014/11/09/roger-federer-atp-finals-novak-djokovic/18775381/.

43. Kimberly K. Smith, "Mere Nostalgia: Notes on a Progressive Paratheory," *Rhetoric and Public Affairs* 3, no. 4 (2000): 506–507. On these pages Smith highlights the importance of nostalgia for "progressive" politics. She defines "progressive" in "admittedly broad" terms: "Progressives, whether capitalist or socialist, advocate industrialization and the further rationalization of society in order to relieve suffering and improve the standard of living; they put their faith in natural and social science, in rational administration and ever-improving technology." In progressives' hands, nostalgia might become a rhetorical weapon against opponents of any of these ideas about historical progress. For a critique of the notion that nostalgia is a psychological defect, see Marouf Hasian Jr., "Nostalgic Longings, Memories of the 'Good War,' and Cinematic Representations in *Saving Private Ryan*," *Critical Studies in Media Communication* 18, no. 3 (2001): 338–358.

44. Quoted in Mark Maeske, "Something in the Air; NFL Observers Say Super Bowl Win Would Make the Patriots the Greatest Team Ever," *Washington Post*, January 27, 2008.

45. Quoted in Frank Fitzpatrick, "Eight Golds; Michael Phelps Pulls It Off," *Philadelphia Inquirer*, August 17, 2008.

46. Thomas Boswell, "Knee Deep in Pain, He Plays Through," *Washington Post*, June 16, 2008.

47. Bill Elliott, "Golf: Tiger's Genuine Gesture Makes Him the All-Time Sporting Great," *The Observer* (England), June 22, 2008; Gary Shelton, "Tiger vs. Sports History: Best Athlete Ever?" *St. Petersburg Times* (Florida), April 10, 2008.

48. "Tiger Woods' Record before and after Thanksgiving Crash," *The Telegraph* (UK), December 5, 2011, http://www.telegraph.co.uk/sport/golf/tigerwoods/8935368/Tiger-Woods-record-before-and-after-Thanksgiving-crash.html.

49. British Broadcasting Corporation, "Masters 2011: Tiger Woods Has Lost His Aura—Nick Faldo," BBC, April 5, 2011, http://news.bbc.co.uk/sport2/hi/golf/9448237.stm; Neil McLeman, "Tiger's No Master: Peter Alliss Says 14-Time Major Winner Has Lost His Aura ahead of Augusta Test," *Mirror* (UK), April 5, 2012, http://www.mirror.co.uk/sport/golf/the-masters-2012-tigers-lost-his-aura-782039.

50. Latour, "How to Be Iconophilic," 421.

51. Rolf Tiedemann, "Historical Materialism or Political Messianism? An Interpretation of the Theses 'On the Concept of History,'" in *Benjamin: Philosophy, History, Aesthetics*, ed. Gary Smith (Chicago: University of Chicago Press, 1989), 185; Benjamin, "Theses," 257, 264.

52. Ronald Walter Greene, "Rhetorical Pedagogy as a Postal System: Circulating Subjects through Michael Warner's 'Publics and Counterpublics," *Quarterly Journal of Speech* 88, no. 4 (2002): 438. Greene addresses in this essay Michael Warner's influential work on circulation. As Warner argues, circulation is organized around a "punctual" temporality characterized by "distinct moments and rhythms, from which distance in time can be measured" (e.g., news publication and delivery schedules, publishing seasons). People can become reflexive about the "temporality of circulation" that shapes their particular social activities. For Warner, "The more punctual and abbreviated the circulation, and the more discourse indexes the punctuality of its own circulation, the closer a public stands to politics"; in contrast, within "continuous flows, action becomes harder to imagine" (Michael Warner, *Publics and Counterpublics* [Brooklyn, NY: Zone Books, 2005], 95–97). For more on how Warner's discursive focus on circulation might fit with Latour's imagistic view, see Finnegan and Kang, "'Sighting' the Public," 393–397.

53. Jeff Chase, "The 50 Biggest Upsets in Sports History," *Bleacher Report*, January 26, 2012, http://bleacherreport.com/articles/1036181-the-50-biggest-upsets-in-sports-history; ESPN, "The List: Biggest Upsets," ESPN Page 2, http://espn.go.com/page2/s/list/top upsets/010525.html; *Sports Illustrated*, "Greatest Upsets in Sports History," http://sports illustrated.cnn.com/multimedia/photo_gallery/0802/biggest.upsets/content.2.html; Mr. Jones and Me, "The 50 Biggest Screw-Ups in Sports History," *Bleacher Report*, March 2, 2010, http://bleacherreport.com/articles/355433-the-50-biggest-screw-ups-in-sports-history-with-videos; ESPN, "ESPN 25: The 25 Biggest Sports Blunders," July 30, 2004, http://sports.espn.go.com/espn/espn25/story?page=listranker/blunderresult; ESPN, "NCAA Tournament at 75: The Top 75 Players," February 15, 2013, http://espn.go.com/mens-college-basketball/story/_/id/8951228/top-75-players; David Ubben, "Who Is the Greatest Big 12 Player Ever?" ESPN, May 17, 2013, http://espn.go.com/blog/ncfnation/post/_/id/78960/who-is-the-greatest-big-12-player-ever; Michael Pinto, "The 50 Greatest College Football Players of All Time," *Bleacher Report*, November 29, 2010, http://bleacherreport.com/

articles/528267-the-top-50-college-football-players-of-all-time; *Sports Illustrated*, "Greatest College Football Players by Number: 1–33," http://sportsillustrated.cnn.com/multimedia/ photo_gallery/0712/cfb.best.player.numbers.1to33/content.1.html; Miguel Delaney, "The 30 Greatest International [Football] Teams of All Time," *Football Pantheon*, June 16, 2011, http://footballpantheon.com/2011/06/the-30-greatest-international-teams-of-all-time/; Tommy Favorolo, "The Best Soccer Team in History: All-Time Starting XI," *Bleacher Report*, March 31, 2011, http://bleacherreport.com/articles/651444-all-time-starting-xi-soc cer-team; David Schoenfield, "Hall of 100: Best Pitcher of All Time," ESPN, December 13, 2012, http://espn.go.com/blog/sweetspot/post/_/id/31469/hall-of-100-best-pitcher-of-all-time; Rick Weiner, "The 50 Greatest Starting Pitchers in MLB History," *Bleacher Report*, November 27, 2012, http://bleacherreport.com/articles/1421701-the-50-greatest-starting-pitchers-in-mlb-history; Dan Tylicki, "The 100 Greatest Hitters in MLB History," *Bleacher Report*, March 12, 2012, http://bleacherreport.com/articles/1098327-the-100-greatest-hit ters-in-mlb-history; Joe Posnanski, "The 10 Greatest Hitters Ever," *Sports Illustrated*, October 14, 2009, http://sportsillustrated.cnn.com/2009/writers/joe_posnanski/10/14/best. hitters/; *Baseball Almanac*, "Top 20 Hitters," http://www.baseball-almanac.com/legendary/ lited20.shtml; Braden Gall, "College Football's Top 50 Quarterbacks of the BCS Era," *Athlon Sports*, March 25, 2013, http://www.athlonsports.com/college-football/college-foot balls-top-50-quarterbacks-bcs-era; Mike Olson, "Top 10 Quarterbacks of All-Time," *Men's Fitness*, http://www.mensfitness.com/training/pro-tips/top-10-quarterbacks-of-all-time; *Sports Illustrated*, "Top 10 Clutch Quarterbacks of All Time," http://sportsillustrated.cnn .com/multimedia/photo_gallery/0608/gallery.NFLclutchqbs/content.1.html; NBC, "NBCSports.com's Top 5 College Quarterbacks of All Time," NBC Sports, http://nbcsports .msnbc.com/id/32696409; Tom Van Riper, "America's Most Disliked Athletes," *Forbes*, February 5, 2013, http://www.forbes.com/sites/tomvanriper/2013/02/05/americas-10-most-disliked-athletes/; Dan Favale, "Most Hated Payer in the History of Every NBA Franchise," *Bleacher Report*, October 4, 2011, http://bleacherreport.com/articles/875254-most-hated-player-in-the-history-of-every-nba-franchise; Adam Hart, "25 Most Hated Athletes of All Time," *Bleacher Report*, June 26, 2011, http://bleacherreport.com/articles/749041-top-twenty-five-most-hated-athletes-of-all-time; Sam Stejskal, "The 10 Most Disliked Ath letes," *Sports Illustrated*, http://sportsillustrated.cnn.com/multimedia/photo_gallery/1202/ most-disliked-athletes/content.1.html; Ed Novelo, "The 50 Dirtiest Players of All Time," *Bleacher Report*, August 9, 2011, http://bleacherreport.com/articles/795051-the-50-dirti est-players-of-all-time; ESPN, "Readers: Dirtiest Pro Players," ESPN Page 2, http://espn .go.com/page2/s/list/readers/dirtiest/players.html; *Sports Illustrated*, "NBA Poll: Dirti est Player," http://sportsillustrated.cnn.com/multimedia/photo_gallery/1204/nba.dirtiest .player/content.1.html; *USA Today*, "The Dirtiest Players in NFL History," November 29, 2012, http://www.usatoday.com/picture-gallery/sports/nfl/2012/11/29/the-dirtiest-players-in-nfl-history/1735087/; Jermaine Spradley, "The 30 Greatest African American Athletes of All Time," *Huffington Post*, August 12, 2012, http://www.huffingtonpost.com/2012/08/12/ greatest-black-athletes-of-all-time_n_1770057.html; Bob Warja, "Top 10 Greatest Black Athletes," *Bleacher Report*, February 5, 2010, http://bleacherreport.com/articles/340194-black-history-month-top-10-greatest-black-athletes; Richie Whitt, "The Top 10 Great est Black Athletes in the History of Ever," *Dallas Observer*, February 17, 2009, http:// blogs.dallasobserver.com/sportatorium/2009/02/the_top_10_greatest_black_athl.php; Kelsey Givens, "Top 50 Female Athletes Ever," *Bleacher Report*, August 4, 2012, http:// bleacherreport.com/articles/791374-top-50-female-athletes-ever; Johnette Howard, "The Thin Line between Better and Best," ESPN, April 30, 2012, http://espn.go.com/espnw/ title-ix/article/7864240/top-40-female-athletes-countdown-introduction; Adam Rank,

"Munoz Tops List of Greatest Mexican-Americans in NFL History," NFL, May 5, 2011, http://www.nfl.com/news/story/09000d5d81fb1d79/article/muoz-tops-list-of-greatest-mexicanamericans-in-nfl-history; Richie Whitt, "The Top 5 Mexican Athletes in the History of Dallas," *Dallas Observer*, May 5, 2009, http://blogs.dallasobserver.com/sporta torium/2009/05/the_top_5_mexican_athletes_in.php; Kyle McAreavy, "The Best Fifteen Left Handed Pitchers Right Now," *Rant Sports*, March 16, 2013, http://www.rantsports .com/mlb/2013/03/16/the-best-fifteen-left-handed-pitchers-right-now/; Elliott Pohnl, "Left Handed Day 2010: The 10 Best Sports Lefties Ever," *Bleacher Report*, August 13, 2010, http://bleacherreport.com/articles/435415-left-handed-day-2010-the-10-best-sports-lefties-ever; "Debate: Who's the Best Lefty Ever?" ESPN, June 5, 2009, http://sports.espn.go.com/mlb/news/story?id=4231338.

54. Bryan Rose, "NFL Ranked as Most Popular American Sport for 30th Consecutive Year," *Sports Illustrated*, April 14, 2014, http://nfl.si.com/2014/04/14/nfl-ranked-as-most-popular-american-sport-for-30th-consecutive-year/; Darren Rovell, "NFL Most Popular for 30th Year in Row," ESPN, January 26, 2014, http://espn.go.com/nfl/story/_/id/10354114/harris-poll-nfl-most-popular-mlb-2nd; Michael Oriard, *Brand NFL: Making and Selling America's Favorite Sport* (Chapel Hill: University of North Carolina Press, 2007), 177.

55. Oriard, *Brand NFL*, 16.

56. Quoted in ibid., 14.

57. Ibid., 16–17.

58. Mark Bowden, "The Hardest Job in Football," *The Atlantic*, January 1, 2009, http://www.theatlantic.com/magazine/archive/2009/01/the-hardest-job-in-football/ 307212/?single_page=true.

59. For an online archive of NFL Films' *America's Game* series, see http://www.nfl .com/videos/nfl-films-americas-game. For an online archive of NFL Films' *A Football Life* series, see http://www.nfl.com/videos/a-football-life.

60. See Michael Butterworth, "NFL Films and the Militarization of Professional Football," in *The NFL: Critical and Cultural Perspectives*, ed. Thomas Oates and Zach Furness (Philadelphia: Temple University Press, 2014), 205–225.

61. Quoted in National Football League, "The Top 100: NFL's Greatest Players to Debut Friday, Sept. 3 at 10 P.M. ET on NFL Network," news release, August 26, 2010, http://www.nfl.com/news/story/09000d5d81a07507/article/the-top-100-nfls-greatest-players-to-debut-friday-sept-3-at-10-PM-et-on-nfl-network.

62. John Hargreaves, "Sport, Culture and Ideology," in *Sport, Culture and Ideology*, ed. Jennifer Hargreaves (London: Routledge and Kegan Paul, 1982), 41.

63. My understanding of "kinesthetic imagination," as well as of the organizational settings within which successive bodies surrogate specific kinesthetic repertoires, comes from Joseph Roach, *Cities of the Dead: Circum-Atlantic Performance* (New York: Columbia University Press, 1996), 27–28.

64. Nick Trujillo, "Machines, Missiles, and Men: Images of the Male Body on ABC's *Monday Night Football*," *Sociology of Sport Journal* 12, no. 4 (1995): 407–409.

65. Tara Magdalinski, *Sport, Technology and the Body: The Nature of Performance* (New York: Routledge, 2009), 3.

66. Latour, "How to Be Iconophilic," 427.

67. These relationships between athletic spontaneity and jazz fit with ideas about "being in the zone" or in a "flow state" that have been prevalent in sport for quite some time. Flow in this sense is often associated with popularizations of Hungarian psychologist Mihaly Csikszentmihalyi's work, which defines "flow" as an inherently pleasurable condition of total absorption in the moment, an effortless unification of mind and body that excludes

thought and emotion. Athletes in such a state describe being on autopilot, floating, being weightless, and being tuned in. See Susan A. Jackson and Mihaly Csikszentmihalyi, *Flow in Sports: The Keys to Optimal Experiences and Performances* (Champaign, IL: Human Kinetics, 1999), 4–5, 11–12. Going much further back (and playing on Marsalis's reference to Zen), Buddhist monk Takuan Soho's writings on swordplay are famous among martial artists as he emphasizes an "unfettered mind" absent of even the smallest intervals within which thought might intrude to create a physical delay. See Takuan Soho, *The Unfettered Mind: Writings from a Zen Master to a Master Swordsman*, trans. William Scott Wilson (New York: Kodansha International, 1986), 19–39.

68. Latour, "How to Be Iconophilic," 427, emphasis mine.

69. Leonard Shapiro and Mark Maske, "Lions' Sanders Retires from NFL," *Washington Post*, July 28, 1999, http://www.washingtonpost.com/wp-srv/sports/nfl/daily/july99/29/sanders29.htm. Payton's record was eventually broken by Emmitt Smith. See Pro Football Hall of Fame, "History: All-Time Rushing Record Holders," http://www.profootballhof.com/history/general/rushers/.

70. NFL Films, *A Football Life: Barry Sanders* (NFL Network, 2013).

71. Quoted in Michael O'Keeffe, "Sacking NFL's Stance: Ex-players Plead Case to Congress," *New York Daily News*, June 27, 2007.

72. Charles K. Ross, *Outside the Lines: African Americans and the Integration of the National Football League* (New York: New York University Press, 1999), 49–50. Also see Oriard, *Brand NFL*, 211.

73. Ross, *Outside the Lines*, 47–50, 79. Also see Oriard, *Brand NFL*, 210–257.

74. See J. R. Woodward, "Professional Football Scouts: An Investigation of Racial Stacking," *Sociology of Sport Journal* 21, no. 4 (2004): 356–375. Also see Daniel A. Grano, "Risky Dispositions: Thick Moral Description and Character-Talk in Sports Culture," *Southern Communication Journal* 75, no. 3 (2010): 255–276; Thomas P. Oates, "The Erotic Gaze in the NFL Draft," *Communication and Critical/Cultural Studies* 4, no. 1 (2007): 74–90.

75. Samuel G. Freedman, "The Year of the Black Quarterback," *New Yorker*, January 29, 2014, http://www.newyorker.com/news/sporting-scene/the-year-of-the-black-quarterback.

76. Mike Freeman, "Moon Angry over Perceived Racial Bias toward Newton," CBS Sports, March 30, 2011, http://www.cbssports.com/nfl/story/14879833/moon-angry-over-perceived-racial-bias-toward-newton.

77. For more on historical and mediated productions of quarterbacking and race, see Grano, "Risky Dispositions"; Oates, "The Erotic Gaze"; Douglas Hartmann, "Rush Limbaugh, Donovan McNabb, and 'A Little Social Concern': Reflections on the Problems of Whiteness in Contemporary American Sport," *Journal of Sport and Social Issues* 31, no. 1 (2007): 45–60; Daniel Buffington, "Contesting Race on Sundays: Making Meaning out of the Rise in the Number of Black Quarterbacks," *Sociology of Sport Journal* 22, no. 1 (2005): 19–37; Andrew C. Billings, "Depicting the Quarterback in Black and White: A Content Analysis of College and Professional Football Broadcast Commentary," *Howard Journal of Communications* 15, no. 4 (2004): 201–210; David McCarthy and Robyn L. Jones, "Speed, Aggression, Strength, and Tactical Naiveté," *Journal of Sport and Social Issues* 21, no. 4 (1997): 348–362; James A. Rada, "Color Blind-Sided: Racial Bias in Network Television's Coverage of Professional Football Games," *Howard Journal of Communications* 7, no. 3 (1996): 231–239; Audrey J. Murrell and Edward M. Curtis, "Causal Attributions of Performance for Black and White Quarterbacks in the NFL: A Look at the Sports Pages," *Journal of Sport and Social Issues* 18, no. 3 (1994): 224–233; Laurel R. Davis, "The Articulation of Difference: White Preoccupation with the Question of Racially Linked Genetic Differences

among Athletes," *Sociology of Sport Journal* 7, no. 2 (1990): 179–187; and Raymond E. Rainville and Edward McCormick, "Extent of Covert Racial Prejudice in Pro Football Announcers' Speech," *Journalism and Mass Communication Quarterly* 54, no. 1 (1977): 20–26.

78. Buffington, "Contesting Race on Sundays," 21.

79. Grano, "Risky Dispositions."

80. Hartmann, "Rush Limbaugh," 55. Also see Mary McDonald, "Mapping Whiteness and Sport: An Introduction," *Sociology of Sport Journal* 22, no. 3 (2005): 245–255; Richard C. King, "Cautionary Notes on Whiteness and Sport Studies," *Sociology of Sport Journal* 22, no. 3 (2005): 397–408; and Douglas Hartmann, "Rethinking the Relationships between Sport and Race in American Culture: Golden Ghettos and Contested Terrain," *Sociology of Sport Journal* 17, no. 3 (2000): 229–253.

81. National Football League, "NFL Network Presents: The Top 100 Players of 2013," news release, April 19, 2013, http://nflcommunications.com/2013/04/19/nfl-network-presents-the-top-100-players-of-2013/.

82. Bill Barnwell, "The Ever-Flawed NFL 100," *Grantland*, June 26, 2013, http://www.grantland.com/story/_/id/9423963/bill-barnwell-breaks-numerous-flaws-nfl-100-list.

83. Brian A. Shactman, "NFL Turns Its 6-Month Season into a 12-Month Business," CNBC, April 26, 2013, http://www.cnbc.com/id/100679711.

84. Jim Steeg, "The Evolution of the NFL Draft," *National Football Post*, April 26, 2012, http://www.nationalfootballpost.com/The-evolution-of-the-NFL-draft.html. Also see Grano, "Risky Dispositions"; Oates, "The Erotic Gaze."

85. Grano, "Risky Dispositions"; Oates, "The Erotic Gaze."

86. Burke writes that eternity is experienced as an "absolute extension of that momentary present which, in time, is forever arising out of the future and receding into the past": it is an "ever standing" moment "without past or future." Expanding on this idea of extension, Burke invokes various images of "stretching" time—making it tense, spreading it out, distending it, extending it, straining it—to explain how we achieve "constant attention to the present" (Burke, *The Rhetoric of Religion*, 145–146, 153).

87. John Durham Peters, "Witnessing," *Media, Culture and Society* 23, no. 6 (2001): 719.

88. See Michael L. Butterworth, "The Passion of the Tebow: Sports Media and Heroic Language in the Tragic Frame," *Critical Studies in Media Communication* 30, no. 1 (2013): 17–33.

89. Greg Gabriel, "Has the RB Position Become Devalued in the NFL?" *National Football Post*, July 19, 2013, http://www.nationalfootballpost.com/Has-the-RB-position-become-devalued-in-the-NFL.html.

90. Michael David Smith, "Jerry Rice's Single-Season Record Falls to Calvin Johnson," Pro Football Talk, December 22, 2012, http://profootballtalk.nbcsports.com/2012/12/22/jerry-rices-single-season-record-falls-to-calvin-johnson/.

91. Walter Benjamin, *The Arcades Project*, trans. Howard Eiland and Kevin McLaughlin (Cambridge, MA: Harvard University Press, 1999), 471.

92. Latour, "How to Be Iconophilic," 425–426.

CHAPTER 3

1. Ray Gamache, "Genealogy of the Sportscast Highlight Form: From Peep Show to Projection to Hot Processor," *Journal of Sports Media* 5, no. 2 (2010): 101; Patrick Saunders, "A Look at Replay through the Years," *Denver Post*, November 17, 2013.

2. Tony Verna, *Instant Replay: The Day that Changed Sports Forever* (Beverly Hills, CA: Creative Book Publishers International, 2008), 6–8, 11.

3. Verna, *Instant Replay*, 13–14, quoting Nelson.

4. Bruce Weber, "Tony Verna, Who Started Instant Replay and Remade Sports Television, Dies at 81," *New York Times*, January 21, 2015, http://www.nytimes.com/2015/01/22/sports/tony-verna-who-started-instant-replay-and-remade-sports-television-dies-at-81.html?_r=0; Matt Schiavenza, "Instant Replay's Quiet Revolutionary," *The Atlantic*, January 19, 2015, http://www.theatlantic.com/entertainment/archive/2015/01/instant-replays-quiet-revolutionary/384641/; Directors Guild of America, "DGA Statement on the Passing of Tony Verna," January 19, 2015, http://www.dga.org/News/PressReleases/2015/150119-DGA-Statement-on-the-Passing-of-Tony-Verna.aspx.

5. John Durham Peters, "Witnessing," *Media, Culture and Society* 23, no. 6 (2001): 707.

6. John Ellis, *Seeing Things: Television in the Age of Uncertainty* (New York: I. B. Tauris Publishers, 2000), 10, 32–33.

7. Benjamin, "Theses on the Philosophy of History," 255, 264; Rolf Tiedemann, "Historical Materialism or Political Messianism? An Interpretation of the Theses 'On the Concept of History,'" in *Benjamin: Philosophy, History, Aesthetics*, ed. Gary Smith (Chicago: University of Chicago Press, 1989), 185.

8. Ellis, *Seeing Things*, 10, 32–33.

9. Peters, "Witnessing," 719.

10. Gary Kamiya, "Running into History: Usain Bolt's Performance Was the Greatest Individual Athletic Feat of Our Time," *Salon*, August 21, 2008, http://www.salon.com/2008/08/21/historic/.

11. See Mary Ann Doane, "Information, Crisis, Catastrophe," in *Logics of Television: Essays in Cultural Criticism*, ed. Patricia Mellencamp (Bloomington: Indiana University Press, 1990), 227; Patricia Mellencamp, "TV Time and Catastrophe, or *Beyond the Pleasure Principle* of Television," in Mellencamp, *Logics of Television*, 242.

12. Margaret Morse, "Sport on Television: Replay and Display," in *Television: Critical Concepts in Media and Cultural Studies*, vol. 2, ed. Toby Miller (New York: Routledge, 2003), 380–381, 388. Morse argues that as a scientific object, the athletic body signifies ideals of human performance while also licensing and rendering "harmless" homoerotic gazing and commentary. For a similar critique of erotic looking and athletic bodies, see Thomas P. Oates, "The Erotic Gaze in the NFL Draft," *Communication and Critical/Cultural Studies* 4, no. 1 (2007): 74–90. For an analysis of the "fetishistic" qualities of replay, see Barry Brummett and Margaret Carlisle Duncan, "Theorizing without Totalizing: Specularity and Televised Sports," *Quarterly Journal of Speech* 76, no. 3 (1990): 235.

13. Phillip Prodger, *Time Stands Still: Muybridge and the Instantaneous Photography Movement* (New York: Oxford University Press, 2003), 25.

14. Kevin MacDonnell, *Eadweard Muybridge: The Man Who Invented the Moving Picture* (London: Weidenfeld and Nicolson, 1972), 14–15.

15. Phillip Prodger, *Muybridge and the Instantaneous Photography Movement* (New York: Oxford University Press, 2002).

16. Rebecca Solnit, *River of Shadows: Eadweard Muybridge and the Technological Wild West* (New York: Viking, 2003), 23, 179.

17. Prodger, *Muybridge*, 224–225.

18. Marianne Hirsch, *Family Frames: Photography, Narrative, and Postmemory* (Cambridge, MA: Harvard University Press, 1997), 117.

19. As Prodger explains, this is part of Muybridge's legacy and one of the lessons to be derived from apocryphal stories about the bet between Stanford and McCrellish: "The oft-repeated tale of Stanford's wager over the position of a horse's legs concerns the need for objective, mechanical evidence. A photograph was required to settle a manner upon which two sets of eyes could not agree." Prodger, *Muybridge*, 136.

20. Morse, "Sport," 386, 391, 382.

21. Ibid., 380–381.

22. Stephanie Marriott, "Time and Time Again: 'Live' Television Commentary and the Construction of Replay Talk," *Media, Culture and Society* 18, no. 1 (1996): 83.

23. Jack Dickey, "Let's Review 50 Years of Instant Replay," *Time*, December 7, 2013, http://ideas.time.com/2013/12/07/lets-review-50-years-of-instant-replay/, emphasis original.

24. Marriott, "Time," 78.

25. Ibid., 84. For a firsthand scholarly account of the viewing experience in this shared space, see Terrence J. Roberts, "The Making and Remaking of Sports Actions," *Journal of the Philosophy of Sport* 19, no. 1 (1992): 15–29.

26. John McGrath, "Instant Replay Should Be a Tool for Accuracy, Not Acrimony," *News Tribune* (Tacoma, WA), November 20, 2013.

27. Gary Pomerantz, "NFL Owners Vote to Extend Replay; Trial Given Another Season," *Washington Post*, March 20, 1987; Leonard Shapiro, "The Owners Blow the Call," *Washington Post*, August 30, 1992; Leonard Shapiro, "Keep the Lights Off in the Replay Booth," *Washington Post*, December 18, 1992; Leonard Shapiro, "Replay Is under Review; Debated Calls Could Spark Return of Revamped System," *Washington Post*, December 9, 1998.

28. David Biderman, "11 Minutes of Action," *Wall Street Journal*, January 15, 2010, http://www.wsj.com/articles/SB10001424052748704281204575002852055561406. Though this report was taken as a revelation at the time, credit is due to Michael R. Real for analyzing just how little game action there is in an NFL broadcast in his seminal essay "Super Bowl: Mythic Spectacle," *Journal of Communication* 25, no. 1 (1975): 31–43.

29. Monica Lamb-Yorski, "Duelling Pens," *Prince Rupert Daily News* (British Columbia), July 6, 2010.

30. David Brown, "MLB Announces Pace-of-Play Changes and Replay Tweaks," CBS Sports, February 20, 2015, http://www.cbssports.com/mlb/eye-on-baseball/25075051/mlb-announces-pace-of-play-changes-and-replay-tweaks; Richard Sandomir, "Baseball; Let's Dawdle, Spit and Play Ball!" *New York Times*, May 30, 1995, http://www.nytimes.com/1995/05/30/sports/baseball-let-s-dawdle-spit-and-play-ball.html.

31. Mike Dodd and Mel Antonen, "Does Baseball Need Instant Replay? Miscues Revive Call for Second Opinion," *USA Today*, October 19, 1999.

32. Quoted in Jordan Schultz, "Adam Silver, NBA's New Commissioner, on Jersey Sponsorships, New Technology," *Huffington Post*, February 24, 2014, http://www.huffingtonpost.com/2014/02/24/adam-silver-nba-commissioner_n_4832968.html; Neal Conan and Tom Goldman, "Judging of Athletic Competitions," *Talk of the Nation*, National Public Radio, August 25, 2004.

33. Jake O'Donnell, "My Apology Letter to the NHL Playoffs," *Sports Grid*, May 30, 2014, http://www.sportsgrid.com/nba/my-apology-letter-to-the-nhl-playoffs/; Ricardo Guerra, "Saving the Beautiful Game: A Radical Revision of the Rules of Football," *Soccerlens*, May 14, 2011, http://soccerlens.com/saving-the-beautiful-game-a-radical-revision-of-the-rules-of-football/69633/.

34. Jeff Blair, "Blatter's Heir Apparent Destined to Fail," *Globe and Mail* (Canada), December 6, 2013. Also see, for example, Scott Phillips, "No Stoppage Time: Financial Implications of Video Replay in MLS," *Business of Soccer*, September 15, 2014, http://www.businessofsoccer.com/2014/09/15/no-stoppage-time-financial-implications-of-video-replay-in-mls/; and Anthony Stewart, "Let Man on the Ground Make Video Decisions," *Townsville Bulletin* (Australia), July 21, 2007.

35. Joe Posnanski, "Upon Further Review: Instant Replay Takes Away from the Immediacy of Sport," NBC Sports, April 18, 2014, http://www.nbcsports.com/joe-posnanski/upon-further-review-instant-replay-takes-away-immediacy-sport.

36. Brett Hutchins and David Rowe, *Sport beyond Television: The Internet, Digital Media and the Rise of Networked Media Sport* (New York: Routledge, 2012), 22, 25. Also see Raymond Boyle, "Television Sport in the Age of Screens and Content," *Television and New Media* 15, no. 8 (2014): 749; David Rowe, "New Screen Action and Its Memories: The 'Live' Performance of Mediated Sport Fandom," *Television and New Media* 15, no. 8 (2014): 756; and Garry Whannel, "The Paradoxical Character of Live Television Sport in the Twenty-First Century," *Television and New Media* 15, no. 8 (2014): 770, 772.

37. Raymond Williams, *Television: Technology and Cultural Form*, ed. Ederyn Williams (London: Routledge, 2003), 90–94.

38. Since Williams originally conceived the term, "flow" has been a way to think about television programming as situated within a larger cultural context where commercial providers exert specific technological, economic, and political limits and pressures that shape but never wholly determine users' experiences and opportunities. Williams anticipated a struggle for control between the intentions of commercial providers and the experiences of viewers that today plays out through more options for user-directed flow (beginning with the remote control and continuing through digital video recorders and online content) and providers' redirection of user choices into various linked commercial holdings (networks, websites, applications, devices, and so on). See Williams, *Television*, 133–134; William Uricchio, "Television's Next Generation: Technology/Interface Culture/Flow," in *Television after TV: Essays on a Medium in Transition*, ed. Lynn Spigel and Jan Olson (Durham, NC: Duke University Press, 2004), 163–182; and Michael Kackman et al., "Introduction," in *Flow TV: Television in the Age of Media Convergence*, ed. Michael Kackman et al. (New York: Routledge, 2011), 1–2.

39. Hutchins and Rowe, *Sport beyond Television*, 30–32. Also see Whannel, "The Paradoxical Character," 774; Brett Hutchins and David Rowe, "From Broadcast Scarcity to Digital Plentitude: The Changing Dynamics of the Media Sport Content Economy," *Television and New Media* 10, no. 4 (2009): 360.

40. Hutchins and Rowe, "From Broadcast Scarcity," 356.

41. Hutchins and Rowe, *Sport beyond Television*, 33–34; Whannel, "The Paradoxical Character," 772; Lawrence A. Wenner, "On the Limits of the New and the Lasting Power of the Mediasport Interpellation," *Television and New Media* 15, no. 8 (2014): 734–735.

42. Quoted in Hutchins and Rowe, *Sport beyond Television*, 20.

43. Hutchins and Rowe, *Sport beyond Television*, 24; Rowe, "New Screen Action," 754; Boyle, "Television Sport in the Age of Screens."

44. Hutchins and Rowe, *Sport beyond Television*, 24; Hutchins and Rowe, "From Broadcast Scarcity," 363; Yair Galily, "When the Medium Becomes 'Well Done': Sport, Television, and Technology in the Twenty-First Century," *Television and New Media* 15, no. 8 (2014): 718, 722; Whannel, "The Paradoxical Character," 773–774; Rowe, "New Screen Action," 755.

45. Quoted in Kackman et al., *Flow TV*, 2.

46. Williams, *Television*, 86.

47. *The Telegraph* (UK), "Sir Geoff Hurst: Goal-Line Technology in 1966 Would Have Stopped 50 Years of German Moaning," August 12, 2013, http://www.telegraph.co.uk/sport/10237139/Sir-Geoff-Hurst-goal-line-technology-in-1966-would-have-stopped-50-years-of-German-moaning.html.

48. Ian Reid and Andrew Zisserman, "Goal-Directed Video Metrology," in *Computer Vision—ECCV '96: 4th European Conference on Computer Vision, Cambridge, UK, April 1996 Proceedings*, vol. 2, ed. Bernard Buxton and Roberto Cipolla (New York: Springer-Verlag, 1996), 647–658.

49. 4RFV, "HD 'Settles' 1966 World Cup Controversy," 4RFV, May 15, 2006, http:// www.4rfv.co.uk/industrynews/51603/hd_settles_1966_world_cup_controversy; *The Sun* (UK), "Think Ball's All Over? It Isn't!—World Cup 25 Days to Go," May 15, 2006.

50. Quoted in *The Telegraph*, "Sir Geoff Hurst."

51. Juliet Macur, "Lance Armstrong Is Stripped of His 7 Tour de France Titles," *New York Times*, October 22, 2012, http://www.nytimes.com/2012/10/23/sports/cycling/arm strong-stripped-of-his-7-tour-de-france-titles.html?_r=0.

52. Dylan Mulvin, "Game Time: A History of the Managerial Authority of the Instant Replay," in *The NFL: Critical and Cultural Perspectives*, ed. Thomas Oates and Zach Furness (Philadelphia: Temple University Press, 2014), 41–42. On these same pages Mulvin introduces two other figures—the "mechanical judge" and the "mechanical manager." Each represents a "relocation" of the mechanical referee's function to legal and managerial spheres.

53. Ibid., 41–42, 51–53.

54. Louis-Georges Schwartz, *Mechanical Witness: A History of Motion Picture Evidence in U.S. Courts* (New York: Oxford University Press, 2009), 4–5.

55. Ibid., 9, 66, 85.

56. John Walters, "Your Lying Eyes," *Newsweek*, April 24, 2014, http://www.news week.com/2014/05/02/your-lying-eyes-248544.html.

57. Quoted in Rachel Shuster, "No Great Clamor for the Return of Instant Replay," *USA Today*, September 23, 1992.

58. FIFA Quality Programme, "Goal-Line Technology: Recommendations for Implementations in Competitions Based on Experiences from the FIFA Club World Cup Japan 2012," 8, http://www.fifa.com/mm/document/fifaqualityprogramme/goal-linetech nology/02/01/77/01/gltweben.pdf. Also see James Dart and Paolo Bandini, "The Hardest Recorded Shot in Football—Ever," *The Guardian*, February 14, 2007, http://www.the guardian.com/football/2007/feb/14/theknowledge.sport.

59. Will Oremus, "Machines, Not Humans, Will Decide What's a Goal in the 2014 World Cup," *Slate*, July 5, 2012, http://www.slate.com/blogs/future_tense/2012/07/05/ fifa_approves_goal_line_technology_for_2014_world_cup_epl_next.html.

60. Ibid., 6.

61. Quoted in *The Independent* (UK), "Tony Verna: Television Producer Who Invented the Instant Replay," January 22, 2015, http://www.independent.co.uk/news/people/tony-verna-television-producer-who-invented-the-instant-replay-9993736.html.

62. Quoted in Seth Stevenson, "The Man Who Saved Tennis (from Bad Line Calls, That Is)," *Slate*, November 6, 2012, http://www.slate.com/articles/sports/doers/2012/11/ hawk_eye_saved_tennis_from_bad_line_calls_paul_hawkins_invention_designed.html.

63. Quoted in Mike Freeman and Richard Sandomir, "Spotlight on N.F.L. Playoffs Exposes Rift over Officiating," *New York Times*, January 15, 2003.

64. Walters, "Your Lying Eyes"; Paul Clemens, "Nearly Perfect in Detroit," *New York Times*, June 5, 2010.

65. Barry M. Bloom, "Limited Instant Replay Debuts Thursday," MLB, http://m.mlb .com/news/article/3370519/; Alan Schwartz and Michael S. Schmidt, "Perfectly Flawed; Replay Gets Another Look after a Gaffe Seen by All," *New York Times*, June 4, 2010.

66. Armando Galarraga, Jim Joyce, and Daniel Paisner, *Nobody's Perfect: Two Men, One Call, and a Game for Baseball History* (New York: Atlantic Monthly Press, 2011), 217.

67. Galarraga, Joyce, and Paisner, *Nobody's Perfect*.

68. Diane Sawyer and John Berman, "Blown Call; Supreme Sportsmanship," *ABC News*, June 3, 2010; Brian Williams, Mike Taibbi, and Bernie Smilovitz, "Ump Apologizes for Making Wrong Call and Ruining a Perfect Baseball Game," *NBC News*, June 3, 2010; George Stephanopoulous, Robin Roberts, and John Berman, "The Great Sportsmen; Bad Call Reveals Good Guys," *ABC News*, June 4, 2010; Matt Lauer and Meredith Vieira, "Umpire Jim Joyce Discusses His Call at Detroit Tigers Game that Cost Armando Galarraga a Perfect Game," *Today*, NBC News, June 4, 2010; Susan Tish, "A Pitcher, an Umpire, and a Lesson in Grace; A Christian Science Perspective," *Christian Science Monitor*, June 9, 2010.

69. John Harper, "The Perfect Crime May Have All of Baseball Going to Videotape," *Daily News* (New York), June 3, 2010; Tyler Kepner and Micheline Maynard, "One Out from Perfection, Undone by the Umpire," *New York Times*, June 3, 2010; Wayne Coffee, "Joyce Miscue Makes Dekinger Replay His," *Daily News* (New York), June 4, 2010; Seth Livingstone and Sean Leahy, "Selig: Baseball People Don't Want Replay," *USA Today*, June 9, 2010; Michael S. Schmidt, "N.F.L.-Style Challenges Join Debate on Replay," *New York Times*, June 9, 2010.

70. *Wall Street Journal*, "Bud, Make It Perfect," June 4, 2010, http://www.wsj.com/articles/SB10001424052748704025304575284824275003954.

71. Father Raymond J. de Souza, "Baseball Should Make It Right," *National Post*, June 4, 2010.

72. *New York Times*, "One Wrong Call after Another," June 6, 2010.

73. Schwartz, "Perfectly Flawed."

74. Neal Conan, "Ump Blows Call, Ruins Galarraga's Perfect Game," *Talk of the Nation*, National Public Radio, June 3, 2010, interviewing Sharp.

75. Mike Lopresti, "For Umps, Blown Calls Leave Lasting Marks," *USA Today*, June 4, 2010.

76. George Vecsey, "Worst Call Ever? Sure. Kill the Umpires? Never," *New York Times*, June 4, 2010.

77. Jeff Connor, "Video Referee Ensures Big-Time Decisions Are Far Less Trying," *Scotland on Sunday*, December 3, 2000.

78. Jonathan Turley, "Olympic Slips and Falls: It Is Time for the Olympic Committee to Get Rid of Out-Dated Procedures," *Jonathan Turley: Res Ipsa Loquitur*, August 13, 2012, http://jonathanturley.org/2012/08/13/olympic-slip-and-falls-it-is-time-for-the-olympic-committee-to-get-rid-of-out-dated-procedures/.

79. Adam Kilgore, "Hard to See Extended Role for Replay Even Though It Might Help," *Washington Post*, July 15, 2012.

80. John Durham Peters, *Speaking into the Air: A History of the Idea of Communication* (Chicago: University of Chicago Press, 1999), 6. Peters relates this "homeopathic" problem to the concept of communication, which, he writes, "is a compensatory ideal whose force depends on its contrast with failure and breakdown." I think this parallels nicely the basic problems of replay.

81. Jere Longman, "NFL Turns to Instant Replays to Help with Some Calls," *Philadelphia Inquirer*, September 4, 1986; Tony Long, "March 11, 1986: NFL Adopts Instant Replay," *Wired*, March 11, 2011, http://www.wired.com/2011/03/0311nfl-owners-ok-instant-replay/.

82. See Glenn Dickey, "Instant Replay Has Some Powerful Allies," *San Francisco Chronicle*, March 17, 1988; Ed Meyer, "NFL Owners Approve Instant Replay for 1989," *Akron Beacon Journal*, March 24, 1989; John McClain, "NFL Owners Approve, Revise Instant Replay," *Houston Chronicle*, March 13, 1990; Jerry Magee, "NFL Makes the Call: Instant Replay Is

Thrown for a Loss in '92," *San Diego Union Tribune*, March 19, 1992; Ira Kaufman, "Further Review Shows Owners Did the Right Thing," *Tampa Tribune*, March 19, 1992; Tim Brown, "For Now, Replay Is Past Its Prime (Time)," *Daily News of Los Angeles*, August 30, 1992.

83. Quoted in *Los Angeles Times*, "Instant-Replay Reversal a 'Major Step Backward'?" March 19, 1992.

84. Quoted in Thom Loverro, "A Botched Call? Opening Games Lasted Longer Even without Instant Replay," *Washington Times*, September 10, 1992.

85. *Seattle Post-Intelligencer*, "Upon Further Review, Replay Returns—Testaverde TD vs. Hawks 'Shook People Up,'" March 18, 1999. Also see Kirk Bohls, "There's No Need to Review This Call: Instant Replay Has No Place in the NFL," *Austin American-Statesman*, August 14, 1996; *St. Louis Post-Dispatch*, "On the Replay Issue, NFL May Play It Again—Replay, Absent since after the 1991 Season, Will Be Put to a Vote Again," March 8, 1997; Ed Bouchette, "NFL Votes Replay Back In," March 18, 1999.

86. Quoted in John Huxley, "In the Can: Refs, Tries and Videotape," *Sydney Morning Herald* (Australia), April 14, 1990.

87. Joseph Maguire, *Power and Global Sport: Zones of Prestige, Emulation, and Resistance* (New York: Routledge, 2005), 87–106; "Aussie Rebels to Follow Euro Lead," *New Straits Times*, October 7, 1996.

88. Dean Ritchie, "Let's Go to the Video/NRL under Pressure to Change Rule," *Daily Telegraph*, March 7, 2000; "NRL Promises Big Boot for Time Wasters," *Townsville Bulletin* (Australia), December 5, 2003; Brian Smith, "Be Patient: Critics Too Quick to Shoot Down Innovations—2008 NRL Season," *Newcastle Herald*, April 11, 2008; Agence France-Presse, "RugbyL: Two Referees to Control NRL Matches," December 11, 2008.

89. *Sydney Morning Herald*, "NRL a Step Closer to Video Referee Bunker," August 27, 2014, http://www.smh.com.au/rugby-league/league-news/nrl-a-step-closer-to-video-referee-bunker-20140827-108zqr.html; Angela Hashaby, "NRL to Trial a Referee Bunker to Make Decisions from the Middle of 2015," *Daily Telegraph* (Australia), August 27, 2014, http://www.dailytelegraph.com.au/sport/nrl/nrl-to-trial-a-referee-bunker-to-make-decisions-from-the-middle-of-2015/news-story/cfe9fd8ed7e70f74622291f0a5524a0a; Brad Walter, "NRL Set for Mid-Season Trial of Video Referee Bunker System," *Sydney Morning Herald*, March 24, 2015, http://www.smh.com.au/rugby-league/league-news/nrl-set-for-midseason-trial-of-video-referee-bunker-system-20150324-1m6p1y.html.

90. Paul Mulvey, "Coaches Call for Video Ref; Row over Wallaby Captain's—Winner," *The Advertiser* (Adelaide, Australia), June 28, 1999.

91. Stephen Jones, "Time to Give Referees a Third Eye—Rugby Union," *Sunday Times* (London), January 3, 1999.

92. Michael Foley, "Video Nasty—Technology to Rule on Tight Decisions Has Been Resisted by the GAA but New Systems Could Be in Place Next Summer," *Sunday Times* (London), September 5, 2010; Steve Deane, "Top 10 Things Rugby Union Nicked from League," *New Zealand Herald* (Auckland, New Zealand), November 26, 2010; Mick Cleary, "New Rules for Television Match Officials Will Not Make Game Boring to Watch, Insist Rugby Chiefs," *The Telegraph* (UK), August 20, 2012, http://www.telegraph.co.uk/sport/rugbyunion/club/9488451/New-rules-for-Television-Match-Officials-will-not-make-game-boring-to-watch-insist-rugby-chiefs.html; Gregor Paul, "IRB Want a Faster Game," *Herald on Sunday* (Auckland, New Zealand), May 11, 2014.

93. S. Rajesh, "Neutral Umpires," ESPN Cricinfo, April 19, 2011, http://www.espncricinfo.com/magazine/content/story/511175.html.

94. Rahul Bhattacharya, "The Match Referee and Third Umpire," ESPN Cricinfo, February 26, 2011, http://www.espncricinfo.com/magazine/content/story/499652.html;

Matthew Engel, "Hallowed Game Given 'Evil Eye,'" *The Age* (Melbourne, Australia), June 26, 1993; "Teenage Sachin Was TV's First Ever Victim," *The Witness* (South Africa), November 14, 2013; Keith Moore, "Hawk-Eye: From Concept to Game Changer," *BBC News*, April 12, 2013, http://www.bbc.com/news/uk-22106087.

95. Aron Pilhofer, "A Replay System that Is a Hit among Players, Fans and Even Officials," *New York Times*, September 8, 2008; Patrick Saunders, "A Look at Replay through the Years," *Denver Post*, November 17, 2013. Hawk-Eye's stated margin of error has been disputed, though it is taken as a given in much of the sport media coverage. For an example of a challenge, see Carl Bialik, "Sports Make Final Call on Technology," *Wall Street Journal*, November 9, 2013, http://blogs.wsj.com/numbers/sports-make-final-call-on-technology-1292/.

96. Stevenson, "The Man Who Saved Tennis."

97. Osman Samiuddin, "The Marginal Decisions that Still Leave Room for Debate in Cricket," *The National*, January 25, 2012, http://www.thenational.ae/sport/cricket/the-marginal-decisions-that-still-leave-room-for-debate-in-cricket#full; Press Trust of India, "Umpiring Decision Review System on the Cards," *NDTV Sports*, June 22, 2008, http://sports.ndtv.com/cricket/news/53230-umpiring-decision-review-system-on-the-cards; ESPN, "Official Debut for Enhanced Review System," ESPN Cricinfo, November 23, 2009, http://www.espncricinfo.com/ci-icc/content/story/436290.html; Sharda Ugra, "Agreement on DRS after Hot Spot Is Made Mandatory," ESPN Cricinfo, June 27, 2011, http://www.espncricinfo.com/ci-icc/content/current/story/520913.html; Sudipto Ganguly, "Decision Review System No Longer Mandatory—ICC," *Reuters*, October 11, 2011, http://uk.reuters.com/article/2011/10/11/uk-cricket-icc-drs-idUKTRE79A1HW20111011.

98. Lawrence Booth, *Arm-Ball to Zooter: A Sideways Look at the Language of Cricket* (New York: Penguin Books, 2007); Paul Rees, "Hot Spot Inventor Calls for Official Use of Snickometer in Winter Ashes," *The Guardian*, July 27, 2013, http://www.theguardian.com/sport/2013/jul/27/hot-spot-snicko-ashes.

99. Nagraj Gollapudi, "Real Time Snicko Could Give DRS the Edge," ESPN Cricinfo, February 6, 2013, http://www.espncricinfo.com/ci/content/story/603632.html; David Clough, "Snicko to the Available to Umpires in Ashes to Help Review System Cut Out Mistakes," *Daily Mail* (UK), November 18, 2013, http://www.dailymail.co.uk/sport/cricket/article-2509713/Ashes-2013-14-Snickometer-used-umpires-Australia-v-England-series.html; *The Guardian*, "Real-Time Snicko to Be Used in First Ashes Test in Brisbane," November 19, 2013, http://www.theguardian.com/sport/2013/nov/19/real-time-snicko-first-ashes-test-brisbane.

100. Ashley Fetters, "How Instant Replays Changed Professional Tennis," *The Atlantic*, September 7, 2012, http://www.theatlantic.com/entertainment/archive/2012/09/how-instant-replays-changed-professional-tennis/262060/.

101. Chris Broussard, "Williams Receives Apology, and Umpire's Open Is Over," *New York Times*, September 9, 2004, http://www.nytimes.com/2004/09/09/sports/tennis/09serena.html?_r=0.

102. Janis Carr, "Players Invite Use of Instant Replay—Most Would Welcome Some Form Available to Eliminate Many Perceived Bad Calls," *Orange County Register* (Santa Ana, CA), September 9, 2004; Charles Bricker, "ITF, USTA Expected to Use Instant Replay," *Sun Sentinel* (Fort Lauderdale, FL), September 9, 2004; Tara Sullivan, "Instant Replay in Sight—Serena Receives Official Apology," *The Record* (Hackensack, NJ), September 9, 2004; Ann Loprinzi, "Instant Replay Could Be Coming to U.S. Open," *The Times* (Trenton, NJ), April 3, 2005; Chris Lehourites, "Instant Replay to Be Used at U.S. Open," *Associated Press*, March 6, 2006; Fetters, "How Instant Replays."

103. *Associated Press*, "Tennis to Debut Instant Replay in Two Weeks," March 7, 2006; Lehourites, "Instant Replay"; Janis Carr, "New Vision: Hawk-Eye—Most Players Say Replays Will Speed Up the Game and Ensure Accuracy of Calls," *Orange County Register* (Santa Ana, CA), March 7, 2006; Michelle Kaufman, "Replay to Debut at NASDAQ," *Miami Herald*, March 7, 2006.

104. Quoted in Greg Garber, "All Eyes on Tennis with Use of Hawk-Eye Replay," ESPN, March 14, 2006, http://sports.espn.go.com/sports/tennis/news/story?id=2356553.

105. Quoted in Cliff Brunt, "RCA Championships Debut Instant Replay for U.S. Open," *Chronicle Herald* (Halifax, Nova Scotia, Canada), July 18, 2006.

106. Fetters, "How Instant Replays."

107. Damien Cox, ""NHL Puts Replay Plan on Fast Forward," *Toronto Star*, January 11, 1991; *Los Angeles Times*, "NHL Adopts Instant Replay to View Goals," June 25, 1991, http://articles.latimes.com/1991-06-25/sports/sp-1247_1_goal-line.

108. Adrian Dater, "NHL Limits Instant Replay, but Is Proud about Getting Goals Right," *Denver Post,* November 18, 2013, http://www.denverpost.com/avalanche/ci_24544095/nhl-limits-instant-replay-but-is-proud-about.

109. John Kryk, "Exclusive: NFL Visits NHL's 'Situation Room' as It Mulls Centralized Replays," *Toronto Sun*, December 12, 2013, http://www.torontosun.com/2013/12/12/exclusive-nfl-visits-nhls-situation-room-as-it-mulls-centralized-replays; Canadian Press, "NHL Centralized Replay Proving to Be Model as MLB Adopts Expanded Review," NHL, January 21, 2014, http://www.nhl.com/ice/news.htm?id=701676; Walter, "NRL Set."

110. Kryk, "Exclusive: NFL Visits."

111. Jason Brough, "Report: NHL Considering Cameras in Posts?" Pro Hockey Talk (NBC), November 20, 2013, http://prohockeytalk.nbcsports.com/2013/11/20/report-nhl-considering-cameras-in-posts/. At the time of this writing (during the 2015 season) the NHL has been testing on-post cameras at various distances from the ice, and has announced that it would like to use the cameras to provide an additional angle for video reviews by the playoffs, if not before, as long as they are sure the system is operable. See Larry Brooks, "The NHL's Added Camera Solution for Improved Instant Replay," *New York Post*, January 17, 2015, http://nypost.com/2015/01/17/the-nhls-added-camera-solution-for-improved-instant-replay/.

112. Les Bowen, "Farewell: Replay a Step Forward," *Philadelphia Daily News*, June 25, 1991; Jarre Fees, "NHL Doesn't Make Use of Replay," *St. Louis Post-Dispatch* (MO), May 9, 1998; Steve Silverman, "Why the NHL Must Expand the Use of Instant Replay," *Bleacher Report*, January 28, 2013, http://bleacherreport.com/articles/1504927-why-the-nhl-must-expand-the-use-of-instant-replay; Canadian Press, "NHL Centralized Replay"; Greg Wyshynski, "NHL Rejects Video Review for High-Sticking Penalties, Unfortunately," *Puck Daddy*, September 15, 2013, http://sports.yahoo.com/blogs/nhl-puck-daddy/nhl-rejects-video-review-high-sticking-penalties-unfortunately-153657110--nhl.html.

113. Barry M. Bloom, "Limited Instant Replay Debuts Thursday," MLB, http://m.mlb.com/news/article/3370519/; Joe Frisaro, "Ump's Calls Upset Sox, Halos," Los Angeles Angels, October 9, 2009, http://m.angels.mlb.com/news/article/7405856/; David Schoenfield, "Five Worst Umpiring Calls in History," ESPN, January 13, 2012, http://espn.go.com/blog/sweetspot/print?id=25570; Thomas Harding and Adam McCalvy, "Ump Admits Missed Call on Utley Hit," Colorado Rockies, October 12, 2009, http://m.rockies.mlb.com/news/article/7438306/; Jim Caple, "Umpire Errors a Real Embarrassment," ESPN, October 21, 2009.

114. Robert Siegel, "A Perfect Game, Ruined by a Bad Call," National Public Radio, June 3, 2010; Scott Simon, "After a Ballgame, 'Nobody's Perfect' Is Just Perfect," National

Public Radio, June 5, 2010; Matt Lauer and Meredith Vieira, "Detroit Tigers Pitcher Armando Galarraga Misses Out On Perfect Game When Umpire Makes the Wrong Call," *NBC News*, June 3, 2010.

115. Quoted in Paul White, "When Baseball Gets It Wrong; Blown Call Is a Case for Instant Replay—and a Lesson in Sportsmanship," *USA Today*, June 4, 2010.

116. Ian Begley, "Selig Confident Replay Will Grow," ESPN, July 27, 2012, http://espn.go.com/new-york/mlb/story/_/id/8206550/bud-selig-says-baseball-expand-instant-replay; Leyland quoted in Walters, "Your Lying Eyes."

117. Walters, "Your Lying Eyes."

118. Joe Lemire, "Welcome to the ROC—MLB's High-Tech Replay Room," *USA Today*, March 26, 2014, http://www.usatoday.com/story/sports/mlb/2014/03/26/mlbs-high-tech-replay-room-opens-sunday/6932553/.

119. Quoted in Mark Feinsand, "Joe Says No to 'Robots;' Girardi: Human Error Should Stay Part of Game," *Daily News* (New York), June 5, 2010.

120. Quoted in Jayson Stark, "The Future of Replay," ESPN, January 17, 2013, http://espn.go.com/mlb/story/_/id/8852971/future-expanded-replay-major-league-baseball.

121. Quoted in Kilgore, "Hard to See Extended Role"; quoted in Lemire, "Welcome to the ROC."

122. Glenn Moore, "FIFA Argues against Instant Video Replay," *The Independent* (UK), October 20, 1995.

123. British Broadcasting Corporation, "1966: Football Glory for England," BBC, July 30, 2005, http://news.bbc.co.uk/onthisday/hi/dates/stories/july/30/newsid_2644000/2644065.stm/; *New York Times*, "Geoff Hurst and Soccer's Zapruder Film," May 29, 2006, http://worldcup.blogs.nytimes.com/2006/05/29/geoff-hurst-and-soccers-zapruder-film/?_r=0.

124. Quoted in Rob Hughes, "Beep of the Future: Too Late for Real; Celta Wins with 'Goal that Never Was,'" *International Herald Tribune*, September 12, 2005.

125. Ibid.

126. John Blau, "Chip-Enabled Ball at 2006 World Cup Soccer Games?" *PC World*, October 25, 2005, http://www.pcworld.com/article/123197/article.html; Eddie Griffin, "The Future of Refereeing? FIFA Using Ball-Chip Technology for Club World Cup," *Soccerlens*, December 11, 2007, http://soccerlens.com/the-future-of-refereeing-fifa-using-ball-chip-technology-for-club-world-cup/4628/; British Broadcasting Corporation, "FIFA Delays Goal-Line Technology," BBC, December 5, 2005, http://news.bbc.co.uk/go/pr/fr/-/sport2/hi/football/internationals/4488318.stm; Alastair Himmer, "Soccer-Goal-Line Technology Here to Stay, Says FIFA President," *Reuters*, Dec 15, 2012, http://www.reuters.com/article/2012/12/15/soccer-fifa-technology-idUSL4N09P0AE20121215.

127. Sam Wallace, "Hand Gaul! Ireland Furious as Henry Snatches Victory," *The Independent* (UK), November 19, 2009, http://www.independent.co.uk/sport/football/international/hand-gaul-ireland-furious-as-henry-snatches-victory-1823317.html; Eliot Van Buskirk, "Soccer Resists Instant Replay despite Criticism," *Wired*, November 30, 2009, http://www.wired.com/2009/11/soccer-resists-the-instant-replay-despite-criticism/.

128. George Vecsey, "An Obvious Case for Instant Replay," *New York Times*, June 27, 2010.

129. Michael Hiestand, "Play It Again Sam—Final Opposition to Instant Replay Crumbling Away," *Courier Mail* (Brisbane, Australia), July 8, 2010, quoting Blatter.

130. Quoted in FIFA Quality Programme, "Goal-Line Technology," 3.

131. Ibid., 4; Fédération Internationale de Football Association, "The IFAB, the Eternal Guardian of the Laws," FIFA, http://www.fifa.com/aboutfifa/organisation/ifab/history

.html; Adam Elder, "Soccer Finally Comes to Its Senses with Goal-Line Tech," *Wired*, July 6, 2012, http://www.wired.com/2012/07/fifa-goal-line-technology/.

132. Shahan Ahmed, "Soccer Should Expand Instant Replay to Review More Crucial Calls," Yahoo Sports, November 11, 2014, http://sports.yahoo.com/news/soccer-should-go-expand-instant-replay-to-review-more-crucial-calls-152833594.html; Patrick Rishe, "2014 World Cup: Expanded Instant Replay, Extra Field Official Would Enhance Soccer's U.S. Popularity," *Forbes*, June 16, 2014.

133. Associated Press, "Sepp Blatter: Use Instant Replay to Challenge Disputed Calls in Soccer," NESN, September 8, 2014, http://nesn.com/2014/09/sepp-blatter-use-instant-replay-to-challenge-disputed-calls-in-soccer/.

134. Chris Sheridan, "Stern: NBA Will Discuss Using Instant Replay," *Associated Press International,* April 29, 2002.

135. Quoted in Fred Kerber, "NBA Governors OK Instant Replay," *New York Post,* July 30, 2002.

136. Jordan Schultz, "Adam Silver, NBA's New Commissioner, On Jersey Sponsorship, New Technology," *Huffington Post*, February 24, 2014, http://www.huffingtonpost.com/2014/02/24/adam-silver-nba-commissioner_n_4832968.html; Barry Petchesky, "Report: NBA to Overhaul Replay System," *Deadspin*, May 19, 2014, http://deadspin.com/report-nba-to-overhaul-replay-system-1578381786; Matt Winkeljohn, "Notebook: Hawks 98, Pacers 85," NBA, April 25, 2014, http://www.nba.com/games/20140424/INDATL/gameinfo.html?ls=iref:nba: serieshubs:mid:seriesschedule; Randy Renner, "Notebook: Thunder 105, Clippers 104," NBA, May 14, 2014, http://www.nba.com/games/20140513/LACOKC/gameinfo.html?ls=iref:nba: serieshubs:mid:seriesschedule; Billy Witz, "NBA's Replay Controversies Could Lead to a Review," *New York Times*, May 15, 2014; Ben Golliver, "Report: NBA to Implement Centralized Instant Replay Review for 2014–2015 Season," *Sports Illustrated*, May 18, 2014, http://www.si.com/nba/point-forward/2014/05/18/nba-instant-replay-off-site-review-adam-silver.

137. National Basketball Association, "Replay Center," NBA, http://official.nba.com/replay/.

138. Jeff Zillgit, "NBA's New Replay Center Helping 'Get the Call Right,'" *USA Today*, February 23, 2015, http://www.usatoday.com/story/sports/nba/2015/02/23/replay-center-instant-review-behind-the-scenes/23888843/; Tim Moynihan, "The NBA's New High-Tech Control Center Is a Hoops Fan's Dream," *Wired*, October 28, 2014, http://www.wired.com/2014/10/nba-replay-center/.

139. Brett Pollakoff, "NBA Replay Center Helped Incorrectly Overturn Call Late during Heat-Wizards," *Pro Basketball Talk* (NBC), March 7, 2015; Dan Devine, "NBA to Publish 'Last Two Minutes' Reports Grading Refs' Late Calls, Non-Calls," *Ball Don't Lie* (Yahoo), February 27, 2015, http://sports.yahoo.com/blogs/nba-ball-dont-lie/nba-to-publish--last-two-minutes---reports-grading-refs--late-calls--non-calls-195852107.html.

140. Quoted in CBC, "FIFA Halts Instant Replay Experiment," CBC Sports, March 8, 2008, http://www.cbc.ca/sports/fifa-halts-instant-replay-experiment-1.695604.

141. Hughes, "Beep of the Future."

142. William C. Rhoden, "Longing for a Return to the Beauty of Imperfection," *New York Times*, September 17, 2012.

143. Ira Berkow, "Sports of the Times; Bloodless Instant Replays," *New York Times*, November 14, 1989; Jonathan Liew, "Look Out, the Machines Have Taken Over," *Daily Telegraph* (UK), July 15, 2013.

144. Leigh Montville, "Get This Right the First Time, Santa, because I'm Not Showing It to You Again," *Washington Post*, December 20, 2002.

145. Quoted in Rhoden, "Longing for a Return."

146. Joe Posnanski, "Upon Further Review: Instant Replay Takes Away from the Immediacy of Sport," NBC Sports, April 18, 2014, http://www.nbcsports.com/joe-posnanski/upon-further-review-instant-replay-takes-away-immediacy-sport.

147. Steve Leszczynski, "Level 3 Referees Course, 2003: Technology and the Changing Face of Rugby," Australian Rugby Union, http://www.rugby.com.au/Portals/18/Files/Refereeing/level3papers/Major_Project_Steve_Leszczynski.pdf.

148. Malcolm Knox, "Video Ref Should Back Off or We'll All Go Mad," *The Age* (Melbourne, Australia), April 19, 2014.

149. Greg Baum, "Playing with Controversy—Cricket," *The Age* (Melbourne, Australia), December 31, 2011; Jessica Rutledge, "Foot-Faults and Expletives Return to U.S. Open," *The Informer* (Hartford, CT), September 9, 2010.

150. Candice Keller, "Computer Games," *The Advertiser* (Adelaide, Australia), March 4, 2009; Christine Brennan, "Umpires Got It Right This Time, but Instant Replay Would Be Wise," *USA Today*, October 21, 2004; Rhoden, "Longing for a Return."

151. Peter McKnight, "Messy, Yes, but We're Stuck with the Human Condition," *Vancouver Sun*, January 23, 2010.

152. Mark Kiszla, "Instant Replay Is for Losers," *Denver Post*, January 6, 2013.

153. Ricardo Guerra, "Saving the Beautiful Game: A Radical Revision of the Rules of Football," *Soccerlens*, May 14, 2011, http://soccerlens.com/saving-the-beautiful-game-a-radical-revision-of-the-rules-of-football/69633/.

154. Berkow, "Sports of the Times."

155. Alan Schwartz, "Ideas and Trends; A Shot Seen 'Round the World," *New York Times*, October 15, 2000.

156. Bob Halloran, "Objectively Speaking, You're All Biased," ESPN, May 6, 2002, http://espn.go.com/page2/s/halloran/020508.html.

157. Schwartz, "Ideas and Trends."

158. *Belfast News Letter*, "Hawk-Eye to Stay! You Cannot Be Serious," June 20, 2006.

159. See, for example, Jeff Powell, "Mugged by Maradona? Jeff Powell Looks Back at the Hand of God 25 Years On," *Daily Mail* (UK), June 21, 2011, http://www.dailymail.co.uk/sport/football/article-2006467/Jeff-Powell-reflects-25-years-Hand-God.html; Eleanor Cooks, "Goal-Line Technology to Be Sanctioned: The Famous Goals that Never Were, from Geoff Hurst to Frank Lampard," *The Telegraph* (UK), July 5, 2012, http://www.telegraph.co.uk/sport/football/competitions/premier-league/9377880/Goal-line-technology-to-be-sanctioned-the-famous-goals-that-never-were-from-Geoff-Hurst-to-Frank-Lampard.html.

160. Michael Nass, *Miracle and Machine: Jacques Derrida and the Two Sources of Religion, Science, and the Media* (New York: Fordham University Press, 2012), 77–79.

161. Quoted in ibid., 77. Nass is analyzing Jacques Derrida's discussion of autoimmune religious responses to contamination and impurity. See Jacques Derrida, "Faith and Knowledge: The Two Sources of 'Religion' at the Limits of Reason Alone," in *Acts of Religion*, ed. Gil Anidjar (New York: Routledge, 2010), 63. The connections to sport here are my own, and I am taking some liberties with Derrida's critique, which focuses on religion in a more formal (i.e., denominational) sense. For more on my justifications for drawing such parallels between denominational and popular religious institutions, see my discussions of "theology" and "religion" in the Introduction.

162. Derrida, "Faith and Knowledge," 63, 79–82.

163. Mulvin, "Game Time," 41–45.

164. Thomas Patrick Oates, "Constructing Replay, Consuming Bodies: Sport Media and Neoliberal Citizenship," in *Sports and Identity: New Agendas in Communication*, ed. Barry Brummett and Andrew W. Ishak (New York: Routledge, 2014), 152–154.

165. Henry Jenkins, *Convergence Culture: Where Old and New Media Collide* (New York: New York University Press, 2006), 3; Henry Jenkins, *Textual Poachers: Television Fans and Participatory Culture*, 20th anniv. ed. (New York: Routledge, 2013), 23–28.

166. Lawrence Grossberg, "Is There a Fan in the House? The Affective Sensibility of Fandom," in *The Adoring Audience: Fan Culture and Popular Media*, ed. Lisa A. Lewis (New York: Routledge, 1992), 64–65.

167. Jenkins, *Textual Poachers*, xxiv–xxxvi, 23–24.

168. See ibid., xxvi, 26, and Jenkins, *Convergence Culture*, 17–18.

169. Norman Chad, "NFL's Instant Replay Officiating Is One Call that Should Be Overruled," *Washington Post*, September 26, 1986.

170. Bruce Weber, "If At First You Don't Succeed," *New York Times*, June 11, 2011.

171. Hiestand, "Play It Again Sam."

172. Anna Clark, "The Human Element," *Pacific Standard Magazine*, December 12, 2013, http://www.psmag.com/books-and-culture/the-human-element-instant-replay-tony-verna-71408. Clark's reference is to the famous film record, shot by Abraham Zapruder, of President John F. Kennedy's assassination.

173. Gordon Thomson, *The Man in Black: A History of the Football Referee* (London: Prion Books Limited, 1998), 5–22. Also see J. A. Mangan and C. Hickey, "Keeping Control: Refereeing the Game," *Soccer and Society* 9, no. 5 (2008): 727–749.

174. Emanuele Isidori, Arno Müller, and Sabri Kaya, "The Referee as Educator: Hermeneutical and Pedagogical Perspectives," *Physical Culture and Sport Studies and Research* 56, no. 1 (2012): 6–7.

175. Ibid., 7; Emily Erikson and Joseph M. Parent, "Central Authority and Order," *Sociological Theory* 25, no. 3 (2007): 258; Sharon Colwell, "The 'Letter' and the 'Spirit': Football Laws and Refereeing in the Twenty-First Century," in *The Future of Football: Challenges for the Twenty-First Century*, ed. Jon Garland, Dominic Malcolm, and Michael Rowe (London: Frank Cass, 2000), 204.

176. Josh Levin, "Zapruder Films for Sports Junkies: How YouTube Is Making Life Miserable for Referees," *Slate*, October 18, 2006, http://www.slate.com/articles/sports/sports_nut/2006/10/zapruder_films_for_sports_junkies.html. Also see Jason Zinoman, "The YouTube Referee Indictment," *New York Times*, December 10, 2006.

177. Tallemong, "SBXL Calls," YouTube, August 7, 2010, https://www.youtube.com/watch?v=SlsPTvoLGgg; Pooriton, "Seahawks Got Screwed," YouTube, July 2, 2007, https://www.youtube.com/watch?v=vURI_Cz-p6s.

178. SuperBowl43XLIII, "Refs 'Steel' Cardinals Victory: Super Bowl XLIII," YouTube, February 6, 2009, https://www.youtube.com/watch?v=BMmd6H-27-s; BaggioFn, "Bad Refereeing against Italy at 2002 World Cup," YouTube, January 8, 2008, https://www.youtube.com/watch?v=2Pm4jD5kU4U; ConspiracyCoverUp's Channel, "Kings Lakers Game 6 Mixtape * RIGGED * 2002," YouTube, December 19, 2011, https://www.youtube.com/watch?v=qjRcTiwVEwo.

179. Mark Andrejevic, "Watching Television without Pity: The Productivity of Online Fans," *Television and New Media* 9, no. 1 (2008): 25, 37, 42–43.

180. Markus Stauff, "Sports on YouTube," in *The YouTube Reader*, ed. Pelle Snickars and Patrick Vonderau (Stockholm: National Library of Sweden, 2009), 240–241.

181. Levin, "Zapruder Films."

182. Bill Reiter, "Fan Revolt Made NFL Come to Senses," Fox Sports, June 2014, http://www.foxsports.com/nfl/story/fans-revolt-made-roger-goodell-and-owners-strike-deal-with-refs-092612.

183. See Stauff, "Sports on YouTube," 241–244.

184. Jodi Dean, *Democracy and Other Neoliberal Fantasies: Communicative Capitalism and Left Politics* (Durham, NC: Duke University Press, 2009), 162; Slavoj Žižek, *The Ticklish Subject: The Absent Centre of Political Ontology* (London: Verso, 1999), 322–323.

185. Stephen Mumford, "Truth Makers for Judgment Calls," *European Journal of Sport Science* 6, no. 3 (2006): 181–182; Victor Lee Austin, "Authority in Sport," *Studies in Christian Ethics* 25, no. 1 (2012): 67–69.

186. Žižek, *The Ticklish Subject*, 323, 327, 330. Also see Dean, *Democracy*, 162–163. Here I am borrowing from Dean's helpful analysis of symbolic efficiency as it relates to judges and doctors.

187. Dean, *Democracy*, 163.

188. Christopher Clarey, "Upon Further Review, It's Time for Instant Replay," *New York Times*, June 24, 2010; Stephen Jones, "Rugby Blurs Video Picture—Rugby Union," *Sunday Times* (London), February 12, 2006; Andrew Longmore, "Cricket: The Law Is by Shepherd, but Only Just—Buchanan: Raise Umpire Standards to Stem Gizmos," *The Independent* (UK), June 10, 2001; Mike Davidson, "Sport Pays Penalty for Officialdom Gone Mad," *Daily Mail* (London), January 11, 1999.

189. Fetters, "How Instant Replays."

190. Henry Winter, "Messy and Confusing, but This Row Cannot Be Allowed to Drag On," *Daily Telegraph* (UK), October 30, 2012.

191. Selena Roberts, "Technology's Cutting Edge Draws Some Blood," *New York Times*, September 24, 2006.

192. Jodi Dean, *Blog Theory: Feedback and Capture in the Circuits of Drive* (Cambridge, UK: Polity, 2010), 6–7.

193. Mark Andrejevic, "The Work of Watching One Another: Lateral Surveillance, Risk, and Governance," *Surveillance and Society* 2, no. 4 (2005): 482–483. Also see Dean, *Democracy*, 163; Dean, *Blog Theory*, 6; Jodi Dean, *Publicity's Secret: How Technoculture Capitalizes on Democracy* (Ithaca, NY: Cornell University Press, 2002), 132; Žižek, *The Ticklish Subject*, 324.

194. For more on the political inertness of the "savvy" consumer, see Andrejevic, "Watching Television," 39.

195. John Durham Peters, "Witnessing," *Media, Culture and Society* 23, no. 6 (2001): 708; Ellis, *Seeing Things*, 9–11.

196. Andrejevic, "Watching Television," 25.

197. Ian Taylor, "'Football Mad': A Speculative Sociology of Football Hooliganism," in *The Sociology of Sport: A Selection of Readings*, ed. Eric Dunning (London: Frank Cass, 1970), 364; Garry Crawford, "The Career of the Sport Supporter: The Case of the Manchester Storm," *Sociology* 37, no. 2 (2003): 219–237. Chas Critcher's critique and extension of Taylor's work (where he makes a very similar argument) is also frequently cited as seminal. See Chas Critcher, "Football since the War," in *Working-Class Culture: Studies in History and Theory*, ed. J. Clarke, Chas Critcher, and R. Johnson (New York: St. Martin's Press, 1979), 161–184. For a representative criticism of hooliganism as a form of "authentic" middle-class resistance, see Anthony King, *The End of the Terraces: The Transformation of English Football in the 1990s* (London: Leicester University Press, 1998), 3–15.

198. See, for example, Leon Davis, "Football Fandom and Authenticity: A Critical Discussion of Historical and Contemporary Perspectives," *Soccer and Society* 16, nos. 2–3 (2015):

422–436; Inghar Mehus, "The Diffused Audience of Football," *Continuum: Journal of Media and Cultural Studies* 24, no. 6 (2010): 897–903; Garry Crawford, *Consuming Sport: Fans, Sport and Culture* (New York: Routledge, 2004), 20, 33–38; Richard Giulianotti, "Supporters, Followers, Fans, and *Flaneurs*: A Taxonomy of Spectator Identities in Football," *Journal of Sport and Social Issues* 26, no. 1 (2002): 25–46; Nicholas Abercrombie and Brian Longhurst, *Audiences: A Sociological Theory of Performance and Imagination* (London: Sage, 1998), 30–32.

199. As it happens, instant replay originated in the 1963 Army-Navy game only weeks after the assassination of President John F. Kennedy. See Verna, *Instant Replay*, 11–12.

200. Oyvind Vagnes, *Zaprudered: The Kennedy Assassination Film in Visual Culture* (Austin: University of Texas Press, 2011), 5.

201. Art Simon, *Dangerous Knowledge: The JFK Assassination in Art and Film* (Philadelphia: Temple University Press, 1996), 2.

202. Ibid., 43.

203. Ibid., 44.

204. Derrida, "Faith and Knowledge," 82.

205. Benjamin, "Theses," 264.

206. Walter Benjamin, *The Arcades Project*, trans. Howard Eiland and Kevin McLaughlin (Cambridge, MA: Harvard University Press, 1999), 475.

207. Ibid.

208. Miriam Hansen, *Babel and Babylon: Spectatorship in American Silent Film* (Cambridge, MA: Harvard University Press, 1991), 111.

209. Ibid.

210. Walter Benjamin, "A Short History of Photography," in *Classic Essays on Photography*, ed. Alan Trachtenberg (New Haven, CT: Leete's Island Books, 1980), 202–203.

211. Walter Benjamin, *The Writer of Modern Life: Essays on Charles Baudelaire*, ed. Michael W. Jennings and trans. Howard Eiland, Edmund Jephcott, Rodney Livingston, and Harry Zohn (Cambridge, MA: Harvard University Press, 2006), 191.

212. Arianne Conty, "They Have Eyes that They Might Not See: Walter Benjamin's Aura and the Optical Unconscious," *Literature and Theology* 27, no. 4 (2013): 473–474.

CHAPTER 4

1. Bruno Latour, "How to Be Iconophilic in Art, Science, and Religion?" in *Picturing Science, Producing Art*, ed. Caroline A. Jones and Peter Galison (New York: Routledge, 2013), 426–427; Cara A. Finnegan and Jiyeon Kang, "'Sighting' the Public: Iconoclasm and Public Sphere Theory," *Quarterly Journal of Speech* 90, no. 4 (2004): 395.

2. Tara Magdalinski, *Sport, Technology and the Body: The Nature of Performance* (New York: Routledge, 2009), 3, 8.

3. Jim Parry, "Part III Introduction," in *Theology, Ethics and Transcendence in Sports*, ed. Jim Parry, Mark Nesti, and Nick Watson (New York: Routledge, 2011), 181.

4. Martha C. Nussbaum, *Love's Knowledge: Essays on Philosophy and Literature* (New York: Oxford University Press, 1992), 365–366.

5. Martha C. Nussbaum, "Transcendence and Human Values," *Philosophy and Phenomenological Research* 64, no. 2 (2002): 446–447; Nussbaum, *Love's Knowledge*, 378–379.

6. Nussbaum, *Love's Knowledge*, 380.

7. Ibid., 372.

8. Ibid., 372–373, 381. For more on the difficulties of dividing between internal and external transcendence, see Paul Taylor, *A Secular Age* (Cambridge, MA: Belknap Press of Harvard University Press, 2007), 627–638.

9. Nussbaum, *Love's Knowledge*, 372.

10. Ibid., 381.

11. Michael Atkinson, "Heidegger, Parkour, Post-sport, and the Essence of Being," in *A Companion to Sport*, ed. David L. Andrews and Ben Carrington (Malden, MA: Blackwell, 2013), 360. For more on differentiations between humanism, transhumanism, and posthumanism, see Sonia E. Miller, "Human, Transhuman, Posthuman: What's the Difference and Who Cares?" *Futures Research Quarterly* 20, no. 2 (2004): 61–67; José Cordeiro, "The Boundaries of the Human: From Humanism to Transhumanism," *World Future Review* 6, no. 3 (2014): 231–239.

12. Humanity+, "Transhumanist Declaration," Humanity Plus, http://humanityplus.org/philosophy/transhumanist-declaration/.

13. Atkinson, "Heidegger, Parkour," 362–364.

14. Ibid., 361.

15. Michael J. Sandel, *The Case against Perfection: Ethics in the Age of Genetic Engineering* (Cambridge, MA: Harvard University Press, 2007), 26–29.

16. Michael J. McNamee, "Transhuman Athletes and Pathological Perfectionism: Recognising Limits in Sports and Human Nature," in *Athletic Enhancement, Human Nature, and Ethics: Threats and Opportunities of Doping Technologies*, ed. J. Tolleneer, Sigrid Sterckx, and Pieter Bonte (New York: Springer, 2013), 185, 188, 193. For a related concern regarding transhumanism and rule structures, see Sigmund Loland, "Normative Theories of Sport: A Critical Review," *Journal of the Philosophy of Sport* 31, no. 2 (2004): 111–121.

17. Mike McNamee, "Whose Prometheus? Transhumanism, Biotechnology and the Moral Topography of Sports Medicine," in *The Ethics of Sport: A Reader*, ed. Mike McNamee (New York: Routledge, 2010), 214.

18. Elaine Graham, "'Nietzsche Gets a Modem': Transhumanism and the Technological Sublime," *Literature and Theology* 16, no.1 (2002): 69–70.

19. Tracy J. Trothen, "Better than Normal? Constructing Modified Athletes and a Relational Theological Ethic," in *Theology, Ethics and Transcendence in Sports*, ed. Jim Parry, Mark Nesti, and Nick Watson (New York: Routledge, 2011), 71–73, 75.

20. Atkinson, "Heidegger, Parkour," 362–364. For more extensive treatments of sport and neoliberalism, see Michael L. Silk and David L. Andrews, eds., *Sport and Neoliberalism: Politics, Consumption, and Culture* (Philadelphia: Temple University Press, 2012).

21. Andy Miah, "Be Very Afraid: Cyborg Athletes, Transhuman Ideals and Posthumanity," *Journal of Evolution and Technology* 13, no. 2 (2003): 1–23.

22. Andy Miah, "From Anti-doping to a 'Performance Policy' Sport Technology, Being Human, and Doing Ethics," *European Journal of Sport Science* 5, no. 1 (2005): 55. Also see Andy Miah, "Rethinking Enhancement in Sport," *Annals of the New York Academy of Sciences* 1093, no. 1 (2006): 301–320.

23. Claudio M. Tamburrini and Torbjörn Tännsjö, "Introduction: Transcending Human Limitations," in *The Ethics of Sports Medicine*, ed. Claudio M. Tamburrini and Torbjörn Tännsjö (New York: Routledge, 2009), vii.

24. Claudio M. Tamburrini, "What's Wrong with Genetic Inequality? The Impact of Genetic Technology on Elite Sports and Society," in Tamburrini and Tännsjö, *The Ethics of Sports Medicine*, 115–117.

25. Tamburrini, "What's Wrong with Genetic Inequality?" 115–117.

26. Eric T. Juengst, "Subhuman, Superhuman, and Inhuman: Human Nature and the Enhanced Athlete," in Tolleneer, Sterckx, and Bonte, *Athletic Enhancement, Human Nature, and Ethics*, 99–100. For a similar argument, see J. Savulescu, B. Foddy, and M. Clayton, "Why We Should Allow Performance Enhancing Drugs in Sport," *British Journal of Sports*

Medicine 38, no. 6 (2004): 667. For more on the randomness of the genetic lottery, see Claudio M. Tamburrini, "After Doping, What? The Morality of the Genetic Engineering of Athletes," *Research in Philosophy and Technology* 21 (2001): 266; Sigmund Loland, *Fair Play in Sport: A Moral Norm System* (New York: Routledge, 2002), 69; Torbjörn Tännsjö, "Genetic Engineering and Elitism in Sport," in *Genetic Technology and Sport: Ethical Questions*, ed. Claudio Tamburrini and Torbjörn Tännsjö (New York: Routledge, 2005), 60.

27. Kutte Jönsson, "Sport beyond Gender and the Emergence of Cyborg Athletes," *Sport in Society* 13, no. 2 (2010): 249, 255–257. Also see Kutte Jönsson, "Who's Afraid of Stella Walsh? On Gender, 'Gene Cheaters,' and the Promises of Cyborg Athletes," *Sport, Ethics and Philosophy* 1, no. 2 (2007): 239–262.

28. See, for example, P. David Howe, "Cyborg and Supercrip: The Paralympics Technology and the (Dis)empowerment of Disabled Athletes," *Sociology* 45, no. 5 (2011): 873–875; Moss E. Norman and Fiona Moola, "'Bladerunner or Boundary Runner'? Oscar Pistorius, Cyborg Transgressions and Strategies of Containment," *Sport in Society* 14, no. 9 (2011): 1270.

29. Atkinson, "Heidegger, Parkour," 359–360; Gerald McKenny, "Transcendence, Technological Enhancement, and Christian Theology," in *Transhumanism and Transcendence: Christian Hope in an Age of Technological Enhancement*, ed. Ronald Cole-Turner (Washington, DC: Georgetown University Press, 2011), 178.

30. Tara Magdalinski, "Restoring or Enhancing Athletic Bodies," in Tolleneer, Sterckx, and Bonte, *Athletic Enhancement, Human Nature, and Ethics*, 237–238.

31. Magdalinski, *Sport, Technology, and the Body*, 3.

32. See, for example, John Hoberman, *Mortal Engines: The Science of Performance and the Dehumanization of Sport* (New York: Free Press, 1992), 100–153; John Hoberman, *Testosterone Dreams: Rejuvenation, Aphrodisia, Doping* (Berkeley: University of California Press, 2006); Rob Beamish and Ian Ritchie, *Fastest, Highest, Strongest: A Critique of High-Performance Sport* (New York: Routledge, 2006); Paul Dimeo, *A History of Drug Use in Sport 1876–1976: Beyond Good and Evil* (New York: Routledge, 2007); Daniel M. Rosen, *Dope: A History of Performance Enhancement in Sports from The Nineteenth Century to Today* (Westport, CT: Praeger, 2009); Rob Beamish, *Steroids: A New Look at Performance-Enhancing Drugs* (Santa Barbara, CA: Praeger, 2011).

33. Hoberman, *Testosterone Dreams*, 194–195.

34. Thomas H. Murrary, Karen J. Maschke, and Angela A. Wasunna, "Preface," in *Performance-Enhancing Technologies in Sports: Ethical, Conceptual, and Scientific Issues*, ed. Thomas H. Murrary, Karen J. Maschke, and Angela A. Wasunna (Baltimore, MD: Johns Hopkins University Press, 2009), ix.

35. Verner Møller, *The Ethics of Doping and Anti-doping: Redeeming the Soul of Sport?* (New York: Routledge, 2010), 4–7.

36. Hoberman, *Mortal Engines*, 101, 110–111.

37. Hoberman, *Testosterone Dreams*, 181–182.

38. Beamish and Ritchie, *Fastest, Highest, Strongest*, 107–109. Also see Maxwell J. Mehlman, *The Price of Perfection: Individualism and Society in the Era of Biomedical Enhancement* (Baltimore, MD: Johns Hopkins University Press, 2009), 121–122.

39. Mehlman, *The Price of Perfection*, 122–125.

40. Ibid., 124–125.

41. Hoberman, *Testosterone Dreams*, 241–243, quoting Samaranch.

42. John Hoberman, "How Drug Testing Fails: The Politics of Doping Control," in *Doping in Elite Sport: The Politics of Drugs in the Olympic Movement*, ed. Wayne Wilson and Edward Derse (Champaign, IL: Human Kinetics, 2001), 245.

43. Hoberman, *Testosterone Dreams*, 194–195, 240. Also see Beamish and Ritchie, *Fastest, Highest, Strongest*, 115, 137–138.

44. Hoberman, *Testosterone Dreams*, 194–195, 240.

45. Beamish and Ritchie, *Fastest, Highest, Strongest*, 110–111.

46. Hoberman, *Mortal Engines*, 101.

47. Beamish and Ritchie, *Fastest, Highest, Strongest*, 110.

48. Bryan Denham, "When Science, Politics, and Policy Collide: On the Regulation of Anabolic-Androgenic Steroids, Steroid Precursors, and 'Dietary Supplements' in the United States," *Journal of Sport and Social Issues* 35, no. 1 (2011): 10.

49. Bryan Denham, "*Sports Illustrated*, the 'War on Drugs,' and the Anabolic Steroid Control Act of 1990," *Journal of Sport and Social Issues* 21, no. 3 (1997): 267.

50. Denham, "When Science, Politics, and Policy Collide."

51. Hoberman, *Testosterone Dreams*, 245–246.

52. Ibid., 249, 195–196, 245–247.

53. Matt Majendie, "The Festina Affair Still Lingers," *The National*, July 14, 2008, http://www.thenational.ae/sport/the-festina-affair-still-lingers; Ian Landau, "The Biggest TdF Scandals: 1998—The Festina Affair," *Outside*, July 15, 2013, http://www.outsideon line.com/1917356/biggest-tdf-scandals-1998%E2%80%94-festina-affair.

54. Landau, "The Biggest."

55. Dag Vidar Hanstad, Andy Smith, and Ivan Waddington, "The Establishment of the World Anti-Doping Agency: A Study of the Management of Organizational Change and Unplanned Outcomes," *International Review for the Sociology of Sport* 43, no. 3 (2008): 228–229.

56. Rosen, *Dope*, 111–114; Nancy Reichman and Ophir Sefiha, "Regulating Performance-Enhancing Technologies: A Comparison of Professional Cycling and Derivatives Trading," *Annals of the American Academy of Political and Social Science* 649, no. 1 (2013): 109.

57. Mehlman, *The Price of Perfection*, 126; Hoberman, *Testosterone Dreams*, 243.

58. Mehlman, *The Price of Perfection*, 126–127.

59. U.S. Anti-Doping Agency, "How and Why Does USADA Exist?" USADA, http://www.usada.org/resources/faq/. WADA oversees the Olympics and the Paralympic Games, as well as the antidoping programs for most of international sport. The USADA is a signatory to the World Anti-Doping Code and exercises authority over USOC-recognized events and athletes (mainly the Olympics, Paralympics, Pan American and Parapan American Games), as well as over international athletes who are competing in the United States. Neither WADA nor the USADA governs U.S. professional or collegiate sport leagues, which have their own antidoping programs.

60. Reichman and Sefiha, "Regulating Performance-Enhancing Technologies," 109–110.

61. See, for example, CBS, "Poll: Fans Say Most Baseball Players Clean," CBS News, March 31, 2008, http://www.cbsnews.com/news/poll-fans-say-most-baseball-players-clean/; Marist University, "4/6: Steroid Scandal: Fans, Public React," Marist Poll, April 6, 2009, http://maristpoll.marist.edu/steroid-scandal-fans-public-react/; Harry Arne Solberg, Dag Vidar Hanstad, and Thor Atle Thøring, "Doping in Elite Sport—Do the Fans Care? Public Opinion on the Consequences of Doping Scandals," *International Journal of Sports Marketing and Sponsorship* 11, no. 3 (2010): 185–199; Marist University, "7/23: More than Six in Ten Fans Believe Connection to Biogenesis Steroid Clinic Too Little to Justify MLB Suspensions," Marist Poll, July 23, 2013, http://maristpoll.marist.edu/723-more-than-six-in-ten-fans-believe-connection-to-biogenesis-steroid-clinic-too-little-to-justify-mlb-suspensions/; Jon Cohen and Peyton M. Craighill, "Poll: Few See Steroids Ruining Sports, but Most Say

Users Should Not Get in Hall of Fame," *Washington Post*, January 8, 2013, http://www.washingtonpost.com/sports/poll-few-see-steroids-ruining-sports-but-most-say-users-should-not-get-in-hall-of-fame/2013/01/08/595b5910-599f-11e2-beee-6e38f5215402_story.html.

62. *Forbes*, "Major League Baseball Sees Record $9 Billion in Revenues for 2014," December 10, 2014, http://www.forbes.com/sites/maurybrown/2014/12/10/major-league-baseball-sees-record-9-billion-in-revenues-for-2014/.

63. See, for example, Larry Siddons, "IOC Expels Six Members in Salt Lake City Scandal," *The Guardian*, March 17, 1999, http://www.theguardian.com/sport/1999/mar/17/ioc-expels-members-bribes-scandal; Jules Boycoff and Alan Tomlinson, "Olympic Arrogance," *New York Times*, July 4, 2012, http://www.nytimes.com/2012/07/05/opinion/no-medal-for-the-international-olympic-committee.html; Andrew Jennings, "Meet the IOC, Ideal Candidates for a Perp Walk," *The Atlantic*, January 22, 2014, http://www.thenation.com/article/meet-ioc-ideal-candidates-perp-walk/.

64. Nielsen, "Nielsen Sports Insights," October 2012, Nielsen, http://www.nielsen.com/content/dam/corporate/us/en/sports/nielsen-sports-newsletter-october-2012.pdf.

65. Richard Sandomir, "NBC Extends Olympic Deal into Unknown," *New York Times*, May 7, 2014, http://www.nytimes.com/2014/05/08/sports/olympics/nbc-extends-olympic-tv-deal-through-2032.html.

66. Ben Rumsby, "BBC Begins Urgent Talks to Avoid Losing Olympics Games to Eurosport," *The Telegraph* (UK), June 29, 2015, http://www.telegraph.co.uk/sport/olympics/11706262/BBC-lose-TV-broadcasting-rights-for-Olympics-Games-to-Eurosport.html; British Broadcasting Corporation, "Eurosport Wins Olympic TV Rights for Europe," BBC, June 29, 2015, http://www.bbc.com/news/entertainment-arts-33311902.

67. Hoberman, *Testosterone Dreams*, 219.

68. Dimeo, *A History of Drug Use in Sport*, 138.

69. Hoberman, *Mortal Engines*, 124–125.

70. Institution of Mechanical Engineers (IMechE), *Sports Engineering: An Unfair Advantage?* (London: IMechE, 2012), 3, https://www.imeche.org/policy-and-press/reports/detail/sports-engineering-an-unfair-advantage.

71. Tony Hadland and Hans-Erhard Lessing, *Bicycle Design: An Illustrated History* (Cambridge, MA: MIT Press, 2014), 402–403; IMechE, *Sports Engineering*, 3.

72. Chester R. Kyle and David R. Bassett Junior, "The Cycling World Hour Record," in *High-Tech Cycling: The Science of Riding Faster*, ed. Edmund R. Burke (Champaign, IL: Human Kinetics, 2003), 182.

73. Matt Pacocha, "Interview: Jean Wauthier, USCI Technical Advisor," *Bike Radar*, June 19, 2010, http://www.bikeradar.com/us/gear/article/interview-jean-wauthier-uci-technical-advisor-26424/.

74. Union Cycliste Internationale, *The Lugano Charter*, October 8, 1996, http://oldsite.uci.ch/imgarchive/Road/Equipment/The%20Lugano%20charter.pdf.

75. IMechE, *Sports Engineering*.

76. Quoted in Pacocha, "Interview."

77. See, for example, Carlton Reid, "UCI Tries to Make Peace with Bike Industry," *Bikebiz*, September 2, 2010, http://www.bikebiz.com/news/read/uci-tries-to-make-peace-with-bike-industry; *Cycling Weekly*, "Bending the (UCI) Rules," October 17, 2013, http://www.cyclingweekly.co.uk/news/bending-the-uci-rules-24159.

78. Dick Marty, Pete Nicholson, and Ulrich Haas, "Cycling Independent Reform Commission: Report to the President of the Union Cycliste Internationale," February 2015, 7–11, 133, http://www.uci.ch/mm/Document/News/CleanSport/16/87/99/CIRC Report2015_Neutral.pdf.

79. Robert Rawdon Wilson, "Cyber(body)parts: Prosthetic Consciousness," *Body and Society* 1, nos. 3–4 (1995): 243.

80. Joshua Hunt, "Cycling's Greatest Hour," *New Yorker*, September 27, 2014, http://www.newyorker.com/news/sporting-scene/cyclings-greatest-hour.

81. Christopher Clarey, "Olympics; EPO Tests Are Approved for Sydney," *New York Times*, August 29, 2000, http://www.nytimes.com/2000/08/29/sports/olympics-epo-tests-are-approved-for-sydney.html.

82. IMechE, *Sports Engineering*, 3.

83. See, for example, Farhad Manjoo, "'Tech Doping'? How Speedo's LZR Suit Breaks Swim Records," *Salon*, April 10, 2008, http://www.salon.com/2008/04/10/speedo_suit/; Randy Starkman, "Sleek Suit Swamps Records," *Toronto Star*, June 24, 2008; Robert Kitson, "Why Swimmers Keep Hammering Their Way to New Heights," *The Guardian*, August 13, 2008; Peter Nichols, "'Technological Doping' Doesn't Suit Rebecca Adlington," *The Guardian*, July 19, 2009, http://www.theguardian.com/sport/2009/jul/19/rebecca-adlington-swimsuit-fina.

84. Andrew Dampf, "Phelps, Space-Age Suits and 108 World Records, SWM," *Associated Press*, December 6, 2008.

85. See, for example, Chris Zelkovich, "Will 'Technology Doping' Be the First Competition Scandal at Sochi Olympics?" Yahoo Sports, February 9, 2014, https://ca.sports.yahoo.com/blogs/eh-game/technology-doping-first-competition-scandal-sochi-olympics-183427240.html; Danielle Elliot, "Winter Olympics 2014: The Fine Line between Innovation and 'Technological Doping,'" CBS News, February 12, 2014, http://www.cbsnews.com/news/winter-olympics-2014-the-fine-line-between-innovation-and-technological-doping/; Jon Bardin, "Is Technological Doping the Strongest Force in the Olympics?" *Los Angeles Times*, July 24, 2012, http://articles.latimes.com/2012/jul/24/science/la-sci-sn-is-technological-doping-the-strongest-force-in-the-olympics-20120724.

86. Ted Butryn, "Cyborg Horizons: Sport and the Ethics of Self-Technologization," in *Research in Philosophy and Technology*, vol. 21, *Sport Technology: History, Philosophy and Policy*, ed. Andy Miah and Simon B. Eassom (Bingley, UK: Emerald Group Publishing, 2002), 112.

87. Manjoo, "'Tech Doping'?"; Jim Morrison, "How Speedo Created a Record-Breaking Swimsuit," *Scientific American*, July 27, 2012, http://www.scientificamerican.com/article/how-speedo-created-swimsuit/; National Aeronautics and Space Administration, "Breaking Record Benefits: A Speedo-NASA Partnership after the 2004 Olympics Resulted in a Swimsuit Worthy of World Records," NASA October 31, 2012, https://www.nasa.gov/offices/oct/home/tech_record_breaking.html#.Va0aVkWsrLc.

88. Dampf, "Phelps, Space-Age Suits"; Kabir Sawhney, "New Suits Taint Swimming Records," *Stanford Daily* (CA), January 12, 2010.

89. Amy Shipley, "FINA Opts to Ban All High-Tech Suits in Unanimous Vote," *Washington Post*, July 25, 2009.

90. Federation Internationale de Natation, "Dubai Charter: On FINA Requirements for Swimwear Approval," FINA, archives.fina.org/H2O/docs/PR/the%20dubai%20charter.

91. Magdalinski, "Restoring or Enhancing," 242.

92. Tara Magdalinski, "Performance Technologies: Drugs and Fastskin at the Sydney 2000 Olympics," *Media International Australia* 97, no. 1 (2000): 65.

93. Christine Brennan, "Sink or Swim? Not with This Suit," *USA Today*, June 30, 2008; Lisa Dillman, "FINA Bans Bodysuits that Have Led to Spate of World Records," *Los Angeles Times*, July 25, 2009, http://articles.latimes.com/2009/jul/25/sports/sp-world-swimming25; Andy Bull, "Michael Phelps Vows Not to Swim until Supersuits Are Banned," *The*

Guardian, July 28, 2009, http://www.theguardian.com/sport/2009/jul/28/michael-phelps-swimsuits-fina-world-championships.

94. Quoted in Karen Crouse, "Scrutiny of Suit Rises as World Records Fall," *New York Times*, April 11, 2008, http://www.nytimes.com/2008/04/11/sports/othersports/11swim.html?_r=0.

95. Quoted in Vahe Gregorian, "Controversy Suits Speedo Just Fine," *St. Louis Post-Dispatch*, August 9, 2008.

96. Laura Bell, "Breaking the Speed Limit—Studies Examine Physiology and Technology to Better Foresee the Ultimate Edge of Human Performance," *Science News*, December 5, 2009; Crouse, "Scrutiny of Suit."

97. Magdalinski, *Sport, Technology and the Body*, 111–115.

98. Ibid., 116–117.

99. Ibid., 111, 117.

100. Karen Crouse, "Swimming Bans High-Tech Suits, Ending an Era," *New York Times*, July 25, 2009, http://www.nytimes.com/2009/07/25/sports/25swim.html?_r=0, quoting Salo and Van Almsick.

101. Anna Kessel, "Born Slippy," *The Guardian*, November 22, 2008, http://www.theguardian.com/sport/2008/nov/23/swimming-olympics2008.

102. Patricia Marx, "Itsy-Bitsy Teeny-Weeny: On the Trauma of Swimsuit Shopping," *New Yorker*, August 3, 2009, http://www.newyorker.com/magazine/2009/08/03/itsy-bitsy-teeny-weeny.

103. *Guardian Unlimited*, "Olympics: Why the Pool Is Way Too Fast for 'Budgie Smugglers,'" August 12, 2008.

104. Phelps quoted in Gregorian, "Controversy Suits Speedo"; Lochte quoted in John Niyo, "Sleek Suits Make Waves at Swim Trials," *Detroit News*, June 29, 2008.

105. Quoted in Alex Brown, "Belief in Purity of Human v Water Contest a Snag for Super Cossie," *Sydney Morning Herald*, April 26, 2008.

106. Karen Crouse, "Phelps Loses, and a Debate Boils Over," *New York Times*, July 28, 2009, http://www.nytimes.com/2009/07/29/sports/29swim.html?pagewanted=all&_r=0, quoting Biedermann and Bowman.

107. *Toronto Star*, "Techno Doping in Rome," August 1, 2009.

108. Sally Jenkins, "Arena X-Glide Body Suit 1, Michael Phelps 0," *Reach for the Wall*, July 28, 2009, http://reachforthewall.com/2009/07/28/jenkins-column/.

109. Ibid.

110. Morrison, "How Speedo Created."

111. Hoberman, *Mortal Engines*, 132. For more on the slippages between drug- and technology-based alterations of athletic bodies, see Cheryl L. Cole, "Addiction, Exercise, and Cyborgs: Technologies of Deviant Bodies," in *Sport and Postmodern Times*, ed. Geneviève Rail (Albany: State University of New York Press, 1998), 261–275; Jennifer K. Wesley, "Negotiating Gender: Bodybuilding and the Natural/Unnatural Continuum," *Sociology of Sport Journal* 18, no. 2 (2001): 162–180.

112. See for example, Sanghamitra Chakraborty, "Doping: Sporting World's Worst Kept Secret," *Times of India*, October 20, 2002; David King, "Doping Dilemma—Supplement Use Widespread as Athletes Look for Any Edge," *San Antonio Express-News*, October 23, 2002; Matthew Pryor, "Kenteris and Thanou Charged over Missed Tests—Olympic Games," *The Times* (London), November 19, 2004; *Salt Lake Tribune*, "Sports on Steroids," December 8, 2004; Carlos Frias, "The Test Players Fear," *Palm Beach Post*, April 2, 2006; Charles Morris, "The Year Drugs Came First," *Financial Times* (London), December 28, 2007; Jay McGwire, *Mark and Me: Mark McGwire and the Truth behind Baseball's Worst-*

Kept Secret (Chicago: Triumph Books, 2010); *Agence France-Presse,* "Cycling: Landis Claims May Be Armstrong's Biggest Test Yet," May 24, 2010; Ben Doherty, "Pumped-Up Dream Deflates in Disgrace," *Sydney Morning Herald,* July 16, 2011; *Agence France-Presse,* "Cycling: Armstrong's Years of Denial," January 18, 2013.

113. Mehlman, *The Price of Perfection,* 125.

114. *Miami Herald,* "Nike Says Swimmers Can Switch to Speedos," July 31, 2008.

115. Quoted in Simon Hart, "UK Athletics Chief Neils De Vos Puts Olympic Gold Rush Down to 'Technological Doping,'" *The Telegraph* (UK), December 1, 2012, http://www.tele graph.co.uk/sport/olympics/9715937/UK-Athletics-chief-Neils-De-Vos-puts-Olympic-gold-rush-down-to-technological-doping.html.

116. UK Sport, "World Class Programme," UK Sport, http://uksport.gov.uk/our-work/world-class-programme.

117. IMechE, *Sports Engineering.*

118. Dan James, "Sports Minister Launches the Australian Sports Technology Network," *Queensland Sports Technology Cluster,* April 30, 2012, http://www.qsportstechnol ogy.com/blog/sportsministerlaunchestheaustraliansportstechnologynetwork.

119. Barrie Houlihan, Jae-Woo Park, and Mayumi Ya-Ya Yamamoto, "National Elite Sport Policies in Preparation for London 2012," in *Handbook of the London 2012 Olympic and Paralympic Games,* vol. 1, *Making the Games* (New York: Routledge, 2013), 268. All of the information I cite for South Korea and Japan is from ibid., 272–276.

120. Chris Hables Gray, *Cyborg Citizen: Politics in the Posthuman Age* (New York: Routledge, 2001), 170.

121. Amy Shipley, "US Olympic Committee Weighs the Highly Charged Option of Government Funding for Its Cash-Strapped Programs," *Washington Post,* January 14, 2010, http://www.washingtonpost.com/wp-dyn/content/article/2010/01/13/AR2010011304258 .html.

122. Blake Z. Rong, "BMW Bobsled Carries Team USA to Winter Olympics Victory," *Autoweek,* February 18, 2014, http://autoweek.com/article/car-news/bmw-bobsled-carries-team-usa-winter-olympics-victory.

123. Matt Majendie, "McLaren: From F1 to a Formula for Winter Olympic Gold," CNN, December 17, 2013, http://www.cnn.com/2013/12/17/sport/mclaren-winter-olym pics-work/index.html; John Branch, "Designers Carve a Fashion Runway at the Games," *New York Times,* February 6, 2014, http://www.nytimes.com/2014/02/07/sports/olympics/ designers-carve-a-fashion-runway-at-the-games.html; Andrew Liszewski, "The World's Fastest Speedskating Suit Has Lockheed Martin DNA," January 16, 2014, *Gizmodo,* http:// gizmodo.com/under-armour-will-debut-the-worlds-fastest-speedskatin-1502673088.

124. Robin Scott-Elliot, "Team GB's Cutting Edge: UK Sport Is More than Ever Using the Latest Military Technology Secrets to Produce Marginal Gains that Lead to Medals," *The Independent* (UK), October 9, 2013, http://www.independent.co.uk/sport/olympics/ team-gbs-cutting-edge-uk-sport-is-more-than-ever-using-the-latest-military-technology-secrets-to-produce-marginal-gains-that-lead-to-medals-8869938.html.

125. Loz Blain, "Ionically Charged Sports Clothing Boosts Athletes' Power Output and Recovery," *Gizmag,* September 11, 2007, http://www.gizmag.com/go/7950/; Mark Carter, "Roush Racing, Redstone Have Successful Partnership that Marries Racing and Military Technology," AL, June 12, 2011, http://www.al.com/sports/index.ssf/2011/06/roush_rac ing_redstone_have_suc.html; April Joyner, "Military Technology Company Protects NFL Players," *Inc.,* February 1, 2013, http://www.inc.com/magazine/201302/april-joyner/military-tech-company-protects-nfl.html.

126. Wilson, "Cyber(body)parts," 243.

127. Donna Haraway, "A Manifesto for Cyborgs: Science, Technology, and Socialist Feminism in the 1980s," *Socialist Review* 80 [15, no. 2] (1985): 67–69.

128. Thomas F. Corrigan et al., "Discourses of the 'Too-Abled': Contested Body Hierarchies and the Oscar Pistorius Case," *International Journal of Sport Communication* 3, no. 3 (2010): 288–307.

129. Magdalinski, "Restoring or Enhancing," 246.

130. Ian Brittain, *The Paralympic Games Explained* (New York: Routledge, 2010), 97.

131. Ibid., 103.

132. Marc Woods, "Paralympics 2012: Everything You Need to Know but May Be Afraid to Ask," *The Guardian*, July 23, 2012, http://www.theguardian.com/sport/2012/jul/23/para lympics-2012-marc-woods; Anne Marcellini et al, "Challenging Human and Sporting Boundaries: The Case of Oscar Pistorius," *Performance Enhancement and Health* 1, no. 1 (2012): 4; Corrigan et al., "Discourses of the 'Too-Abled,'" 289; Ivo Van Hilvoorde and Laurens Landeweerd, "Disability or Extraordinary Talent—Francesco Lentini (Three Legs) versus Oscar Pistorius (No Legs)," in *Ethics, Dis/Ability and Sports*, ed. Ejgil Jesperson and Mike McNamee (New York: Routledge, 2009), 19; *Los Angeles Times*, "Obituaries/Passings/Lis Hartel," February 15, 2009, http://articles.latimes.com/2009/feb/15/local/me-passings15.S2.

133. Howe, "Cyborg and Supercrip," 873–875.

134. Wilson, ""Cyber(body)parts," 243; Magdalinski, "Restoring or Enhancing," 244; Corrigan et al., "Discourses of the 'Too Abled,'" 300.

135. Norman and Moola, "'Bladerunner,'" 1270.

136. Corrigan et al., "Discourses of the 'Too Abled,'" 294–295; International Association of Athletics Federation, "IAAF Council Introduces Rule Regarding 'Technical Aids,'" IAAF, March 26, 2007, http://www.iaaf.org/news/news/iaaf-council-introduces-rule-re garding-techni. In Rule 144.2 the IAAF banned the use of technical aids in competition.

137. *Pistorius v. IAAF, Award of 16 May 2008*, CAS 2008/A/1480 (CAS 2008), juris prudence.tas- cas.org/sites/CaseLaw/Shared%20Documents/1480.pdf. In addition to the official CAS (Court of Arbitration for Sport) document, I am also relying here on summaries of the Pistorius case provided in Corrigan et al., "Discourses of the 'Too Abled,'" 294–295; and Norman and Moola, "'Bladerunner,'" 1271.

138. C. L. Cole, "Oscar Pistorius's Aftermath," *Journal of Sport and Social Issues* 33, no. 1 (2009): 3.

139. PTY, Deepak Vasa-Informit-RMIT Training, "Pistorius v International Association of Athletics Federations (IAAF)(2008) 3 (1) ANZSLJR 2," *Australian and New Zealand Sports Law Journal* 3, no. 1 (2008): 145–164.

140. Colleen Barry, "Amputee Runner Oscar Pistorius Wins Appeal," *Associated Press*, May 16, 2008; *Guardian Unlimited*, "Pistorius Fails to Make South Africa's Team for the Olympics," July 18, 2008; Chris Lehourites, "Pistorius Lived Out Dream by Running at Olympics," *Associated Press*, February 14, 2013.

141. Magdalinski, "Restoring or Enhancing," 249.

142. Silvia Camporesi, "Oscar Pistorius, Enhancement and Post-humans," *Journal of Medical Ethics* 34, no. 9 (2008): 639.

143. Cole, "Oscar Pistorius's Aftermath," 3–4.

144. Norman and Moola, "'Bladerunner,'" 1273–1274.

145. Marcellini et al., "Challenging Human and Sporting Boundaries," 8.

146. Jeré Longman, "An Amputee Sprinter: Is He Disabled or Too-Abled?" *New York Times*, May 15, 2007, http://www.nytimes.com/2007/05/15/sports/othersports/15runner .html?pagewanted=all&_r=0; Ellen Goodman, "The Future of Sport in an Age of Cyborgs," *Boston Globe*, May 28, 2007.

147. Longman, "An Amputee Sprinter."

148. Paul Root Wolpe, "Oscar Pistorius, an Inspiration and a Question," *CNN Wire,* August 6, 2012.

149. Anders Sandberg, "Olympic Blade Runner Challenges Our View of Humanity," *New Scientist,* August 13, 2012, https://www.newscientist.com/article/mg21528775-500-olympic-blade-runner-challenges-our-view-of-humanity/.

150. Longman, "An Amputee Sprinter"; Neal Conan, "Prosthetics in Sports: Disability or Advantage?" National Public Radio, May 31, 2007.

151. Ebenezer Samuel, "Blade Runner: Pistorius's Olympic Quest Sparks Debate on Track," *New York Daily News,* June 1, 2008.

152. Tracy J. Trothen, "The Trans-athlete and the Religion of Sport: Implications of Transhumanism for Elite Sport's Spiritual Dimension," in *Religion and Transhumanism: The Unknown Future of Human Enhancement,* ed. Calvin Mercer and Tracy J. Trothen (Santa Barbara, CA: ABC-CLIO, 2015), 351–352.

153. For debates over whether transhumanism is a secular, or even formally religious, faith, see Robert M. Geraci, "There and Back Again: Transhumanist Evangelism in Science Fiction and Popular Science," *Implicit Religion* 14, no. 2 (2011): 141–172; Hava Tirosh-Samuelson, "Transhumanism as Secularist Faith," *Zygon* 47, no. 4 (2012): 710–734; Anders Sandberg, "Transhumanism and the Meaning of Life," in *Religion and Transhumanism: The Unknown Future of Human Enhancement,* ed. Calvin Mercer and Tracy J. Trothen (Santa Barbara, CA: ABC-CLIO, 2015), 3–22.

154. Patrick D. Hopkins, "Transcending the Animal: How Transhumanism and Religion Are and Are Not Alike," *Journal of Evolution and Technology* 14, no. 2 (2005): 13.

155. McKenny, "Transcendence," 183–185. For similar arguments about how denominational religions (especially Christianity) and transhumanism differ according to "techniques" of transcendence, see Heidi Campbell and Mark Walker, "Religion and Transhumanism: Introducing a Conversation," *Journal of Evolution and Technology* 14, no. 2 (2005): ii; Todd Daly, "Life-Extension in Transhumanist and Christian Perspectives: Consonance and Conflict," *Journal of Evolution and Technology* 14, no. 2 (2005): 64; Donald M. Braxton, "Does Transhumanism Face an Uncanny Valley among the Religious?" in *Religion and Transhumanism: The Unknown Future of Human Enhancement,* ed. Calvin Mercer and Tracy J. Trothen (Santa Barbara, CA: ABC-CLIO, 2015), 337; Ronald Cole-Turner, "Introduction: The Transhumanist Challenge," in *Transhumanism and Transcendence: Christian Hope in an Age of Technological Enhancement,* ed. Ronald Cole-Turner (Washington, DC: Georgetown University Press, 2011), 4–5; James J. Hughes, "The Politics of Transhumanism and the Techno-millennial Imagination, 1626–2030," *Zygon* 47, no. 4 (2012): 757–776. For many scholars who have examined the overlaps and oppositions between religious and transhumanist transcendence, technological intervention is the basic dividing line. Some, however, do not see religious and technologically grounded transcendence as antithetical. For examples of this argument, see Arthur Saniotis, "Attaining Transcendence: Transhumanism, the Body, and the Abrahamic Religions," in *Religion and the Body: Modern Science and the Construction of Religious Meaning,* ed. David Cave and Rebecca Sachs Norris (Boston: Brill, 2012), 158–161; Michael S. Burdett, "Contextualizing a Christian Perspective on Transcendence and Human Enhancement: Francis Bacon, N. F. Fedorov, and Pierre Teilhard de Chardin," in *Transhumanism and Transcendence: Christian Hope in an Age of Technological Enhancement,* ed. Ronald Cole-Turner (Washington, DC: Georgetown University Press, 2011), 32–33.

156. For a discussion of how Nussbaum's distinction between internal and external transcendence relates to religion and secularity, see Robert Merrihew Adams, *Finite and Infinite*

Goods: A Framework for Ethics (New York: Oxford University Press, 1999), 50–77; Nussbaum, "Transcendence and Human Values," 445–452; Taylor, *A Secular Age*, 618–639.

157. Finnegan and Kang, "'Sighting' the Public," 395.

158. Hilvoorde and Landeweerd, "Enhancing Disabilities," 2226.

159. Lauren Reichart Smith, "The Blade Runner: The Discourses surrounding Oscar Pistorius in the 2012 Olympics and Paralympics," *Communication and Sport* 3, no. 4 (2015): 390–410; Howe, "Cyborg and Supercrip"; *Agence France-Presse*, "Blade Runner Oscar Pistorius Was One of the World's Most Inspirational Sportsmen," February 15, 2013; Mark Purdy, "The Heart of an Olympian," *San Jose Mercury News*, August 5, 2012.

160. Eric Wilson, "Model and Front-Runner," *New York Times*, July 13, 2011, http://www.nytimes.com/2011/07/14/fashion/oscar-pistorius-a-model-and-front-runner.html?_r=0.

161. Purdy, "The Heart of an Olympian."

162. Simon Allison, "Oscar Pistorius Guilty of Murder as Court Overturns Previous Conviction," *The Guardian*, December 3, 2015, https://www.theguardian.com/world/2015/dec/03/oscar-pistorius-conviction-reeva-steenkamp-upgraded-murder.

163. Rebecca Davis, "Oscar Pistorius and the Paradox of the Disabled Super-Athlete," *Daily Maverick*, July 7, 2014, http://www.dailymaverick.co.za/article/2014-07-07-oscar-pistorius-and-the-paradox-of-the-disabled-super-athlete/#.Vfw6hbSdLzI.

164. Drew Griffin and David Fitzpatrick, "Not Everyone Surprised at Oscar Pistorius' Fall from Grace," CNN, March 7, 2013, http://www.cnn.com/2013/03/06/world/africa/pistorius-image/; Harriet Alexander, "Oscar Pistorius Ex-girlfriend: 'It Could Have Been Me,'" *The Telegraph* (UK), September 12, 2014, http://www.telegraph.co.uk/news/world news/oscar-pistorius/11091309/Oscar-Pistorius-ex-girlfriend-It-could-have-been-me.html.

165. Derman quoted in Sydney Lupkin, "Disability Does Not Justify Pistorius Shooting, Groups Say," ABC News, July 2, 2014, http://abcnews.go.com/Health/disability-jus tify-pistorius-shooting-groups/story?id=24401355; Roux quoted in Davis, "Oscar Pistorius and the Paradox."

166. Peter Bansel and Browyn Davies, "Assembling Oscar, Assembling South Africa, Assembling Affects," *Emotion, Space and Society* 13, no. 4 (2014): 41.

167. See ibid., 42. Bansel and Davies offer an excellent critique of a "culture of violence" narrative that emerged in coverage, especially related to an influential *Time* article written by Alex Perry. See Alex Perry, "Pistorius and South Africa's Culture of Violence," *Time*, March 11, 2013. Also see Leslie Swartz, "Oscar Pistorius and the Melancholy of Intersectionality," *Disability and Society* 28, no. 8 (2013): 1157–1161.

168. Sarah Lyall, "Torment on the Stand, but Is It an Act?" *New York Times*, April 19, 2014, http://www.nytimes.com/2014/04/20/sunday-review/torment-on-the-stand-but-is-it-an-act.html; Terrence McCoy, "The Weeping Oscar Pistorius and a Final Question: Has It All Been an Act?" *Washington Post*, October 15, 2014, http://www.washingtonpost.com/news/morning-mix/wp/2014/10/15/the-weeping-oscar-pistorius-and-a-final-question-has-it-all-been-an-act/; Michael Sokolove, "The Adrenaline-Fueled Life of Oscar Pistorius," *New York Times*, February 14, 2013, http://6thfloor.blogs.nytimes.com/2013/02/14/the-adrenaline-fueled-life-of-oscar-pistorius/?ref=magazine.

169. Quoted in Clare Harvey, "What's Disability Got to Do with It? Changing Constructions of Oscar Pistorius before and after the Death of Reeva Steenkamp," *Disability and Society* 30, no. 2 (2015): 301.

170. Glazer quoted in Lupkin, "Disability Does Not Justify"; Harvey, "What's Disability," 302.

171. Aislinn Laing, "Oscar Pistorius Re-enacts Reeva Steenkamp Shooting in Extraordinary Leaked Video," *The Telegraph* (UK), July 5, 2014, http://www.telegraph.co.uk/news/

worldnews/oscar-pistorius/10949067/Oscar-Pistorius-re-enacts-Reeva-Steenkamp-shooting-in-extraordinary-leaked-video.html; Jonathan Pearlman, "Oscar Pistorius Video: What Is The Evidence Room?" *The Telegraph* (UK), July 7, 2014, http://www.telegraph.co.uk/news/worldnews/oscar-pistorius/10950556/Oscar-Pistorius-video-what-is-The-Evidence-Room.html.

172. Aislinn Laing, "Pistorius Lawyers Slam 'Unlawful' Broadcast of Steenkamp Shooting Re-enactment," *The Telegraph* (UK), July 6, 2014, http://www.telegraph.co.uk/news/worldnews/oscar-pistorius/10949897/Pistorius-lawyers-slam-unlawful-broadcast-of-Steenkamp-shooting-re-enactment.html; Hood quoted in Stephanie Findlay, "Oscar Pistorius Re-enacts Steenkamp Shooting in Leaked Video," *Hamilton Spectator* (Ontario), July 6, 2014, http://www.thespec.com/news-story/4617703-oscar-pistorius-re-enacts-steenkamp-shooting-in-leaked-video/.

173. Haraway, "A Manifesto," 68.

174. Claire F. Sullivan, "Gender Verification and Gender Policies in Elite Sport: Eligibility and 'Fair Play,'" *Journal of Sport and Social Issues* 35, no. 4 (2011): 401–402. Also see Kathryn Henne, "The 'Science' of Fair Play in Sport: Gender and the Politics of Testing," *Signs: Journal of Women in Culture and Society* 39, no. 3 (2014): 787–812.

175. John M. Sloop, "Riding in Cars between Men," *Communication and Critical/Cultural Studies* 2, no. 3 (2005): 194.

176. Robert McRuer, *Crip Theory: Cultural Signs of Queerness and Disability* (New York: New York University Press, 2006), 1–31; James L. Cherney and Kurt Lindemann, "Queering Street: Homosociality, Masculinity, and Disability in Friday Night Lights," *Western Journal of Communication* 78, no. 1 (2014): 3.

177. I am leaving out a full treatment of connections between queer theory, disability studies, and sport since this is outside the scope of my chapter. For examples of how these bodies of scholarship come together in sport studies, see Benita de Robillard, "'Our Caster' and 'The Blade Runner': 'Improper' Corporealities Cripqueering the Post/Apartheid Body Politic," *Image and Text: A Journal for Design* 24, no. 1 (2014): 79–115; and Jayne Caudwell, "Queer-in the Sociology of Sport," in *The Ashgate Research Companion to Queer Theory*, ed. Noreen Giffney and Michael O'Rourke (Burlington, VT: Ashgate, 2009), 219–236. For broader treatments of queer theory and sport, see Gamal Abdel-Shehid, *Who da Man? Black Masculinities and Sporting Cultures* (Toronto: Canadian Scholars' Press, 2005), 139–149; Jayne Caudwell, ed., *Sport, Sexualities and Queer/Theory* (New York: Routledge, 2006); Samantha King, "What's Queer about (Queer) Sport Sociology Now? A Review Essay," *Sociology of Sport Journal* 25, no. 4 (2008): 419–442; Sheila Scraton and Anne Flintoff, "Gender, Feminist Theory, and Sport," in *A Companion to Sport*, ed. David L. Andrews and Ben Carrington (Malden, MA: Blackwell, 2013), 96–111. For an analysis of queer theory in relationship to technologized bodies within and beyond sport, see de Robillard, "'Our Caster' and 'The Blade Runner'"; Nikki Sullivan and Samantha Murray, "Introduction," in *Somatechnics: Queering the Technologisation of Bodies*, ed. Nikki Sullivan and Samantha Murray (Burlington, VT: Ashgate, 2009), 1–10.

178. Donna J. Haraway, *Simians, Cyborgs, and Women: The Reinvention of Nature* (New York: Routledge, 1991), 212–213.

179. Sheila L. Cavanagh and Heather Sykes, "Transsexual Bodies at the Olympics: The International Olympic Committee's Policy on Transsexual Athletes at the 2004 Athens Summer Games," *Body and Society* 12, no. 3 (2006): 89.

180. Ibid., 89.

181. *The Gender Recognition Bill [HL]*, U.K. House of Commons (2004), 52.

182. For more on common connections between sexual identity and performance-

enhancing drugs in sport, see C. L. Cole, "Testing for Sex or Drugs," *Journal of Sport and Social Issues* 24, no. 4 (2000): 331–333.

183. Laura A. Wackwitz, "Verifying the Myth: Olympic Sex Testing and the Category 'Woman,'" *Women's Studies International Forum* 26, no. 6 (2003): 553–560; Cavanagh and Sykes, "Transsexual Bodies," 75–102; Sullivan, "Gender Verification;" Katrina Karzakis, Rebecca Jordan-Young, Georgiann Davis, Silvia Camporesi, "Out of Bounds? A Critique of the New Policies on Hyperandrogensim in Elite Female Athletes," *American Journal on Bioethics* 12, no. 7 (2012): 3–16; Henne, "The 'Science' of Fair Play." For more on male genitalia as a regulatory preoccupation in sport, see Laurel Westbrook and Kristen Schilt, "Doing Gender, Determining Gender: Transgender People, Gender Panics, and the Maintenance of the Sex/Gender/Sexuality System," *Gender and Society* 28, no. 1 (2014): 45. For a critique of the presumed connection between androgens (especially testosterone) and athletic performance, see Lance Wahlert and Autumn Fiester, "Gender Transports: Privileging the 'Natural' in Gender Testing Debates for Intersex and Transgender Athletes," *American Journal of Bioethics* 12, no. 7 (2012): 19–21.

184. Diane Marie Keeling, "*His*tory of (Future) Progress: Hyper-Masculine Transhumanist Virtuality," *Critical Studies in Media Communication* 29, no. 2 (2012): 133–134.

185. Heather Walton, "The Gender of the Cyborg," *Theology and Sexuality* 10, no. 2 (2004): 35–36, 39.

186. Sullivan, "Gender Verification," 414.

187. John M. Sloop, "'This Is Not Natural': Caster Semenya's Gender Threats," *Critical Studies in Media Communication* 29, no. 2 (2012): 89–92.

188. Nikki Sullivan, "The Somatechnics of Intersexuality," *GLQ* 15, no. 2 (2009): 314.

189. Heather Graham, *Representations of the Post/Human: Monsters, Aliens and Others in Popular Culture* (New Brunswick, NJ: Rutgers University Press, 2002), 219–220.

190. Walton, "The Gender of the Cyborg," 42.

CHAPTER 5

1. Nielsen, "Football TV Ratings Soar: The NFL's Playbook for Success," Nielsen, January 28, 2011, http://www.nielsen.com/us/en/insights/news/2011/football-tv-ratings-soar-the-nfls-playbook-for-success.html.

2. Bill Carter, "The Top Attraction on TV? No Script, but Plenty of Action," *New York Times*, December 20, 2010; Derek Thompson, "The Fragile Dominance of the NFL," *The Atlantic*, September 22, 2014, http://www.theatlantic.com/business/archive/2014/09/nfl-scandals-could-destroy-football-and-pay-tv/380568/.

3. Nielsen, "Football TV Ratings Soar"; Nielsen, "Super Bowl XLV Most Viewed Telecast in U.S. Broadcast History," Nielsen, February 7, 2011, http://www.nielsen.com/us/en/insights/news/2011/super-bowl-xlv-most-viewed-telecast-in-broadcast-history.html; Nielsen, "Super Bowl XLVII Draws 108.7 Million Viewers, 26.1 Million Tweets," Nielsen, February 5, 2013, http://www.nielsen.com/us/en/insights/news/2013/super-bowl-xlvii-draws-108-7-million-viewers-26-1-tweets.html.

4. National Football League, "NFL, YouTube Announce Partnership including Official Channel," NFL, January 26, 2015, http://www.nfl.com/news/story/0ap3000000463404/printable/nfl-youtube-announce-partnership-including-official-channel.

5. Ben Kelson, "Judge Approves Deal in Concussion Lawsuit," *New York Times*, April 23, 2015; Rick Kissell, "Ratings: NFL Draws Record Audience for Opening Week," *Variety*, September 17, 2015, http://variety.com/2015/tv/news/nfl-record-ratings-for-opening-week-1201595991/.

6. Thompson, "The Fragile Dominance."

7. See, for example, Ann C. McKee et al., "Chronic Traumatic Encephalopathy in Athletes: Progressive Tauopathy following Repetitive Head Injury," *Journal of Neuropathology and Experimental Neurology* 68, no. 7 (2009): 709–735.

8. Joseph A. Slobodzian, "2,000 Ex-players Join to Sue the NFL on Head Trauma," *Philadelphia Inquirer*, June 8, 2012, http://articles.philly.com/2012-06-08/news/32102176_1_concussions-nfl-funded-dave-duerson; Paul M. Barrett, "Will Brain Injury Lawsuits Doom or Save the NFL?" *Bloomberg Business*, January 31, 2013, http://www.bloomberg.com/bw/articles/2013-01-31/will-brain-injury-lawsuits-doom-or-save-the-nfl#p3; Ken Belson, "Judge Delays Ruling in N.F.L. Concussion Case and Brings In Mediator," *New York Times*, July 9, 2013.

9. Steve Fainaru and Mark Fainaru-Wada, "Youth Football Participation Drops," ESPN, November 13, 2013, http://espn.go.com/espn/otl/story/_/page/popwarner/pop-warner-youth-football-participation-drops-nfl-concussion-crisis-seen-causal-factor. For a contrarian view of the forces behind declining youth football participation, see Bob Cook, "Why Is Football Participation Declining? The Answer Isn't Concussions," *Forbes*, November 26, 2013, http://www.forbes.com/sites/bobcook/2013/11/26/why-is-football-participation-declining-the-answer-isnt-concussions/; Bob Cook, "Youth Football, despite Reported Declines, Is about as Popular as Ever," *Forbes*, September 25, 2014, http://www.forbes.com/sites/bobcook/2014/09/25/youth-football-despite-reported-declines-is-about-as-popular-as-ever/.

10. The NFL and the NFLPA (the league players' union) endowed USA Football in 2002 as a national governing body for youth football. The organization is funded through grants from NFL charitable foundations, and its board of directors is constituted partly by NFL executives. See National Football League, "NFL Celebrates USA Football Month with Launch of USA Football's Heads Up Football Initiative," NFL, August 15, 2012, http://www.nfl.com/news/story/0ap1000000050353/article/nfl-celebrates-usa-football-month-with-launch-of-usa-footballs-heads-up-football-initiative; Steve Alic, "NFL Foundation Grant Will Support USA Football Programs, including Heads Up Football and NFL FLAG," *USA Football*, March 24, 2014, http://usafootball.com/blogs/roger-goodell/post/8307/nfl-foundation-grant-will-support-usa-football-programs%2C-including-heads-up-football-and-nfl-flag; USA Football, "Directory," USA Football, http://usafootball.com/contact_us.

11. See, for example, Gary Mihoces, "Heads Up: Good Play or Good Ploy?" *USA Today*, August 28, 2013, http://www.usatoday.com/story/sports/nfl/2013/08/27/heads-up-youth-football-nfl-roger-goodell/2711317/; Rick Maese, "Tackling a Crisis: Under Fire because of the Risks of the Game, the NFL Is Promoting New Techniques for Younger Players," *Washington Post*, October 24, 2013, http://www.washingtonpost.com/sf/sports/wp/2013/10/24/tackling-a-crisis/; Steve Fainaru and Mark Fainaru-Wada, "Questions about Heads Up Tackling," ESPN, January 10, 2014, http://espn.go.com/espn/otl/story/_/id/10276129/popular-nfl-backed-heads-tackling-method-questioned-former-players; Drew Magary, "I Got Certified to Coach Heads Up Football and It Was a Joke," *Deadspin*, May 29, 2014, http://deadspin.com/i-got-certified-to-coach-heads-up-football-and-it-was-a-1583159680; Mike Florio, "John Madden Doesn't Believe in the Heads Up Football Program," Pro Football Talk, August 5, 2014, http://profootballtalk.nbcsports.com/2014/08/05/john-madden-doesnt-believe-in-the-heads-up-football-program/; Ken Belson, "To Allay Fears, N.F.L. Huddles with Mothers," *New York Times*, January 29, 2015.

12. Bryant Gumbel, "Troy Aikman," HBO, January 25, 2011, http://www.hbo.com/real-sports-with-bryant-gumbel/episodes/0/166-episode/video/troy-aikman-preview.html?autoplay=true.

13. Quoted in Gumbel, "Aikman"; Joe DeLessio, "9 NFL Players Who Wouldn't Let Their Sons Play Football," *New York Magazine*, November 14, 2014, http://nymag.com/daily/intelligencer/2014/11/9-nflers-who-wont-let-their-sons-play-football.html#.

14. Obama quoted in Franklin Foer and Chris Hughes, "Barack Obama Is Not Pleased," *New Republic*, January 27, 2013, http://www.newrepublic.com/article/112190/obama-interview-2013-sit-down-president; Reed quoted in Susan Reimer, "Loving Football as a Fan, Fearing It as a Parent," *Baltimore Sun*, January 31, 2013.

15. Quoted in Eddie Guy and Mick Rouse, "The Season from Hell: Inside Roger Goodell's Ruthless Football Machine," *GQ*, February 1, 2015.

16. Quoted in Belson, "To Allay Fears."

17. Jonah Lehrer, "The Fragile Teenage Brain," *Grantland*, January 19, 2012, http://grantland.com/features/jonah-lehrer-concussions-adolescents-future-football/.

18. Eric Sondheimer, "High School Football Coaches See Fear of Injuries Draining Talent Pool," *Los Angeles Times*, September 24, 2015, http://www.latimes.com/sports/highschool/la-sp-freshman-football-sondheimer-20150925-column.html; Kevin Thomas, "Thin Rosters Have Some Football Teams on the Edge," *Portland Press Herald*, October 5, 2015, http://www.pressherald.com/2015/10/04/participation-in-varsity-football-at-several-maine-high-schools-has-fallen/.

19. See, for example, Ken Belson, "Football's Risks Sink In, Even in Heart of Texas," *New York Times*, May 12, 2014; Ken Belson, "As Worries Rise and Players Flee, Football Is Cut," *New York Times*, September 29, 2015.

20. See, for example, Tom Scocca, "NFL Playoffs, the Super Bowl," *Slate*, January 10, 2011, http://www.slate.com/articles/sports/sports_nut/features/2011/nfl_playoffs_the_super_bowl/this_is_the_concussion_bowl.html; Ben McGrath, "Does Football Have a Future?" *New Yorker*, January 31, 2011, http://www.newyorker.com/magazine/2011/01/31/does-football-have-a-future; Evan Weiner, "Could Football Fade Away like Boxing?" *Sport Digest*, November 5, 2013; Melissa Harris-Perry, "Melissa Harris-Perry for November 10, 2013, MSNBC," MSNBC, November 10, 2013, http://www.nbcnews.com/id/53522765/ns/msnbc-t/melissa-harris-perry-show-sunday-november-th/; Mark Purdy, "Players' Fear, Risk Becoming Pivotal Factors in NFL," *San Jose Mercury News*, March 18, 2015.

21. Kevin Grier and Tyler Cowen, "What Would the End of Football Look Like?" *Grantland*, February 13, 2012, http://grantland.com/features/cte-concussion-crisis-economic-look-end-football/. Also see Gregg Doyel, "Death of Football? That's Crazy, until You Start Thinking about It," CBS Sports, February 24, 2012, http://www.cbssports.com/nfl/story/17423602/death-of-football-thats-crazy-until-you-start-thinking-about-it; James Bukes, "The End of Football?" *Pittsburgh Post-Gazette*, December 14, 2014. *Slate* writer Will Oremus argues that the pathway Grier and Cowen lay out is unlikely, as brain injury symptoms build over time and typically occur postcareer, when medical and liability insurance policies may not provide coverage. See Will Oremus, "After Further Review," *Slate*, May 10, 2012, http://www.slate.com/articles/sports/sports_nut/2012/05/the_end_of_football_why_concussion_lawsuits_won_t_bring_down_the_game_.html.

22. Dan Rather, "Knocking Heads," *Dan Rather Reports*, March 3, 2009; Frederic J. Frommer and Howard Fendrich, "Goodell Defends NFL's Handling of Head Injuries," *Associated Press*, October 29, 2009; John Culhane, "Concussions and Cigarettes," *Slate*, July 26, 2011, http://www.slate.com/articles/sports/sports_nut/2011/07/concussions_and_cigarettes.html; Steve Hummer, "Hard Knocks' Toll—Former Players Claim the NFL Concealed the Long-Term Costs of Repeated Hits to the Head," *Atlanta Journal-Constitution*, January 29, 2012; Andrew Sullivan, "Is Big Football the Next Big Tobacco?" *The Dish*,

March 28, 2012, http://dish.andrewsullivan.com/threads/is-football-the-next-big-tobacco/; Greg Risling, "Concussion Lawsuits Are Next Big US Litigation," *Associated Press*, June 30, 2012; Bryan Burwell, "NFL Wants Everyone to Forget What It Did, but We Should Refuse," *St. Louis Post-Dispatch*, September 3, 2013.

23. Travis Vogan, *Keepers of the Flame: NFL Films and the Rise of Sports Media* (Urbana: University of Illinois Press, 2014), 46.

24. Quoted in Michael Oriard, *Brand NFL: Making and Selling America's Favorite Sport* (Chapel Hill: University of North Carolina Press, 2007), 14.

25. Vogan, *Keepers of the Flame*, 55.

26. Ibid., 57–59. Also see Maurice Halbwachs, *On Collective Memory*, ed. and trans. Lewis A. Coser (Chicago: University of Chicago Press, 1992), 49–50.

27. Teresa Bergman, "Can Patriotism Be Carved in Stone? A Critical Analysis of Mt. Rushmore's Orientation Films," *Rhetoric and Public Affairs* 11, no. 1 (2008): 89–112; Greg Dickinson, Brian L. Ott, and Eric Aoki, "Spaces of Remembering and Forgetting: The Reverent Eye/I at the Plains Indian Museum," *Communication and Critical/Cultural Studies* 3, no. 1 (2006): 27–47; Greg Dickinson, Brian L. Ott, and Eric Aoki, "Memory and Myth at the Buffalo Bill Museum," *Western Journal of Communication* 69, no. 2 (2005): 85–108; Teresa Bergman, "A Critical Analysis of the California State Railroad Museum's Orientation Films," *Western Journal of Communication* 67, no. 4 (2003): 427–448; Victoria J. Gallagher, "Memory and Reconciliation in the Birmingham Civil Rights Institute," *Rhetoric and Public Affairs* 2, no. 2 (1999): 303–320.

28. Carole Blair, Marsha S. Jeppeson, and Enrico Pucci Jr., "Public Memorializing in Postmodernity: The Vietnam Veterans Memorial as Prototype," *Quarterly Journal of Speech* 77, no. 3 (1991): 263–288; Carole Blair and Neil Michel, "Reproducing Civil Rights Tactics: The Rhetorical Performances of the Civil Rights Memorial," *Rhetoric Society Quarterly* 30, no. 2 (2000): 31–55; Carole Blair and Neil Michel, "The AIDS Memorial Quilt and the Contemporary Culture of Public Commemoration," *Rhetoric and Public Affairs* 10, no. 4 (2007): 596; Roseann M. Mandziuk, "Commemorating Sojourner Truth: Negotiating the Politics of Race and Gender in the Spaces of Public Memory," *Western Journal of Communication* 67, no. 3 (2003): 272; Robert Hariman and John Louis Lucaites, "Public Identity and Collective Memory in U.S. Iconic Photography: The Image of 'Accidental Napalm,'" *Critical Studies in Media Communication* 20, no. 1 (2003): 38.

29. Phil Patton, *Razzle-Dazzle: The Curious Marriage of Television and Professional Football* (New York: Dial Press, 1984), 1–2.

30. Tex Maule, "The Best Football Game Ever Played," *Sports Illustrated*, January 5, 1959, http://sportsillustrated.cnn.com/vault/article/magazine/MAG1133692/index.htm.

31. Mark Bowden, *The Best Game Ever: Giants vs. Colts, 1958, and the Birth of the Modern NFL* (New York: Atlantic Monthly Press, 2008).

32. Ibid., 18.

33. Patton, *Razzle-Dazzle*, 4.

34. Bowden, *The Best Game Ever,* 15.

35. Mary Ann Doane, "Information, Crisis, Catastrophe," in *Logics of Television: Essays in Cultural Criticism*, ed. Patricia Mellencamp (Bloomington: Indiana University Press, 1990), 222–239; Anna McCarthy, *Ambient Television: Visual Culture and Public Space* (Durham, NC: Duke University Press, 2001), 210.

36. Walter Benjamin, "Theses on the Philosophy of History," in *Illuminations*, ed. Hannah Arendt and trans. Harry Zohn (New York: Harcourt, Brace and World, 1955), 256.

37. Joanne H. Wright, *Origin Stories in Political Thought: Discourses on Gender, Power, and Citizenship* (Toronto: University of Toronto Press, 2004), 8, 11.

38. Edward W. Said, *Beginnings: Intention and Method* (Baltimore: Johns Hopkins University Press, 1975), 41–42.

39. Michel Foucault, "Nietzsche, Genealogy, History," in *The Foucault Reader*, ed. Paul Rabinow (New York: Pantheon Books, 1984), 78–79. Also see Wright, *Origin Stories in Political Thought*, 9.

40. Foucault, "Nietzsche, Genealogy, History," 79.

41. All citations related to ESPN's special refer to the TV movie *The Greatest Game Ever Played*, directed by Marc Kinderman (Stamford, CT: Televersemedia, 2008).

42. For a representatively moralistic understanding of the 1958 championship as an antidote for cultural amnesia, see Ihsan Taylor, "The Best Game Ever: Interview with Mark Bowden," *New York Times*, December 25, 2008, http://fifthdown.blogs.nytimes.com/2008/12/25/the-best-game-ever-interview-with-mark-bowden/?_r=0.

43. Taylor, "The Best Game Ever."

44. Michael Hiestand, "Colorizing 'Greatest Game' a Real Clock-Eater," *USA Today*, December 12, 2008.

45. Quoted in *Street and Smith's SportsBusiness Journal*, "ESPN's 'Greatest Game Ever Played' Documentary Debuts Saturday," December 12, 2008, http://www.sportsbusinessdaily.com/Daily/Issues/2008/12/Issue-62/Sports-Media/Espns-Greatest-Game-Ever-Played-Documentary-Debuts-Saturday.aspx.

46. Bowden describes the broadcast as conveying a scene in "spooky black and white," in which television audiences "saw spectral players battling in shades of white and gray against a stark black backdrop. . . . This was more like mortal combat from some dark underworld. As in some medieval rite, the players on both sidelines were draped in long capes. A master cinematographer could not have lit the scene more dramatically" (Bowden, *The Best Game Ever*, 2–3).

47. Quoted in *Street and Smith's SportsBusiness Journal*, "ESPN's 'Greatest Game Ever Played.'"

48. Quoted in Patton, *Razzle-Dazzle*, 2–3.

49. Ibid.

50. Bowden, *The Best Game Ever*, 213–214.

51. Hannah Arendt, *On Revolution* (New York: Viking Press, 1963), 10–11.

52. René Girard, *Violence and the Sacred*, trans. Patrick Gregory (Baltimore, MD: Johns Hopkins University Press, 1972), 8.

53. Ibid., 79–80; Kenneth Burke, *Permanence and Change: An Anatomy of Purpose*, 3rd ed. (Berkeley: University of California Press, 1984), 14–17, 283–291; Kenneth Burke, *A Grammar of Motives* (Berkeley: University of California Press, 1969), 406–408.

54. Wright, *Origin Stories*, 11.

55. Girard, *Violence*, 307.

56. Arendt, *On Revolution*, 10–11.

57. Blair and Michel, "The AIDS Memorial Quilt"; Hariman and Lucaites, "Public Identity and Collective Memory."

58. Mark Yost, *Tailgating, Sacks, and Salary Caps: How the NFL Became the Most Successful Sports League in History* (Chicago: Kaplan, 2006), 70.

59. Ibid., 74–79.

60. Kurt Badenhausen, "The NFL Signs TV Deals Worth $27 Billion," *Forbes*, December 14, 2011, http://www.forbes.com/sites/kurtbadenhausen/2011/12/14/the-nfl-signs-tv-deals-worth-26-billion/.

61. Craig R. Coenen, *From Sandlots to the Super Bowl: The National Football League, 1920–1967* (Knoxville: University of Tennessee Press, 2005), 180.

62. Ibid., 180–186; Richard C. Crepeau, *NFL Football: A History of America's New Pastime* (Champaign: University of Illinois Press, 2014), 136–137.

63. Crepeau, *NFL Football*, 137; Coenen, *From Sandlots*, 182; Al Hirshberg, "He Calls the Signals for Pro Football," *New York Times*, November 23, 1958.

64. Coenen, *From Sandlots*, 185–186; Crepeau, *NFL Football*, 137.

65. Coenen, *From Sandlots*, 185.

66. See *New York Times*, "House Gets New Bill Proposing Antitrust Easing for Pro Sports," January 16, 1959; *New York Times*, "Senate Gets Bill to Govern Sports," May 12, 1961; *New York Times*, "N.F.L. Gains Right to Pool TV Pacts," October 1, 1961.

67. Coenen, *From Sandlots*, 185–188; Crepeau, *NFL Football*, 135–137; Michael Schiavone, *Sports and Labor in the United States* (Albany: State University of New York Press, 2015), 51–80.

68. Coenen, *From Sandlots*, 185–186.

69. Schiavone, *Sports and Labor*, 58.

70. Frank Gifford and Peter Richmond, *The Glory Game: How the 1958 NFL Championship Changed Football Forever* (New York: HarperCollins, 2008), 234.

71. Oriard, *Brand NFL*, 28.

72. Schiavone, *Sports and Labor*, 57–58.

73. Ibid., 53.

74. Ibid., 57–58.

75. Ibid., 60–79.

76. Ibid., 80–81.

77. Ibid., 82–84; Crepeau, *NFL Football*, 178–181.

78. *USA Today*, "Retirees Send Letter to NFL Asking for Input in CBA Talks," July 14, 2011, http://usatoday30.usatoday.com/sports/football/nfl/2011-07-14-lockout-retired-cba_n .htm; Judy Battista, "Retired Players File Complaint, Complicating the N.F.L. Talks," *New York Times*, July 5, 2011.

79. D. Orlando Ledbetter, "Owners Approve Deal," *Atlanta Journal-Constitution*, July 22, 2011.

80. Battista, "Retired Players."

81. Bowden, *The Best Game Ever*, 226.

82. The National Football League Players Association and the National Football League Management Council, *Bert Bell/Pete Rozelle NFL Player Retirement Plan*, April 1, 2007, 1, 19, https://nflalumniasssociation.files.wordpress.com/2011/03/nfl-player-retire ment-plan.pdf.

83. McGrath, "Does Football Have a Future?"

84. Mark Fainaru-Wada and Steve Fainaru, *League of Denial* (New York: Random House, 2013); Steve Fainaru, Mark Fainaru-Wada, Michael Kirk, and Mike Wiser, "League of Denial: The NFL's Concussion Crisis," *Frontline*, PBS (Boston, MA: October 8, 2013). Considering ESPN's investments in the NFL, Fainaru-Wada and Fainaru have often been asked why it allowed them to write their book. For their account of ESPN's stake in the debate, see *League of Denial*, 20–22. Initially ESPN connected the efforts of its investigative reporting team with the *Frontline* series based on *League of Denial*, but in 2013 the network cut ties with the PBS project, apparently due to pressure from the NFL. See James Andrew Miller and Ken Belson, "N.F.L. Pressure Said to Lead ESPN to Quit Film Project," *New York Times*, August 24, 2013.

85. Peter Keating, "Congress Questions NFL Record-Keeping on Disabled Players," ESPN, December 4, 2007, http://sports.espn.go.com/nfl/news/story?id=3139465.

86. Quoted in ibid.

87. Goodell quoted in ibid.; Judy Battista, "N.F.L. and Players Union Agree to Alter Disability Plan," *New York Times*, December 12, 2007.

88. Bowden, *The Best Game Ever*, 216–217.

89. Quoted in Rick Maese, "'Greatest Game' Another Workday for Johnny U, the Modest Hero," *Baltimore Sun*, December 28, 2008, http://www.baltimoresun.com/sports/ravens/bal-sp.maese28dec28,0,2811270.column.

90. William Nack, "The Wrecking Yard," *Sports Illustrated*, May 7, 2001, http://sports illustrated.cnn.com/vault/article/magazine/MAG1022464/index.htm.

91. Quoted in ibid.

92. Ibid.

93. Quoted in Michael O'Keeffe, "Sacking NFL's Stance: Ex-players Plead Case to Congress," *New York Daily News*, June 27, 2007.

94. See, for example, Gridiron Greats (http://www.gridirongreats.org/), an organization that has been successfully publicized by Hall of Fame player and coach Mike Ditka, among others, and disabled retiree Dave Pear's website (http://davepear.com/blog/), which has become a popular hub for retiree news and advocacy.

95. Bruce Laird, "Baltimore Colts' Alumni Form Advocacy Organization," *NFL Former Players* (blog), January 20, 2007, http://nflretirees.blogspot.com/2007/01/baltimore-colts-alumni-form-advocacy.html. See the group's website at http://fourthandgoalunites.com/.

96. Mike Freeman, "Pension Pay Raised for Pre-1977 Players," *New York Times*, May 19, 2002.

97. Judy Battista, "Owners Add $10 Million for Ailing Ex-players," *New York Times*, October 25, 2007.

98. Quoted in Freeman, "Pension Pay."

99. Clifton Brown, "Ex-players Say Increase in Pensions Is Needed," *New York Times*, February 2, 2007; William Rhoden, "After Peace, Can Upshaw Fight for N.F.L. Players Past or Present?" *New York Times*, February 2, 2006.

100. Quoted in Brown, "Ex-players."

101. Quoted in Charles Chandler, "Ex-players Say NFL Neglects Retirees—Hall of Famers: League, Union Leader Fall Short in Providing Benefits," *Charlotte Observer*, January 15, 2006.

102. Les Carpenter, "Upshaw Defends His Handling of Claims," *Washington Post*, September 5, 2007.

103. Rhoden, "After Peace."

104. Fitzsimmons quoted in Steve Fainaru and Mark Fainaru-Wada, "NFL Board Paid $2M to Players while League Denied Football-Concussion Link," PBS, November 16, 2012, http://www.pbs.org/wgbh/pages/frontline/sports/concussion-watch/nfl-board-paid-2m-to-players-while-league-denied-football-concussion-link/; Sarah E. Gaunt, letter to retired player (name redacted), "Bert Bell/Pete Rozelle NFL Retirement Plan," Baltimore, MD, August 5, 1997, http://espn.go.com/pdf/2012/1116/otl_player6_award_letter.pdf; Sarah E. Gaunt, letter to Robert P. Fitzsimmons (re: Mike Webster), "Bert Bell/Pete Rozelle NFL Retirement Plan," Baltimore, MD, May 8, 2000, http://espn.go.com/pdf/2012/1116/otl_may_2000_letter.pdf; Paul Scott, letter to Gerald Sullivan, "NFL Player Benefits," Baltimore, MD, November 28, 2005, http://espn.go.com/pdf/2012/1116/otl_sullivan_disability.pdf.

105. Stephanie Kuzydym, "From Three-Leather Strap to Chronic Traumatic Encephalopathy: Timeline of History of Concussions and NFL," *Cleveland Plain Dealer*, July 9, 2014.

106. Quoted in Fainaru-Wada and Fainaru, *League of Denial*, 215–216.

107. See, for example, David McNabb, "Recent Head Injuries Underscore Concerns," *Dallas Morning News*, October 25, 1994; *Associated Press*, "Concussions: More than Head-

aches," October 26, 1994; Bill Livingston, "Playing the Hits Is NFL's Disgrace," *Cleveland Plain Dealer*, October 26, 1994; Don Banks, "NFL Wakes Up to Concussions," *St. Petersburg Times* (FL), October 30, 1994; Jim Jenkins, "Concussions to Be Subject of Forum," *Sacramento Bee* (CA), November 6, 1994; Gordon Forbes, "Revamping Rules to Safeguard QBs Again Jarring Issue," *USA Today*, November 8, 1994; Kent Pulliam, "Hard Knocks—Rash of Concussions Prompts Concern," *Washington Times*, November 10, 1994; Jonathan Rand, "No Rules Can Stop QB Pain: Top Passers Find Staying Healthy Difficult in the NFL." *Kansas City Star*, November 13, 1994; Dave Anderson, "The N.F.L. Is Asking for Tragedy," *New York Times*, November 27, 1994.

108. Dave Anderson, "The N.F.L.'s Quiet Career Killer," *New York Times*, November 28, 1992; *Associated Press*, "Bears' Hoge Forced to Quit because of Head Injuries," October 18, 1994; McNabb, "Recent Head Injuries."

109. The earliest indications in the research were summarized by Jeffrey T. Barth and colleagues in 1989. See Jeffrey T. Barth et al., "Mild Head Injury in Sports: Neuropsychological Sequelae and Recovery of Function," in *Mild Head Injury*, ed. Harvey S. Levin, Howard M. Eisenberg, and Arthur L. Benton (New York: Oxford University Press, 1989), 257–275.

110. Fainaru-Wada and Fainaru, *League of Denial*, 216–218.

111. Ibid., 220–221.

112. Quoted in Peter Keating, "Doctor Yes," *ESPN the Magazine*, November 6, 2006, http://sports.espn.go.com/nfl/news/story?id=2636795.

113. Duff Wilson, "Medical Adviser for Baseball Lists Exaggerated Credentials," *New York Times*, March 30, 2005; Howard Markel, "The I.D. of the M.D. from Guadalajara," *New York Times*, April 3, 2005.

114. Fainaru-Wada and Fainaru, *League of Denial*, 239–241.

115. Lindsay Beyerstein, "FRONTLINE Wins November Sidney Award for Exposing the NFL's Concussion Crisis," *Sidney Hillman Foundation*, November 2013, http://www.hillmanfoundation.org/sidney-awards/frontline-wins-november-sidney-award-exposing-nfl%E2%80%99s-concussion-crisis.

116. Fainaru-Wada and Fainaru, *League of Denial*, 242–244.

117. Quoted in Gina Shaw, "Could Neurology Have Done More to Avert the NFL Concussion Crisis?" *Neurology Today*, September 10, 2013, http://mobile.journals.lww.com/neurotodayonline/_layouts/oaks.journals.mobile/post.aspx?blogId=1&postId=256/.

118. Quoted in Michael Farber, "The Worst Case: Doctors Warn that Repeated Concussions Can Lead to Permanent Brain Dysfunction," *Sports Illustrated*, December 19, 1994, http://www.si.com/vault/1994/12/19/132920/the-worst-case-doctors-warn-that-repeated-concussions-can-lead-to-permanent-brain-dysfunction.

119. Elliot J. Pellman et al., "Concussion in Professional Football: Repeat Injuries—Part 4," *Neurosurgery* 55, no. 4 (2004): 868–870. In 1997 the American Academy of Neurology would recommend withholding concussed athletes from competition for between one week and one month (or longer) depending on the grade of concussion, arguing: "Repeated concussions can cause cumulative brain injury in an individual injured over months or years" (American Academy of Neurology, "Practice Parameter: The Management of Concussion in Sports [Summary Statement]," *Neurology* 48 [1997]: 581–585). The NFL criticized and ignored these guidelines, and trainers and physicians commonly returned symptomatic players to the field after insufficient neurological testing (James McKinley, "A Perplexing Foe Takes an Awful Toll: There's No Consensus on Handling Concussions," *New York Times*, May 12, 2000).

120. Fainaru-Wada and Fainaru, *League of Denial*, 251. Two reviewers for the MTBI's fourth paper—Julian Bailes and Kevin Guskiewicz—recommended that the paper be re-

jected by the journal. Both were leading thinkers on sport and head trauma. They both had published, with their colleagues, influential studies suggesting that repeat head trauma was common in the NFL, that players with previous concussions were more likely to have additional concussions in the future, and that players with repeat head trauma experienced slower recovery of neurological function and long-term neurodegenerative issues. The fourth MTBI paper directly contradicted these and similar findings from the existing scholarship. Apuzzo decided to publish the study over the objections of Bailes, Guskiewicz, and Cantu (who also had reservations). Apuzzo offered the reviewers a chance to voice their concerns in the comments section following the published article. See Pellman et al., "Concussion in Professional Football: Repeat Injuries—Part 4," 873, 875.

121. Elliot J. Pellman et al., "Concussion in Professional Football: Injuries Involving 7 or More Days Out—Part 5," *Neurosurgery* 55, no. 5 (2004): 1110.

122. Elliot J. Pellman and David C. Viano, "Concussion in Professional Football: Summary of the Research Conducted by the National Football League's Committee on Mild Traumatic Brain Injury," *Neurosurgical Focus* 21, no. 4 (2006): 1–10.

123. Fainaru-Wada and Fainaru, *League of Denial*, 19.

124. Ibid., 18, 150–151.

125. Bennet I. Omalu et al., "Chronic Traumatic Encephalopathy in a National Football League Player," *Neurosurgery* 57, no. 1 (2005): 129.

126. Fainaru-Wada and Fainaru, *League of Denial*, 270–276.

127. Ibid., 279.

128. Omalu et al., "Chronic Traumatic Encephalopathy," 129, 131.

129. Ira R. Casson, Elliot J. Pellman, and David C. Viano, "Chronic Traumatic Encephalopathy in a National Football League Player," *Neurosurgery* 58, no. 5 (2006): E1003. The call for retraction was based on what MTBI doctors deemed "two serious flaws": a "misinterpretation of [Omalu et al.'s] neuropathological findings" in relation to the characteristics of CTE, and an inadequate review of Webster's medical history. The letter was based on misrepresentations of both the existing literature and Omalu et al.'s argument. The MTBI doctors argued that Omalu et al. diagnosed Webster with CTE based on a "complete misunderstanding of the relevant medical literature on [CTE] of boxers (dementia pugilistica)," even though their paper used characteristically different criteria to claim a new syndrome. Rerouting the analysis of Webster's brain through dementia pugilistica, however, allowed the MTBI to reinforce its long-standing position that CTE was a problem unique to boxing and had never been found in football.

130. Fainaru-Wada and Fainaru, *League of Denial*, 262–266, 333.

131. Robert Dvorchak, "Wecht: Long Died from Brain Injury—Had Head Trauma from NFL Days," *Pittsburgh Post-Gazette*, September 14, 2005.

132. Jonathan D. Silver, "Suicide Ruling in Long's Death Hasn't Ended Controversy," *Pittsburgh Post-Gazette*, January 26, 2006; Fainaru-Wada and Fainaru, *League of Denial*, 331.

133. Chuck Finder, "Final Days Were Troubled for Former Steeler," *Pittsburgh Post-Gazette*, June 10, 2005; Dvorchak, "Wecht: Long Died."

134. Bennet I. Omalu et al., "Chronic Traumatic Encephalopathy in a National Football League Player: Part II," *Neurosurgery* 59, no. 5 (2006): 1086–1093.

135. Quoted in Ed Bouchette, "Surgeon Disputes Findings—Disagrees with Wecht that Football Killed Long," *Pittsburgh Post-Gazette*, September 15, 2005; Robert Dvorchak, "Cause of Death Sparks Debate—Steelers Doctor Says Concluding Football Led to Long's Demise Is Bad Science," *Pittsburgh Post-Gazette*, September 16, 2005.

136. Quoted in Silver, "Suicide Ruling."

137. See, for example, Stella Karantzoulis and Christopher Randolph, "Modern Chronic Traumatic Encephalopathy in Retired Athletes: What Is the Evidence?" *Neuropsychological Review* 23, no. 4 (2013): 350–360; Hal S. Wortzel, Robert D. Shura, and Lisa A. Brenner, "Chronic Traumatic Encephalopathy and Suicide: A Systematic Review," *BioMed Research International* 2013, no. 134 (2013): 1–6; Hal S. Wortzel, Lisa A. Brenner, and David B. Arciniegas, "Traumatic Brain Injury and Chronic Traumatic Encephalopathy: A Forensic Neuropsychiatric Perspective," *Behavioral Sciences and the Law* 31, no. 6 (2013): 721–738; Christopher Randolph, "Is Chronic Traumatic Encephalopathy a Real Disease?" *Current Sports Medicine Reports* 13, no. 1 (2014): 33–37; Grant L. Iverson, "Chronic Traumatic Encephalopathy and Risk of Suicide in Former Athletes," *British Journal of Sports Medicine* 48, no. 2 (2014): 162–164; Benjamin Levin and Anish Bhardwaj, "Chronic Traumatic Encephalopathy: A Critical Appraisal," *Neurocritical Care* 20, no. 2 (2014): 334–344; Joseph C. Maroon et al., "Chronic Traumatic Encephalopathy in Contact Sports: A Systematic Review of All Reported Pathological Cases," *PLoS ONE* 10, no. 2 (2015): 1–16.

138. Alan Schwartz, "Expert Ties Ex-player's Suicide to Brain Damage," *New York Times*, January 18, 2007.

139. Jackie MacMullan, "I Don't Want Anyone to End Up like Me," *Boston Globe*, February 2, 2007, http://www.boston.com/sports/football/patriots/articles/2007/02/02/i_dont_want_anyone_to_end_up_like_me/?page=full; Alan Schwartz, "Dark Days Follow Hard-Hitting Career in N.F.L.," *New York Times*, February 2, 2007.

140. Alan Schwartz, "Before Suicide, Duerson Said He Wanted Brain Study," *New York Times*, February 20, 2011.

141. Alan Schwartz, "N.F.L. Players Shaken by Duerson's Suicide Message," *New York Times*, February 21, 2011.

142. Mike Lopresti, "Dave Duerson's Suicide Renews Questions about Football Safety," *USA Today*, February 21, 2011, http://usatoday30.usatoday.com/sports/columnist/lopresti/2011-02-21-dave-duerson-suicide_N.htm.

143. Keating, "Doctor Yes."

144. Ken Murray, "Chair of Concussion Committee Resigns—Pellman Faced Growing Criticism in NFL Position," *Baltimore Sun*, February 28, 2007.

145. Patrick Hruby, "The NFL: Forever Backward," *Sports on Earth*, February 8, 2013, http://www.sportsonearth.com/article/41492872/.

146. Alan Schwartz, "Two Authors of N.F.L. Study on Concussions Dispute Finding," *New York Times*, June 10, 2007.

147. National Football League, "NFL Outlines for Players Steps Taken to Address Concussions," NFL, August 14, 2007, http://www.nfl.com/news/story/09000d5d8017cc67/article/nfl-outlines-for-players-steps-taken-to-address-concussions. The original pamphlet can be accessed at https://www.documentcloud.org/documents/802804-3-nfl-concussion-pamphlet.html.

148. Alan Schwartz, "N.F.L. Acknowledges Long-Term Concussion Effects," *New York Times*, December 21, 2009.

149. Crepeau, *NFL Football*, 184–185.

150. Doyel, "Death of Football?"

151. Quoted in Judy Battista, "N.F.L. Super Bowl Ad Will Stress Safety," *New York Times*, January 31, 2012.

152. For an archived copy of the commercial, see National Football League, "NFL Evolution—Health and Safety," NFL, http://www.nfl.com/videos/nfl-super-bowl-commercials/09000d5d826b4cb9/Health-Safety.

153. Matt Crossman, Twitter post, February 4, 2013, 6:27 A.M., https://twitter.com/mattcrossman_/status/298437723470045185.

154. See, for example, Chris Chase, "NFL Evolution Ad Features Three Players Suing the NFL," *USA Today*, February 4, 2013, http://www.usatoday.com/story/gameon/2013/02/04/nfl-evolution-concussion-mel-gray-rick-upchurch-ollie-matson/1890231/; Nathan Fenno, "NFL's 'Evolution' Commercial Opens Window to Ex-players' Pain," *Washington Times*, February 4, 2013, http://www.washingtontimes.com/news/2013/feb/4/nfl-evolution-com mercial-opens-window-ex-players/?page=all; Hruby, "The NFL: Forever Backward."

155. Brett Hutchins and David Rowe, "From Broadcast Scarcity to Digital Plentitude: The Changing Dynamics of the Media Sport Content Economy," *Television and New Media* 10, no. 4 (2009): 356.

156. Kevin Clark, "The League that Runs Everything," *Wall Street Journal*, September 15, 2014, http://www.wsj.com/articles/the-league-that-runs-everything-1410736053.

157. Alan Schwartz, "N.F.L. Scolded over Injuries to Its Players," *New York Times*, October 29, 2009; Lynn Zinser, "Goodell Defends N.F.L.'s Handling of Head Injuries," *New York Times*, October 28, 2009, http://www.nytimes.com/2009/10/29/sports/football/29injury.html?pagewanted=all; Alan Schwartz, "N.F.L. Union Says It Shares Blame on Head Injuries," *New York Times*, November 1, 2009.

158. Alan Schwartz, "N.F.L. Acknowledges Long-Term Concussion Effects," *New York Times*, December 21, 2009, quoting Aiello.

159. Anita B. Brody, "In RE: National Football League Player's Concussion Injury Litigation," 2:12-md-02323-AB (U.S. Dist. Ct. for the Eastern Dist. of PA 2015), 130–131, https://s3.amazonaws.com/s3.documentcloud.org/documents/2039302/n-f-l-concussion-settlement-ruling.pdf.

160. National Football League, "NFL Moves Kickoffs to 35-Yard Line; Touchbacks Unchanged," NFL, March 22, 2011, http://www.nfl.com/news/story/09000d5d81ee38c1/article/nfl-moves-kickoffs-to-35yard-line-touchbacks-unchanged; Jason M. Breslow, "With Eye on Concussions, NFL Adopts New Rule on Helmet Hits," *Frontline*, PBS, March 22, 2013, http://www.pbs.org/wgbh/pages/frontline/sports/concussion-watch/with-eye-on-concussions-nfl-adopts-new-rule-on-helmet-hits/; Darin Gantt, "Injury Timeout Proposal Unanimously Approved by NFL Owners," Pro Football Talk, March 24, 2015, http://profootballtalk.nbc sports.com/2015/03/24/injury-timeout-proposal-unanimously-approved-by-nfl-owners/.

161. Steve Fainaru and Mark Fainaru-Wada, "NFL's Progress on Concussions Blurred by Inconsistencies," *Frontline*, PBS, December 13, 2012, http://www.pbs.org/wgbh/pages/frontline/sports/concussion-watch/nfls-progress-on-concussions-blurred-by-inconsistencies/.

162. Associated Press, "NFL Sees Spike in Reported Concussions," ESPN, December 13, 2010, http://sports.espn.go.com/nfl/news/story?id=5914797.

163. PBS, "Concussion Watch," *Frontline*, PBS, http://www.pbs.org/wgbh/pages/front line/concussion-watch/#; Robert Collins, "NFL Sees a Drop in Concussions, but Problems Linger," *Frontline*, PBS, December 5, 2014, http://www.pbs.org/wgbh/pages/frontline/sports/nfl-sees-a-drop-in-concussions-but-problems-linger/.

164. Alan Schwartz, "N.F.L. Scolded"; Alan Schwartz, "Leaders of N.F.L. Head Injury Study Resign," *New York Times*, November 25, 2009.

165. Alan Schwartz, "N.F.L. Overhauls Concussion Committee," *New York Times*, March 17, 2010; Alan Schwartz, "Criticism for New N.F.L. Doctors," *New York Times*, May 25, 2010; Alan Schwartz, "Concussion Committee Breaks with Predecessor," *New York Times*, June 2, 2010.

166. Alan Schwartz, "Dementia Risk Seen in Players in N.F.L. Study," *New York Times*, September 30, 2009; David R. Wier, James S. Jackson, and Amanda Sonnega, "National Football League Player Care Foundation: Study of Retired Players," *University of Michigan Institute for Social Research*, September 10, 2009.

167. Jason M. Breslow, "76 of 79 Deceased NFL Players Found to Have Brain Disease," *Frontline*, PBS, December 30, 2014, http://www.pbs.org/wgbh/pages/frontline/sports/concussion-watch/76-of-79-deceased-nfl-players-found-to-have-brain-disease/.

168. Quoted in Daniel Kaplan, "NFL Plans to Attack Medical Foundation of Concussion Claims if Cases Aren't Settled," *Street and Smith's SportsBusiness Journal*, November 24, 2014, http://www.sportsbusinessdaily.com/Journal/Issues/2014/11/24/Law-and-Politics/NFL-concussions.aspx.

169. Associated Press, "Ex-Viking Appeals Lawsuit Settlement," *St. Paul Pioneer Press* (MN), August 18, 2015; Mark Craig, "NFL Concussion Settlement—Players See a Rigged Endgame," *Star Tribune* (Minneapolis, MN), February 22, 2015.

170. Julie Beck, "The NFL's Continuing Concussion Nightmare," *The Atlantic*, September 21, 2015, http://www.theatlantic.com/health/archive/2015/09/researchers-find-brain-damage-in-96-percent-of-former-nfl-players/406462/.

171. Mark Sappenfield, "Chris Borland Retires: What Can the NFL Do about Its Concussion Problem?" *Christian Science Monitor*, March 17, 2015; Todd D. Milewski, "Chris Borland's Retirement, Citing Head Injury Fears, Seen as Watershed Moment for NFL," *Capital Times* (Madison, WI), March 17, 2015; Vahe Gregorian, "Chris Borland's Abrupt Retirement from NFL Another Step toward Enlightenment," *Kansas City Star*, March 17, 2015.

172. Bryant Gumbel, "Monsters No More/Mr. Sunday Night/The Toast of Beijing/Urban Renewal," *Real Sports with Bryant Gumbel*, season 21, episode 1, HBO, January 20, 2015.

CHAPTER 6

Note: I borrow the format for this chapter from two authors who have influenced my thinking throughout this book: Walter Benjamin, whose "Theses on the Philosophy of History" should be an obvious connection, and Jean-Marie Brohm, whose final chapter in *Sport—a Prison of Measured Time* is "Theses towards a Political Sociology of Sport." See Walter Benjamin, "Theses on the Philosophy of History," in *Illuminations*, ed. Hannah Arendt and trans. Harry Zohn (New York: Harcourt, Brace and World, 1955), 255–266; Jean-Marie Brohm, "Theses towards a Political Sociology of Sport," in *Sport—a Prison of Measured Time*, trans. Ian Fraser (Worcester, UK: Pluto Press, 1989).

1. Quoted in Pete Thamel, "N.C.A.A. Sued over Licensing Practices," *New York Times*, July 21, 2009.

2. Erin Buzuvis, "What Effect Will the NLRB Decision Have on Title IX?" *Title IX Blog*, March 27, 2014, http://title-ix.blogspot.com/2014/03/what-effect-will-nlrb-decision-have-on.html.

3. Joe Nocera, "Let's Start Paying College Athletes," *New York Times*, January 1, 2012.

4. Michael McCann, "What the Appeals Court Ruling Means for O'Bannon's Ongoing NCAA Lawsuit," *Sports Illustrated*, September 30, 2015, http://www.si.com/college-basketball/2015/09/30/ed-obannon-ncaa-lawsuit-appeals-court-ruling.

5. Ben Strauss and Marc Tracy, "N.C.A.A. Must Allow College to Pay Athletes, Judge Rules," *New York Times*, August 9, 2014.

6. Quoted in Marc Tracy, "N.C.A.A. Votes to Give Richest Conferences More Autonomy," *New York Times*, August 8, 2014.

7. Strauss and Tracy, "N.C.A.A. Must Allow."

8. Nick Dorzweiler, "What Kain Colter Really Learned at Northwestern," *Deadspin*, August 21, 2015, http://deadspin.com/what-kain-colter-really-learned-at-northwestern-1725648553.

9. Quoted in Ben Strauss and Steve Eder, "College Players Granted Right to Form Union," *New York Times*, March 27, 2014.

10. Quoted in John Walters and Michael Depaoli, "The NCAA's Fishy Argument against a Union for Players," *Newsweek*, May 9, 2014; Mark Guarino, "NCAA and College Sports: Is It Time to Pay Athletes to Play?" *Christian Science Monitor*, May 18, 2014.

11. National Labor Relations Board, "Board Unanimously Decides to Decline Jurisdiction in Northwestern Case," NLRB, August 17, 2015, https://www.nlrb.gov/news-outreach/news-story/board-unanimously-decides-decline-jurisdiction-northwestern-case.

12. Michael Tarm, "Ruling to Allow College Athletes to Unionize Is Thrown Out," *Associated Press*, August 18, 2015.

13. Ben Strauss, "N.L.R.B. Rejects Northwestern Football Players' Union Bid," *New York Times*, August 18, 2015.

14. Ben Strauss, "N.C.A.A. Appeal of Ruling in O'Bannon Case Is Heard," *New York Times*, March 18, 2015; Marc Tracy and Ben Strauss, "Court Strikes Down Payments to College Athletes," *New York Times*, October 1, 2015.

15. Quoted in Mark Schlabach, "Court Strikes Down Payment Plan; Agrees NCAA Violates Antitrust Laws," ESPN, September 30, 2015, http://espn.go.com/ncaa/story/_/id/13777916/appeals-court-nixes-plan-pay-student-athletes-ed-obannon-case-agrees-ncaa-violates-antitrust-laws.

16. Tracy and Strauss, "Court Strikes Down"; Schlabach, "Court Strikes Down."

17. Sara Ganim, "Student-Athlete? Fans Buying Only the Latter Part of the Term, Poll Says," *CNN Wire*, January 12, 2015.

18. Marist University, "Many Fans Think College Sports Programs Break NCAA Rules. . . . Education Should Be a Priority, Say Most," Marist Poll, March 26, 2013, http://maristpoll.marist.edu/326-many-fans-think-college-sports-programs-break-ncaa-ruleseducation-should-be-a-priority-say-most/.

19. Nocera, "Let's Start."

20. Linda Greenhouse, "High Court Ends N.C.A.A. Control of TV Football," *New York Times*, June 28, 1984; *National Collegiate Athletic Association v. Board of Regents of the University of Oklahoma et al.*, 104 S. Ct. 2948 (1984).

21. Ronald A. Smith, "Intercollegiate Athletic Associations and Conferences," in *Sports in America from Colonial Times to the Twenty-First Century: An Encyclopedia*, vols. 1–3, ed. Steve A. Riess (New York: Routledge, 2015), 490–491; Ronald A. Smith, *Pay for Play: A History of Big-Time College Athletic Reform* (Urbana: University of Illinois Press, 2011), 180–182; Taylor Branch, "The Shame of College Sports," *The Atlantic*, September 7, 2011, http://www.theatlantic.com/magazine/archive/2011/10/the-shame-of-college-sports/308643/?single_page=true.

22. Chris Smith, "College Basketball's Most Valuable Teams: Louisville on Top, Kansas Close Behind," *Forbes*, March 6, 2015, http://www.forbes.com/sites/chrissmith/2015/03/16/college-basketballs-most-valuable-teams-louisville-on-top-kansas-close-behind/; Chris Smith, "College Football's Most Valuable Teams 2014," *Forbes*, December 22, 2014, http://www.forbes.com/sites/chrissmith/2014/12/22/college-footballs-most-valuable-teams-2014/. Every year *Forbes* calculates the total value of college teams based on a host of variables including ticket and merchandise sales, contributions, television revenues, NCAA and conference distributions, and expenses such as those related to coaches' salaries.

23. Patrick Rishe, "College Football Coaching Salaries Grow Astronomically due to Escalating Media Rights Deals," *Forbes*, November 20, 2012, http://www.forbes.com/sites/prishe/2012/11/20/college-football-coaching-salaries-grow-astronomically-due-to-escalating-media-rights-deals/.

24. *USA Today*, "NCAA Salaries, NCAAF Coaches," http://sports.usatoday.com/ncaa/salaries/, accessed on November 27, 2015; *USA Today*, "NCAA Salaries, NCAAB Coaches," http://sports.usatoday.com/ncaa/salaries/mens-basketball/coach/, accessed on November 27, 2015.

25. For more on student fee subsidies, see Knight Commission on College Athletics, "How Student Fees Boost College Sports amid Rising Budgets," Knight Commission, September 22, 2010, http://www.knightcommission.org/index.php?option=com_content&view=article&id=596:september-22-2010-how-student-fees-boost-college-sports-amid-rising-budgets&catid=8:fiscal-integrity; David Ridpath, "Who Actually Funds Intercollegiate Athletic Programs?" *Forbes*, December 12, 2014, http://www.forbes.com/sites/ccap/2014/12/12/who-actually-funds-intercollegiate-athletic-programs/; Brian Burnsed, "Growth in Division I Athletics Expenses Outpaces Revenue Increases," NCAA, August 20, 2014, http://www.ncaa.org/about/resources/media-center/news/growth-division-i-athletics-expenses-outpaces-revenue-increases. For more on the finances of individual big-money programs (based on 2015 figures), see *USA Today*, "NCAA Finances," http://sports.usatoday.com/ncaa/finances, accessed on December 1, 2015. To cite just some examples (based on 2015 numbers), the University of Oregon athletic program had more than $190 million in revenues, more than $110 million in expenses, and more than $2 million in total subsidies; the University of Alabama had more than $150 million in revenues, more than $120 million in expenses, and more than $5 million in total subsidies; the same numbers for the University of Wisconsin were around $127 million, $125 million, and $8 million respectively; among the top fifty programs (by total revenue) only six did not take subsidies.

26. National Collegiate Athletic Association, "Division I Results from the NCAA GOALS Study on the Student-Athlete Experience," NCAA, November 8, 2011, http://www.ncaa.org/sites/default/files/DI_GOALS_FARA_final_1.pdf.

27. Dennis Dodd, "Pac-12 Study Reveals Athletes 'Too Exhausted to Study Effectively,'" CBS Sports, April 21, 2015, http://www.cbssports.com/collegefootball/writer/dennis-dodd/25157011/pac-12-study-reveals-athletes-too-exhausted-to-study-effectively.

28. Smith, *Pay for Play*, 96; Andrew Zimbalist, *Unpaid Professionals: Commercialism and Conflict in Big-Time College Sports* (Princeton, NJ: Princeton University Press, 1999), 22–26; Allen L. Sack and Ellen J. Staurowsky, *College Athletes for Hire: The Evolution and Legacy of the NCAA's Amateur Myth* (Westport, CT: Praeger, 1998), 95–109.

29. Sharon Terlep, "NCAA to Allow Big Sports Schools to Offer Full Cost-of-Attendance Scholarships," *Wall Street Journal*, January 17, 2015, http://www.wsj.com/articles/ncaa-to-allow-big-sports-schools-to-offer-full-cost-of-attendance-scholarships-1421542833; National Collegiate Athletic Association, "Cost of Attendance Q&A," NCAA, September 3, 2015, http://www.ncaa.com/news/ncaa/article/2015-09-03/cost-attendance-qa; Jake New, "More Money . . . If You Can Play Ball," *Inside Higher Ed*, August 12, 2015, https://www.insidehighered.com/news/2015/08/12/colleges-inflate-full-cost-attendance-numbers-increasing-stipends-athletes/.

30. PBS, "Interview—Andrew Zimbalist; Money and March Madness," *Frontline*, PBS, March 29, 2011, http://www.pbs.org/wgbh/pages/frontline/money-and-march-madness/interviews/andrew-zimbalist.html; Ahmed E. Taha, "Are College Athletes Economically Exploited?" *Wake Forest Journal of Law and Policy* 2, no. 1 (2011): 71–72.

31. Ragomi Huma and Ellen J. Staurowsky, *The $6 Billion Heist: Robbing College Athletes under the Guise of Amateurism*, National College Players Association and Drexel University Sport Management, 2012, http://www.ncpanow.org/news/articles/body/6-Billion-Heist-Study_Full.pdf.

32. See Robert Brown, "Research Note: Estimates of College Football Player Rents," *Journal of Sports Economics* 12, no. 2 (2011): 200–212.

33. Branch, "The Shame."

34. Lawrence Grossberg, *Cultural Studies in the Future Tense* (Durham, NC: Duke University Press, 2010), 16.

35. Rudolf J. Siebert, "The Critical Theory of Society: The Longing for the Totally Other," *Critical Sociology* 31, nos. 1–2 (2005): 57–113.

36. Eduardo Mendieta, "Introduction: Religion as Critique, Theology as Social Critique and Enlightened Reason," in *The Frankfurt School on Religion: Key Writings by the Major Thinkers*, ed. Eduardo Mendieta (New York: Routledge, 2005), 11.

37. Theodor W. Adorno and Walter Benjamin, *The Complete Correspondence 1928–1940*, ed. Henri Lonitz and trans. Nicholas Walker (Cambridge, MA: Harvard University Press, 1999), 66–67. Also see Susan Buck-Morss, *The Origin of Negative Dialectics: Theodor W. Adorno, Walter Benjamin, and the Frankfurt Institute* (New York: Free Press, 1977), 6.

38. Jeffrey H. Mahan, "Reflections on the Past and Future of the Study of Religion and Popular Culture," in *Between Sacred and Profane: Researching Religion and Popular Culture*, ed. Gordon Lynch (New York: I. B. Taurus, 2007), 52; Gordon Lynch, "What Is This 'Religion' in the Study of Religion and Popular Culture?" in *Between Sacred and Profane: Researching Religion and Popular Culture*, ed. Gordon Lynch (New York: I. B. Taurus, 2007), 136–137; Jeffrey Scholes and Raphael Sassower, *Religion and Sports in American Culture* (New York: Routledge, 2014), 4.

39. David Kaufmann, "Beyond Use, within Reason: Adorno, Benjamin, and the Question of Theology," *New German Critique* 83 (Spring/Summer 2001): 151, 168–169; Siebert, "The Critical Theory of Society," 62.

40. Mendieta, "Introduction: Religion as Critique," 10–11; Max Horkheimer, "Thoughts on Religion," in *Critical Theory: Selected Essays*, trans. Matthew J. O'Connell (New York: Herder and Herder, 1972), 129–131; Benjamin, "Theses," 259.

41. James Hay, Stuart Hall, and Lawrence Grossberg, "Interview with Stuart Hall, June 12, 2012," *Communication and Critical/Cultural Studies* 10, no. 1 (2013): 16–17.

42. Samuel McCormick, "Neighbors and Citizens: Local Speakers in the Now of Their Recognizability," *Philosophy and Rhetoric* 44, no. 4 (2011): 432; Walter Benjamin, *The Arcades Project*, trans. Howard Eiland and Kevin McLaughlin (Cambridge, MA: Harvard University Press, 1999), 463, 475; Buck-Morss, *The Dialectics of Seeing*, 218–219; Rolf Tiedemann, "Historical Materialism or Political Messianism? An Interpretation of the Theses 'On the Concept of History,'" in *Benjamin: Philosophy, History, Aesthetics*, ed. Gary Smith (Chicago: University of Chicago Press, 1989), 185.

43. Hay, Hall, and Grossberg, "Interview with Stuart Hall," 16.

44. Ben Carrington, "Sport without Final Guarantees: Cultural Studies/Marxism/Sport," in *Marxism, Cultural Studies and Sport*, ed. Ben Carrington and Ian McDonald (New York: Routledge, 2009), 20–21.

45. David L. Andrews and Michael D. Giardina, "Sport without Guarantees: Toward a Cultural Studies that Matters," *Cultural Studies ↔ Critical Methodologies* 8, no. 4 (2008): 397.

46. Walter Byers, *Unsportsmanlike Conduct: Exploiting College Athletes* (Ann Arbor: University of Michigan Press, 1995), 388.

47. Ted Striphas, "Keyword: Critical," *Communication and Critical/Cultural Studies* 10, nos. 2–3 (2013): 325. Striphas borrows this clinical definition of "critical" from Raymond Williams's book *Keywords*, as well as from Williams's concept "structure of feeling," which describes a latent cultural consciousness that is lived though not yet fully articulated. See

Raymond R. Williams, *Keywords: A Vocabulary of Culture and Society*, rev. ed. (New York: Oxford University Press, 1983).

48. Mahan, "Reflections"; Lynch, "What Is This 'Religion,'" 136–137; Susan Buck-Morss, *The Dialectics of Seeing: Walter Benjamin and the Arcades Project* (Cambridge, MA: MIT Press, 1989), 245; Horkheimer, "Thoughts on Religion," 129–131; Benjamin, "Theses," 259.

49. Buck-Morss, *The Dialectics of Seeing*, 245.

50. Heather L. Reid, "Sport and Moral Education in Plato's Republic," *Journal of the Sociology of Sport* 34, no. 2 (2007): 160–175; Debra Hawhee, "Emergent Flesh: Phusiopoiesis and Ancient Arts of Training," *Journal of Sport and Social Issues* 25, no. 2 (2001): 141–157; Debra Hawhee, *Bodily Arts: Rhetoric and Athletics in Ancient Greece* (Austin: University of Texas Press, 2004).

51. Hay, Hall, and Grossberg, "Interview with Stuart Hall," 16–17; Benjamin, *Arcades*, 463, 475.

52. Smith, *Pay for Play*, 51–53.

53. Ibid., 57–58.

54. Ibid., 63–66.

55. *National Collegiate Athletic Association v. Board of Regents*.

56. Branch, "The Shame." For more on college sport and full-program apparel contracts, see Samantha King, "Nike U: Full-Program Athletics Contracts and the Corporate University," in *Sport and Neoliberalism: Politics, Consumption, and Culture*, ed. David L. Andrews and Michael Silk (Philadelphia: Temple University Press, 2012), 75–89.

57. Keenan Mayo, "Under Fire for Hypocrisy, NCAA Quits the Jersey Business," *Bloomberg Business*, August 8, 2013, http://www.bloomberg.com/bw/articles/2013-08-08/under-fire-for-hypocrisy-ncaa-quits-the-jersey-business.

58. Grossberg, *Cultural Studies in the Future Tense*, 8, 20.

59. Brohm, *Sport*, 5, emphasis original.

60. Ibid., 7.

61. Benjamin, *Arcades*, 475. Also see Peter Gilgen, "History after Film," in *Mapping Benjamin: The Work of Art in the Digital Age*, ed. Hans Ulrich Gumbrecht and Michael Marrinan (Stanford, CA: Stanford University Press, 2003); Joshua Gunn, "Benjamin's Magic," *Telos* 119 (Spring 2001): 71.

62. Buck-Morss, *The Dialectics of Seeing*, 250.

63. Walter Benjamin, "The Work of Art in the Age of Mechanical Reproduction," in *Illuminations*, ed. Hannah Arendt and trans. Harry Zohn (New York: Harcourt, Brace and World, 1955), 238–239.

64. Miriam Hansen, *Babel and Babylon: Spectatorship in American Silent Film* (Cambridge, MA: Harvard University Press, 1991), 110–111.

65. John Durham Peters, "Witnessing," *Media, Culture and Society* 23, no. 6 (2001): 707.

66. Walter Benjamin, "A Short History of Photography," in *Classic Essays on Photography*, ed. Alan Trachtenberg (New Haven, CT: Leete's Island Books, 1980), 202–203; Walter Benjamin, *The Writer of Modern Life: Essays on Charles Baudelaire*, ed. Michael W. Jennings and trans. Howard Eiland, Edmund Jephcott, Rodney Livingston, and Harry Zohn (Cambridge, MA: Harvard University Press, 2006), 191; Arianne Conty, "They Have Eyes that They Might Not See: Walter Benjamin's Aura and the Optical Unconscious," *Literature and Theology* 27, no. 4 (2013): 473–474.

67. Steve Eder and Greg Bishop, "High-Stakes Games: Critical Step for Suit Seeking Payment for College Athletics," *New York Times*, June 20, 2013.

68. Richard Lapchick et al., "The 2014 Racial and Gender Report Card: College

Sport," Institute for Diversity and Ethics in Sport (University of Central Florida), March 3, 2015, 1–9, http://nebula.wsimg.com/308fbfef97c47edb705ff195306a2d50?AccessKeyId =DAC3A56D8FB782449D2A&disposition=0&alloworigin=1.

69. Ibid., 4–6. The 2014 Report Card categorized 1 percent of male FBS football players as "other." These race and class inequities have been summarized by some reformers through the image of a plantation economy. In his article "The Shame of College Sports" Branch expresses appropriate caution in employing this analogy: "College athletes are not slaves. Yet to survey the scene—corporations and universities enriching themselves on the backs of uncompensated young men, whose status as 'student-athletes' deprives them of the right to due process guaranteed by the Constitution—is to catch an unmistakable whiff of the plantation." This has been until recently a fairly marginalized argument, but it now circulates more commonly in news reports. Most fans and journalists do not realize that the analogy traces back to Byers, the architect of the contemporary NCAA, who wrote in 1995, "The college player cannot sell his own feet (the coach does that) nor can he sell his own name (the college will do that). This is the plantation mentality resurrected and blessed by today's campus executives." See Branch, "The Shame"; Byers, *Unsportsmanlike Conduct*, 390–391. I am not including the plantation analogy in the main text as the controversies surrounding it (including criticisms from both the political right and political left) warrant more attention than I can give to them in this chapter.

70. Alicia Jessop, "The Elephant in the Room in Student-Athletes' Unionization Attempt: Title IX," *Forbes*, January 31, 2014, http://www.forbes.com/sites/aliciajes sop/2014/01/31/the-elephant-in-the-room-in-student-athletes-unionization-attempt-title-ix/; Mechelle Voepel, "Title IX a Pay-for-Play Roadblock," ESPN, July 15, 2011, http:// espn.go.com/college-sports/story/_/id/6769337/title-ix-seen-substantial-roadblock-pay-play-college-athletics. For more on the historical, political, and legal details of Title IX, see Deborah Brake, *Getting In the Game: Title IX and the Women's Sports Revolution* (New York: New York University Press, 2010); Nancy Hogshead-Makar and Andrew Zimbalist, eds., *Equal Play: Title IX and Social Change* (Philadelphia: Temple University Press, 2007).

71. Nicole M. Bracken and Erin Irick, "2004–2010 NCAA Gender-Equity Report," National Collegiate Athletic Association (Indianapolis, IN), January 2012, 32; Women's Sports Foundation, "Pay Inequity in Athletics," Women's Sports Foundation, July 20, 2015, http://www.womenssportsfoundation.org/home/research/articles-and-reports/equity-issues/ pay-inequity; National Women's Law Center, "Title IX and Men's Sports: A False Conflict," NWLC, August 2015, http://nwlc.org/resources/title-ix-and-mens-sports-false-conflict/.

72. Buzuvis, "What Effect"; ESPN, "Pay-For-Play: Dr. Ellen Staurowsky," ESPN: Sports Nation, July 15, 2011, http://espn.go.com/sportsnation/chat/_/id/39354.

73. Brake, *Getting In the Game*, 69–70.

74. Ibid., 70–71.

75. For arguments about these possibilities and projections about revenue redistribution, see Allen R. Sanderson and John J. Siegfried, "The Case for Paying College Athletes," *Journal of Economic Perspectives* 29, no. 1 (2015): 129–132; Dave Zirin, "An Economist Explains Why College Athletes Should Be Paid," *The Nation*, March 27, 2015, http://www .thenation.com/article/economist-explains-why-college-athletes-should-be-paid/; Editorial Board, "Pay for Play and Title IX," *New York Times*, March 23, 2014.

76. Antonio Gramsci, *Selections from the Prison Notebooks of Antonio Gramsci*, ed. and trans. Quintin Hoare and Geoffrey Nowell Smith (New York: International Publishers, 1971), 195; Stuart Hall, "The Problem of Ideology—Marxism without Guarantees," *Journal of Communication Inquiry* 10, no. 2 (1986): 41.

77. Lawrence Grossberg, "The Circulation of Cultural Studies," *Critical Studies in Mass Communication* 6, no. 4 (1989): 415.

INDEX

DANIEL A. GRANO is an Associate Professor in the Department of Communication Studies at the University of North Carolina at Charlotte.